CHRISTOPHER HARDING

Japan Story

In Search of a Nation,
1850 to the Present

PENGUIN BOOKS

PENGUIN BOOKS

UK | USA | Canada | Ireland | Australia
India | New Zealand | South Africa

Penguin Books is part of the Penguin Random House group of companies
whose addresses can be found at global.penguinrandomhouse.com

First published by Allen Lane 2018
First published in Penguin Books 2019
001

Set in 9.24/12.35 pt Sabon LT Std
Typeset by Jouve (UK), Milton Keynes
Printed and bound in Great Britain by Clays Ltd, Elcograf S.p.A.

A CIP catalogue record for this book is available from the British Library

ISBN: 978-0-141-98537-4

To my parents and to my wife
With love and gratitude
For all the things I can think of
And all those a more perceptive son and husband
Would have noticed by now

Contents

PART FOUR
Modernity 2.0? (1940s to 1960s)

PART FIVE
Twisted Visions (1950s to 1990s)

PART SIX
Raising Spirits (1990s to 2010s)

List of Maps

A Note to the Reader

Japanese names appear in this book in the standard Japanese order of family name followed by given name. Where a Japanese scholar is publishing in English, their name appears in the standard English language order of given name followed by family name.

Macrons are used to indicate elongated vowel sounds except in the case of place names that are well established in English (e.g. Tokyo).

Passages have been set in *italic* where events, conversations between historical characters or storylines from Japanese literature are being paraphrased or condensed.

English translations of Japanese book titles have been given in brackets after the Japanese. Those books that have also been published in English appear in *italics*. The date of the original publication in Japanese is given in brackets after the title.

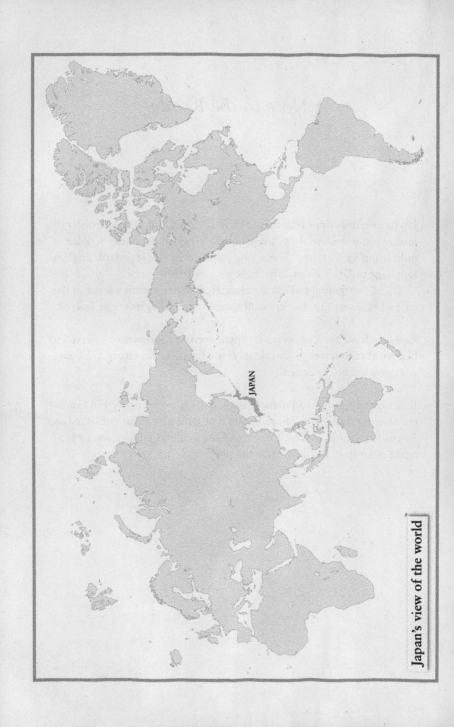

JAPAN

Japan's view of the world

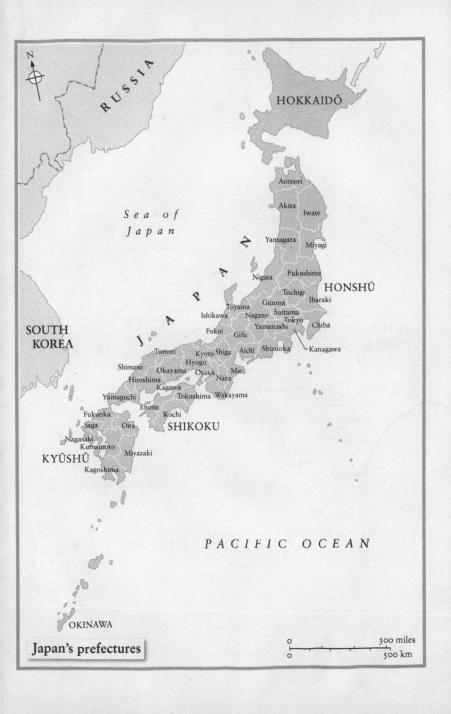

N

RUSSIA

HOKKAIDŌ

Sea of Japan

Aomori

Akita

Iwate

Yamagata

Miyagi

Nigata

Fukushima

HONSHŪ

Tochigi

Ibaraki

Toyama

Gunma

Ishikawa

Nagano

Saitama

Tokyo

Fukui

Gifu

Yamanashi

Chiba

SOUTH KOREA

JAPAN

Tottori

Kyoto Shiga

Aichi

Shizuoka

Kanagawa

Shimane

Okayama

Hyogo

Osaka

Mie

Hiroshima

Nara

Kagawa

Yamaguchi

Tokushima

Wakayama

Ehime

Kochi

Fukuoka

SHIKOKU

Saga

Oita

Nagasaki

Kumamoto

KYŪSHŪ

Miyazaki

Kagoshima

PACIFIC OCEAN

OKINAWA

Japan's prefectures

0   300 miles

0   500 km

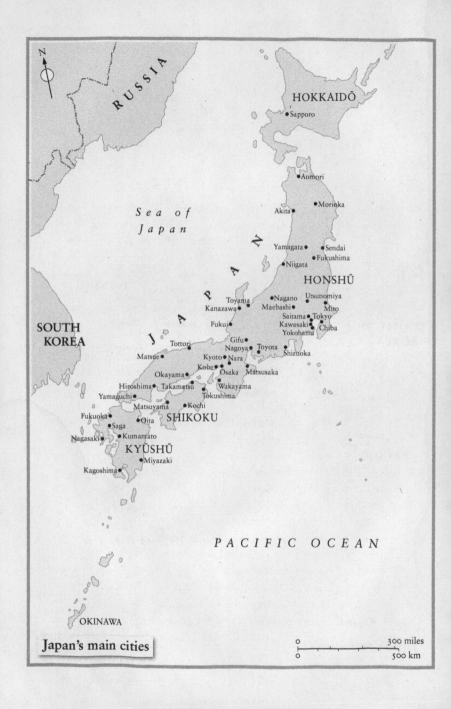

Japan's main cities

Prologue
Harumi and Heisaku

My kimono, the colour of rust. Central Tokyo, cars whizzing around me. Sitting inside a car with my friend, a mountain of boiled eggs in front of us. My sister's sickroom. Standing, staring at her water-blue futon as she sleeps. She's frowning. Flowers in a garden. Someone's fingers. Three men in a coffee shop. Flowers again – a field of yellow flowers. Inside a plane. A banyan tree. An Indian book-shop, shelves heavy with books. I worry they're going to spill down on top of me. A man removing his glasses . . .

Harumi stopped speaking, and opened her eyes. A face appeared briefly in a dusty shaft of daylight: tired but noble, framed by thin grey hair. A black scarf was tucked inside a kimono of dark silk.

'You're ill. You're suffering.'

The man's words were slightly slurred and indistinct; his eyesight had mostly gone, years before, and now a series of strokes were eating away at his powers of movement and speech. And yet this was the softest voice that Harumi had ever heard. She wasn't being handed a diagnosis, nor being idly discussed as a case study. She was being seen, in a way no one – herself included – had ever managed before. Many years later Harumi remembered that voice as sending cool water coursing through a mind and body so desiccated, so brittle, that she feared the lightest of touches would break her.

The voice belonged to Kosawa Heisaku, a devout Buddhist and Japan's first Freudian psychotherapist. Sitting in a chair behind Setouchi Harumi, who was lying on his couch, he stayed mostly silent as she allowed thoughts, images, fantasies and worries to tumble out of her, at random and uncensored, into the musty wooden stillness.

Harumi and Heisaku: two lives – overlapping for a few brief months in the mid-1960s – which together spanned most of Japan's tumultuous modern era. As a boy in the early 1900s, the young Heisaku's heart had been set racing by the crackle of gunfire resounding across the fields near his home. Japan's new professional, conscript army on manoeuvres, immaculate in European-style uniforms and tiny, tight moustaches, had been hurriedly established a generation before, amidst the menace of heavily armed Western steamships materializing off the country's coast. This army's stunning victories over China and then Russia were already immortalized in vivid posters and commemorative postage stamps pored over by the young boy and thousands like him. A little over a century later, an octogenarian Harumi would protest against her country's faded sense of purpose. A precipitous return to nuclear power after triple disasters in 2011 – earthquake, tsunami and nuclear meltdown – threatened, she would say, to further shake people's confidence in Japan and its leaders. Proposed revisions to Japan's pacifist constitution, opening up the prospect of renewed self-assertion in East Asia, seemed to her a poor and dangerous substitute for real political direction.

Heisaku and Harumi: two lives lived at the reflective, apprehensive fringes of modern Japan. Harumi was in her forties when they met, a novelist approaching her lowest point just as all around her the heyday of the *akarui seikatsu* – the 'bright life' – animated a city many of whose neighbourhoods had been reduced to ashes and bone just twenty years before. Tokyo was now the pulsating centrepiece of Japan's 'economic miracle'. Music and fashion filled the bars and streets, critics hailed a golden age of literature and cinema, and brand new super-fast shinkansen trains were being rolled out just in time to serve as a symbol of Japan's progress as the world's athletes and sports fans limbered up for the city's hosting of Asia's first Olympic games.

Harumi had in recent years come through the ignominy still attached to divorce. She had successfully battled accusations of pornography against her early writing – literature remained for the most part a man's world, with intimate writing by women not always welcomed. And she had built friendships amongst Tokyo's celebrated community of writers and artists. She would soon stand next to Mishima Yukio as he rang the bell at the home of Kawabata

Yasunari, his hand clenched white-knuckle tight around a congratu-
latory bottle of *sake* as he steeled himself to celebrate with Kawabata
the Nobel Prize in Literature that he felt should have been his. Harumi
had found richness too in her relationships with the tangle of competing men who inspired one of her greatest works: *Natsu no Owari*
('The End of Summer').

And yet of late she had started to worry her friends. A wry, probing
conversational style had become more and more intense, verging on
the obsessive. She would start talking and be unable to stop, sometimes running on for a whole night. One day she came close to injuring
herself absently trying to walk up the descending escalator in one of
Tokyo's exclusive department stores.

The old consulting room to which all this had led her, with its ageing couch and chair, testified to a life of great industry drawing to a
marginal, faintly disappointed close. Heisaku's bookshelf proudly
announced the latest psychological insights of the 1930s, 40s and
50s – a series of exciting new dawns already for the most part forgotten by a newer generation of psychologists and therapists. Outside,
beyond the curtained window, lay the Tokyo suburb of Den-en-chōfu.
Japan's pre-war attempt at the British and American 'garden city'
ideal of affordable houses set out along wide tree-lined streets had
long since turned into a celebrity- and politician-infested Beverly Hills.

Over the last thirty years, Heisaku had ministered to hundreds of
people both here and further afield. Farmers and brothel-owners,
civil servants, schoolgirls and sushi chefs had all passed across the
couch on which Harumi now lay. He had failed, however, to claim
his nation as a whole for Freud. Even now, with American culture
cascading through Japan's music and film scenes, its schools and universities, its fashion and forms of politics and commerce, somehow
America's fascination with psychoanalysis and therapy was failing to
rub off. Through his window this increasingly frail man looked on in
puzzlement as his fellow Tokyoites said 'yes' to pop, television and
short skirts, and mostly 'no' to the inner world that Freud had so
vividly opened up for him.

Puzzlement there may have been for Heisaku, but not surprise. His
two heroes in life – Sigmund Freud and a medieval Japanese Buddhist

3

saint called Shinran – both taught that people, even entire societies, become deeply attached to particular images of themselves, to the point where they can't or won't see anything else. They get hooked on particular stories about who they are and what they are for. It is easy to see why. A good story offers purchase on life. It helps to herd the happenings and anxieties of past, present and future into some coherent, meaningful whole. But cherished stories can become so powerful that people suffer in serving them – and suffer too if forced to probe or part with them. And though a story may give shape to a single life or nation, it risks doing so at the cost of a steady loss of the ability to see, think and imagine otherwise – about one's self or one's home.

The world outside Heisaku's window – peaceful, prosperous, lively and safe – provided fuel for a particularly compelling story about Japan. It was a powerful force in the country's mainstream politics and media, widely accepted abroad (indeed, partly fashioned there), and altogether too good to give up. It was a story, almost a morality tale, of successful, hard-won modernization. A modest Asian country rises rapidly and purposefully to a parity of sorts with the advanced seafaring empires of the West; briefly, it descends into corruption and cruelty and is deservedly crushed; but then it soars again, becoming Asia's economic giant. Modern state-builders, imperialists and militarists make way for a peaceful supremacy fashioned from high technology, the sweat of pliant salarymen, and later a 'soft power' of tourism and cherry blossoms, intelligent anime and cutesy pop.

Japan's dramatic rise, fall and resurgence across the twentieth century was real enough. But this by itself didn't explain a seemingly unshakeable commitment at home and around the world to this one story about Japan, all but eclipsing a wealth of conflicting, complicating evidence emerging from the late nineteenth century onwards. When the post-war boom years finally turned to bust in the 1990s – fears for their financial future, compounded by apprehension over China's rise and later the tick-tick-tick of a demographic time bomb (ageing society, low birth rate) – there was a deep sense of shock amongst people in Japan. This was not the country that politicians and much of the media had led them to believe they were living in, and working for. There was surprise abroad too, combined with a stubborn commitment to the modernization story. Coverage of the country's struggling economy was offset by a continuing, fascinated association of 'Japan' with neon signage, bustling commuter hubs, quirky habits and fads, and the latest things to be achieved with moulded plastic and electronic circuitry. Even the country's social problems seemed ultra-modern: young people exchanging human relationships for animal-petting cafés; robot care-givers for the elderly.

Where did this story derive such power? First, from an investment in Japan by outsiders of tremendous hope; a need, born in the latter half of the nineteenth century but never really disappearing, to see vindicated there the claims that Western-style modernization and modernity had made for themselves: rapid progress in understanding and controlling the physical and social worlds, albeit with jolts and reversals along the way; ever-improving standards of living; and the eventual banishing to museums, memorials and history books of all that is wrong or unsettling in human thought and behaviour. A second source was the great hope invested by many Japanese in clos-ing the gap between what mid nineteenth-century critics (Japanese and Western alike) insisted was a feudal backwater and the major industrial, trading and military powers of Europe and America.

Japan ended up serving as modernity's poster-child not once but twice. First around the turn of the twentieth century, when the West-ern world was tickled and gratified by the sight of besuited ex-samurai suddenly going about civilized urban business, from banking to tram-riding to democratic politics. And then for a second time, in the 'bright life' era of Harumi and Heisaku's meeting. The period in between, with its bloody ideological and military conflicts, was rel-egated to the status of a bump in the road. The popular phrase 'dark valley' said it all – a troubling but temporary stretch of terrain, passed through and left behind.

Western observers tempted to paint Japan in primary colours extolled, alongside the thrillingly modern, a culture marked by depth and subtlety of insight, from its pre-modern poetry to its film-making. Here was a second influential story about Japan, developed, as the modernization story was, through a combination of Japanese and Western efforts. It told of a land especially blessed, perhaps by the gods, with a distinctive genius emerging in its people and their cul-ture across enormous stretches of time, preserved by seeking always to balance the reception of outside ideas with a clear sense of what makes Japan 'Japan'.

China long weighed heaviest with the tellers of this second story. Acutely aware of Chinese influence on Japanese culture – from rice cultivation to written language, from Buddhist thought and architecture to the values by which people lived and rulers ruled – some sought to create a clear distinction between the 'rationalistic Chinese' and the more intuitive, poetical Japanese. Others pitted an understated Japanese refinement against the commercial grasping and general barbarism of odiferous early modern European traders, pointless trinkets filling the holds of their enormous ocean-going vessels.

Modern Western technology, from steam power to machine tools, gave the boldest of these storytellers little more than momentary pause for thought. It was soon claimed that such astonishing material advancement could only have been purchased at the cost of the Western soul. With help from Western romantics who fell hard for what they soon discovered of the philosophy and aesthetics of the 'East', there emerged in this story of national exceptionalism a promising sub-plot: a spiritually bankrupt 'West' is saved by a far-away Asian country where intuitive wisdom and closeness to nature have always been properly valued and preserved. In Japan, modernity would be achieved without the tragic side effects so obvious in Europe and America – the greed, the arrogance, the slums.

In the middle decades of the twentieth century, with the United States first on Japan's doorstep and then for seven years actually across the threshold and running its affairs, much was made of the gulf between American and Japanese 'selves' and psychological types. Differences were explored and speculated upon between American versus Japanese family structures, parenting styles, norms of behaviour, even toilet habits. Americans were said to be individualistic and assertive, head-based this-or-that people; Japanese preferred the warm embrace of the group, of rules, and also of ambiguity, raised with a 'both-and' sensibility that Westerners were liable to mistake for passivity or an inability to make decisions.

Where poets, intellectuals, politicians, soldiers and psychologists had all helped to weave versions of this second story down the years, by Harumi and Heisaku's time major contributions were on the horizon from the worlds of mass media and tourism. People at home in Japan and abroad could barely believe the pace at which the country bounced back from wartime devastation. As the Tokyo Olympics opened to great international fanfare in the autumn of 1964, and Ian Fleming bestowed on Japan the singular honour of serving as backdrop for a James Bond book – *You Only Live Twice*, complete with fantasy love interest 'Kissy Suzuki' – a market began to open up, both domestic and international, for scholarly insights into what made the Japanese tick. Japanese travel and advertising companies began to encourage locals and visitors alike not just to see something of the country – but to see it as special.

These two stories were not merely interpretations of events in Japan. Much in the country's modern history turned on their power actually to shape reality: operating separately or in uneasy combinations (could the country be a beacon of a universal modernity and yet 'unique' at the same time?), while suppressing rival accounts of 'Japan' – of people and projects and movements that didn't quite fit.

*

Harumi sought out Heisaku because her own story was starting to kill her. As it melted gradually away on his couch, she experienced not so much a loss as an unburdening. In place of *ikiru*, to live, she discovered *ikasareru*, to be lived or lived *through*. In place of *umareru*, to be born, was *umaresaserareru*, to be borne forth, *by* something. And in place of her plans and schemes and everything she usually paid attention to in the world, all the rest of life: rich, active and forever moving her along. After years of living within a single story, Harumi learned to imagine otherwise about herself – and radically so.

Over the next ten years she moved from Freud via Carl Jung and Christianity to Buddhism, shaving her head and taking the vows of a Buddhist nun. With the new name of Setouchi Jakuchō she became one of the best-known Buddhists in Japan, finishing one century and beginning the next as the scourge of her country's underperforming politicians and a comforter of the distressed. She often credited Heisaku with inspiring her personal style, used in her public talks and one-to-one meetings. And though most Japanese came to know her name, while few knew Heisaku's, the two of them shared the same calling: ministering to modern, malfunctioning stories.

This was spiritual and psychological work ideally suited to the country and the age in which Harumi and Heisaku met. People have always sought, told and lived according to stories. But there was a rare urgency and intensity to this across much of the modern era in Japan. In the mid-1800s, a country that had previously controlled its contact with the outside world was forced dramatically to ramp up those relationships – 'opened up' to the West at gunpoint, during the high noon of European colonialism and the early years of American expansionism. Acute strategic insecurity and a cascade of incoming ideas – from science and technology through to philosophy, politics and the arts – brought two related and enduring crises: of independence and identity.

Japan's great novelist Natsume Sōseki likened his country's experience here to a person who is awakened by a fire-bell and jumps out of bed. It was a shock that shaped the decades to come. People were subject to unprecedented interventions in their lives from leaders motivated by ambition and anxiety for Japan's standing in the world. The rhetoric of national emergency was an almost constant feature of life right up to the mid-1900s. These leaders were intent upon harnessing new technologies – from a nationwide network of classrooms to factories, discussion groups and broadsheets – in order to impress upon people the threat from abroad and the need to meet it by building a unified and purposeful modern nation. The devastation of Japan's mid twentieth-century wars did not put an end to these hectoring intrusions; they took on the gentler, more intimate form of a deeply influential mass media – newspapers, radio and television – whose critics charged that it combined wide reach with a narrow notion of the nation.

Alongside being pressured to play their allotted part in an evolving national story – on pain, depending upon the times, of being deemed selfish, anti-social, un-Japanese, or even treasonous – people in modern Japan had to sift for themselves a dizzying array of insights about the world, domestic and foreign, historical and contemporary. The opportunities and difficulties involved were felt earliest and most acutely in rapidly changing late nineteenth- century cities, and in particular by a burgeoning middle class whose members strove to fashion rationales that could bring order and contour to the unwieldy present, and offer reassuring projections for the future.

Tokyo's transformation by the early 1900s was treated by enthusiast and critic alike as paradigmatic, a sign of things to come for the rest of Japan. Leafing lovingly through 'One Hundred Famous Views' of that great city, completed by the woodblock print artist Hiroshige as recently as the 1850s, a pessimist might glance out of the window and conclude that the bitterest of exchanges had been made. The soft burble of river water washing languidly along beneath willow trees and rainbow-curved wooden bridges, past the occasional family on foot, paper umbrellas in hands – for the screech of iron-wheeled rickshaws, the incessant clop and clatter of horse-drawn buses, the din of traffic. A crystal-clear sky above low-rise homes and welcoming, open-fronted shops, its spaciousness deepened rather than disturbed by the birds and kites that dotted it by day and the glow of lantern light from below at night – for an ever-worsening chaos of construction, of mixed styles and materials and qualities, eating up street space and thrusting ever upwards, their façades sprouting national flags, shop signs and advertising posters, telegraph lines spooling outwards from the brickwork to form a thickening lattice with the tram wires running above the streets. And the people! You rarely saw more than handfuls at a time in Hiroshige. But here they were pouring in from across the country, bustling and jostling, dodging around the tram traffic and hurriedly getting on with who knew what . . .

This was not merely a problem of under-planned urbanization or a rather prosaic dislike of the new. Where the early architects of Japan's modernization story saw in the city proof of progress, others detected imposition and imposture. They encountered modernity not as a natural development but as a 'thing', a foreign import. They tried to touch it and trace its contours, recall its 'before' and identify its potential 'after'; probe its logic, and search for any space that might be left – uncontaminated – around or beneath it. Like Indian contemporaries scouring their cultural landscape for pockets of life free from the taint of British colonialism – the privacy of home life, spirituality, the feted purity of women's hearts – Japanese novelists, philosophers, ethnologists and others sought some means with which to survive this interloper.

There was keen interest from the country's commentariat in those who couldn't or didn't want to cope. An individual's distress, it was thought, could be read alternately as a sign of society's success or of its taking a wrong turn. From the 1870s, Japanese newspapers debated *shinkei suijaku* (nervous exhaustion, or 'neurasthenia') and its relationship with the challenges of modern life: new kinds of bureaucratic tasks; an ever-quickening pace of life into which people were bullied and then trapped; the pressure to dress, eat, read and behave in certain ways; and various public responsibilities in building up the nation. Attention later shifted to *hanmon* (existential distress), thought to affect the young especially, and by the early 1930s one could find talk of *sarariman no kyōfu*: the anxiety of Japan's first generation of salaryman, whom a consumerist society pressured into wanting more than he could afford. His lot in life was to shuttle on crowded trains between an insecure job where his skills were treated as commodities rather than gifts, and a home life marred by an atmosphere of 'icy separation' from a wife who blamed him rather than society for her dreams going unfulfilled. One could see the desperate fallout from this, claimed the author of *Sarariman: Kyōfu no jidai* ('Salaryman: Age of Anxiety') (1930), in men's 'boisterous dancing' in the new urban dance halls, or in their 'silent endurance'.

All sorts of physical, dietary, spiritual and psychological 'cures' were advertised for addressing modernity's ills. They were joined in the 1930s by extreme political 'solutions': the violent removal of creeping Anglo-American influence in Asia, responsible, it was felt, for alienating people from their cultural roots. And yet Japanese distress was not, as the ideologues promised, eliminated through force of arms. For all the world-class achievements in science and sport, technology, business and the arts that soon filled the pages of postwar newspapers, the parsing of people's pain for clues to society's ills went on. Particular attention was paid to the young, from school refusal in the 1960s to *hikikomori* in the early twenty-first century: men (for the most part) who physically avoided or rejected society by shutting themselves away at home. As Japan prepared to host the Summer Olympics for a second time, in 2020, *karō utsubyō* and *karōshi* were never far from the headlines – people made to strive so hard for some civic or corporate ideal that they worked themselves into depression, and even to death.

Here was a nation wrestling with itself across more than a century and a half, searching for the right guiding story or stories. The process played out across politics and music, art and philosophy, conflict at home and abroad, family and work life, dance and religion, literature, folklore and film. It is still going on.

This book explores those struggles, reflecting along the way on stories in general: how they are seeded and how they grow and spread like vines, supporting or entangling whole societies; how they take unexpected turns; how they may be lost and recovered. This seems, in the early twenty-first century, to matter more than ever. We know now the unpredictable paths that modernization can take, the surprising range of flavours in which 'modernity' comes, and the frightening speed at which national purpose can unravel and people, or peoples, be forced to think again. Modern Japan offers a compelling case study in the sort of wrestling that lies behind – and ahead – of us all.

*

At the end of each session Harumi would pause by Heisaku's front door for a moment, stepping back into her shoes. 'He would compliment me on my kimono or my handbag,' she later recalled – 'alas, never on my looks . . .' These were basic gentlemanly gestures for a man of Heisaku's generation. And yet Harumi found that they were the final, essential element in each of their encounters: somehow a reminder that she was being seen in a much broader, richer way than she was usually able to see herself – a reminder that there was more there to see.

Stories are a very human compromise. We cannot simply inhabit them, unquestioning, but nor are we able fully to discern them, see around them, and so decide for ourselves how tightly they should grasp us. To live and flourish somewhere in between requires, for nations as for individuals, effort without end. But, as Harumi found, this is the only home we have.

Kosawa Heisaku (1897–1968) and Setouchi Harumi (1922–),
pictured in the 1960s.

PART ONE

Weaving, Tearing
(1850s to 1910s)

I
Japan Goes Global

The encounter ended with the gift of a small piece of white cloth. The American Commodore Matthew C. Perry delivered it to his samurai interlocutors along with a message that he had crossed the Atlantic, sailed around Africa and India, and finally crept up the coast of China to convey. Written on vellum, bound in blue silk velvet, and presented in a box of rosewood and gold, it was from his president, Millard Fillmore. The President gently and respectfully encouraged his 'great and good friend' the Emperor of Japan to open up his country – to trade, to friendship and to the supply of passing American vessels with fuel, food and water.

The choreography of Perry's visit, in July 1853, was more forceful than his president's prose. Reading up on Japan in the New York Public Library, he had come to believe that only firm displays of power and intent would get through to its people. So when he stepped ashore near the entrance to Edo Bay, he did so in the company of one hundred sailors, one hundred Marines, and two military bands. Perry marched up the beach with the two largest and most threatening-looking men of his squadron by his side, both given extra weapons to wear for the occasion.

Hosts far outnumbered guests. Thousands of samurai were arrayed along the beach and up a nearby hill; on foot and on horseback, armed with swords, spears and guns. But they struck Perry as a small and effeminate bunch, drawn up in ragged formation with local villagers allowed to gawp through the gaps at their foreign visitors. Perry thought that his own men, by contrast, exuded strength and discipline, despite some being kept up the night before by the sound of Japanese carpenters hurriedly constructing a pavilion in which to welcome them. Cannon fire advertised the advanced military might lying just out to sea. Here, on the beach, the proud strains of 'Hail, Columbia' completed the effect.

Then came the piece of cloth. In the midst of all the red-carpet ceremony – drawn out by the laborious back and forth of interpretation via Dutch – the message conveyed by the handing over of that single object cut right through. Should you refuse my president's generously expressed requests, Perry made clear, there will be a war. And you will need *this* to surrender with.

Point made, and promising to return for an answer the following year, Perry led his four towering vessels out to sea. Hulls coated in pitch, and two spewing smoke from their funnels, they soon entered into Japanese folklore as the *kurofune*, the 'black ships' – omens of dark days ahead.

Japan's ruling Tokugawa shogunate and its allies were in disarray. They had avoided outright conflict with the Americans, 200-year-old flintlocks resting unused (and possibly unloaded) in samurai hands as the very latest in steam-powered technology cruised away into the distance. But their hold on Japan's borders and internal politics alike had been slipping for some time now. These exquisitely rude and troublingly persistent foreigners, likened by one Japanese commentator to 'flies around a bowl of rice', looked like being the final straw.

How different it had all been at the beginning. In the second half of the 1500s, three great warlords had worked steadily to stitch the country back together again under one rule, following centuries of rivalry and conflict between powerful regional lords. Tokugawa Ieyasu was the last of the three, winning a decisive battle at Sekigahara in 1600 and receiving from the Emperor in Kyoto three years later his formal appointment as Shogun: 'barbarian-subduing generalissimo'. He proceeded to subdue Emperor, provincial rivals and foreign powers alike.

With the Emperor, Ieyasu employed culture as political chloroform. Japan's capital, Kyoto, was to remain a place of refined study, ritual and poetry – and very little else. Anything that looked like debate or the pursuit of power would attract the unforgiving attentions of Tokugawa samurai retainers. A large contingent was soon quartered within menacingly easy reach of the Imperial Palace, in a new residence built by the ever-vigilant Ieyasu: Nijō Castle was constructed with 'nightingale floors', designed to emit a bird-like squeak when stepped on – depriving would-be assassins of the element of surprise.

The Tokugawa shogunate had its main base in a former fishing village called Edo, which underwent rapid development from the early 1600s as a centre of national power. Hilly areas were flattened out, watery ones filled with earth. Thousands of labourers were conscripted to ransack a far-away peninsula for its granite. They brought the enormous pieces to Edo by barge, and then honed and stacked them to form a steeply angled defensive perimeter, nearly eleven miles long, for an enormous castle compound. Life within those walls, whose tops passers-by had to crane their necks to make out, remained largely a mystery to an expanding city population whose homes and shops and livelihoods were arranged around them. Few would ever get close to the intricate corridor networks, the screens of gold leaf and delicate brushwork, and the fragrant, polished wood amidst which Japan's first family set about forging and ruling a nation.

Japan's regional lords (*daimyō*) – around two hundred of them in the early 1600s – were kept in line via a signature Tokugawa mix of persuasion and coercion. An alternate attendance system (*sankin kōtai*) required *daimyō* and their staff to reside every other year in this emerging de facto capital, inside sprawling homes newly constructed outside the castle compound – the more loyal they were, the closer they lived to those soaring structures. Edo was soon a city of half a million souls: samurai residing in the 'high city'; those who served their needs populating the 'low city'. During the year they spent back in their largely independent domains, with their own up-and-coming castle towns, *daimyō* were required to leave their wives and children behind in Edo – effectively as hostages.

Along with the obvious surveillance advantages of *sankin kōtai* – the system was set up so that at any one time, half of all *daimyō* would be in Edo, and mostly within sight of the castle – came the benefit of all but bankrupting many of these lords. They were forced to make ruinously expensive journeys with a large retinue (some had more than a thousand retainers and servants in tow) to and from ruinously expensive Edo residences, which considerations of relative status forced many to build and furnish in grand style. In addition, the shogunate required contributions of money and labour from *daimyō*: towards building a bridge, a shrine or a castle like Nijō, or else shoring up coastal defences. In return for all this, the shogunate recognized and guaranteed domain (*han*) borders, meaning that *daimyō* need worry much less about their neighbours than they had in recent centuries.

When it came to foreign powers, the Tokugawa strategy was careful management backed by threat of force. Iberian traders and missionaries had been active in Japan in the second half of the 1500s, the latter rapidly gaining themselves a reputation – the Jesuits in particular – for being at least as interested in politics and lucrative trade as in matters purely religious. By 1600, convert numbers were close to 300,000 (according to missionary tallies), boosted as they were elsewhere in Asia through mass conversions required by powerful figures of people under their control. In Japan's case, that often meant *daimyō*, moved by some mixture of the gospel and prospective gains from Portuguese trade. Amidst worries about loyalties being undermined by mixed allegiances, along with rumours that Europeans had started selling Japanese women into slavery and dressing their spies up as missionaries (scoping the country out for an invasion attempt), the warlord Toyotomi Hideyoshi had ordered the expulsion of all foreign missionaries back in 1587. Ten years later, he crucified twenty-six Christians at Nagasaki, including six non-Japanese: a warning to all the rest.

After a short hiatus, the new Tokugawa shogunate took up the theme. Fresh persecutions were launched in the 1610s, while an Edict in 1636 expressed the shogunate's position with particular clarity:

> No Japanese ship nor boat whatever, nor any native of Japan, shall presume to go out of the country; whoever acts contrary to this shall die ... All persons who return from abroad shall be put to death. Whoever discovers a Christian priest shall have a reward of 400 to 500 sheets of silver. All Namban ['southern barbarians': Portuguese and Spanish people] who propagate the doctrine of the Catholics, or bear this scandalous name, shall be imprisoned. The whole race of the Portuguese with their mothers, nurses, and whatever belongs to them, shall be banished to Macao.

Christian churches and monasteries were burned, incoming missionaries executed and wealthy convert families exiled. From the 1640s
onwards, the business-minded Dutch found themselves the only acceptable Europeans: less hungry than the Catholic Portuguese for converts
or for the country's gold and silver – another concern for the shogunate
was the trading away of its precious metals. But even the Dutch had to
be wary of overstepping the mark. The drill onboard their vessels
entering Nagasaki Bay was the same every year. Sailors prepared to
surrender their guns and ammunition to the authorities, together with
the ship's rudder and sails. Bibles were nailed down into wooden
barrels, not to be retrieved until the ship left Japanese waters again.

A handful of Europeans succeeded, over the decades that followed,
in making pioneering links between Western and Japanese medicine
and botany. But for the most part, the Dutch presence in Tokugawa
Japan was limited to traders who looked forward to doing a little business, playing billiards, drinking coffee (which first made its way into
Japan in the 1690s, thanks to the Dutch), and perhaps paying for the
company of a local woman or two – all from the confines of a small
man-made island called Dejima, shaped like a fan and connected to the
Nagasaki mainland by a single, guarded bridge. There was to be no
free travel within Japan, no politics, and most certainly no religion.

The shoguns' power over the next two hundred years, and the
single story of purpose and legitimacy that they sought to tell about
themselves and a newly unified Japan, was built on firm foundations:
military supremacy, control of huge swathes of richly taxable rice
paddy, a thicket of legal and sumptuary codes, co-option of Buddhism's popular appeal and temple networks, the sponsoring of
Neo-Confucian thought (with its welcome emphasis upon filial duty),
and finally the many fruits of an unprecedented peace. There was a
reason why Perry was met, in 1853, by poorly drilled troops toting
museum pieces: while Westerners had spent much of the past two and
a half centuries honing the technologies of war through repeatedly
tearing themselves and others apart, Japan had largely flourished.

'Settled agriculture' had come to mean something again, after the
deadly disruptions of earlier decades. Cottage industries from *sake* to
silk production had blossomed, while sea-borne trade spanned the length
of the archipelago, from fur-clad Ainu people in the far north down to

the tropical Ryūkyū islands in the south; across to China and Korea, and further beyond, courtesy of the Dutch. A modest proportion of the nation's children received an education at schools run by temples or regional domains, or else at small, private institutions. Tourists tramped new roadways in search of great places and monuments, guidebooks in hand. Print-making and satirical storytelling emerged as just two of the many arts chronicling and enlivening city life in places like Edo, Osaka and Kyoto. Bureaucratic statecraft – orders and judgement from on high; organized self-surveillance from below, in groups of five or more households – was itself developed almost to the point of an art form.

Detail from a sketch of Edo Castle

The shogunate achieved stability at the cost of flexibility, with the codification of everyday life stretching even into which foods and fabrics people of differing social status might enjoy: fine silks for samurai, down through the plainer kind for townspeople – merchants and artisans – finishing at rough cotton for lowly peasants. For a long while, these arrangements seemed to be just what a war-torn country needed, to recover its balance. But they were too brittle to cope well with longer-term change, and by the early 1800s the rot appeared to be setting in. Japan found itself beset by weak leadership and a flagging economy, alongside periodically failing crops. Society was in turmoil as low-born farmers and merchants got steadily richer, while samurai families – on inadequate stipends and forbidden from working in potentially lucrative professions – slipped into poverty.

Crop failures and fluctuations in the monetary system caused pain around the country. But some were able to pass it on. The shogunate could lean on *daimyō* for rice or cash; the *daimyō* in turn pressurized their samurai retainers. Merchants could hike prices or alter their rates of exchange, while wealthier country families could make new demands of, or dispense with the paid labour of, weaker ones. For those at the bottom, however, there was only desperation. Famine and forced migration became so bad at times that the authorities took to the surveillance of pregnant women and young mothers to prevent a loss of rural productivity through abortion and through a practice known by the agricultural euphemism of *mabiki*: 'thinning out the seedlings' to ensure better growth for the rest – infanticide.

A guiding principle in the Neo-Confucian ethics of the time was mutuality. Within the social order, as within each family, the higher could expect of the lower, but the lower could expect from the higher too. Service travelled one way, care the other. What this meant in practice was that protest against insufficiently solicitous superiors was a right, even a duty – in the interests of restoring the social order. Many of the tens of thousands of protestors whom the leaders of late Tokugawa Japan saw as enemies were in fact quite clearly its products: they saw themselves not as rebelling against traditional values of sincerity, selflessness and self-cultivation, but as practising them properly.

To top things off, Westerners began once again to make mischief. In 1808 a Dutch ship was noticed sailing into Nagasaki Bay, a little later

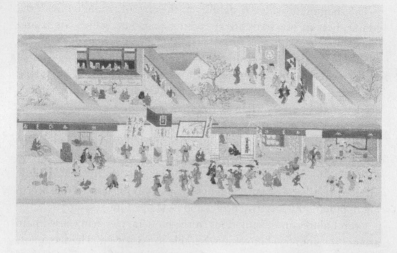

Detail from a street scene in Edo's theatre district, section from *Theatres of the East* (*Azuma yarō*) by Furuyama Moromasa (c.1710–30)

in the season than usual. A small party of Dutch residents on Dejima rowed out to greet it – and was promptly captured. The ship was in fact British: HMS *Phaeton*, flying a Dutch flag as camouflage. Her teenage captain made a curt request for supplies for his ship, in return for which he declared he would spare the lives of the Dutch. He followed this up with threats to destroy the other ships in the harbour, along with an admonitory volley of cannon and gunfire. The Dutch and Japanese scrambled their coastal defences: ageing cannons that mostly failed to fire, and a small handful of troops. Before reinforcements could arrive, the local magistrate had provided the supplies and a well-timed wind had seen the *Phaeton* breeze safely out of the bay.

The magistrate disembowelled himself and the enquiries into foreign mischief began, in the course of which the Japanese made the belated discovery that America was now an independent country. It had, it turned out, been in Dutch interests to keep this from them. For similar reasons, the Japanese had been given a very late and very misleading account of the French Revolution. Thanks to the regime's seclusion policy, there were few alternative sources about global affairs against which self-interested Dutch censoring of the international news could be checked.

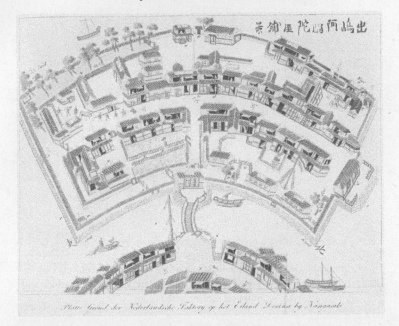

出嶋阿蘭陀国屋舗景

Plan Grond der Nederlandsche Faktory op het Eiland Desima by Nangasaki

Ground plan of Dejima

Blame did not lie solely with the Dutch, however. There had been few official attempts in Japan to make the most of having these well-travelled Europeans around for the last century and a half. On their yearly pilgrimages to Edo to pay their respects, the Dutch had found themselves invited to crawl and jump and dance rather than speak. People seemed to find their bodies and mannerisms hilarious, from the red hair to the thick-soled Dutch clogs which made some Japanese suspect that their wearers, just like dogs, possessed feet whose heels didn't touch the ground. Mothers took to hushing their children with whispered threats about the demonic and malodorous Dutch coming to snatch them.

The shogunate had relaxed the rules on imported Western knowledge in 1720, opening the way for crusading *rangakusha* – practitioners of 'Dutch learning' (*ran* from 'Oranda', Holland; *gakusha* meaning 'scholar') – to begin gathering in and around Nagasaki, hoping to absorb what they could from the books, artworks and artefacts that made it into Japan via Dejima. The physician Sugita Genpaku (1733–1817) pored

A Banquet on Dejima: some of Japan's first coffee-drinkers, relaxing amidst the mixed Western and Japanese decor typical of the era (tables and chairs on tatami-mat floors)

over a Dutch anatomy text for hours on end, struggling with friends to guess at the meaning of words by their placement near pictures and their frequency of recurrence. Sugita recalled once spending a 'long spring day' wrestling with a single line: 'the eyebrows are the hair growing above the eyes'. He went as far as performing autopsies on executed criminals – a rare transgression for his times – in order to compare the contents of hacked-open, torn-back torsos with Chinese and then with Dutch accounts. The former were woefully adrift, the latter spot on.

But such information had always to be shared with caution. Despite *rangakusha* protestations that they were acquiring new knowledge for the furtherance of regional or national interests (in Sugita's case, to secure the health of his lord), the shogunate in Edo could be acutely sensitive to having its prerogatives over policy and security infringed upon. The military scholar Hayashi Shihei pointed out that a nation made up of small islands could not afford to rely for its security upon tactics rooted in Chinese treatises like *The Art of War* (fifth century BC), which focused on expanses of inland terrain. It ought instead to maintain a strong navy and credible coastal defences. For his troubles, Hayashi found his book, *Kaikoku*

Heidan ('Military Defence of a Maritime Nation') (1787), burned, and the blocks on which it was created destroyed. He himself was placed under house arrest, where he soon died, a deeply disillusioned man.

Other voices in Japan had sought to warn about the intensifying threat from abroad. The world's great powers had stayed away from Japan until the 1800s not out of fear or respect but out of lack of interest. There had been richer pickings elsewhere, from India to China to South East Asia. That time was now coming to an end. The Russians had pushed ever eastward across their continent during the 1700s, arriving at the Pacific and eventually heading for Nagasaki, seeking trade (Nikolai Rezanov, bearing a letter from Tsar Alexander I, was made to wait there for six months in 1804–5 and was then sent packing). The Americans had pushed ever westward during that century and since, arriving on the other side of the same vivid-blue expanse with much the same thoughts about Japan in their heads. President Fillmore, in his letter to the Emperor delivered in 1853, wrote proudly of his country stretching 'from ocean to ocean', its 'great State of California' lying 'directly opposite the dominions of your imperial majesty'.

This moment, of no longer being able to fob off or fend off the neighbours, seemed to be captured by an Edo artist named Hokusai, working away in the early 1830s at thirty-six landscape prints depicting Mount Fuji. In some of the pictures, Fuji dominated the scene completely, its perfectly gradual gradient drawing the eye skywards. In others, it provided the serene backdrop for Tokugawa Japan going about its peaceful, confident, highly civilized business: people building, crafting, selling, fishing and leaning languidly over temple balconies to appreciate the awesome mountain.

But in one picture, Fuji appears differently. It has shrunk far away into the background, framed by tempestuous waters whose undulations and claw-like curling spray dominate the scene. Three boats ride the waves, their oarsmen too small and indistinct for us to know their thoughts. They may be mastering a stormy sea, thrilling at the possibilities that travel may soon open up. Or perhaps they are nervously hunkering down, clinging on for dear life as an approaching wall of water looms and threatens to engulf them.

A great many *daimyō*, samurai retainers and commoners alike had acquiesced in their country's new political arrangements after 1600

Hokusai's *Great Wave off Kanagawa* (*c*.1830)

more out of weariness with war than any particular affection for the Tokugawa family. Amongst the most important of those who never learned to love the shogunate were the rulers of two great domains: Satsuma, on the southern island of Kyūshū, and Chōshū, just across the water on the westernmost tip of Japan's main island of Honshū.

Satsuma's dominance over the Ryūkyū Kingdom to the south-west of Japan had brought it wealth and allowed it to build useful trading contacts with China and Korea – quietly flouting Tokugawa control of Japan's contact with the outside world. Its warriors donned full armour every year on the anniversary of Sekigahara, visiting a temple near the castle town of Kagoshima to meditate on what had been for them an epochal defeat. In Chōshū, mothers had their boys sleep with feet pointing eastwards – an insult to Edo – and told them never to forget Sekigahara, even in their dreams.

The weaker the Tokugawa shogunate looked, especially in the wake of Perry's visit, the fresher that memory appeared: a seizure of power, which could always be reversed. It had long been traditional for senior figures in the household of the Chōshū *daimyō* to appear before their lord at the first cockcrow of each new year. 'Has the time come to begin the subjugation of the *bakufu* [the Tokugawa military government]?' they would ask. The intoned reply – 'It is still too early' – never seemed likely to change. Until now.

*

Such were the swirling waters into which Perry sailed his ships for a second time, returning as promised in 1854 for his answer. The shogunate had concluded that in the circumstances there was only one answer it could give. Irony became one of the first things Japan learned at the hands of the modern West, as its representatives sat down to sign a 'Treaty of Peace and Amity' surrounded by five hundred American sailors and Marines, while a thousand more Americans waited aboard ten heavily armed ships out at sea, lest the friendship not get off on the right foot. Three American bands blared out martial music in celebration.

Signed at a fishing village later renamed Yokohama, this treaty and a successor in 1858 covering trade became for Japan an opening of the international floodgates. Soon the British, the Russians, the French and others were clamouring for similar deals. They managed to secure access to Japanese markets with guaranteed low import tariffs, together with the promise, as in China and elsewhere, of 'extraterritoriality': when non-Japanese committed crimes in 'treaty ports' like Yokohama, they would be tried under their own, rather than Japanese, jurisdiction.

Political unrest and economic woe followed, as stories of intrusive and overbearing foreigners did the rounds in the treaty ports and beyond. A five-man Commission for Foreign Countries, established in 1858, made its way through seventy-four members in just ten years as it struggled to work out what to do about Japan's newfound and unwanted popularity abroad. Younger, low- and middle-ranking samurai began to band together as *shishi*, or 'men of high purpose', a great many of them hailing from south-western domains including Satsuma and Chōshū. Where the nation's leaders appeared unable to deal with foreigners and guide the country forward, these activists resolved to intervene directly: intimidating their political enemies and attacking non-Japanese who set up home in the treaty ports.

The British diplomat Ernest Satow, serving in Japan in the 1860s, reported that such was the widely acknowledged risk during these years of 'coming to an untimely death at the hands of an expert swords-man' that he had bought himself a revolver, powder, bullets and caps. 'No one leaves their compound without a weapon,' he claimed. 'Most sleep with one under their pillow.'

Preying particularly on expat minds were the events of July 1861. Laurence Oliphant, stationed with the British Legation in Edo, was enjoying the sight of a comet passing overhead one night when he heard a dog begin to bark, followed closely by the sound of a Japanese watch-man's rattle. He rushed out of his room, and down a dark corridor:

> Just as I turned the corner I came upon a tall black figure, with his arms above his head, holding a huge two-handed sword. I could only see indistinctly that the figure had a mask on, and seemed in armour. Short time for observation, had to dodge the sword, and get back a step to get at him with my whip, yelling loudly. He made no sound; we were at it for a minute or two . . .

Others at the Legation seized hold of their guns and rushed in. Joined by their Japanese guards, they successfully fought off the attackers across the course of a busy, bloody night. Only in daylight did Oli-phant, badly wounded, discover what had really saved his life: an enormous wooden beam running across the ceiling of his quarters, badly damaged by heavy sword blows that had been intended for him.

The number of actual killings by *shishi* ran into the tens rather than the hundreds, mostly of Japanese perceived to be collaborating with foreigners or otherwise participating in a treasonously wrong-headed foreign policy. What mattered more was the atmosphere of heightened crisis that their actions helped to create, together with a growing sense in south-western domains especially that, as in 1600 so now in the mid-1860s, the time was ripe for radical change. The shogunate was mired in a mix of too-little-too-late interest in West-ern technology and interminable dithering over how to deal with foreign pressure. Meanwhile, a mismanaged economy ensured that inflation, unemployment and hunger were amongst the early rewards of participation in the global economy. Riots broke out in city and countryside alike, alongside millenarian predictions of world renewal and joyously fatalistic festivities – of drink, dance, food, and sex. *Ee ja nai ka?!* ran the refrain. *Who cares anymore?!*

Leading figures in Satsuma and Chōshū began to go their own way, using relationships that Satsuma had built up with Western traders – including the Scottish merchant Thomas Blake Glover, based in Nagasaki – to purchase and later manufacture up-to-date guns, ships and cannon. The two domains concluded a secret alliance in 1866, agreeing to help one another should the shogunate, desperately building up and re-equipping its own forces, seek to impose its will on them. They need not have worried. A punitive expedition sent from Edo against Chōshū that year was so underwhelming – the best troops were needed to stop Edo and Osaka going up in flames, while some domains refused outright to contribute forces – that Chōshū men alone were able to see off the threat. The Shogun, Tokugawa Yoshinobu, found himself faced with an impossible military, political and economic situation, just as influential imperial courtiers in Kyoto (sentenced to poetry all those years ago by Tokugawa Ieyasu) decided that the time had come to retake the reins of power from a family that had well and truly forfeited the right to hold them.

In 1867, Yoshinobu reluctantly allowed leaders from Tosa domain, allied with Satsuma and Chōshū, to persuade him to resign. Sitting amidst the splendour of Nijō Castle, built by Tokugawa Ieyasu, he gave up the title so hard-won by his illustrious ancestor. Yoshinobu expected that in exchange he would sit at the head of a new ruling council of *daimyō*. Instead, early in 1868, radicals from Satsuma and Chōshū led a coup in Kyoto and gained control of the young boy-emperor Mutsuhito, who was encouraged to proclaim his own full restoration to power. The confiscation of all Tokugawa lands was announced, forcing Yoshinobu into all-out conflict.

The 'Boshin War' dragged on into 1869, with anti-Tokugawa troops multiplying as a mix of samurai and commoner conscripts joined up from across Japan's domains. Tokugawa forces found themselves pushed ever northwards, right up to the island of Ezo (soon to be known as Hokkaidō) where they established a short-lived, quasi-independent state, complete with elections to its leadership. They finally surrendered to 'imperial forces' – as the rebel samurai now styled themselves – in the summer of 1869.

Back down south, a fresh epoch had begun the year before. In the past, the era name in Japan, decided by imperial court officials, had often changed several times across the reign of a single emperor. Now, the era would only change with the succession of a new emperor, who would posthumously bear its name. This new era and this new Emperor were to be known as 'Meiji': 'enlightened rule'.

The young man on whom all this was being staked found himself evicted from the refined comfort of Kyoto towards the end of 1868 – 'Meiji 1' of the new age – and paraded all the way to Edo, where he was installed in the imposing castle that had once belonged to the Tokugawa family. That great city, peacefully surrendered except for outbreaks of sporadic resistance and opportunistic criminality, acquired a new name: 'Tokyo', or Eastern Capital. Here, the Emperor was to be fashioned into an effective figurehead – the centrepiece of an as-yet embryonic national narrative.

The new regime's Charter Oath, issued in 1868, struck an artfully general and conciliatory tone:

1. Deliberative assemblies shall be widely established and all matters decided by public discussion.
2. All classes, high and low, shall be united in vigorously carrying out the administration of affairs of state.
3. The common people, no less than the civil and military officials, shall all be allowed to pursue their own calling so that there may be no discontent.
4. Evil customs of the past shall be broken off and everything based upon the just laws of Nature.
5. Knowledge shall be sought throughout the world so as to strengthen the foundation of imperial rule.

Alongside high-sounding ideals ran necessarily grubbier, more urgent priorities. A guiding principle was established: *fukoku kyōhei*, 'enrich the state, strengthen the military'. Japan had to avoid being next after once-mighty China on Western colonialism's 'To Do' list, and must secure revision of the humiliating international trading agreements now widely disparaged as 'unequal treaties'. The new Japanese state and its story were to be forged in an atmosphere if not of outright panic then of acute anxiety, mixed with powerful and urgent determination.

Every resource, including every human resource, was devoted to the self-strengthening task. An effective military needed reasonably up-to-date hardware, which in turn meant the finance, raw materials, technology, infrastructure and expertise necessary for building up industrial capacity. Japanese students and scholars, businessmen and diplomats toured the world in search of all of this, in the years after 1868, while at home a small clique of rebels-turned-statesmen oversaw an unprecedented concentration of national power: Ōkubo Toshimichi, Mori Arinori and Saigō Takamori from Satsuma domain; Kido Takayoshi, Yamagata Aritomo and Itō Hirobumi from Chōshū; Itagaki Taisuke from Tosa; and Ōkuma Shigenobu from Hizen. Together these men and their allies revived a centuries-old executive body known as the Dajōkan, or Council of State. They exchanged Japan's hundreds of old domains, run by great regional families, for just fifty 'prefectures' controlled ultimately from the new capital – in whose Kasumigaseki district they established European-style ministries (including Public Works, Industry and Education), developing national policies and issuing national directives.

Transformation proceeded apace across the 1870s. A new banking system began dealing in the yen as the national currency, replacing the old Tokugawa *koban*. A combination of government and private capital helped to establish high-tech mining and the industries of the future, including cotton-spinning and silk-reeling. Telegraph and postal services were set up, and via a Fundamental Code of Education (1872) a national schooling system was established. Pupils, a few clad in the shiny-buttoned military-style uniforms favoured by their Prussian counterparts, learned modern values first from American textbooks and then via role models from Japanese history and legend – from good-hearted soy-sauce vendors up to the great Tokugawa Ieyasu himself (his descendants might have let the country down, but he himself was revered as a great nation-builder). For those occasions where education botched the job, a Tokyo police force based on a French model stood ready to keep His Majesty's subjects in line.

A limited railway entered operation, its brick and glass station buildings serving as models of modern architecture. Tax payable in rice, based on harvest size and local agreement, was replaced by a centrally assessed land tax, payable in cash. Conscription was introduced, to an army based on the French, and then later on the evidently superior Prussian, model – the Japanese kept a sharp eye on the

Franco-Prussian War of 1870–71 as they now did on most goings-on in Europe and beyond. Japan's navy, comprising mostly volunteers, was based on Britain's Royal Navy.

The scale of this task was enormous, involving a rapidly rising population destined to reach 42 million by the turn of twentieth century – larger than that of the United Kingdom or France. But one of the advantages of being a relative latecomer to modernity – which was how Japan's first leaders regarded their situation – was that you could learn not just from its hits but from its evident misses too: avoiding London's slums and the coal smog draped over Liverpool, all but blocking out the daylight (one Japanese official wrote of the 'sad and pitiful' history of British industrialization), and avoiding the excessive ceding of political power to the general public that marred the English and French systems.

Everything could be assessed in advance and then adapted to suit the new nation's needs and evolving self-image. The postal system was based on Britain's General Post Office (GPO). But where the GPO employed women – as sub-postmistresses, postwomen and clerical workers – it was decided that a Japanese system could only be staffed by men. And with Tokyo's transport still underdeveloped, and its population swelling with rural migrants not entirely to be trusted, to the original Parisian model was added a dense network of *kōban*: police boxes housing one or two officers, so that city-dwellers could more easily get hold of a police officer – or vice versa.

But while there was general consensus amongst Japan's leaders on the practical measures required to strengthen the country, and on the basic need for unity of national purpose, precisely what that purpose ought to be beyond security and revising the treaties was less easily agreed. Argument, trial and error, and changes of direction were to be significant features of the years ahead, both at the apex of politics and out across the country. Sometimes, what *seemed* modern ended up governing decision-making in building the country's capacities. For a hugely expensive new silk-reeling plant in 1872, pure economics dictated the use of wood for fuel and a simple design that could be easily repaired. This way, Japan could get a major export industry moving relatively quickly. But wood was redolent of the past. It was primitive. *Coal* was the fuel used in the modern West (though Tokugawa Japan, too, had been known for its production; President

Fillmore had noted as much in his letter to the Emperor). So it had to be coal for the new plant – and French coal at that. And it had to be a complex modern design, which it turned out few in Japan could operate and even fewer could put right when it went wrong.

Elsewhere, modernization could be a matter of pure caprice. Early Meiji Japanese might have learned much more than they did from the Italians or the Americans. But at the crucial moment both countries were riven by war, leaving Britain, France and Prussia better placed to provide models and expertise. One of Japan's first and most influential teachers of medicine at the new Tokyo University, Erwin von Bälz, was recruited on the basis of a chance meeting with a Japanese patient in Leipzig. And though large numbers of Japanese went abroad to learn from the world's best, many of those trips were planned on the basis of limited knowledge about what 'best' was, and where it could be found. Time away was often limited to mere months, so that the connections made, and the imprimatur gained of some famous European scholar, were sometimes of greater significance than anything that was actually learned.

Japan's determining of its own borders, too, was an uncertain, exploratory affair. On the basis that a great power must be a colonizing, civilizing one – the logic of the day – territories towards the north and south of the archipelago became subject to colonial experiments, alternating between attempts at assimilating their inhabitants as true 'Japanese' (still a developing concept) and keeping them at arm's length. The net result was that northern Ainu and the people of the southern Ryūkyū Kingdom found their homelands absorbed into Japan, as Hokkaidō and Okinawa prefectures respectively, while they themselves remained peripheral peoples, in unflattering contrast to whose histories and habits 'mainland' Japanese defined and celebrated their own.

These territorial moves were also part of a search for natural resources and fresh markets to help the new economy grow, and for the kind of rightful sphere of security and influence that few Western powers could deny Japan without risk of glaring hypocrisy. The Korean peninsula in particular was regarded as too close for comfort to south-western Japan: it was, as Yamagata Aritomo put it, 'a dagger pointed at Japan's heart'. And yet once Japanese influence began to extend into mainland Asia, there arose a question of enormous difficulty and significance: where should that influence end?

Portrait of Commodore Perry, from the *Black Ship Scroll*

Foreign Ship: one of the American 'Black Ships'

＊

Riding on the Nagasaki road the other day, I met with another strik-ing illustration of the entire absence of modesty which astonishes Europeans on their first visit to Japan. A little urchin, seated at the door of a neat and substantial dwelling-house, gave the alarm of the approach of a Tojin [foreigner], and as I passed I had the pleasure of seeing the whole family rush out into the street to gaze at me.

I retained my presence of mind sufficiently to notice that this family group represented three generations. There were two very old women, one unmistakable old man; then paterfamilias with his wife; lastly some half dozen boys and girls, from about eighteen to six years of age. They were all stark naked, and to all appearance perfectly unconscious of the fact, as they stared at me in open-eyed wonder. After having passed some little distance I looked back; they were still at their doors quietly chatting, and, I suppose, criticizing my appearance. I wondered whether they would dress for dinner.

> Historian and traveller Edward Barrington de Fonblanque,
> visiting Japan in the 1860s

A powerful sense pervaded Japan, from the late 1860s onwards, that the eyes of the world were upon it. A range of newly established journals and newspapers featured much discussion of how other countries were doing things – from planning parties to planning cities, from raising children to selling insurance. Details might differ, yet there were certain standards, it was thought, to which any civilized country must adhere.

So the tut-tutting of visitors like Edward Barrington de Fonblanque mattered. There were anxious calls for curbs on bathing naked in public or urinating in the street. More profoundly the search for a new national purpose, in which people far beyond the political elite soon began to engage, was subject to two potentially conflicting pressures: the need to rediscover something lost or forgotten – 1868 was, after all, billed as a 'restoration' of imperial rule rather than a revolution – and a desire for foreign approval. Some of the earliest and lasting impressions of Japan amongst Westerners were products of these pressures. Samurai culture was proudly advertised as a Japanese equivalent of Europe's chivalric tradition, in Nitobe Inazō's bestselling *Bushidō: The Soul of Japan* (1900) – published in English, for foreign consumption. Zen Buddhism was repackaged, around the same time, to suggest the power of intuitive Japanese spirituality while accommodating Western yearnings for experiential over dogmatic religion.

There was an attempt, early on, to guide Japan's modernization according to a basic principle of *wakon-yōsai*: 'Japanese spirit, Western techniques'. But spirits and techniques, it was soon discovered, are not so easily distinguished or disentangled. Spirit shapes technique: social and political institutions are derived, somewhere along the line, from assumptions about what human beings most fundamentally are, and what is natural and good for them both as individuals and in communities. Great feats of science and engineering also have their intimate, human underpinnings and inspirations. Techniques, in turn, shape spirits. Education systems, jobs markets, media, medicine, governmental arrangements – all these things create certain types of people over time.

Highbrow publications and societies dedicated to tackling such challenges began to proliferate, run and populated by scholars, journalists, politicians, businessmen and members of the emerging civil service. The *Meirokusha*, 'Meiji 6 Society' – established in the sixth year of the new era – counted amongst its members some of the most influential commentators of the day. Fukuzawa Yukichi excoriated the conservative Confucian scholars of the recent past as 'rice-consuming dictionaries', while recalling through tears of gratitude the heroic painstaking of inquisitive *rangaku* pioneers like Sugita Genpaku. He urged upon Japan modes of learning that were practical and pragmatic, helping to build a modern nation from the roots upwards rather than simply importing modernity in some 'finished' foreign form. Other prominent *Meirokusha* members included the great statesman Mori Arinori, founder of Japan's modern education system and ambassador to the United States and then China, and the philosopher Nishi Amane, who took on the mammoth task of importing and categorizing modern Western philosophical knowledge for a Japanese readership.

In all of this, talk of a 'Japanese spirit' was more a rallying cry than a solid and agreed-upon point of reference. It offered a useful rhetorical gloss, a sense of unity and naturalness, to a process of going global that in fact combined short-term pragmatism, elite self-interest, experimentation and compromise, and ad hoc decision-making in the hasty fabrication of a new order. It provided, too, a means of bringing together two emerging images of modern Japan which it was by no means certain were actually compatible: Asia's modernizing vanguard, and a place whose history, culture, sensibilities and blood-line

Fukuzawa Yukichi (1835–1901)

made it quite unlike any other. No wonder that a celebrated chron-
icler of the new nation's birth pangs, the novelist Natsume Sōseki,
found the concept distinctly slippery:

> Admiral Tōgō [a Meiji-era naval hero] possesses the Japanese spirit,
> and the local fishmonger has it as well. Swindlers and murderers also
> have the Japanese spirit. Since it is a spirit it is always blurry and
> fuzzy; there is no one in Japan who hasn't had it on the tip of his
> tongue, but there's no one who has actually seen it.

As with 'Japanese spirit', so with Japan's story at this point. To their
cheerleaders, of whom there were many across the globe, the Meiji
leaders were pulling off the world's most painstaking and thoughtful
national overhaul. To their various emerging critics at home, from the
mid-1870s into the early 1880s, the country either lacked a clear sense
of itself or was rapidly acquiring an unwelcome one: an Asian facsimile of Western life, which farmers and factory girls sweated to fund; a
place where new political freedoms were once seemingly promised
and then withheld; a nation led and populated by imposters.

2

Blood Tax

Woe betide any new government that can't keep its schoolteachers onside. In 1884, a young teacher in the south-western city of Okayama saw her small school for women, which she helped run from home with her mother, closed down by the local authorities when some of the staff and students dared to attend a political meeting one summer evening. A year later the same teacher, Kageyama Hideko, was plotting to smuggle explosives into Korea, hoping to launch a violent coup there that would eventually bring democracy to Japan.

Kageyama was not the only one embarking on a radical trajectory in 1884. Hundreds of miles to the east in Gunma prefecture, north of Tokyo, a second schoolteacher, Miura Momonosuke, was helping to recruit hundreds of farmers, gangsters, hunters and sumo wrestlers for military training in the mountains. The plan was to make the most of an upcoming imperial visit to attack local government troops and take prisoner several of the Emperor's high-ranking officials. Meanwhile, in Saitama prefecture, just next door to Gunma, as many as 3,000 schoolteachers, artisans, tradesmen and farmers gathered one day at a village shrine, wearing makeshift uniforms – white headbands, short coats and tight trousers – and carrying an assortment of weapons including rifles, swords and bamboo spears. They listened to men, rumoured to be gangsters, address them as the 'Poor People's Army' . . .

For all that Tokyo's new governing elite sought to restructure Japan's affairs according to their own designs throughout the 1870s, a great many others around the country were determined to have their say in what the ultimate meaning and implications of the 1868 restoration ought to be. Teachers, farmers and other commoners were set to press their cases across the turbulent mid-1880s. But first, Japan's leaders were forced to contend with some seriously disgruntled samurai.

The rigid Tokugawa class system had positioned samurai one rung above the country's farmers, below whom came artisans and then merchants, with society's outcasts at the very bottom: *hinin* or 'non-people' (vagrants, some types of singers and dancers, executioners), alongside whole communities of *eta* ('full of filth'), their leather-working profession regarded as unclean because of its close connection with dead flesh. A highly diverse class of people, in terms of wealth and standing, the samurai spent the largely peaceful Tokugawa years trying to get used to a shift from warrior work to office work, as administrative servants to their lords. Long and short swords had still been thrust proudly into waistbands each morning, but the likelihood of their being used diminished by the day. *Bushidō*, the legendary 'way of the warrior', was an outcome not of medieval warfare but in fact of this early modern peace. It emerged from the 1600s onwards, bound up more with ideals of service, frugality, honour and pursuit of the arts than with violent conflict.

By the late 1700s, lower-ranking samurai especially found that these virtues were not getting them very far. Stipends were worth less and less all the time: they were not reassessed to keep up with inflation, and needy *daimyō* would sometimes 'borrow' a portion before paying them out. Meanwhile, all around them in cities like Edo and Osaka the vulgar merchant class seemed to be hoarding most of the wealth and to be having most of the fun. Some samurai turned to drink – stories abounded of men being confined by embarrassed families to wooden cages – while others pawned their armour or, through gritted teeth, conceded to merchants their daughters' hands in marriage.

The restoration of 1868 had failed to improve matters, despite its leaders being samurai themselves. Disaffected samurai of the old Satsuma domain acquired a valuable figurehead in 1873 when Saigō Takamori turned his back on the Council of State in Tokyo – disgusted at the collapse of the clique's plan to provoke war with Korea – and returned home to the soothing hot springs of what was now Kagoshima prefecture. Branches of a 'private academy' began to spring up in the region, to whose young students Saigō was a hero. He worked with them, hoping to pass on something of the old samurai values before the last generation of natural-born samurai died out.

To Saigō's former friends in the capital, these schools looked very much like military training camps. Alongside instruction in Chinese, French and English, 'schooling' was being offered in the use of weapons and artillery. Spies from Japan's new police force were duly sent to investigate, towards the end of 1876. Some of these agents were caught and questioned, and a rumour began to circulate that at least one of them had confessed a government plot to assassinate Saigō. Coming around the same time as the arrival in Kagoshima of a ship sent by the government to remove munitions stored in the town, it was enough to convince Saigō's supporters that if action were to be taken against Tokyo, it was now or never.

Saigō himself did not declare an uprising. He agreed to go to Tokyo to 'remonstrate' and 'question', setting out early in 1877 with around 12,000 of his student soldiers. The number rose to as many as 42,000 as others joined his cause. Fearing what might come next – especially after an attack by Saigō's men on government troops at Kumamoto Castle – Tokyo sent tens of thousands of troops from its new army of conscripted commoners to stop him.

Violent clashes erupted, continuing on for months as 6,000 government soldiers were killed and three times that number from amongst the rebels ended up dead or wounded. Eventually, Japan's new regime prevailed. It was able to supply its men with modern weapons and to produce half a million rounds of small-arms ammunition every day (albeit at ruinous expense), while the rebels had to make do with what they had. The American captain of a Mitsubishi Steamship Company vessel, used by the government to transport troops and supplies, later recalled seeing caches of confiscated rebel arms: old-fashioned match-lock rifles, together with piles, ten feet high, of worn-out swords.

The 'Satsuma Rebellion', as it became known, reached its denouement when a wounded Saigō retreated to a cave to perform ritual suicide. It was the last and greatest of a series of uprisings in the 1870s by former samurai who had hoped that 1868 would be a

Surrender of the Rebels (Tsukioka Yoshitoshi, c.1880)

means of refashioning their world rather than overturning it – and who believed that for all its rapid achievements the new order was not yet set in stone.

They were wrong, at least as far as their own class was concerned. The payment of samurai stipends had made up almost a third of government spending early on; at first they had been reduced and then, in 1876, converted into government bonds – often for small sums that were easily frittered away. Samurai were encouraged to become business entrepreneurs, but while some succeeded, many failed. In the newspapers, where old-school samurai were not much loved to begin with – their arrogance, sophistry and empty bravado regarded as part of the toxic Tokugawa brew that Japan had at last left behind – much fun was had over shambolic *bushi shōhō*: 'warrior business-management'.

And yet Saigō was regarded in some quarters as a hero after his death, eventually receiving a posthumous imperial pardon. Before the century was out, a statue of Saigō stood proudly in Tokyo's Ueno Park. The samurai class might be dead and gone, but the samurai ideal – for better and frequently for worse – had a long future ahead of it in modern Japan.

*

Saigō Takamori (1828–77)

Rumours About 'Saigō Star': when Mars reached its closest approach to earth in 1877, seeming to emit powerful light, there were rumours that the great Saigō Takamori was inside, alive and well

The early years after 1868 were also marked by hundreds of distur-
bances by farmers concerned about the impact – especially during
times of crop failure – of the country's rigid new tax arrangements.
In Okayama, people campaigned to have their old feudal lord re-
instated, along with the lower taxes he used to request. For similar
reasons, villagers in Hiroshima tried to prevent their *daimyō* and his
entourage from leaving when the domains were abolished.

Communication between the country's leadership in Tokyo and
the majority of Japanese who lived and worked in the countryside
was as yet far from perfect, compounded by a dismissive attitude
towards rural people held by educated urbanites like Fukuzawa
Yukichi – who declared them so woefully ignorant that they practic-
ally 'invited oppression'. Various attempts were made by the Meiji
leaders to improve that situation, and to persuade people of their
vision for Japan. But there was a risk their actions could backfire –
alienating the countryside even further, and even radicalizing it.

An early initiative was the 'Great Promulgation Campaign',
launched in 1870. Buddhist and Shinto priests were sent out across
the land as peripatetic political agents, spreading Three Great Teachings: respect for the gods and love of country; principles of Heaven
and the Way of Man; and reverence and obedience to the Emperor
and court. By 1876, a total of more than 10,000 'evangelists' had
been signed up to share a message that in practice boiled down to
three more prosaic points: pay your taxes, send your children to
school and comply with military conscription. At the same time,
Japan's numerous Shinto shrines were united in a single national
framework, ranked in order of importance with the Ise Grand Shrine
at the top – with whose rites everyone else had to harmonize theirs.
This was also to be a means of reaching the population with whatever religious or political messages their new rulers sought to send.

Unfortunately, the Great Promulgation Campaign was not universally well received. People complained that the sermons were dull and
the teachers were dullards, constantly arguing with one another –
Shinto and Buddhist speakers were often tempted to slip sectarian
asides into supposedly 'national' teachings. One group of samurai
became so enraged that they travelled to the Great Teaching Institute
and tried to burn it down.

Another option for Japan's governing elite, as with their counter-parts in the West, was fostering a loyalist newspaper industry. Most of the influential early Meiji papers were linked to members of the ruling clique. The conservative *Tokyo Nichi Nichi Shimbun* had permission to report imperial court news, and functioned for a while almost as an official mouthpiece for the Chōshū faction within the leadership. Increasingly, however, large national newspapers served not just to encourage a sense of national cohesion but to lay bare a lack of elite consensus about what shape Japan's future should take.

Education and conscription, the two final major means by which rural Japan came into contact with the new state, were similarly double-edged. By the mid-1870s the country was home to around 20,000 primary schools, most of them using Buddhist temples and private homes for their premises. But many people simply didn't see the benefit: forking out extra taxes *and* losing the labour of their children for extended periods seemed a poor deal without clear evidence of improved job prospects. Moreover, in the early years before curricula and teacher training could be ironed out, it was possible for people like the future explosives courier Kageyama to become teachers, and to blur the line between education and politics.

The demand that every man give three years of service to the regular army, followed by four to the reserves, was similarly unpopular – made more so by a rather unnecessary digression on foreign culture contained within the text of the Conscription Edict of 1873: 'Western people call this a "blood tax" ... This is because one protects one's country verily with one's blood.' It said much about how fed up many in rural Japan were with the new regime's rapidly multiplying demands upon their time and wealth, and the degree to which they suspected its motives, that a rumour swiftly gained traction in some parts of the country that the government now wanted literally to syphon off blood out of the veins of conscripts so that it could be sold abroad, possibly as wine. Some even claimed to have spotted men in white coats roaming the countryside carrying large glass receptacles. The choice of targets in the violent protests that ensued – involving many tens of thousands of people – made clear people's wider grievances: money-lenders, wealthy farmers, merchants, schools, machinery at state-run mines and local government offices.

When trouble like this broke out, rural leaders tried to remonstrate with the authorities, as they had in the Tokugawa past. The rural poor shouldn't be asked to fund so many new and dubious government initiatives all at once. Tax payments ought to reflect the productivity of the land. Moneylenders charging exorbitant rates during hard times should be brought to justice. And yet the rules appeared to have changed. A certain amount of negotiation was still possible, particularly where influential landowners were doing the asking. But isolated rural demonstrations that would once have caused embarrassment and a rethink were now sometimes simply fired upon, charged into and pushed back. Administrators, police forces and the new conscript army were often not local people anymore, with the knowledge or power or desire to put things right. They were agents of a distant central authority, with a job to do.

Ultimately, the only means of addressing grievances now was to find ways of influencing that central authority directly – not least via representative government of some kind. It was a conclusion that people across Japan were reaching during the 1870s and into the early 1880s.

In 1879, a man by the name of Chiba Takusaburō found work as a primary school teacher in a mountain town called Itsukaichi, not far from Tokyo. A decade earlier, he had served in the Tokugawa warrior ranks as they retreated northwards. Later he became a drifter, studying medicine and the tenets of the Pure Land Buddhist sect, joining the Russian Orthodox Church (at that time making minor inroads into northern Japan) and later assisting a Catholic missionary. In Itsukaichi, he made a brand-new discovery. A group of farmers drawn from five local villages were engaging in the most unusual of late-night fireside conversations: they were planning a draft constitution for Japan.

Chiba's record of those discussions was unearthed many decades later, along with a worm-eaten treasure trove of books on British, French and German constitutional law – with Chiba's comments scrawled in red in the margins. Incredibly, the Itsukaichi Constitution was far from the only document of its kind: evidence of more than thirty such constitutions was later found, all around Japan. A movement for 'Freedom and People's Rights' (*jiyū minken*) was underway with small political societies like Chiba's springing up everywhere. Drawing on people's experiences of life before and since 1868, their aspirations for the future, longstanding beliefs in a just reciprocity between ruler and ruled, and incoming Western models and concepts, many of these societies were championing a form of constitutional monarchy in which people's rights would be carefully elaborated and protected.

It all helped to pile pressure on Japan's leaders, already reeling from samurai rebellions and splits amongst themselves. Itagaki Taisuke had left the Council of State along with Saigō in 1873 – over policy towards Korea, and also because of resentment about the dominance of national politics by Satsuma and Chōshū men. Itagaki petitioned the Emperor in 1874 to establish a representative assembly. And while this request came to nothing in the short term, Itagaki emerged as a leader in the Freedom and People's Rights movement. By 1881 the government found itself forced to act on a long-held plan to risk some degree of representative democracy in Japan. An imperial rescript was issued, promising a constitution by 1890. A few days earlier, Itagaki had formed Jiyūtō, the 'Freedom Party'. This was followed the next year by Rikken Kaishintō, Constitutional Progressive Party, also led by a former clique member who had fallen out with his colleagues – Ōkuma Shigenobu.

Itagaki, Ōkuma and their allies rooted their politics in translations of Western political treatises. Itagaki's group preferred French revolutionary ideas while Ōkuma's group built on English constitutional thought. Like Chiba and his friends, these elite-led parties worked on the fundamentals of a constitution for Japan, while trying to familiarize the public with concepts that were new and foreign. 'Free-ness' – was that moral or metaphysical? Was it about movement in some ethereal sense? 'Rights' – to do what, why and in defiance of whom?

The effort to make meanings clear here was fraught with risk – of confusion, misunderstanding, raising false hopes, or upsetting important allies. The selection of a word that would correspond to the French word *liberté* involved the careful weighing of at least four options. *Jishu* suggested self-mastery; *fuki*, unfetteredness; while *jiyū* and *jizai* implied following one's intentions without restriction. The last two were close to what was needed, but carried unfortunate connotations of having one's way at the expense of others. That left Fukuzawa Yukichi and other advocates of *jiyū* with a struggle on their hands to make it respectable while preventing it from dissolving into the 'freedom' of anarchy or barbarism. Long after *jiyū* won out – and was used in Itagaki's party's name – advocates of 'freedom' remained vulnerable to charges of living self-seeking lives that ignored the needs of others and the state. It was to become a favourite means of opposing new ideas down the decades in Japan, as elsewhere in the world: the conflation of political dissent with anti-social behaviour.

The emergence of these new political parties and the enthusiasms of their activists was looked upon with concern amongst leaders in Tokyo, amidst a snowballing economic crisis. In 1881 the pressure of paying old domain debts and samurai stipends, of putting in place the rudiments of a modern state despite terrible trade terms imposed by the unequal treaties, and finally the costly defeat of Saigō Takamori's Satsuma Rebellion had brought the government to the brink of bankruptcy. Foreign loans – save one, for a railway line – were not an option: Japan's leaders needed only to glance out into the world, most notably to Egypt, to find cautionary tales of countries whose relationship with European powers began with inward investment and ended in colonization. Instead, an urgent deflationary drive was launched.

By drastically reducing the amount of money in circulation, and raising taxes, the country's finances and the immediate future of Japanese industry was eventually secured. But as rice and silk prices crashed, much of rural Japan fell into deep debt. People found themselves forced to take out new, high-interest loans to repay the ones they had taken out in good times, in order to invest in modern equipment. Anger escalated, and Japan's leaders had to learn swiftly how to balance use of the carrot with the stick. Itagaki was a talented speaker, but he was also a man with a weakness for being blown off-course by well-timed bribes: once with a welcome back into government, before Jiyūtō was established; and then again at the height of the party's national impact in 1882, with an all expenses paid fact-finding trip to Europe – though it is not clear that he was aware of the government's role in funding his journey. Other rights activists encountered a police force that was increasingly well-informed and well-resourced. Many a political or 'lecture' meeting was broken up, often violently. Some groups took to having their meetings on barges in the middle of rivers and lakes, to guarantee undisturbed deliberations.

It was amidst these heightened tensions, particularly in the country-side, that the Okayama schoolteacher Kageyama Hideko moved to Tokyo and became involved with plotters raising funds for the Korean Revolutionary Movement. Her dedication to the cause impressed the radical Freedom and Popular Rights leader and Jiyūtō member Ōi Kentarō, who had initially had his doubts about letting a young woman in on his scheme. Kageyama was asked to help carry the explosives for the group, from Osaka to Nagasaki in late 1885. From there, they would make the crossing to Korea and join activists who were hoping to install a new, reformist government.

But word spread about the Korea plot, and Ōi, Kageyama and the others were rounded up at an inn in Nagasaki while waiting for their ship. When the police turned up, Kageyama tried to feign ignorance of the plot, but an incriminating letter of hers was discovered in her bedding. Still, under interrogation she insisted that she was just in Nagasaki to 'see the sights' – only then to be goaded by the police: surely someone like her, who claimed to be a woman of principle, ought to give an honest account of her actions? Kageyama conceded the point and spilled the beans.

All in all, 200 people were arrested in 1885 in what became known as the 'Osaka Incident', named after the city where the plans had first been hatched. Put on trial for crimes against the state, posses-sion of weapons and inciting riots, Kageyama received a prison sentence, becoming the first woman in modern Japan to be imprisoned for international political activism. She later recalled in her writings the journey to the prison on the Ise Peninsula: the pleasure of the beautiful, inspiring scenery somewhat dampened by 'my persimmon-coloured, tight-sleeved [prison] garb and . . . a rope around my waist'.

Ōi, for his part, was not going down without a speech. He per-suaded the court to let him speak for three days about his motivations, in the course of which he claimed that he had done it all for the sake of Korean democracy. After all, he said, Koreans, like ordinary Japanese, were presently caught between Western aggression and reactionary elites at home – power in Japan, he believed, simply having been passed in 1868 from one narrowly self-interested group to another. The judges were unmoved and handed Ōi a six-year prison term. He appealed, alleging political persecution – to which they responded by upping his sentence to nine years.

Ōi used his time in prison to develop his political vision, going on after his (very) early release in 1889 to try his hand at both electoral politics and violent unrest. He supplied a bomb, from the Osaka Incident stockpile, to an ultra-nationalist group opposed to what they saw as the appeasement of Western powers by Japan's Foreign Minister – Ōkuma Shigenobu, who had been tempted back to the government fold. The bomb took Ōkuma's leg off.

Feted in the press as 'Japan's Joan of Arc', Kageyama spent her jail time leafing through love letters from Ōi, helping other women in her prison learn how to read and write, and beginning to set out her call for women's rights in Japan. This was something she thought that egotistical male radicals were still rather neglecting, happy as they were to spend money that might have gone to political causes on drinking and prostitutes instead.

Where Kageyama's original career in school-teaching had fallen prey to the state's clampdown on political discussion, her fellow teacher Miura Momonosuke was a victim of the serious economic harm being done to the countryside in the interests (as many a rural radical saw it) of propping up an illegitimate urban leadership. He began his plotting and training in Gunma prefecture, in 1884, after losing an appeal to a high-interest loan company for repayments to be postponed. He had links with Ōi Kentarō's radical wing of Jiyūtō, and also with local gangsters, including Yamada Jōnosuke. Heavily involved in the illegal gambling industry, Yamada, like Miura, was losing out to various government policies of recent years. Its deflationary drive impoverished his gambling customers. A new anti-gambling law saw well over a thousand people punished in Gunma in a single year. And rocky consumer markets damaged Yamada's silk-farming business.

Working with the mob was useful at a time when the state was beefing up its police force. In April of 1884, Miura helped to hide a gangster in his storehouse, following a fatal sword attack on a policeman conducting surveillance of a gambling den. Later that month the favour was repaid; after police threatened to break up a meeting at which Miura and others were speaking – and at which a revolutionary song about the skies raining blood had just been sung – Yamada rushed in with around one hundred of his men, forcing the police to flee.

It was later at Yamada's house that the bigger incident was planned out, set for 1 May when the Emperor was due to arrive to open a new stretch of railway. But local police started to become suspicious when an unusually large number of people began to gather near the train station. They called off the opening ceremony as a precaution. Miura's group moved to Plan B: they gathered together thousands of farmers a couple of weeks later, attacked the boss of a local moneylending company, robbed some wealthy farmers nearby and launched an assault on a police station. When expected reinforcements failed to arrive, large numbers of the attackers, Miura included, ended up getting arrested. While Kageyama taught and wrote behind bars, Miura began a sentence of seven years' imprisonment with hard labour.

Mere months after the 'Gunma Incident' reached its climax, it was the turn of the Poor People's Army in Chichibu, Saitama prefecture, to make its anger felt at what the country and people's lives were turning into. As in Gunma, the traumatic impact of a collapse in silk prices came together with calls for political rights and responsible government to create a broad base of potential recruits for armed rebellion. Making their way to their village meeting point, 3,000 volunteers were divided into two battalions by their commander – the sometime gangster Tashiro Eisuke – and sent into action. Two local towns were promptly captured, government offices and money-lenders' homes were attacked (Tashiro himself was reportedly in debt to three separate loan companies, in addition to a mortgage on his land), and supplies were stolen – albeit with receipts issued bearing the stamp 'Headquarters of the Revolution'. From their new bases, the Poor People's Army sent out recruiting parties to nearby villages, sometimes claiming to be from Jiyūtō.

But as with the Satsuma, Osaka and Gunma incidents, so too with Chichibu: a new state that had yet to achieve clarity in its political arrangements proved nevertheless to have its internal security well in

Freedom and Popular Rights
activist Kageyama Hideko
(1865–1927)

Dajōkan councillor turned
party organizer Itagaki
Taisuke (1837–1919)

hand. Police and military police units rushed to the scene, and aside
from a skirmish or two lost because some of them had brought along
the wrong bullets for their guns, they were quickly successful in putting down the rag-tag rebellion. It was all over within days: more
than thirty people dead, 200 arrested, and another 200 fleeing the
scene. Tashiro was captured and carried away in a bamboo cage,
becoming one of seven to receive a death sentence.

*

The conservative *Tokyo Nichi Nichi Shimbun* dismissed the people
of the Chichibu rebellion as 'villainous gamblers and radical wander-
ers'. Another paper homed in on the destruction of moneylenders'
records, suggesting that the whole thing was about personal self-
interest and nothing more. Such interpretations mattered: the
newspapers were becoming immensely influential in shaping the ways
in which an ever-larger constituency of urban readers thought about
far-off events in rural, regional Japan. Today's unacceptable outliers

in Japan's constantly evolving modern story were the gamblers and the debtors leading good people astray. Tomorrow's would be over-educated women, traitorous socialists, uppity industrial workers and venal politicians and businessmen.

Meanwhile, the sense of dislocation between rural and urban worlds that was betrayed in some of the press reaction to the incidents of 1884 and 1885 was set to intensify into the twentieth century. Urbanites would discover too late the implications of failing to keep happy those parts of the country that supplied the lion's share of their food and of recruits to the army.

For now, what most exercised the minds of city-dwellers were questions of high politics, culture and how to deal with the outside world. With radical movements largely quashed by the mid-1880s, what should responsible politics look like? Why were the unequal treaties *still* in place – had the country's leaders spent so much time trying to live like foreigners that they had forgotten how to be firm with them? Might Japan even be losing its cultural memory, and with it any clear sense of what the future ought to look like?

3

The Dancing Cabinet

The navy band struck up, and the guests paraded in. Ball gowns and gentlemen's frock coats from all points on Europe's fashion compass hung off wearers poised to put long hours of dance tuition to the test. German beer and American cocktails were on hand to steady nerves, while in the kitchen a French chef was preparing a banquet of his native cuisine, selections to be made by aspiring gourmands from a menu printed entirely in French. The taste and warm haze of imported English cigarettes would round off the whole experience nicely.

In other rooms nearby, billiards and cards could be played. There was even a corridor designed especially for promenading up and down. But this upper floor ballroom was the centrepiece, filling rapidly with Tokyo's international great and good, gas lights picking out their faces as they danced the night away at the annual imperial birthday ball. The Rokumeikan, as it was called, had been completed in 1883, at ruinous – even insulting – expense, given Japan's straitened economic circumstances in the mid-1880s. It was intended as a place where the country's elites might socialize on equal terms with influential foreigners; the name meant 'Deer Cry Hall', and was inspired by a Chinese poem lauding the spending of precious time with strangers.

Advocates for the building lauded a grand, appropriately global design: a large stuccoed mansion dominated by verandas and colonnades, the brainchild of a British architect, Josiah Conder. Detractors spied only a mess of incompatible features from around the world, thrown together and plonked down amongst Japanese pines, ponds and old stone lanterns. Here was a monument to the most curiously self-defeating of national policies; a metaphor in mortar for just how

The Rokumeikan – 'Deer Cry Hall'

lost, how estranged from its history and culture Japan had become in a few short years.

Similar social gatherings were increasingly being held in private homes too. Most notorious was a masquerade ball – reputedly Japan's first – thrown in 1887 at the residence of one of the era's most influential governing elites: Itō Hirobumi. Fairy queens and pirates hobnobbed with goblins, beetles and butterflies, as the man himself appeared as a Venetian nobleman and his daughter as an Italian peasant girl. Precisely what went on below the chandeliers that particular night remains a mystery. But etiquette seemed to go missing along the way, and Itō was later rumoured to have tried to seduce a young married woman.

Itō's hope, together with his childhood friend and fellow Chōshū rebel Inoue Kaoru, who commissioned the Rokumeikan, had been to use grand social occasions to show the world just how far Japan had come. They might also show, by example, Japan's middling and lower orders something of how to interact properly with foreigners – as opposed to shooting or stabbing them, as had briefly been tried in the febrile 1850s and 1860s.

But by the late 1880s the Rokumeikan became synonymous instead, amongst Japanese journalists and commentators, with the ridiculous and harmful presumptions of a small, deluded clique. The Council of

State having been exchanged in 1885 for a cabinet system of government – Inoue as Minister of Foreign Affairs, Itō as Japan's first Prime Minister – some talented satirist spotted the chance to coin a phrase: 'the dancing cabinet'. It stuck.

Partly this was a problem of perceived indecency. Japanese journalists were as adept as their international counterparts at professing moral anxiety as a pretext for basking in the salacious:

> A beautiful woman leans her head against a man's shoulder and turns her fair face toward the man's ears. Her bare arm circles the man's neck, and her undulant bosom touches the man's chest, rising and falling with her breathing. Her legs intertwine with the man's like vines on a pine tree. The man's strong right arm firmly encircles the small of the woman's back; with each move he presses her ever more tightly to his body. The light ... in the beautiful woman's eyes is steadily directed at the man, but she is too dazzled to see anything. The music stirs her, but she does not hear the sounds. She hears instead the echoes of a distant waterfall and moves as in a dream, her body clinging to the man's. When a woman reaches such a state, where is the innate modesty of the virtuous maiden?

But the indecencies that really concerned critics were cultural as much as social or sexual. These soirées were beginning to epitomize what a retrospective piece forty years later in the *Japan Times* would call the era's 'mad rush to adopt Western customs and habits'. Itō's masquerade ball in particular had 'astonished the public': 'those who saw [a] dignified Premier and other officials appearing in strange costumes thought it an insane and foolish event.'

Western visitors to Japan, too, discovered much that was ripe for satire. The French cartoonist Georges Ferdinand Bigot, who lived in the country for nearly twenty years, lampooned local ladies learning ballroom dance, and the narcissism of elite culture more broadly. In one of his sketches, two people dressed in European costume admire themselves in a mirror – two monkeys stare back. A second Frenchman, Pierre Loti, thought the Rokumeikan's Japanese patrons were involved in a 'contemptible imitation' of European culture, rather sniffily likening the building itself to a casino that one might find in a French spa town.

Monday at the Rokumeikan
(Georges Ferdinand Bigot, 1887)

Imitation (Georges Ferdinand Bigot, 1877)

Western satirizing of this early cultural love-in between Japan and the West cut both ways, of course, with much of it taking the form of long-term ex-pats scorning the vulgarity of their own countrymen blundering through 'the East' for the first time. A favourite target was the wealthy tourist, possessed of more money than taste, fawning over fakes and expecting everything to be for sale. Japan resident Osman Edwards offered up a little ditty on the subject, to fit the tune of Yankee Doodle:

> Doodle San will leave Japan
> With several tons of cargo;
> Folks will stare when all his ware
> Is poured into Chicago.
>
> There's silk, cut velvet, old brocade
> And everything that's *jōtō* [high class],
> And ancient bronzes newly made
> By dealers in Kyoto.

For the Japanese, there was a deadly serious political context to their concerns about what Itō and his colleagues got up to of an evening. These self-appointed leaders of the new Japan were failing, still, to have the widely despised unequal treaties of a generation before revised. Just how much this mattered, and just what foreigners seemed really to think of Japan, became apparent in late 1886 when a cargo ship called the *Normanton*, travelling from Yokohama to Kobe, was wrecked and sank. Somehow its British and German crew found safety aboard the lifeboats, while twelve Indian and Chinese crewmen and twenty-five Japanese passengers were left behind in the water. All twenty-five of the Japanese died.

Inoue Kaoru ordered an urgent investigation, only to find himself hampered by the extraterritoriality rules that remained part of the unequal treaties. A British investigation exonerated the captain, John William Drake, of any wrongdoing. Only after Inoue was reduced to bringing charges in the British Court for Japan was a three-month prison sentence for Drake finally won. Compensation claims by families continued to be rejected. An outraged Japanese press covered the whole affair in heavy detail, with one writer at the

Tokyo Nichi Nichi accusing Drake of treating his Japanese passengers 'like luggage'.

It would take Japan's vanquishing of its erstwhile cultural mentor China in a short war in 1894–5, to help finally achieve treaty revision on acceptable terms. Just as Commodore Matthew C. Perry had thought the Japanese susceptible only to great demonstrations of power, the same appeared to be true in reverse: where carefully costumed civility attracted ridicule from Western counterparts, a naked display of military power succeeded.

Where Japan's elite had the Rokumeikan as an aspirational point of contact with foreign culture, its middle and lower classes had the streets of the treaty ports and the new capital. These continued to fill with immigrants from across Japan, getting around on horse-drawn buses or iron-wheeled rickshaws (the word itself comes from the Japanese *jinrikisha*: 'person-powered vehicle').

Following a fire in 1872, the Ginza district of Tokyo was rebuilt as a model neighbourhood of brick and gas lighting, down which self-consciously 'modern' men and women could be seen strolling in curious combinations of clothing. It was a gift to writers of 'cheap, amusing literature' (*gesaku*) like Kanagaki Robun: kimono worn over trousers, gingham umbrellas come rain or shine, shabby second-hand Western suits for the financially constrained early-adopter, and the occasional ostentatious gesture to consult the time on a watch that might be embarrassingly cheap or solid gold.

Alongside Sunday rest and Christmas, a major contribution to these new rhythms and sights of urban Japanese street life were its fads – or as Basil Hall Chamberlain, a British professor of Japanese at Tokyo Imperial University, referred to them: 'fashionable crazes'.

1873 was the rabbit year. There had been none of these little rodents in Japan. Hence, when imported as curiosities, they fetched incredible prices, as much as $1,000 being sometimes paid for a single specimen. Speculations in $400 and $500 rabbits were of daily occurrence . . . 1874–5 were the cock-fighting years . . . Waltzing and gigantic funerals marked 1886–7. The following year took quite a new departure, setting mesmerism, table-turning and planchette in fashion; and 1888 lifted wrestling from a vulgar pastime to a fashionable craze, in which the then prime minister . . . led the way. 1889 saw a general revival of all native Japanese amusements, Japanese costume, anti-foreign agitation, etc. This was the great year of reaction. 1893, the whole nation went mad over Colonel Fukushima's successful ride across Siberia. 1896, stamp-collecting. 1898–1900, garden-parties . . .

There were vogues for squeaky brogues – special inserts made of 'singing leather' could be purchased. And the eating of meat went from being something done for medicinal reasons only to an experiment by curious urbanites to see whether it really was one of the ingredients of Western success. Beef had been eaten by injured soldiers of the Boshin War, to aid their recovery, and was soon permanently on the menu in army and navy barracks. From there, it made it onto civilian menus, a transition slowed slightly in Tokyo because supply was somewhat at the mercy of the fabled *bushi shōhō* (warrior business-management). The people involved treated their clients so arrogantly, were so shameless in trying to rig prices, and were sufficiently relaxed about quality control that their enterprise was quickly wound up by red-faced officials. Nevertheless, Western patrons of high-class restaurants were soon enjoying a warm feeling of cultural superiority as they watched their Japanese friends chase a piece of meat patiently around the plate with inexpertly wielded knives and forks. Rougher outlets offered chopsticks to their patrons: these were the cramped, steamy spaces – known as 'stew restaurants' – where experiments were made in marinading beef in familiar flavours like miso and soy sauce. All this quickly caught on: by 1877, Tokyoites in search of beef had nearly 600 establishments from which to choose.

Elsewhere, more radical modernizing suggestions were being made: English as the national language, Christianity for the national religion, even organized intermarriage with foreigners – the most direct way, it was speculated, of injecting into the Japanese bloodstream whatever it was about Westerners that had first powered them to Japan's shores in their spectacular, terrifying steamships.

These were extreme ideas, never likely to materialize. But some still found the general trend worrisome. Modernity seemed to have a way of rendering hollow, quaint or picturesque so much that they valued about their country's long past: the powerful, paradigmatic stories told in kabuki plays and poetry, in history and fiction, in music and fashion, and in the art and architectural styles that still made up most of the landscape. Were these things now just to be fodder for the international exhibitions – beginning with Vienna in 1873 – at which 'Japan' was enthusiastically marketed by government and entrepreneurs alike? Was the Japanese past just a source of *objets d'art* with which Doodle San could fill his home?

If not, then where was the grand narrative about Japan that could truly interweave the best of the modern West with the country's aesthetic and moral inheritance? For people of the psychoanalyst Kosawa Heisaku's father's generation, hard at work in these closing years of the 1800s, *wakon-yōsai* – 'Japanese spirit, Western techniques' – was turning out in practice to be a kind of bifurcation in their own beings. An urban middle-class man might wear a suit to work and then a kimono at home, where in a 'Western room' – positioned to the fore while a 'Japanese room' lurked deeper within – he could read in his newspaper an anxiety-producing running commentary on how his country was doing compared with the British or the Germans. How were split, anxious personalities like these to be restored and modernity domesticated?

Real moral and cultural commitment was called for here, not just the blend of shallow pragmatism and embarrassing dilettantism that critics associated with Japan's leaders, cut off from the people as they were by lengthy travels abroad and the alien sensibilities acquired in the process. For women and men who worried about these sorts of things, the problem by the mid-1880s was not their prime minister's rather craven interest in wearing the mask of a Venetian nobleman. It was that the man behind the mask, too, appeared to be an imposter.

*

This evening so cold and chill
That the mallards' wings are white with frost
As they skim the reedy shore,
How I think of Yamato!

These lines, attributed to a member of Japan's imperial family in 706, were included in the country's first known anthology of poetry: *Man'yōshū*, or *The Ten Thousand Leaves*. Compiled in the mid-700s, it featured more than 4,000 poems spanning courtly culture and the coarser existences of the lesser born – albeit with many of the book's 'peasants' and 'soldiers' being courtiers imaginatively garbed in the lives of others. Nature, and especially the changes wrought by the seasons, appeared everywhere as backdrop and as metaphor for fleeting moments of grace: playfulness and delight, the poignancy of loss and grief, tiny captured glimpses of great cycles of vitality bursting forth, then withering away. Life was apprehended as brief, seasonal and sorrowful.

A language that 'rhymes too readily', and with which care must therefore be taken to avoid vulgar versifying, had been brought together here with a broader aesthetic based on the evocative power – to the intellectually and emotionally initiated – of the minimal and the allusive. The result was a poetic tradition dominated by the thirty-one syllable *tanka* ('short poem') version of *waka* ('Japanese poem'), usually created using the pattern: 5-7-5-7-7. The original Japanese version of the poem above ran:

> Ashi e yuku
> Kamo no hagahi ni
> Shimo furite
> Samuki yūhe ha
> Yamato shi omohoyu

Argument raged across the Meiji era as to whether there was any role for literature like this in the new, modernizing nation. In the year of Itō's masquerade ball, a thesis on 'Reform of National Literature and *Waka*' counselled that the content of Japanese poetry must at the very least be made manlier – 'conducive to a spirit of bravery'. Other critics suggested doing away with traditional forms entirely.

And yet the long-standing association in Japan of poetry with the life of the imperial court was thought too precious to lose. A preference emerged for reworking rather than rejecting. The old Imperial Poetry Bureau was re-established in 1869 and a New Year's poetry competition inaugurated, to which, after 1874, commoners were permitted to contribute. Beginning in the early 1880s, the winning poems were printed in the daily newspapers, those from imperial and commoner pens appearing side by side. Over the course of his lifetime, the Emperor Meiji himself – no doubt with the assistance of the Imperial Poetry Bureau – was said to have composed more than 90,000 verses. Haiku poets, meanwhile, were recruited by the government to help them communicate the new national morality – Emperor, taxes, conscription – to the masses. Matsuo Bashō, the great Tokugawa-era master of the haiku form, was quite literally deified – worshipped as the god Hana-no-moto Daimyōjin.

Part of the impetus for the preservation of poetry as a living form could be traced back to late Tokugawa *kokugaku* ('national learning') scholars like Motoori Norinaga (1730–1801). He claimed to find in ancient and classical Japanese poetry and prose an unrestrained response to the beauty of life, which stood in stark contrast to ponderous Chinese poetry – drily rationalistic and excessively concerned with rigid standards of behaviour. Various versions of this 'Japanese' aesthetic were developed before and well after Motoori's time, but in general they tended to be defined and energized by three sets of tensions, each giving the other two much of their force.

The first was between emotion and its refined restraint, present in *waka* poetry and informing, too, the design of masks used by principal dancers in the 'Nō' style of theatre. The second was between complexity on the one hand and an understated rustic simplicity, bordering on loneliness (*wabi*) on the other – it was part of the potter or shrine-builder's highly developed skill to allow their finished product to radiate a sense of the raw, imperfect clay or wood from which it was fashioned. Under the influence of Zen, a version of the tea ceremony was developed from the late 1400s called *wabicha* – tea based on *wabi* – in which elegant Chinese kettles and vessels were exchanged for ceramics from regions of Japan like Bizen, known for their natural and imperfect, 'withered' (*sabi*) appearance. The final tension was between the enjoyment of life and an awareness that everything in nature is constantly passing away. This awareness, often referred to as *mono no aware*, was less an unfortunate, melancholy disposition than a prized human capacity to be moved by the world.

To have a modern Emperor who could appreciate and express all this in poetry of his own was all the more important because of the associations suggested by thinkers like Motoori between Japanese aesthetics and emotions, on the one hand, and, on the other, the country's ancient and mythical history and its imperial bloodline. Back in the early 700s, not long before the *Man'yōshū* anthology was compiled, two chronicles had appeared: the *Kojiki* ('Records of Ancient Matters') and the *Nihon shoki* ('The Chronicles of Japan'). The oldest extant writings in Japanese, they were produced at a time when a kingdom was coming together – the 'Yamato' period – that did not yet encompass the whole of modern-day Japan, but to whose emperors Meiji could nevertheless trace his family line all the way back.

The *Nihon shoki* offered a creation story that gave Japan pride of place. It told of a country created as a 'drifting land' by the brother and sister *kami* (gods) Izanagi and Izanami. Izanagi thrust his spear into the ocean; when he withdrew it, drops of brine from its tip formed into small islands. Among the *kami* later to emerge from Izanagi's body were Amaterasu, the Sun Goddess, and her brother Susanoo, the Wind God. Appointed to rule over the high plains of heaven, Amaterasu sent her grandson, Ninigi, to pacify and rule this drifting land, giving him three treasures: a bronze mirror, a sword and a curved jewel. Ninigi's great-grandson Jimmu became the land's first Emperor in 660 BCE, from which point the *Nihon shoki* traced an imperial line for more than a thousand years right up to the early 700s, mythology shading into history along the way.

These powerful, ancient convictions about Japan's special place in the world were given new life by *kokugaku* thinkers like Hirata Atsutane (1776–1843), who suggested that via the performance of certain rituals the emperor in every age was able to connect his people to the gods and to awaken in them the spirit that Motoori liked to call *yamato-gokoro* – 'Yamato-heart'.

Of the various ways in which such ideas filtered through to the modern era, one was expressed in the 1880s by Kuga Katsunan, the influential editor of the newspaper *Nihon*. He insisted that Japan had its own distinctive forms of behaviour and politics, formed naturally and organically across many centuries, the value and truth of which was deducible not through scientific reason (whose modern reification

Izanagi and Izanami Creating the Islands of Japan
(Kobayashi Eitaku, *c*.1885)

was itself a matter of culture rather than nature or necessity) but via appeal to the emotions.

These forms, he argued, were politically and psychologically indispensable to the successful building up of Japan as a competitive modern nation. 'If the culture of one nation', Kuga wrote, 'is so influenced by another that it completely loses its own unique character, that country will surely lose its independent footing.' Here was a warning with powerful resonance in the era of the dancing cabinet: if as Japanese we all end up capering around in foreign finery, aping foreign manners and mannerisms, then the colonization of our country that our leaders claim to fear will have been achieved without a shot being fired.

Kuga also wished to impress upon his readers that there was no such thing as 'the West': each Western nation possessed its own particular genius, had mapped its own route to progress and had made its own contributions to world development. Such varied and complementary talents amongst nations was the stuff of real and creative internationalism, he insisted, and Japan ought to play its part rather than being content with mere borrowing or imitation.

Kuga's ideas were developed by Miyake Setsurei, who claimed in an essay entitled 'The Japanese: Truth, Goodness and Beauty' that in working for the good of one's country one works for the good of mankind. For the Japanese, this meant making use of the unique opportunity of being the first Asian country to approach economic and technological parity with the modern West, by reaching deep into their culture to find ways of being in the world that would balance those offered up and lived out by Westerners. Japan should pursue balance too, he added, by building up its military strength to the point where Asian countries need no longer fear being overrun by European colonialism.

For popular nationalists like Kuga and Miyake, discerning the finer details of all this became an urgent priority in the late 1880s and 1890s. What precisely *was* the 'national essence' (*kokusui*) running through Japan's past, aesthetics and emotional life, and what was the proper role of the imperial institution in guaranteeing its preservation?

Japan by the late 1880s thus found itself home to at least three powerful and conflicting sets of ideals. A great many liberals, some of whom were prepared to condone violence in the pursuit of their aims, thought that in questions of politics and rights Japan had much to learn from the likes of America, Britain and France. They believed the country's leaders had become too comfortable in their power, and risked betraying the great promise of 1868. A newer nationalist line of thought urged a more critical stance towards Western culture, seeking to tease out and promote some kind of national essence as the basis for education, behavioural norms and policy-making. Both approaches were overtly and self-consciously forward-looking, though they differed fundamentally in their conceptions of what 'progress' might be and how it would happen.

Finally, there were traditionalist conservatives like Motoda Eifu, who served as personal tutor to the Emperor. Motoda saw much good in Confucian standards and patterns of relationship as the foundation for a successful society in any era. Fearing for his country's future, he produced an imperial rescript in 1879 warning of 'foreign civilizations' whose 'only values are fact-gathering and technique'. It led them, he said, to lack the attention to sincerity and morality for which Confucius remained the best guide.

Inside many Japanese swirled elements of all three sets of ideals, and the era was famous for political U-turns by great thinkers. Timing, too, was enormously significant in helping to settle matters between competing visions for modern Japan. Traditionalists and the new nationalists found themselves enjoying influence – in the press and at the Emperor's ear – just as Japan's political leaders were completing their work on a long-awaited Constitution.

*

The move from a Council of State to a cabinet system of government had been made in 1885 in preparation for the publication and promulgation of a document whose compilation was carried out without public discussion (as, its defenders were keen to point out, the Constitution of the United States had been), but with careful reference to what worked and what did not in Europe. Itō had travelled there in the early 1880s, returning having learned two crucial things: how to hold a cigar like Bismarck, and how to adapt Prussia's constitutional monarchy to fit Japan's unique situation – a divine Emperor at the head of a 'vast village community', as Itō put it.

Promulgated in 1889, the Constitution of the Empire of Japan (*Dai-Nippon Teikoku Kenpō*) was presented as a gift from the Emperor, in whom sovereignty resided on the basis of his divine ancestry – as recorded in Japan's two ancient chronicles. The ceremonial events of that great day, 11 February, began with a visit by the Emperor to the Place of Awe, the most sacred part of the newly built imperial palace in Tokyo. There he promised Amaterasu, the Sun Goddess and great mother of the imperial line, that he would protect Japan's ancestral form of government and uphold this new addition to it. He repeated his promise at the Ancestral Spirits Sanctuary before worshipping for a while at the Sanctuary of the *Kami*.

Messengers were then sent out to shrines and places of remembrance across the country, bringing the news to the gods and to deceased leaders of the 1868 restoration of imperial rule.

The Emperor proceeded to exchange his ritual robes for the military uniform of a modern European monarch, and enter the Throne Room, where national and prefectural politicians, peers and select members of the press awaited him. Reading out a short speech, he handed – literally made a gift of – the new Constitution to Japan's Prime Minister. A specially installed telegraph line informed the Imperial Guard outside of what had just occurred, and a 101-gun salute was fired off – duly answered in kind by battleships moored at Shinagawa and Yokohama, and by the crackle of fireworks and the ringing of temple bells.

Under the terms of the new Constitution, the Emperor was supreme commander of the armed forces, and would make all appointments to the judiciary, to the new Diet's Upper House (or House of Peers), and to the Cabinet. The Lower House of the Diet, the House of Representatives, was to be elected on the basis of a limited franchise: just 5 per cent of the adult male population, based primarily on age (twenty-five or over) and the amount of tax paid. In 1890, the year of Japan's first election under the new Constitution, that meant around 450,000 people, or a little over 1 per cent of Japan's total population. The Lower House was set up so as to have an influential rather than a decisive role in governance, drafting legislation (a function shared with the ministries and with the dependably conservative and loyalist House of Peers) and passing the annual budget.

The real purpose of the Diet, for Meiji leaders like Itō and especially his hardline Chōshū ally Yamagata Aritomo – who regarded party politics as an immoral tussle over power, and 'public opinion' as a barely legitimate concept – was in fact two-fold. First, as a safe means of letting the opinionated feel important and effective; and secondly, as yet another way (alongside schools, conscription, newspapers and imperial rescripts) in which the will of those really in charge might be communicated to the public. That real power lay with the executive: the Cabinet, with its Ministers of State, who remained separate from the Lower House ('transcendent' was the preferred term) and independent of any interference by the judiciary.

The only true leverage enjoyed by elected politicians under the new Constitution was the ability to refuse to pass the annual budget.

People's freedoms were, on paper, extensive, spanning movement, property, free speech, religion, assembly and privacy of correspondence. But all were vulnerable to restriction by law or by (very flexible) considerations of the public peace. Similarly, although management of the press via legislation seemed at first to augur a more liberal regulatory regime, the Cabinet could still use imperial directives to intervene with editors and publishers. A Newspaper Law in 1909 added to those powers, enabling the complete banning of a particular edition of a publication (and the seizure of all copies) without resort to the courts. In the early days of the Meiji era, the Council of State had encouraged journalistic discussion of national matters, but had made clear that books and newspapers would be subject to scrutiny and 'irresponsible criticism' would not be tolerated. In this new constitutional era, the thinking remained very much the same.

Japan's first ever nationwide elections, in 1890, were greeted with a 97 per cent turnout amongst eligible voters. The two major parties by 1890 were a reformed Jiyūtō and Kaishintō, channelling anger at government leaders for their failure to revise the unequal treaties and for the high taxes to which they were subjecting the wealthy farmers and merchants who made up the majority both of the voting public and their newly elected representatives. Most of the latter were young – two-thirds were below the age of forty-three – and from this point on Japan began to establish a tradition of returning the same people, and often their sons or other relatives after them, time after time to public office. Other new electoral traditions included government bribery of Diet members (Yamagata enjoyed an imperial palace purse of nearly a million yen to this end in 1892) and the use of the police and hired thugs to try to swing key election outcomes. No party whose members or allies controlled the Home Ministry ever lost a Lower House election.

It is impossible to know in advance how a Constitution will work out in practice. In the case of the Meiji Constitution, an early effect of having 'transcendent' rather than party cabinets was that battle lines emerged as much between the executive and the House of Representatives as between parties in the House. Many a time the House would try to bring down individual ministers, using its power of budget

Itō Hirobumi (1841–1909)

Illustration of the Imperial Diet of Japan (Gotō Yoshikage, 1890): upper
left, the Emperor looks on as proceedings get under way

approval to try to get its way. The government could, if necessary,
have the previous year's budget renewed without the need for approval,
but in an era of escalating costs this was far from an ideal solution.

The anger that sometimes lit up the Lower House was understand-
able. For the first two and a half decades after its establishment in
1885, Cabinet government looked very much like the old Council

of State. Japan's premiership circulated almost entirely around a small band of Satsuma-Chōshū men and their protégés. Itō Hirobumi held the post four times, Yamagata Aritomo twice. Matsukata Masayoshi, Satsuma architect of the famously radical and radicalizing deflation of the mid-1880s, also served twice as prime minister during this period, as did Katsura Tarō (Chōshū, mentored by Yamagata) and Saionji Kinmochi of the pre-1868 imperial court. Kuroda Kiyotaka (Satsuma) and Ōkuma Shigenobu (Saga) both served once.

Meanwhile, an Imperial Rescript on Education in 1890 helped to embed further the victory for traditionalists and new nationalists that the Constitution represented. Education was a passion of the Emperor's, and he had long encouraged his tutor, Motoda Eifu, to write books that would help instil in the young a degree of filial piety and loyalty towards the imperial institution. Together, Motoda, the Minister of Education, and a third man named Inoue Kowashi – referred to by contemporaries as 'Itō's brain' – came up with the 1890 Rescript in response: the influence of Neo-Confucian virtues and *kokugaku* visionaries could not have been clearer:

> Ye, Our subjects, be filial to your parents, affectionate to your brothers and sisters; as husbands and wives be harmonious, as friends true;
>
> Bear yourselves in modesty and moderation; extend your benevolence to all; pursue learning and cultivate arts, and thereby develop intellectual faculties and perfect moral powers;
>
> Always respect the Constitution and observe the laws; should emergency arise, offer yourselves courageously to the State; and thus guard and maintain the prosperity of Our Imperial Throne coeval with heaven and earth.

A copy of the Rescript was issued to all schools, where it was bowed to and recited in unison by students every day. Both the Rescript and portraits of the Emperor were to be saved from fire or other disasters at all costs – including human life: hagiographical accounts emerged of head teachers dying while trying to save these sacred items from harm.

But like the Constitution, imperial rescripts were highly ideological documents capable of being put to unpredictable uses. They offered standards to which an individual might hold not just him- or herself, but others too – not least people in positions of power. For those attending ceremonies for the promulgation of the new Constitution in early 1889, the absence of Japan's influential Minister of Education, Mori Arinori, must have seemed odd. And yet there was good reason for it: he had just been stabbed, and would shortly die. The attacker left a note, accusing Mori of profaning the divine presence and offending the imperial family on a visit to the Grand Shrine at Ise. Mori had allegedly entered without removing his shoes, and had then used his cane to move aside the curtain that protected from view the sacred mirror (one of the three treasures mentioned in Japan's ancient chronicles), so that he could take a quick look. An investigation subsequently found his attacker's claims to be false, but such 'patriotic' attacks on Japan's politicians were only just beginning. A higher authority and standard had been articulated, well beyond them, to which a sufficiently heartfelt appeal would later become capable of justifying the most violent actions.

A few years before his untimely death, Mori Arinori had divorced his wife. They had tried out an 'egalitarian marriage', but Mori claimed that it had rendered his wife 'flighty and peculiar'. Japan's early experiments with modernity were never just a matter of grand places, public spaces and great events. There was also trial and error within intimate relationships and the sheltered four walls of the home. Family was no longer a place of escape from whatever was happening in the outside world. It was a crucible, in which many women and men faced for the first time the deep uncertainties of the journey on which their leaders had set them.

4

Happy Families

March 1908, and the arrival of the post was no longer something Hiratsuka Haruko looked forward to. Today's item was a small package. Opening it, she discovered a series of pornographic images, sent by a stranger. Other days brought letters containing sarcastic proposals of marriage, alongside offers of a less wholesome sort. A friend from Hiratsuka's Buddhist meditation group turned up at her door offering to wed her, apparently out of pity. Journalists, too, clamoured outside, and then abused her in print: immoral home-wrecker, who ought to be sent to the slums; poisoner of young minds; shameless ingrate; madwoman. Japan Women's College, from which Hiratsuka had recently graduated, were kind enough to send round a messenger – to let her know in person that she had been expelled from their alumni association.

Such were the wages of sin. Hiratsuka had offended gravely against a story about the nature of Japanese womanhood, developed across recent decades and now commanding a visceral attachment (in public at least) throughout much of urban society. The power of this narrative lay in its synthesis of diverse womanly virtues – drawn from around the world and from across Japan's old class system – and its production in a kind of cultural surround-sound: the law, police officers, schools, newspapers and magazines, fiction and fantasy, and of course the family.

If the Constitution and Imperial Rescript on Education had worried some as a step back from the aspirations of 1868's Charter Oath, the same was true of the new Meiji Civil Code in its final 1898 incarnation. For a while it had looked as though Japan might adopt a French-style civil code, and a man with no less a name than Gustave

Emile Boissonade de Fontarabie had been brought across from the Sorbonne to advise. And yet officials worried that an emphasis on individual rights and private property might put at risk the household, or *ie*, as the primary social unit, and with it the filial piety and respect for ancestors that was by this point so widely regarded as a good and natural legacy of an older era. In fact, this traditional family had always been a fantasy: households of that older era were often home to a range of people beyond immediate family – concubines and adopted children, apprentices and servants – and afforded relatively little of the civilized privacy so valued by Japan's early modernizers. Much of this modern official thinking was instead a matter of pragmatism: a society premised on hierarchy, cooperation and public duty would be more conducive to achieving the swift economic and military development that Japan's leaders knew they needed.

Under the new arrangements, the *ie* was the country's basic legal unit (rather than the individual). Its headship passed from father to eldest son, conferring privileges including the allowing or disallowing of marriages for daughters up to the age of twenty-five and sons up to the age of thirty. Under a new Family Registry System, all families were required to register their members with the authorities, and without family membership a person could not enjoy legal rights.

As in many parts of the West in these years, women were denied a range of legal and educational privileges enjoyed by men. In Japan, they were forbidden from testifying in a court of law, bringing legal proceedings, or involving themselves in financial or business matters without their husband's permission – restrictions they shared with people designated under the law as 'quasi-incompetent persons'. A woman could initiate a divorce in cases of extreme cruelty or desertion, but not on the basis of adultery. A man, on the other hand, would be quite within his rights to seek divorce on such grounds, along with a two-year prison sentence for both his wife and the gentleman in question. If a marriage ended, the children belonged to – and so stayed with – the *ie*. The wife would be the one to leave.

A woman wanting to change any of this had a struggle on her hands. She did not have the vote, and she was banned, after 1890, from any kind of participation in politics. Much time would be spent instead at home, where a visit from a police officer would not be uncommon, encouraged as Japan's constabulary were to take a careful paternal interest in women's activities and whereabouts and to blend law enforcement with moral guidance.

Where the law and the police placed limits on women's prerogatives, the state bureaucracy went to great lengths to spell out their duties. In a country run almost on a permanent war footing – with periods of actual conflict marked by changes of pace more than tone – women, men and children alike were viewed as productive assets of the state. And assets needed to be developed, honed and protected. While boys were prepared for service in a range of professions, the highest of which required study at one of Japan's imperial or private universities, girls pored over textbooks on *kaji* ('domestic things'). They learned about nutrition and laundry, family finances and hygiene, until they were ready to set up and run households of their own. No prospect yet of a university education. Instead, vocational colleges were for the time being the rarely reached summit of institutional female learning in Japan.

To interpret all this as women mattering less than men would be to underestimate the ambition of Japan's political elite. When Mori Arinori as Education Minister exhorted middle-class women to become *ryōsai kenbo* – 'Good Wives, Wise Mothers' – he was not banishing them from the public sphere. He was radically expanding that sphere. As the text of a Ministry of Education publication entitled *Meiji Onna Daigaku* ('The Meiji Greater Learning for Women') put it in 1887: 'the home is a public place.'

'Home' and 'homemaker' were rapidly evolving ideas across the late nineteenth century in Japan. Onto the figure of the modest and frugal samurai wife was grafted the get-your-hands-dirty hard work ethos of rural women, together with a range of Anglo-American ideas about domesticity that were captured in the loan word *'hōmu'*.

Iwamoto Yoshiharu, the Anglophile Christian editor of *Jogaku Zasshi* ('Women's Education Magazine'), claimed the credit for popularizing this term, which he took to mean the establishment of a secure domestic environment where the real, loving core of a family – parents and children – could flourish, as far away as possible from the human household clutter of times gone by: the servants and extended or adopted family members who compromised true familial affection and cohesion.

The multigenerational household was never in danger of disappearing, but increasingly an urban middle-class ideal was established – later extended down the social scale – whereby 'home' was associated with a moral and hygienic environment sealed off from strangers and bad influences, while remaining porous to the public good and conducive overall to parents' shaping of healthy imperial subjects. Its spirit was captured in a new word, *katei* ('household' – literally 'home-and-garden'), popularized via a publication boom around the turn of the twentieth century. Alongside newspaper *katei* columns were *Katei Zasshi* ('Household Magazine') in 1892, followed by *Katei no Tomo* ('Household Friend') in 1903, later to become the highly influential *Fujin no Tomo* ('Woman's Friend'). Advice was offered on everything from recipes to the price of domestic essentials, alongside virtual tours of real-life 'model' households run by the wives of successful politicians or businessmen.

One such account, appearing in a book called *Katei no Kairaku* ('The Pleasures of the Home') (1901), described a 'family meeting' held at 3 p.m. every Saturday afternoon. Tea would be prepared in the household head's room and the family ushered in, offering one another formal greetings as they entered. The head would then read aloud from the newspaper for the edification, in turn, of his parents, his younger siblings, and finally his children. Tea and sweets followed, after which the *koto* (a traditional Japanese stringed instrument) was played and a young boy sang the national anthem. Variations on this 'family time' theme included the giving of speeches, the telling of anecdotes and gathering around a baby to gaze smilingly into its face.

Japan's business community made the most of the opportunities here. Architects and house-builders worked on homes in which the family could be separated more effectively from servants and guests – though not from one another: there was little recognition of any need for individual space. Kitchen design allowed women to enhance productivity by standing up while they worked, at units along the wall or at mobile worktables. From 1904, advertisements hit the newspapers for Japan's first gas-burning rice cooker, complete

A family meeting pictured in the 1902 edition of *Katei no Kairaku* ('The Pleasures of the Home'): the head of the household, top right, seats himself on a cushion.

with slogans like 'With just one match' and 'No need for a maid' – the latter so catchy a concept that the device itself came to be known as a *gejo irazu* ('maid not required'). The same year, Mitsukoshi opened as one of Japan's first department stores, operating as a mixture of shop, product exhibition space, tourist spot, children's playground and even salon for intellectual conversation – putting consumer culture in grander, purposeful perspective. Discussion highlights were published in Mitsukoshi's own magazine.

There was no escaping this Meiji family, even in fiction. Male writers revealed themselves in their writings as sons who rhapsodized about rather than really knew their mothers, and who sought desperately as a result to fix the womanly and the maternal as comforting social and emotional, even spiritual categories. Many a Japanese boy continued to miss his mother long after he left home. Kosawa Heisaku's Freudian free associations regularly returned to his own mother: bathing with her at the turn of the twentieth century; her joy when later he used to come home from boarding school, making him *amazake* (a sweet rice drink) that was so tasty he licked the cup clean – 'like a baby,' he recalled, 'just moving onto solid food'.

Childhood baths with mother helped set the novelist Tanizaki Junichirō off on his career, too – a lifetime of writing longingly about women:

> The flesh of her thighs was so marvellously white and delicate that many times . . . I would find myself looking at her body with amazement. It seemed to me that her skin grew whiter as I looked at it . . . Women before the turn of the century did not go out much into the light and air: they wrapped their bodies in voluminous robes and lived secluded in rooms that remained dim even at noon. No doubt that explains why their skins were so fair. My mother's skin retained its wonderful fairness until I was a young man of twenty-six or twenty-seven.

In this way, mothers, wives, mistresses, sisters and daughters could all find themselves imprisoned on pedestals, forced to be the ultimate answer to every male doubt about Japan's modernity; the means by which every loss might be recovered. There was even an ideal type for failed marriages: the wife who suffers, beautifully and patiently, emerged from centuries of celebration in Chinese and Japanese literature to become a staple of Meiji-era fiction by men.

An emerging trend for writing by women at turns impressed, titillated and terrified the reading public. Shimizu Shikin started to work at *Jogaku Zasshi* in 1890 shortly after her first marriage, marred by her husband's infidelities, ended in divorce. In her first story, '*Koware Yubiwa*' ('The Broken Ring'), published in the magazine, Shimizu described marriage as like drawing lots. Men have a life outside the home, she pointed out, so an unlucky draw need not be defining or disastrous for them. Women are less fortunate.

In place of the stoically suffering wife, Shimizu's writing offered a new image: a woman whose life truly begins only when she escapes her marriage. A mother teaches her daughter modestly to conceal herself from visitors to the house, introducing her to Chinese biographies full of women who went as far as cutting off parts of their bodies to demonstrate their fidelity. When the mother dies, the daughter is able to open up a new world of books and magazines. She first tries to change her husband, before later divorcing him, refusing to accept that sorrow is a natural part of the female condition.

As a journalist, Shimizu criticized both the mainstream men who limited women to a narrowly functional education (they could sense that it was wrong, but were unable to forgo its sheer convenience) and the People's Rights activists who fought for women's rights in public, but 'lord[ed] it over their wives and children' at home. Some were known to rail energetically against prostitution and then visit brothels to unwind, while the Freedom and Popular Rights leader Ōi Kentarō's busy schedule of travel, writing, and activism was matched by an equally hectic private life – as Shimizu herself discovered, to her cost.

One of Shimizu's closest friends was Kageyama Hideko, the Okayama schoolteacher and explosives courier who had been arrested in the Osaka Incident. Both Kageyama and Ōi were released early from prison as part of an amnesty timed to coincide with the promulgation of the new Constitution in 1889. Welcomed into Osaka station with great cheers and a shower of flowers – a scene repeated across the city that afternoon as she travelled around in a rickshaw with her father – Kageyama went back to the station the next day to greet Ōi off the train from his own release. His prison love letters had finally worn her down: Kageyama went to live with him, and they had a child together. But Ōi refused her the equal marriage she wanted, and one day she received an odd letter from him, asking after her health and professing his love for her. Kageyama was perplexed: she was quite well.

It turned out that Ōi had mixed up two different letters, sending Kageyama a missive meant for Shimizu, with whom he had started an affair and also fathered a child. Shimizu received the letter intended for Kageyama. The two women's friendship came to an abrupt end, Shimizu suffered a second nervous breakdown (Ōi's letter had been enquiring after the first), and both women left Ōi for better prospects.

Remarrying, Shimizu carried on producing acclaimed work, but struggled to avoid compromising. A woman who just a few years before had used *Jogaku Zasshi* to excoriate Meiji-era marriage now found herself writing the magazine's *katei* column. 'How to Select a Wet Nurse' and 'Delicious Sweet Potatoes' were amongst her offerings. Shortly after her husband returned from five years of work in Europe, Shimizu stopped writing altogether. Rumour had it that she had retired from writing – had 'broken her brush' – under duress. Her son Yoshishige later recalled an exchange in which Shimizu suggested resuming her work as a writer, from home. 'Ha!' replied her husband. 'But the *tensai* (genius) is now a *gusai* (stupid wife).'

*

Far above and beyond any school-teaching or magazine column, the ultimate lesson in 'family' was provided by Japan's imperial household. Great ceremonial occasions offered ideal opportunities, and one of the greatest was the promulgation of the Constitution in 1889. In Tokyo, festival floats snaked through the streets underneath evergreen arches, passing by buildings decorated with flags and lanterns. People walked alongside them, eating rice cakes and mandarins. Sumo wrestlers grappled with one another. *Sake* flowed, and an ultra-modern light-show sparked up. Several people drank themselves to death.

Erwin von Bälz – the Tokyo Imperial University professor of medicine, recruited almost at random by a Japanese exchange student in Leipzig – wondered uncharitably to himself how many of the people gadding about the streets of Tokyo this day actually knew what was *in* the Constitution. But of course that wasn't the point. Content mattered less than choreography: the celebration of the archetypal Japanese family, stretching far back in time – even beyond time, to Japan's formation out of droplets from the spear-tip of a great god. The choice of 11 February for the day's ceremonies had been quite deliberate: Empire Day (*Kigensetsu*) was a national holiday created back in 1873 to commemorate the accession of Japan's first Emperor, Jimmu, which experts working with the *Kojiki* and *Nihon Shoki* set at 660 BCE.

And yet the ideal of the *kazoku kokka* ('family state'), developed by

Japanese thinkers building on Western 'organic state' theories, did not at first sit easily with a population accustomed to imagining the imperial institution as distant and secluded. Much time and money had to be spent on changing their minds. The Meiji Emperor found himself carted (or rather palanquined) around the country on imperial processions and tours, the first of which, from Kyoto to Tokyo in late 1868, may have been the first time a Japanese emperor laid eyes on Mount Fuji.

On one such tour, in the early 1870s, residents of Kamakura and Enoshima simply did not believe they were looking at the real Emperor. Others complained that whereas a *daimyō* and his retinue processing by would have guaranteed a good turnout and brisk business at street stalls, not many people bothered with the Emperor, so it was hardly worth the effort of cleaning the roads. The attitude seemed to be quite pervasive. One year, the police found themselves tasked with 'encouraging' people to come out of their homes for public celebrations of the Emperor's birthday.

At least the younger generation could be trained. Where adults might mill around in the background when imperial tours came through, mothers breastfeeding their babies, children could be dragooned into straight lines, bowing and breaking into '*Kimi ga yo*' – the song adopted as Japan's national anthem in 1888, its excessively upbeat original melody, written in a rush by a British military bandmaster named John William Fenton, quickly replaced with something more suitable.

By the time of the Constitution's promulgation, these anxieties about popular enthusiasm for the Emperor prompted a search for some appropriate expression of celebration for the big day. Performances of '*Kimi ga yo*' was the natural choice, but schoolchildren aside there was as yet no tradition in Japan of large groups singing in unison. It was decided that a cheer would be better. The Education Minister Mori Arinori suggested *hōga*: 'respectful congratulations'. But this ran perilously close to *ahō ga* – 'the idiot'. Given Japanese satirists' fondness for wordplay, it didn't seem a risk worth taking. Instead, an ancient cheer was modified and popularized: *Tennō heika banzai*! 'May His Majesty the Emperor live for ten thousand years!'

*

If the effectiveness of a new ideology can be judged by how far its opponents end up forced to fight it on its own terms, then 'happy families' – from humble household up to imperial palace – was by the early twentieth century a roaring success. Many radicals found themselves trapped either into working with it or making recklessly direct moves against it. Very much in the latter vein was a 1908 magazine article entitled 'The First Enemy':

> The first enemy that we meet as soon as we enter society are parents and masters . . . yes, the parents are the enemy of children, and masters of servants. If you really love justice and freedom, you must beat . . . your parents.

A magazine called *Sekai Fujin* ('Women of the World') – one of three socialist women's journals active around this time – was fined so heavily for carrying this piece that it was no longer able to afford the 500-yen 'guarantee' fee payable to the authorities by anyone wishing to publish on current affairs. It was forced to operate instead as a 'learned journal', resulting in fresh fines (and the imprisonment of its editor) when inevitably it exceeded its limited new academic brief.

The man behind bars was Ishikawa Sanshirō, led by some combination of love, chivalry and publishing pragmatism to put his name to what was really Kageyama Hideko's latest venture. Since leaving Ōi Kentaro, Kageyama had married again – acquiring in the process the name 'Fukuda', by which she was later better known – had three children, suffered the early death of her husband and ushered her offspring into Ishikawa's adopted family instead: Japan's small band of socialists.

Many in this group were Christians, including Ishikawa, with whom Fukuda now began to attend a church near Tokyo University. They were attracted by the social gospel and by what they saw as Jesus Christ's embodiment of the *jinkakusha* (man of character) ideal, which seemed to them so sorely lacking elsewhere in the politics of their times. Japan's socialists, whether Christian or not, took a powerfully and unashamedly moral approach in their early campaigning, seeking not to overthrow the bourgeoisie but to establish a middle class in Japan that possessed a sense of decency and purpose, and which everyone might one day be able to join.

Women's rights, however, continued to be something of a blind spot for many a male radical. Back in the early 1880s, a man had been so embarrassed at being slated to speak on the same stage as the female activist Kishida Toshiko that he faked a toothache at the last minute to get out of it – prompting Kishida to ask the crowd what kind of man would 'get such a terrible toothache at the mere sight of a woman'. Journalists proved little better: many of Kishida's speeches are lost to history because newspaper coverage of them focused so heavily on what she was wearing. Kishida herself had well understood the deeply insidious nature of what was going on here. The transition from an old Tokugawa theme of 'Respect Men, Despise Women' (*danson-johi*) to the ladies-first gentlemanliness of the Rokumeikan era was little more than a minor makeover. 'Ah, you men . . .' Kishida sighed, 'you talk of reform but not of revolution.'

Now, a generation later, when Japan's socialists organized meetings for and featuring women – carefully billed as 'academic lectures', to circumvent the law – men rarely bothered turning up. And though Fukuda Hideko's group liked to imagine their tight-knit, constantly imperilled organization as an 'extended family' (complete with pet dog 'Maru', short for 'Marx'), the benefits of having comrades to see you off to jail and welcome you home again were perhaps outweighed by Fukuda finding herself referred to as 'mother-in-law', while other women – whether married to group members or not – were cast as 'wives'. It always seemed to be a female member who was tasked with the cooking. One signed off an article for the group's magazine by saying that she had plenty more to say but had to head off now to make dinner.

Elsewhere, socialists seemed to draw deeply on Meiji images of womanhood in seeking to win women to their creed: women should 'fall in love with socialism', wrote one, apparently on the basis that women were ruled by romance; others explored the ways in which women's natures – humane, conciliatory, full of sympathy – suited them to the socialist cause.

The publication of Fukuda's magazine, *Sekai Fujin*, was made possible through expertise acquired in the course of producing her successful autobiography. *Warawa no Hanshōgai* ('Half of My Life') (1904) was reprinted more than forty times. The magazine was intended as a way of pushing a serious, committed political agenda. It campaigned first and foremost for a revision of the law forbidding women's participation in politics, so that all other issues that concerned Meiji women – from education to prostitution and concubinage – might be more effectively tackled. It informed women about their rights (and their many vulnerabilities) under the Civil Code. And it carried articles on women's suffrage movements around the world, to remind Japanese women that they were not alone.

Parliamentary campaigns to amend the law in favour of allowing women to participate in political meetings were successful in the Lower House but were constantly frustrated by Japan's conservative Upper House, which thereby showed itself to be working very much as the crafters of the Constitution had intended. Fukuda watched from the gallery on one occasion as the measure was voted down by 300 votes to just 4, later condemning the men of that House as bigoted, ignorant and illogical. The cause was not finally won until 1922.

Some regarded falling foul of the police, as Fukuda's magazine often did, as potentially beneficial for a movement's credibility. Witnessing skirmishes with law enforcement, including on one occasion the descent into violence of a socialist cherry-blossom viewing party (perhaps the event's sheer incongruousness was regarded as grounds for intervention), could be an effective way of showcasing injustice and persuading new people of the progressive nature of a cause. But Fukuda finally ended up in poverty after her magazine's fine in 1908, cooking and washing for her children in the mornings and selling kimono fabric in the afternoons to make ends meet. Suffering now with beriberi, Fukuda – Okayama schoolteacher, bomb-carrier, socialist and sometime radical Christian – had one last great piece of writing in her. 'The Solution to the Woman Problem' was published in February 1913, and it suggested quite openly that the only way now truly to achieve emancipation for women was all-out communism.

Unsurprisingly, the magazine that carried Fukuda's firecracker of a farewell saw its February issue immediately banned. The editor's father was unhappy, but not surprised. When it came to embarrassing her family, his daughter, Hiratsuka Haruko, had form. The incident in question, five years before in 1908, had been the cause of all those unpleasant items arriving for her in the post – the pornography, the fake marriage proposals. It had all begun with a single, and singularly strange, letter, containing the following thoughts:

> The moment that any woman dies is the most beautiful moment in her life. I will kill you. I am an artist. I am a poet. I am an envoy of beauty. I must observe your last dying moment, which will be the most beautiful moment in your life.

The sender was a man with an awkwardly large head and body, his physical movements as ponderous as his speaking style. Or so it had seemed to Hiratsuka, sitting in his classroom. Morita Sōhei was a lecturer in Western literature at a literary society for women, known as the Keishū Bungakukai. Having read Hiratsuka's first novel, *Ai no Matsujitsu* ('The Last Day of Love'), which appeared in the society's magazine, Morita came to feel all the more keenly his wife's relative dullness of spirit and the soulless slog of his career. The woman in *Ai*, by contrast, was a force of nature: she jumped out of her lover's bed to interrogate him smartly and mercilessly over all the things they disagreed on, ignored his pleas to marry him regardless, and then left him for an independent career as a high school teacher.

Much Japanese fiction of this era, and perhaps especially a first novel, was deeply autobiographical. And so, in Hiratsuka, the author of *Ai*, Morita felt himself face to face with someone who drove the proverbial coach and horses through Japan's drab womanly ideal and who seemed to have stepped, instead, straight out of one of the plays he taught – D'Annunzio's *The Triumph of Death* or Ibsen's *A Doll's House*.

Hovering somewhere between fiction and real life too was the plan Morita now hatched, which he imagined ending with him whiling away his life in a 'lone cell in a snowbound Sakhalin jail, observing the changes in myself'. His letter to Hiratsuka, on 21 March 1908, was written to let her know that the time had at last come for her to run away with him – and be killed.

Hiratsuka had become attracted to Morita by this point, despite his many flaws, including a tendency to trip over tree roots during romantic walks through the park. He somehow appealed to an 'irresponsible playfulness' in her, she decided. She packed a bag and dashed off to meet Morita – taking with her a dagger, a family heirloom, with which he could do his deed.

Together, the two of them left Tokyo by train and then rickshaw, travelling north via Ōmiya, in Saitama prefecture, all the way up to Shiobara, in the mountainous north of Tochigi prefecture. Finally, they trekked together on foot up a snowy mountain road. There at the edge of a steep drop, as night fell, they poured whisky over their letters to one another and set them alight. Morita at last brandished the dagger, but cried out suddenly that he couldn't kill anyone, not even Hiratsuka (this seems to have been intended as a compliment). He threw the dagger, still in its black leather sheath, down into the dark valley below and collapsed into the snow, wailing.

Hiratsuka persuaded him to get up, and the two spent the rest of the night trudging through the snow, until they were found the next morning by a couple of policemen and returned to their homes: Morita to write the autobiographical novel (*Baien*, 'Smoke'), for which Hiratsuka suspected he had concocted this whole episode as inspiration; Hiratsuka to face a very angry father and some very excited journalists. Not only had two highly educated assets of the state gone AWOL on a mad-cap adventure. It was widely (and wrongly) assumed that they had had a passionate sexual relationship. In fact, Hiratsuka had refused Morita's advances, condemning him to an afterlife, once that fact became known, of tittering commentary about a man twice unable to plunge his dagger when the crucial moment came.

The moral charge sheet against Hiratsuka looked for a time as though it could hardly be more comprehensive. And yet the same newspapers that helped to compile it found themselves, just a few years later, carrying adverts for Hiratsuka's new magazine: *Seitō* ('Bluestocking'). It was probably not her father's first wish that money put aside for his daughter's wedding should be spent instead on setting up a women's literary monthly. But in 1911 the epoch-making first issue appeared nonetheless, with an opening statement from Hiratsuka – now taking the pen-name Raichō ('thunderbird') – that featured a refrain hallowed ever since in histories of Japanese feminism:

In the beginning, woman was the sun, and a true being.
Now woman is the moon.
She lives through others, and shines through the light of others.

The first line reminded readers that while Japan's great national family might have an emperor at its head, it had a goddess at its originary heart. *Seitō* – both the magazine and the associated society – was intended as the means by which the brilliance of Japan's women, long overshadowed, could finally be shared.

What started as a literary venture, giving women writers the chance to meet and to hone and demonstrate their talents, could hardly avoid becoming political. In 1912, goaded by criticism over a misleadingly reported fact-finding visit to the Yoshiwara red-light district (this time, pelted rocks replaced malicious mail), Hiratsuka penned a ground-breaking piece in the highly respected journal *Chūō Kōron* ('The Central Review'). It was entitled 'A New Woman':

I am the Sun . . .[which is] renewed day by day. A 'new woman' places
a curse on 'yesterday' . . . not satisfied with the life of an oppressed old
woman, made ignorant, made a man's slave and treated as nothing but
a lump of meat by male selfishness. A new woman seeks to destroy old
morals and laws, which were created for men's convenience.

The next year in *Seitō*, a couple of months after its February issue was banned for publishing Fukuda's advocacy of communism, Hiratsuka did away with literary allusions altogether, in a stark denunciation of where happy families had left Japan's women:

The so-called women's virtues exist only for men's convenience. The
lives of many wives are no more than being their husbands' slaves during the daytime and their prostitutes at night . . . If love arises from
such marriages, it must be only a pretence, and no more than the result
of calculating interests and convenience in many cases.

As per their training, and the Meiji family ideal, the police played it gently with the mostly middle-class women of *Seitō*. They professed to be more disappointed than angry. When this latest piece was published, two of *Seitō*'s members were called to the Metropolitan Police Department's Special Higher Police Section for a meeting. There they

The imperial family at home, in *A Mirror of Japanese Nobility*
(Toyohara Chikanobu, 1887)

were told that this particular (April) issue would not be banned, but
they should be careful not to 'disturb the conventional virtues of
Japanese women' in this way again.

Hiratsuka ignored the advice and republished her piece in a book.
This time, it was banned immediately. But by now the 'new woman'
genie was well and truly out of the bottle. Hiratsuka's challenge to
women, to free their creative spirits and face up to what an 'un-
ethical, unlawful and unreasonable marriage system' was really asking
of them, would steadily gain ground into the 1920s and beyond.

*

If upper-middle-class literary women ended the Meiji era in a stronger
position, it was a very different story for their sisters on the political
left. Efforts by socialists to formally organize in 1901 had been frustrated by the police, who shut down the Social-Democratic Party
within hours of it being launched. A second attempt, in 1906 – this
time as the Japanese Socialist Party – lasted just a year, after which
influential voices began to advocate a rejection of parliamentarian-
ism in favour of direct action.

Such became the approach of a women's rights activist by the name
of Kanno Suga (or Sugako). She was first caught up in the 'Red Flag

'In the beginning, woman was the sun': Amaterasu, the Sun Goddess, depicted in *The Origins of Sacred Dance at the Heavenly Cave* (Utagawa Toyokuni III, *c.*1856) *above*; Hiratsuka Raichō (1886–1971), pictured (*below, far right*) at a new year's party for her Seitō group in 1913.

Incident' in June 1908, a relatively minor matter of protestors parading around with flags bearing the words 'anarchism' and 'anarcho-communism', but a useful opportunity for police to round some of them up and to demonstrate a hard line. Newspaper reporting of the trial did not take Kanno entirely seriously:

To the [judge's] question, 'Is your objective anarchism?' ... Kanno Sugako said: 'Yes, I am an anarchist rather than a socialist. My thoughts have progressed.' In her stylish outfit of arrow-patterned silk kimono and loosely tied satin purple sash, she said this audacious thing ...

Badly treated throughout her life by callous women and violent men, by the police, and by judges and journalists, Kanno found herself becoming involved in 1910 in a plot to rid Japan of the single most important symbol of what the country had become: the Emperor.

By this time, the theory was well advanced amongst anarchist converts like the factory worker and fellow plotter Miyashita Takichi that the emperor story was no more than a myth dreamed up by government-friendly ideologues and put about by state-trained schoolteachers. Alternative histories, treasonous in the extreme, cast the emperors of Japan down the ages as bloodsuckers, killers, thieves and the helpless puppets of shoguns.

Miyashita made and successfully tested a bomb, and after lots were drawn, the honour of throwing the first device fell to Kanno. All was set. But then Miyashita's friend betrayed him to the police who, it turned out, already had their eye on Miyashita. Tin canisters and chemicals were discovered and soon Miyashita, Kanno and the other conspirators were rounded up. At a secret trial held in December 1910, Kanno referred to her intended victim casually by his personal name:

Emperor Mutsuhito, compared with other emperors in history, seems to be popular with the people and is a good individual. Although I feel sorry for him personally he is, as emperor, the chief person responsible for the exploitation of the people economically. Politically he is at the root of all the crimes being committed, and intellectually he is the fundamental cause of superstitious beliefs. A person in such a position, I concluded, must be killed.

The Emperor was destined to live on until his natural death in 1912, at which time the sheer scale of the public mourning seemed a powerful vindication of the role he had been given in the happy families system and in the official story of the nation more broadly. It was Kanno, along with eleven others, who were to be killed.

In the week after her death sentence was handed down, on 18 January 1911, Kanno wrote to friends, largely rejected the ministrations of the prison chaplain (though she had been a practising Christian for a number of years), and made requests of the director of prison instruction, a man by the name of Tanaka:

> I described the kind of coffin I wanted made for me and how I wanted to be dressed after death. I was afraid that the supporters of the emperor and champions of patriotism might dig up my corpse and hack it to bits. I did not want to look too shabby when this happened.

On 25 January, just a few days after writing that she was 'sacrificing my little body for a glimmer of hope', Kanno mounted the scaffold. She sat down, and a white cloth was placed over her face. Two thin cords were looped around her neck. At some point before the floorboard supporting her was suddenly removed, she is said to have offered up her own version of that great, family-unifying cheer of 1889: '*Ware shugi no tame shisu* ['We die for the cause'] – *banzai!*'

PART TWO

Resistance is Fertile
(1900s to 1930s)

5

Contesting the Cosmos

Winter 1465. A band of men, around 150 in all, gather in the cold near the top of a mountain – armed. Together they troop down the mountainside, enter the great city below, and put a group of its buildings to the torch.

Their letter of warning a week before had been full of accusations against the inhabitants of these buildings. Of duping the 'ignorant' and 'lowly' of the city. Of befouling the place with false ideas. It had to stop. Those ignorant and lowly types were, after all, *their* concern – in this life, from how they behaved to the taxes they paid, and in the next.

The men turn to leave, reassured by the promising spit and crackle of a fire taking hold, and content that the meaning of this act will not be missed: upstarts cannot be tolerated. Others around this city like to divide the world up, for the sake of comfort or convenience or their own careers: the seen kept separate from the unseen, politics from priestly affairs, military from moral leadership. But the men of the mountain know better, as do the vanquished pretenders whose HQ is beginning to collapse into the flames: this is a world in which gods, nature and human societies are all profoundly interconnected. To understand this, and to persuade others of the wide-ranging rights and prerogatives it gives you, is true power. And there can be no sharing it.

The attackers make their way back up Mount Hiei, returning to their temples and the daily round of Buddhist monastic life. Below, the odour of burned-out buildings, belonging to the rival Jōdo Shinshū sect, wafts through the city of Kyoto. Up here, the precious wood and stone, brass, silver and gold amidst which the monks live offer testament to centuries of successful persuasion and hard-won privilege, which they remain firmly resolved always to defend, against any and all enemies.

Theirs is a migrant religion made good. Buddhism arrived at the Yamato court from China and Korea in the mid-500s, just as the leaders of Japan's fledgling national polity were busy weaving themselves into a compelling cosmic fabric that traced their origins back to the *kami*, or gods. While the emperor across the water in China fretted the possession and loss of the 'mandate' of heaven, the emperor here was a *child* of heaven. He was a god on earth.

Buddhism's early advocates struggled to match this. Worries at court that the *kami* would take offence at Buddhism's very presence in this land seemed to be confirmed when a series of natural disasters struck. A Buddhist image brought over from Korea was duly thrown into a canal. The temple that had housed it was destroyed.

But Buddhism clung on, its priests performing prayers and rituals in protective support of a sceptical court. Over time, the relationship developed into *ōbō-buppō*: imperial law and the Buddha's Law are as inseparable – so the saying went – as the 'wings of a bird' or the 'wheels on an axle'. Further afield, people took up popularized forms of Buddhist prayers and practices as an extra layer of insurance amidst the precarity of village life. In an unpredictable world, you covered your bases. And in an ultimately unknowable world, you didn't expect to meet life's biggest questions with anything but a judicious blend of partial answers.

Buddhism and Shinto grew steadily closer as the centuries passed, their deities and places of worship mixing and mingling. Shinto's stories and rituals focused on purity, on fertility of crop and creature, and on the life that courses through nature. Buddhism came to be valued for its insights into the world beyond, and for its ritual ability to mediate between the two. Buddhist ideas even found their way into a seventeen-article constitution created in the early 600s, for an entity now calling itself 'Nihon': the source of the sun. Marco Polo eventually brought the Chinese rendering of the name – 'Jihpen' – back to Europe.

Japanese students returned from trips to the Asian mainland loaded with the latest scriptural and ritual learning, alongside ideas about art and architecture that began to revolutionize Japan's landscape.

Low thatched houses found themselves in the shade of towering new multi-storey temples of heavy wood topped with cascading tiles, their cavernous interiors housing precious paintings and awesome statues.

By 1465, then, there was much for the warrior monks of Mount Hiei's large and powerful Tendai sect, founded back in the early 800s, to celebrate. But there was also much to lose: extensive territories, money, a certain hold on the imaginations and consciences of the devoted, and ready access to political power down in the city below and out across the plains beyond. Defending it all was an impossibly complex task. There was preaching and prayer, monastic ritual and sutra study; education in the community and work in government posts; funerals; oversight of the people and produce of temple lands; and the running of various side ventures, from commerce to combat to the incineration of rival infrastructure.

The appearance over the last two hundred years or so of new, self-consciously reformist sects like Jōdo Shinshū had made all this much harder. But the far greater setback for Tendai, and a lesson to all religious communities in Japan, was yet to come. Where Tendai's warrior monks descended Mount Hiei to deliver their particular form of justice, just over a century later, in 1571, a much-feared military leader ascended it to administer his. Sick and tired of religious organizations overplaying their hand in the politics of a war-ravaged country, which he was struggling to reunify, Oda Nobunaga led a samurai army hacking and burning its way through all that the monks had built. Several thousands died. Hundreds of temples were razed to the ground.

It seemed that for all their accomplishments across ten centuries in the realms of art, the spirit and realpolitik, the basic calculus had not changed for Japan's Buddhist sects. They continued to depend for survival on political and public support that was hard won, easily lost, full of temptation and often complicated to reconcile with the values they espoused – of compassion and the avoidance of attachment to the pleasures and pains of the material world. Such was the baggage that they would carry with them into a brutally competitive and profoundly uncertain modern era.

*

In 1885, a student at Tokyo University decided to bite the hand that fed him. Inoue Enryō turned his back on the people who had funded his education, and on the profession of his father, who had fully expected his son to follow in his footsteps as a Buddhist temple priest once he completed his studies. As one of a tiny first generation of Japanese to attend a university – Tokyo, the first and most prestigious of them, had only opened its doors eight years previously – Inoue could be forgiven a little unpredictability and self-indulgence. It was natural that an ambitious young person discovering all that a university and a booming city had to offer should develop a certain distance from – even a little contempt for – his provincial origins. But in fact nothing of the sort was going on here. Inoue was abandoning his father's world in order to save it.

That world had been through a tough few years. Buddhism had survived Japan's sixteenth-century unification process, and had gone on to enjoy great privilege as part of the Pax Tokugawa from 1603. But its various sects struggled once that regime hit the rocks in the 1860s. There had been signs earlier on of trouble to come: resentment of Buddhist power and privilege; nativist ideologues harping on Buddhism's 'immigrant' status in Japan – manifestly, claimed one, the product of an 'inferior Indian mind'. Then, as the intellectual cheerleaders of the new Japan cast around for reasons why their country faced a gargantuan game of catch-up with the West, their attention came to rest on the economic and imaginative stranglehold of Buddhism on the Japanese population.

The pages of new, elite journals were heavy with rueful reflection. Western nations had been busy these last centuries developing technologies so advanced that they struck some Japanese as bordering on the magical. They had fashioned a global order so tightly contoured to their own interests that for a while it seemed that the best Japan could hope for was to get off a little more lightly than China when it came time to be gobbled up into one or more foreign empires. Meanwhile, in Japan those same centuries had been largely squandered by Buddhist leaders accumulating and violently defending vast wealth, fomenting intrigue and conflict, hoovering up people's tax money and perpetuating – with flat-out cosmological lies – popular ignorance and ignominy.

Payback time, for gross disservices to the nation, had finally arrived.

With a revitalized Shinto providing a cultic support system for the new state – from foundational stories to its prize symbol, the Emperor himself – there was little need any more for Buddhism. So a policy was announced in 1868 that reversed the trend of a millennium: *shimbutsu bunri* – the separation out of Shinto and Buddhism.

Shrines and temples would no longer share sacred ground. Deities would no longer do double duty – buddhas and bodhisattvas had been regarded as *kami*, *kami* as emanations of buddhas and bodhisattvas. Buddhist temples would lose their cherished and lucrative Tokugawa prerogative of registering local births, marriages and deaths. And people's taxes would be pumped instead into a revitalized and reordered Shinto infrastructure.

Worse was to come. Such was the anger against Buddhism in some quarters – much of it stoked by people with vested career interests in Shinto – that *shimbutsu bunri* morphed, in the early 1870s, into *haibutsu kishaku*: 'Abolish Buddhism, destroy Shakyamuni!' (the historical Buddha). Buddhist temples were attacked and looted of sutras and other precious objects, some of which found their way into the hands of grateful Western museum curators. Statues were decapitated, lands confiscated, and tens of thousands of temples closed or destroyed. Many thousands of monks and nuns were forced out of the religious life and into the mundane world of marriage and meat-eating.

Jōdo Shinshū (or 'Shin') had by this time long-since recovered from the fire of 1465 and had become the country's largest Buddhist organization. Its two branches, Eastern and Western, were quick to try to mollify the country's modernizing leaders after 1868: loaning money, building roads, providing army chaplains and supporting the steady expansion of Japanese influence in Asia by sending missionaries to the mainland, from Pusan to Shanghai.

Just about weathering the *haibutsu kishaku* storm, Shin leaders felt secure enough by the mid-1870s to withdraw from the government's much-mocked 'Great Promulgation Campaign' once it became clear that its real aim was the promotion of Shinto as a state religion. Seeing a culture war on the horizon, with education likely to be a major battleground, they instead rushed to set up their own schools, dormitories and universities, where they could whisper into the ears of promising young intellectuals and future leaders.

Inoue Enryō, born in a Shin temple in 1858, was a product of these hasty efforts to once again try to secure Buddhism's place in Japan. He was the first person to be sent by Shin's Eastern branch to acquire a cutting-edge education at Tokyo University. And where older Buddhists hoped to survive the new age by clubbing together, cleaning up their collective act and encouraging the development of a better class of Buddhist priest, Inoue set out to embrace – even to shape – the whole spirit of that age.

Everything, Inoue saw, was suddenly up for debate. A full-on contest for the cosmos was brewing, spanning questions of truth, salvation, knowledge, the role of government and the fate of nations, as well as the worth and mission of the Japanese people both historically and into the future. A mere priest was ill-equipped for this fight – ordained back in 1871, Inoue now claimed to feel 'ashamed' of appearing in public with his shaved head and his rosary beads, which he associated with bigotry and gullibility.

Instead, while studying at Tokyo University he found that the big questions of life had become the preserve of a range of intellectual disciplines recently imported in modern form from the West, including the natural sciences. Their questing empiricism and nation-building pragmatism was clearly the future. And their newness to most Japanese, combined with what looked like inherent flexibility and porous borders between disciplines – especially those that touched on the complexities of the human inner life – meant that there was room for someone of an entrepreneurial cast of mind to come along and steer them towards his own purposes.

Inoue's first step was to sort these disciplines into a hierarchy. The natural sciences were unrivalled in their capacity to examine the phenomenal, relative realm – the 'concrete objects' of the world. But they were ultimately transcended by philosophy, part of whose job it was to set the parameters for what counts as 'science' in the first place: what makes for legitimate objects and methods of inquiry. But neither science nor philosophy were of much use when it came to investigating the 'intangible truth': what Inoue variously called *risō* (the Ideal), *shin'nyo* (thus-ness, or such-ness), and *zettai* (the Absolute). To get at *this*, Inoue claimed, one needed Buddhism.

Buddhism old and new in the 1880s: traditionally robed Buddhist monks
(*left*) and Inoue Enryō (*right*)

Presenting himself now as a philosopher – a bias-free truth-seeker –
Inoue set to work as one of his generation's most influential teachers,
preachers and propagandists. Until recently there hadn't been a word
in Japanese for 'philosophy'. As with other imported forms of thought,
such as *liberté*, old Chinese characters and Japanese words were being
repurposed – in some cases new words created – to try to capture new
concepts (or, rather, whatever influential thinkers, in the right place at
the right time, claimed were the essence and true intent of those
concepts). Western-style philosophy came to be called *tetsugaku*: an
abbreviation of a Japanese phrase meaning 'the science or study of
seeking wisdom'. It was perfect for Inoue's expansive needs – in contrast to 'religion', which, rendered now as *shūkyō* ('the teaching of a
(particular) school'), was lumbered with narrow, sectarian connotations that would prove difficult to dislodge across future decades.

Inoue's pitch to the Japanese public was similar to that of other
cultural nationalists across Asia at this point, not least neo-Hindu
thinkers in India. They were determined to meet Western claims of
intellectual supremacy with more than meek agreement or a feeble
rearguard action in defence of their own ideas. The first rhetorical
move was to laud the recent achievements of Western power and

knowledge – before pointing out just how recent they were. The slow trudge of 'Western thought' across millennia could then be set alongside ancient Asian traditions that had reached the same, and then more profound conclusions far earlier and far less laboriously. In fact, in the time it had taken Westerners to acquire *most* of the truth, Asia's leading lights had got hold of the whole shebang and their descendants had mislaid it, contaminating and confusing it with superstitions of all sorts.

It was at this point, for Inoue, that one of those new Western disciplines came in handy: psychology. Buddhism, he argued, thoroughly deserved much of what had been thrown at it in recent years in Japan. Many of its leaders really had been on the take, happy to let what Inoue called *gumin* – 'benighted people', or, less charitably, 'stupid people' – believe tall tales of ghouls and goblins, as long as they paid their taxes and forked out for Buddhist funerals.

But thanks to the insights of psychology, together with Inoue's own brand new discipline of *yōkaigaku* – 'monsterology' – people could now be taught to distinguish between 'true mystery' and the entirely explicable pseudo-mysteries thrown up by over-active and under-educated imaginations. Valuable human faculties of awe, wonderment and non-rationality could be restored to their proper purpose: making that all-important leap from the point where science, philosophy and reason end, out into the Absolute.

Suggestibility, a misguidedly maligned human capacity, had its part to play. Of course, it had been abused by bad priests in the past. But it could also be honed for the good – as 'faith'. Inoue was one of the first in Japan to write about the promise of psychotherapy here, as a means of generating faith and, in turn, both bodily and spiritual healing. At his new institution, 'Philosophy Hall', Inoue set about teaching modified forms of Buddhist rituals and prayers as a form of early psychotherapy. No longer intended to have any instrumental effect on the external world, they were designed instead to encourage and support people in developing the sort of trust and faithfulness that would help them restore contact with the Absolute.

It would also make them good citizens. Inoue's goals dovetailed rather felicitously with those of Japan's new leaders on this point, the latter needing a population of well-nourished bodies and well-balanced minds to help turn their blueprint for the nation into reality. Japan's first psychiatrists earned government trust and money by helping to pull up the weeds – deviants, criminals and the uneducable – and to till the soil for the next generation. Inoue, for his part, took an official government list of harmful superstitions and added many more, demonstrating that false and true religion really were two entirely different beasts – and that true religion was crucial to the national interest. To hammer home that point, and give substance to his cherished slogan – *gokoku airi*: 'defence of the nation through love of truth' – Inoue turned his guns on what he claimed was modern Japan's *real* religious curse: Christianity.

*

One day in March 1865, a French Catholic priest was at home, staring out of the window at the cross atop his new church next door when he heard a commotion. A group of around a dozen Japanese women, men and children were rattling the doors of the small wooden church, trying to get in.

This wasn't good. Land like this, Oura Hill in Nagasaki, had recently been granted to foreigners so that they could build places of worship. But the understanding was that they would keep their religion to themselves. No Japanese were allowed in such structures. Edicts against Christianity had long been plastered across wooden noticeboards up and down Japan. They were a legacy of the now-faltering Tokugawa regime in its early, state-building days – their creation and posting not just about banning something, but about demonstrating the *power* to ban something. This very church, dedicated all of four weeks ago, was established in memory of the twenty-six Christians who were executed for their faith not far from here in 1597, and whom the Catholic Church had recently recognized as saints.

It was therefore with a certain amount of trepidation that Fr Petitjean went out to meet the group. Even if they hadn't come here with some act of anti-Christian or anti-foreigner vandalism on their minds, they could still be a danger. He kept the church doors locked for a reason: anyone found inside could end up in serious trouble with the authorities – and he along with them. But Petitjean sensed something unusual about this group. They didn't seem to be a threat. Nor did they look like the usual tourist types, here for a look at the strange foreign architecture that had started to spring up around the Nagasaki hills (one of the most notable examples being the home of Thomas Glover: built a couple of years before and soon to become a base of operations for his tea sales, money-lending, arms-dealing and assistance to the founders of Mitsubishi, and later famed as the setting for Puccini's *Madama Butterfly*).

So Petitjean decided to let them inside, and when he went to offer a prayer, he was surprised to find that three of the women followed him down the aisle to the altar. Kneeling down beside him, one of them leaned in and spoke, her voice low: 'All of us share with you the same heart.' Fr Petitjean could scarcely believe what he was hearing. He had discovered Japan's legendary *kakure kirishitan* (hidden Christians). Or, rather, they had discovered him.

Tokugawa purges in the early 1600s had reduced a Japanese Christian community of 300,000 people or more – out of a national population of 15 million – officially to zero. People were made to recant, on pain of death. And in order to prove their change of heart, many were forced, each year, to step on copper plates featuring images of the Virgin Mary or Christ. Based on European Christian imagery, these were carefully crafted by apostates for maximum authenticity and emotional impact. The lucrative privilege of hosting this practice, known as *fumi-e* (picture-treading), and issuing the certificate that went with it, had been yet another Buddhist perk of the period.

But some of those who stepped on the plates followed it up later behind closed doors with *conchirisan* (from the Portuguese for 'contrition') and *orashio* ('oratio': prayers). They continued to worship in secret, often using Buddhist imagery as cover, so that over the years a fusion of Catholicism and Buddhism emerged that featured a forgiving motherly God based on the Virgin Mary. She was depicted with her son Jesus in images that looked, for the purposes of official scrutiny, like the Buddhist deity Kannon cradling a child in her arms. The first question the women at the altar asked Petitjean was: '*Sancta Maria no go-zō wa doko?*' 'Where is the statue of the Blessed Mary?'

A *fumi-e* ceremony (*left*) and a *fumi-e* plate of the *Crucifixion*,
seventeenth century, worn from treading (*right*)

Statue of 'Maria Kannon', seized in Nagasaki in 1856

Petitjean had heard stories about the *kakure kirishitan*, but no one knew whether any of their communities had survived into the modern era. It turned out that quite a few had, many of them with a thousand or more members each. Some began to visit Petitjean's church, while he and other priests strayed well outside the boundaries of the treaty port – and the corresponding treaties – to meet and pray with them. Villagers began to build small chapels. Petitjean wrote them a catechism, using terms thought likely to be familiar. The *kirishitan* were advised that they could now, at long last, drop their pretence of loyalty to their local Buddhist temples.

It was all too soon. Some *kirishitan* refused to pay for the re-roofing of a temple. Others shunned the services of their local Buddhist priest for funerals. And in 1867 the local authorities, who had so far turned a blind eye to what was going on, finally snapped. Troops were sent in, property destroyed and large numbers of *kirishitan* were arrested and imprisoned.

The young rebel samurai who seized power the following year took an even harder line at first. To them, international diplomatic sponsorship of freedom of religion looked very much like covert support for Christian missionary activity – which was, in turn, the thin end of a colonial wedge: even the most rudimentary reading of recent history suggested that after the Bible comes the sword. Christianity was, in any case, a clear ideological threat to the new state, and the story its leaders wanted to tell about the Emperor. As one official put it, there was no room in Japan for 'a second son of God'.

So just three days after the 1868 order to separate out Buddhism from Shinto, a second order was issued. Tokugawa-style wooden noticeboards, informing people of the continued prohibition of 'the evil sect of Christianity', were renewed. Christianity ended up sharing space on them with such apparently commensurate corruptions as murder and arson.

The inevitable Western diplomatic outcry achieved no more than a slight rewording of the notices. 'Christianity' and a generalized category of 'evil sects' now appeared in two separate sentences, linked by association rather than by syntax. Meanwhile, thousands of *kirishitan* in south-western Japan were hauled from their homes and deported to other parts of the country. Only by 1873 was the new government sufficiently secure, and coming under sufficiently sustained pressure from foreign governments and domestic liberals, to relax its treatment of Christianity. The noticeboards came down, and the deportees came home.

This soon looked like a mistake. During the 1870s and early 1880s, advocates for Christianity seemed to gain ground. Everywhere you looked, elite men and women who had lost the war of 1868–9, and their *daimyō* to the subsequent swapping of domains for prefectures, were off in search of a new lord. Many found one thanks to the preaching of Western missionaries and other Western teachers. Recalcitrant villagers had been one thing; the prospect on the horizon now was altogether different: the fusing of national with personal crises, and the rise as a result of Christian samurai.

For young men especially, raised on a Neo-Confucian diet that emphasized the virtue of personal sacrifice for a greater goal, post-1868 Japan could feel one day like a world of unimaginable opportunity and another like a 'moral void', as one convert to Christianity put it. Coming into contact, at just this point, with the purposeful Puritanism of American Civil War veterans teaching at English-language schools ended up becoming an 'education' in the widest possible sense.

Men like Captain Leroy L. Janes at the Kumamoto Yōgakkō (School for Western Learning) and William S. Clark at Sapporo Nōgakkō (Agricultural College) had not set out to be missionaries. But these were small schools, where it was hard to separate out ideas from the people who espoused them, and where probing both teaching and teacher for their ultimate source of coherence and values led inevitably to God and the Bible. Conversions, when they came, could be highly emotional affairs, sometimes bubbling up and over as young men watched their teachers pray.

Once again, the descending and ascending of mountains came to be associated with the making of grand cosmic statements. In 1875, a group of thirty-five young men influenced by Janes's Bible classes and his revivalist spirit climbed up Mount Hanaoka, outside Kumamoto, and there pledged themselves to Christianity. Their relatives shared none of their enthusiasm. The mother of one threatened to kill herself when she found out what had happened. The father of another talked about beheading his son. A third student was thrown into solitary confinement. Janes's school was shut down.

And yet the Kumamoto converts understood their embrace of Christianity as the fulfilment of Japanese ethics, not their repudiation. The boys on the mountaintop pledged themselves to Christianity *and* to Japan, sharing Inoue's conviction that faith was essential to the nation's future. When converts in Yokohama issued a 'statement of faith' in 1872, they mixed material from the 'Basis of the Evangelical Alliance' (a Protestant ecumenical document of the era) with articles rooted in their samurai backgrounds: filial piety, submission to teachers and respect for authorities, along with a rejection of selfishness and physical pleasure.

High-profile Christians of the early 1900s like Uchimura Kanzō and Ebina Danjō talked openly about Christianity as a new form of *bushidō*, the 'way of the warrior'. This was to be a new, 'sanctified *bushidō*' or 'baptized *bushidō*'. In fact, the whole Meiji-era reinvention and popularization of *bushidō*, largely for foreign export, owed a great deal both to American Christianity and to the ethos of the British public school. Nitobe Inazō, the author of *Bushidō: The Soul of Japan* (1900), was himself a Christian convert, an alumnus of William S. Clark's Sapporo school.

Very soon, Japanese Christian leaders were emerging. For all the romance of those early, intimate encounters with a Janes or a Clark, many of the foreign missionaries in Japan were markedly less popular. They were *bata-kusai*: they 'stank of butter'. In other words, they understood Christian conversion in terms of the wholesale adoption of Western lifestyles and mores, which some wag had managed to connect with a fondness for dairy products.

Instead, as with counterparts across modern Asia and Africa, Japanese Christians insisted that the gospels went beyond culture and were as open to being understood through Japanese matrices as through Greek or Roman, British or Indian ones. What was more, if the people shipped over to Japan by various missionary societies were anything to go by, then Western Christianity was in trouble: sorely lacking in precisely the sort of selfless *bushidō* spirit that Japan's new Christians believed themselves to possess. It was therefore not a question of passive acceptance of Christianity by Japan, but of Japan turning Christianity into something better.

For Uchimura Kanzō, who led moves to insulate Japanese Christianity from what he regarded as utterly irrelevant foreign denominationalism, the Apostle Paul himself had been a 'true samurai': independent, money-hating and loyal. With a blend of doubt and sneering disdain reminiscent of that used by cultural nationalists like Inoue Enryō, Uchimura observed:

> In matters of electricity, dentistry, cattle-breeding, horse-raising, and swine-keeping, we can and may learn from Americans; but in matters of fine art, high philosophy and spiritual religion . . . is it not a shame to modern Japanese to be taught and led . . . by essentially materialistic, this-worldly Americans?

Protestant Christian numbers in Japan rose from just fifty-nine in 1873 to more than 30,000 two decades later. That figure would treble again by the time the Meiji Emperor was laid to rest in 1912. But as the 1880s wore on, the unequal treaties remained in place and 'dancing cabinet'-style antics were less tolerated, public opinion became increasingly critical of – in some quarters, actively hostile towards – Western power and culture. Pressure was growing for a more coherent, demanding and exclusive form of Japanese identity to be worked out and asserted. More and more across the coming decades, Buddhists and Christians alike would find themselves facing the same questions. What does your religion do for this country? And which comes first?

*

Anyone with access to an up-to-date map could see why such questions about identity and loyalty mattered. A new wave of Western imperialism was crashing over Africa in the 1880s, engulfing parts of Asia too – from Burma to Vietnam – and might soon be lapping at Japan's still rather quaintly defended shores. Russia was building a Trans-Siberian railway across to Vladivostock, which Yamagata Aritomo confidently predicted would soon turn into a push south into the Korean peninsula. Russia had always wanted a warm-water port, and this was one obvious way of getting it – albeit thousands of miles from where it would have been most useful. Hawkish on Japan's internal and external security, Yamagata Aritomo had fought in the Boshin War and led troops against the rebellious Saigō Takamori. In 1890, during a speech to the new Japanese Diet, he famously described Korea as a dagger pointed at Japan's heart. Governance on the peninsula was weak, and China was in no state to prop it up. Western powers were circling. If Japan didn't take control, then some other country soon would – most likely Russia.

As far as Yamagata was concerned, talk of 'international cooperation' was for the birds, and for professional diplomats. What Japan really needed was strong borders and a 'line of advantage' beyond them. That line clearly put the Korean peninsula within Japan's natural orbit. And yet foreign powers whose own reach stretched thousands of miles around the globe seemed conspicuously unwilling to allow Japan just a few hundred miles of extra-territorial influence.

A short conflict with China in 1894–5, over Korea, was easily won by Japan. But almost immediately the Russians, together with Germany and France, intervened to deprive the Japanese of some of the tastiest morsels offered up during peace talks. These included the Liaotung Peninsula, a small but strategically valuable portion of Manchuria, in north-east China. Japanese diplomats looked on helplessly as this 'triple intervention', supposedly made for the 'peace of Asia', resulted in a European feeding frenzy upon a weakened China – including the forced leasing to Russia of the very peninsula the Japanese had just been forced to give back. Construction work soon began on precisely the sort of rail links running south from eastern Russia that Yamagata expected and feared.

It was a sign of the public mood at the time, with expectations whipped up only to be dashed, that an imperial rescript had to be rushed out telling people to remain calm. Military expenditure was ramped up, a reputation-boosting alliance with Britain forged in 1902, and negotiations opened with Russia. One possible solution to dangerously overlapping spheres of interest in East Asia was that the Russians should recognize Japanese dominance on the Korean peninsula while the Japanese accepted Russian dominance of Manchuria, to the north. But neither side was fully committed to the idea, while at home in Japan there were calls to settle the issue in battle. In February

1904, the Japanese navy provided the moment that many had been waiting for since the humiliations of nearly a decade before: a surprise attack on the Russians.

The ensuing conflict – with its machine-gun nests, trench fortifications and barbed wire – earned itself a place on a grim list of small modern wars in the early 1900s that were later regarded as foreshadowing the extraordinary carnage of 1914 to 1918. But it made heroes out of General Nogi Maresuke and Admiral Tōgō Heihachirō. The latter's ships rewarded the Russian Baltic Fleet for an epic 10,000-mile mobilization – from the Baltic, around Western Europe and Africa and across the Indian Ocean – with destruction almost down to the last vessel. There were Japanese victories on land too, including a successful siege of Port Arthur, on the Liaotung Peninsula. By May 1905, both sides had suffered heavy losses – running to more than 100,000 soldiers killed – and both were struggling to keep the conflict going. Japan's leaders appealed in secret to President Theodore Roosevelt to help end it. Following negotiations in Portsmouth, New Hampshire, a peace treaty was signed in September 1905. Roosevelt was later awarded the first Nobel Peace Prize ever granted to a statesman.

There had been no outright victory for Japan, in the end. But the Russo-Japanese War was a sensation nonetheless: an upstart Asian nation had seriously embarrassed a grand old global power. In the

Yamagata Aritomo (1838–1922)

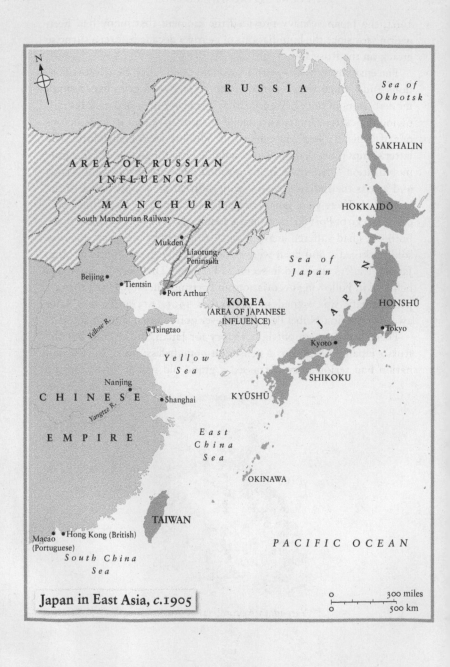

Japan in East Asia, c.1905

racialized rhetoric of the age, yellow had given white what-for. Writing in his diary, India's future prime minister, Jawaharlal Nehru, described a 'great pick-me-up for Asia'. Nationalists from Vietnam to Indonesia to Iran also spotted a turning point in world history. For Japan, the conflict achieved two things. It completed what the alliance with Britain had set in motion: the emergence of Japan as a top-tier nation. And it solidified in the minds and in the public rhetoric of Japan's leaders the triumph of their national story. This really was an exceptional place and people, whose values and spirit continued to drive and shape a process of rapid modernization the like of which existed nowhere else in the world.

But at home, the pressures of the war had quickly begun to tell. As media rhetoric snowballed – Japan in peril; with us or against us – Buddhists, Christians and pacifists all came under attack. Buddhist and Christian organizations did what they could to fend off public hostility by buying government bonds and sending money and gifts to the troops. For pacifists, on the other hand, inflaming public opinion was largely the point. When her brother applied to join a special squad, the poet Yosano Akiko wrote a piece urging him, and the country, to step back from a conflict for which there was no pressing need, and to return instead to the concerns of an older era:

> Oh, my brother, I weep for you.
> Do not give your life.
> Last-born among us,
> You are the most beloved of our parents.
> Did they make you grasp the sword
> And teach you to kill?
> Did they raise you to the age of twenty-four,
> Telling you to kill and die?
> Heir to our family name,
> You will be master of this store, old and honoured, in Sakai.
> Brother, do not give your life.
> For you, what does it matter
> Whether Port Arthur fortress falls or not?
> The code of merchant houses says nothing about this
> Brother, do not give your life.

His Majesty the Emperor
Goes not himself into the battle.
Could he, with such deeply noble heart,
Think it an honour for men
To spill one another's blood
And die like beasts?

Much the worst thing to be during these years was a pacifist *and* a Christian. This was thanks in large part to scepticism that had been building up over the last twenty years in Japan about the compatibility of Christianity with commitment to the nation. The Christian leader Uchimura Kanzō had caused a national sensation back in 1891 when a copy of the Imperial Rescript on Education was unveiled at a Tokyo school where he was teaching. Staff and students alike were expected to bow deeply, but when his turn came, Uchimura first hesitated and then offered a slight nod of the head. Amidst the furious reaction that followed – including accusations of *lèse-majesté* – Uchimura was forced to resign.

Journalists took up the story, and Japan's first full professor of philosophy at Tokyo Imperial University, Inoue Tetsujirō, weighed in. Where in the Bible, Inoue asked, may one find Jesus Christ extolling

Woodblock print (artist unknown; 1904). The caption in Japanese at the top reads: 'Japanese Suicide Squad Fight Bravely in a Naval Battle at Port Arthur during the Russo-Japanese War'

the nation state, or showing anything but 'cold indifference' towards his own parents? How can an ideal of indiscriminate love be compatible with Japanese values like loyalty to family and nation? Will the Sermon on the Mount produce effective soldiers? And why should we let Christians teach in our schools when their connections with Western missionaries may mean that they secretly prefer England or America to Japan? Christians either couldn't or wouldn't assimilate. Instead they clung to the spectacular folly, as another critic put it, of a worldwide religion accidentally kicked off by a young girl trying to explain away an illegitimate pregnancy.

Serious historical and theological arguments were marshalled against all of this, but more influential in the long run was a race to the bottom in religiously inflected militarist rhetoric and tokenism during the Russo-Japanese War. Urban Christian leaders like Ebina Danjō tried to rally parishioners to a vision of war as an opportunity to do God's work. Christian publications eulogized soldiers who supposedly quoted scripture to one another in the thick of the action, or who were seen – in the words of one piece – 'Dying in Battle While Longing for the Bible'.

Despite such efforts, the perception remained about Japan's Christians that 'they' – as though a single, sinister bloc – were ambiguous in their patriotism and lukewarm about war. Inoue Enryō was only too happy to see such sentiments on the rise. For him, the war with Russia was just the kind of national emergency that could help him to put flesh on the bones of his claims about Buddhism and the state naturally supporting one another. The conflict doubled for him, rather conveniently, as a timely crusade against a contemptible Christianity – both at home and abroad, where the blessing of Russian soldiers with Orthodox icons before battle had clearly been to no avail. One of the most grief-inducing signs of the old Buddhism's betrayal of the Japanese people, Inoue believed, was that promising young men were left desperate enough to embrace a view of the world that boasted neither scientific credibility nor the capacity to inspire true selflessness. In such circumstances, the defeat of the Russians and their religion would be a win for modernity, for compassion and for common sense.

*

In the end, the big religious winner of the Russo-Japanese War was in fact Japan's civil religion, of faith in the state, which Japanese leaders had done so much over the last three decades to instil. For all his enthusiastic preaching around the country, and his undoubted influence on generations to come – across the sciences, religion and philosophy – Inoue Enryō's claims of ultimate authority for even a radically reformed Buddhism were badly out of date. That much-cherished power had passed away, if ever it had been truly possessed. And it was not coming back.

Religion could, and did, however, inspire creativity and resistance at the level of individuals and small, committed groups. The Christian minister Kashiwagi Gien was outspoken in blaming the Russo-Japanese War on the evils of capitalism, and in denouncing the use of religion to justify violent conflict. The Buddhist priests Takagi Kemmyō (Shin) and Uchiyama Gudō (Sōtō Zen) were later caught up in the 1910 plot to assassinate the Emperor. But the idea that either Christianity or Buddhism could provide a binding force for broad-based social or political organization, to the point where either became a cultural threat to the state, now looked rather unlikely.

And yet Japan's leaders found that their successful war against Russia bestowed mixed blessings on the domestic front. In September 1905, violence suddenly erupted across Tokyo, and rioters began to head towards the Imperial Palace. The cosmos could, it seemed, be brought to heel. Urban Japan would be another matter.

6

Haunting the Orient

> *Yoru fukete*
> *nemuri shinamu to*
> *seshi kimi no*
> *kokoro wa tsui ni*
> *kōri no gotoshi.*

> As the night grew late,
> And you thought that you would go
> To sleep and death,
> At the end your heart
> Must have been like ice.

Saitō Mokichi was a *waka* poet and an admirer of Japan's great *Man'yōshū* anthology. He was also a psychiatrist, who encountered so many suicides in his time that he diagnosed himself with 'phobia telephonica': a fear of being wakened in the night to hear of yet another person who had taken their life. He eventually developed a special short button-up kimono sash to replace the traditional seven- or eight-foot long *obi* that too many people in extreme distress found irresistible as a means of hanging themselves.

But the man who died on 24 July 1927, and for whom Saitō wrote this poem, had been a friend as well as a patient. Saitō had helped him open up to poetry. The man, in turn, had shared with Saitō his troubling visions: translucent cogwheels, in constant motion, through which he was forced to look out onto the world around. Saitō supplied him with Veronal, a barbiturate, to help him sleep through the unusually hot nights that summer. It may have been this prescription that he used to end his life.

Akutagawa Ryūnosuke was just thirty-five years of age when he died, and already a celebrated writer. He had first made his name producing beautifully crafted historical fiction, but in recent years had turned more and more towards modern Japanese literature's dominant form: the 'I-novel'. Classical *zuihitsu* – fragmented personal reflections along the lines of Sei Shōnagon's *The Pillow Book* (completed in the year 1002) – met European Romanticism and Naturalism to produce a powerfully influential style of closely autobiographical fiction. Stories tended to be structured around moment-by-moment reactions to life, with an unforgiving focus on the author's own feelings and failings.

In Akutagawa's hands, the I-novel became a devastatingly effective means of tracking what critics felt urban Japan was becoming in the 1910s and 1920s. One of his final pieces was *Haguruma* ('Spinning Gears'), whose narrator 'Mr A' tries with mounting desperation to put together a combination of distractions – writing, rifling through the shelves in bookshops ('like a compulsive gambler'), riding Tokyo trains and taxis – to try to make life livable a little while longer.

At one point, Mr A goes to confide in an old man who lives in the attic of a Bible publishing house, working as a handyman by day and spending the rest of his time in prayer and reading. 'Drugs are not going to help you,' counsels the man. 'Wouldn't you like to become a believer?' 'If only I could,' replies Mr A. He can readily believe in the devil and in sin, but not so easily in God or in miracles. Nor does he share the handyman's happy conviction that darkness in the world is a matter of shadows cast by supreme light.

Akutagawa's death was national news. Thanks in part to the 'vague anxiety' about the future that he famously described in his suicide note, his passing was interpreted by intellectuals around the country as a final defeat for the internationalism and open, cultured life for which Akutagawa had seemed to stand. Something had happened to Japan, between the end of the Russo-Japanese War and the loss of this star author in 1927, which seemed to justify Mr A's view of life over the old man's. This was not a world of light, throwing a few unavoidable shadows. There was a deep, creeping darkness here, which simply overtook the likes of Mr A a little earlier than others.

This era of uncertainty was born amidst unprecedented violence, as large-scale protests in Tokyo in the summer of 1905 revealed the pain of a country that had pushed itself to the absolute brink against Russia. Japan had achieved the hoped-for international respect that it turned out ballroom dancing didn't bring. And peace terms seemed passable: Japan took over the Russian lease of the all-important Liao-tung Peninsula (acquiring in the process the Russian-built South Manchuria Railway), and received acknowledgement of its legitimate interest in Korea. But this conflict had cost more than six times Japan's ordinary yearly income. Taxes had skyrocketed, enormous foreign loans had been taken out, families had seen brothers and sons sent far away, and almost every vessel in Japan's merchant marine fleet had been requisitioned and thrown into the fight. So where, pro-testors wanted to know, were the permanent territorial gains – beyond the southern portion of chilly Sakhalin? The Sino-Japanese peace ten years before had brought Japan a hefty indemnity in silver – where was the money this time around?

Anger built as the crowd moved from Hibiya in central Tokyo towards the nearby Imperial Palace – on the site of the old Edo Castle, still with something of the old moats and sloped granite walls remaining. Speech-makers insisted that if the people were to be made to sweat so hard for the empire, they should have their say in how it was run. Some protestors hoped to have the peace agreement rejected altogether, and for their armed forces to fight on in search of real gains.

Bungled crowd control worsened an already tense situation, and soon rioting broke out, spreading across Tokyo and from there into other major cities. Hundreds of buildings were destroyed, including the Home Minister's private residence and nearly three-quarters of all the *kōban* (police boxes) in the capital. Trams were targeted and torched – a reflection of anger at recent transport price hikes – while the offices of pro-government newspapers were attacked. In the end, an army that protestors hoped to see return to the Russian front was set on them instead. Order was belatedly restored.

Japan's modern leaders were well practised at dealing with difficult individuals or publications – they could be imprisoned, fined or shut down. What haunted them now, and into the 1910s and early 1920s, was the spectre of the *gunshū*, the crowd: the potential for a tide of uncontrollable urban public anger to force them out of power. Japan was on the verge of becoming a mass industrial society, and anyone who had travelled abroad of late knew what that might some day entail: extreme poverty, a snowballing of anti-government feeling and the spread of radical alternative ideologies. Could Japan's constitutional arrangements, barely a generation old, cope with this emerging world? Or would the Hibiya riots turn out to be just the tiniest of tasters?

*

Paint toys underground. Peddle cotton goods overground. Nanny children. Feed adults their beef and sushi. Type in an office. Trail customers around a shop. Help a pharmacist. Sleep in a toilet. Find a house. Furnish that house, haggling hard and counting every cost: tea serving tray (1 yen), potted plant (35 sen), pickled wasabi (5 sen), tissue paper (20 sen), noodles for the people downstairs (30 sen). Serve in a café. Chat to the men. Avoid the men. Run away from the men. Back to peddling again. 'If you had slipped me a bomb, I would gladly have thrown it . . .'

Such was the Tokyo life of Hayashi Fumiko, a young woman whose literary montage of people and places, prose and poetry, songs and shopping receipts –published as *Hōrōki* (*Diary of a Vagabond*) at the end of the 1920s – captured the relentlessness of a city that offered endless opportunity but rarely much security. A scruffy university student manning a night-stall tries to persuade passers-by to purchase his calculators by chiding them for their stupidity. *What's 89,503 plus 275,460? Don't know? Need one of these?* A shop owner sleeps at night in front of his safe, just in case. Hayashi herself struggles to earn enough to stay alive, though the thrill and variety of life around her keeps her going – as does her search for friends or lovers behind whose subdued façades might lurk an incendiary passion to match her own. 'I fell in love with the Buddha', one of her poems begins, 'when I kissed his faintly cold lips . . .'

Soon, more than half of Tokyo's rapidly growing population – which doubled from 2 to 4 million between 1895 and 1923 – would, like Hayashi, be first-generation immigrants from the countryside: strangers to one another, in a city sprawling ever further outwards.

Akutagawa Ryūnosuke (1892–1927) (*above*) and
Hayashi Fumiko (1903–51) (*below*)

Part of the pomp of Commodore Perry's return trip to Japan in 1854, in search of an answer to his off-key overtures of the year before, had been the putting on of a little show. A quarter-sized railroad – steam locomotive, carriage and a circle of track – was laid out and fired up, steam whistle and all. Japanese onlookers were duly impressed. One man hitched himself a 20-mile-an-hour ride, balancing perilously on top of the carriage and gripping its roof as his robes flapped in the wind and his body convulsed with laughter.

Across the 1910s and 1920s, thanks to a mix of private and government money, and using track and rolling stock imported from Britain and elsewhere, railway lines helped to define Japan's capital city and to guide its expansion. Where new lines were laid, department stores, commuter housing complexes and restaurants followed almost overnight. Towns and villages were consumed one after another as the city rolled on. New neighbourhoods like Shinjuku appeared, home to Hayashi and an eclectic range of other incomers whose lives she wove into her chronicle.

This was a city of poles, posts and wires: telegraph and telephone services had been installed in the 1890s, with street lighting and then domestic electricity following on behind. A constant stream of trams, workers and shoppers began to flow between ever more tightly packed buildings, vying for space on the street with noisy processions of fashion models, cars, singers and clapperboard men all advertising the latest products. Kirin Beer rose above it all with tethered advertising balloons and aeroplanes that showered leaflets onto the swarm of potential custom below.

As popular song transitioned from live performance art to vinyl record and radio – Asia's first transmissions went out across Tokyo, Osaka and Nagoya in 1925 – it became clear that Japan's urbanites were utterly fascinated by their rapidly changing lives. They were willing to pay good money to have them celebrated and satirized, rendered in rich prose or picked apart by almost anyone with 'gaku' ('-ology') in their job title. 'Tokyo March', the theme song for a film of the same name, became a bestseller in 1929 for its racy depictions of love lives in four famous areas of the city: Shinjuku, Ginza, Asakusa and Marunouchi:

Dancing to jazz, drinking in the small hours
And with the dawn, a flood of tears for the dancer . . .
Vast Tokyo is too small for love.

Other music of the era took a more perverse pride in the city. 'Tokyo Bushi' (1919) pictured a place infested with 'uppity intellectuals', 'crawling with 3 million people who live without making their own rice', and home to 'life-or-death' struggles to board jam-packed public transport. Other city songs capitalized on the remarkably short memories of the recently arrived, waxing nostalgic over far-away home towns where life was simpler and sweeter.

'Tokyo March' was quickly blacklisted for its outrageous suggestiveness by Japan's new national broadcaster, Nippon Hōsō Kyōkai (Japan Broadcasting Corporation). NHK's reins were being held tightly by a state deeply anxious about its potential power over the masses. There was pre-censorship and a total ban on political discussion. Circuit-breakers could be used to cut a live transmission if it began to contravene the rules. Presenters were required to use a 'coldly neutral' voice, while avoiding potentially inflammatory words like 'extremely' or 'absolutely'.

Film-makers had to put up with much of the same. There was to be no politics and no suggestion of class strife. No depictions of crime that might encourage it or tip people off about how to commit one. No material that ran counter to family values, and only the most sparing of references to the imperial family. America's popular Keystone Cops films – slapstick silent comedies featuring an over-zealous, bungling constabulary – were banned in Japan, on the basis that they might damage respect for the police.

In trying to get music and popular culture to do their bidding, Japan's leaders tried to use some elements of it proactively, setting out to shape the nation's sensibilities at home and to advertise its special aesthetic qualities abroad. A memorable early experiment took place in 1872 at the opening of Shimbashi Station, the Tokyo terminus for Japan's first railway line, linking the capital with Yokohama. The theme was Japan as a place where the eternal meets the ultra-modern. Presiding over the ceremony was the Meiji Emperor (whose official wardrobe ran from Shinto robes to the military uniforms of a

European monarch), while wafting through the grand new pavilions of stone, glass and painted metal came the strains of two contrasting musical traditions. A *gagaku* recital – music for strings, wind instruments and voices, heard for centuries at religious sites and the imperial court – was intended to remind gathered Western dignitaries of the new nation's continuity with the past and its refined, sacred aesthetic (for similar reasons, *gagaku* instruments and notation scrolls were sent for display at Expos in Paris and Vienna). Meanwhile, a tune from Japan's new Naval Band, established by the bandmaster John William Fenton – on loan from the British Legation in Yokohama – announced Japanese intentions to emulate Europe's successful marriage of musical pomp with military power.

But it wasn't long before Japan's new military bands were being criticized in the press for abetting – with polkas and quadrilles – the humiliating prancing and promenading of the country's elites at the Rokumeikan. Modern musical tastes were not as straightforwardly governable as Japan's leaders would have liked – and they themselves sometimes changed their minds about what they wanted for the country.

The pale-pigmented cypress masks and slow, minimalist movements of Nō theatre were first frowned upon as 'backward', and then later saved – along with their ensembles of drummers and flautists – when similarities were noticed between Nō and the respected tradition of European opera. In Hiroshima, the authorities at one point disapproved so strongly of the old-fashioned, 'vulgar' *shamisen* and *koto* that only geisha and blind people in need of work were permitted to touch them. But such strictures could not hope to survive these instruments' renewed popularity out in the country, achieved thanks to their use in theatre and cinema productions of old Japanese tales of heroes, villains and lovers. Their players were amongst the first musicians to be herded into recording studios and required to condense their art into the three and a half minutes that a 78 rpm record could hold (a discipline with which one musician struggled so badly that he ended up asking a technician to just come in and knock him on the head when his time was up).

Here, then, were the real taste-makers: the men and women of Japan's record industry. They understood that musical appeal was all about time, and timing. To early Meiji Japanese, the piano and the violin, along with songs like 'Auld Lang Syne', had sounded distinctly Western. For the next generation, they had been part of the fabric. 'Auld Lang Syne' had morphed into '*Hotaru no Hikari*' ('Glow of the Firefly'), while few ever knew that a second childhood classic, '*Chōchō*', about a butterfly fluttering between leaves and cherry blossoms, was very well travelled: its melody had started life in Germany, as '*Hänschen klein*' ('Little Hans'), before journeying to Japan by way of the United States, where it was 'Lightly Row'.

By the 1920s, *shamisen* and *koto* melodies rooted in the sophisticated sadness of the *miyako bushi* scale (E-F-A-B-C-E) were capable of evoking urban longing for a bygone era. An upbeat A-C-D-E-G-A folk scale, meanwhile, conjured the lost simplicity of *furusato* (hometown) life – now mired, for most record-buying city types, somewhere between dim anecdotal remembrance and pure fantasy. Songs addressing contemporary city work-lives, night-lives and love-lives made use of appropriately syncretic scales known as *yonanuki*: Western major and minor scales with fourths (*yo*) and sevenths (*na*) removed (*nuki*).

Even where the authorities went out of their way to crack down on certain sorts of music, their reach had its limits. Capitalism usually found a way, as it did with 'Tokyo March'. The collective hand-wringing ended up being useful for newspaper circulation, while the record company Nippon Victor built on the free publicity by giving away a thousand copies of the song on record at cafés and bars across the city.

Some Japanese actively set out to develop music's subversive potential. Meiji-era *enkashi* used narrative song to circumvent government restrictions on political speech, hawking as many copies of their lyrics as they could – satirizing the crony politics of the day and calling for popular rights – before the police appeared and they were forced to move on. Some accompanied themselves on guitar or violin. Others found that *a cappella* music made for a less encumbered get-away.

Industrialization, meanwhile, came with its own grim soundtrack, of protest and despair. Much of middle-class urban culture was driven by a search for orientation, in a place and time where everyday assumptions went swiftly out of date. How should I relate to my boss? How do I make friends? How should I meet and treat a lover? How do I furnish my home? What's good – and not – to wear and eat these days? But while the average university graduate, working in education or finance or the state bureaucracy, might be able to afford the kind of life described in 'Tokyo March' – complete with the record-player required to sing along at home – it was rapidly clear that the rise of a mass society would be far less kind to others. Even the most committed of revellers would have struggled to tap their feet to 'Song of the Living Corpses':

> My family was poor.
> At the tender age of twelve
> I was sold to a factory . . .
> I was carried away by sweet-sounding words.
> My money was stolen and thrown away.
> Unaware of the hardships of the future,
> I was duckweed in the wind.

Japan's survival in a highly competitive early twentieth-century global economy relied to a considerable extent on industries like silk-reeling and cotton-spinning. These depended in turn on the labour of young girls, who often relocated across great distances from rural to urban Japan. The 'sweet-sounding words' of recruiters paid on a commission basis persuaded hard-up parents to part with a daughter. Sometimes the daughter herself decided that mill-work could be her contribution to dire family finances, or perhaps her ticket to freedom.

'Song of the Living Corpses' goes on to describe arrival at the gates of a cotton mill, a terrifying medical examination and a meal of 'low-grade rice mixed with sand'. The girl in the song innocently asks what the side-dish will be. She laments her 4.30 a.m. starts, ushering in interminably long working days spent in vast, chairless machinery rooms, everyone wearing the same blue uniforms with blue-socked feet wedged into hemp-straw sandals.

At the end of their shifts, which could last for up to fifteen hours, girls returned to locked dormitories where the few with any energy left could 'attend' the school that they and their parents had been promised. It often turned out to be no more than a casual conversation held in a corridor. Meanwhile, cramped conditions proved ideal for the flourishing of tuberculosis, while other workers suffered beatings and sexual abuse ('Let's wrench the balls of the hateful men!' ran another factory song of the era, 'Mr Overseer, Mr Supervisor, you'd better watch out!'). Competition with rival manufacturers around the world dictated that the factory machines, and with them the whole sorry system, had to run twenty-four hours a day.

Around half of all workers ran away during the first few months of employment, even though they knew that their families could be made to repay the money offered by the recruiter. Most moved on to new factories, in the hope of better conditions. Others took work in urban offices or shops – the first, perhaps, of a string of jobs of the sort Hayashi had eventually escaped.

Strikes – of which there were hundreds annually during much of the 1910s and 1920s – were sometimes successful in achieving lower working hours and improvements in food or sleeping conditions. And in some industries, where technical training took time, managers found they would rather make deals with their employees than see them go elsewhere. These were some of the roots of a phenomenon for which Japan would later become known worldwide: labour–management relations based not on antagonism but on quasi kin-like cooperation in everything from job security to welfare benefits. From complaint boxes to good company housing, industrial giants like Mitsubishi found that fostering strong worker identification with their employer was clearly the way to go.

It was becoming clear in the 1910s that the old political status quo could not last for long. Japan's 1889 Constitution had been crafted by a small revolutionary elite, with their own interests and talents in mind. Their personal relationships, spanning the Diet, civilian and military bureaucracies, and of course the Emperor himself, knitted the system together and helped it to run reasonably smoothly. But these men were beginning to leave the scene now, replaced by people who relied for their influence on more circumscribed – and therefore obsessively guarded – powerbases. Elected politicians were forced to strike a balance between conspicuous flag-waving on the one hand, helping a popular military to fill its coffers, and on the other consideration for the finances of their relatively wealthy and naturally tax-averse voter base. Politics gained, in the process, a reputation for factionalism and gridlock. Critics found it increasingly hard to distinguish between politicians running the system and gaming it for their own interests.

The new Emperor after 1912 was in no position to guide or mediate. His father and predecessor was revered as a great figurehead, who had successfully managed the transition to the role of a modern monarch and helped his era to live up to the hopes of those who named it at its outset: 'Meiji' – 'enlightened rule'. But the man whose era was given the name 'Taishō' – 'great righteousness' – suffered serious physical and mental incapacitation, complicated by a drinking habit, which proved difficult to conceal from the public. On one occasion, when he was about to give a speech to the Diet, the Emperor rolled up his scroll and peered out through it at his audience, as though through a telescope. Turbulent times called for an emperor who would exude calm and continuity, albeit from an enigmatic distance. Emperor Taishō was poorly suited for the role.

Instead, the 1910s witnessed rising popular pressure for true parliamentary governance in Japan, as opposed to the all but advisory role initially envisaged for the Diet. Before his death in 1909, Japan's great constitutional strategist Itō Hirobumi had advised fellow

Tokyo in the 1920s

leaders that in order to safeguard the Meiji settlement they would need to hold their noses and work more closely with Diet members, allowing political parties to become a serious force in the country. Itō himself became president of a new party: Seiyūkai, or the Friends of Constitutional Government Party. Other elites and their protégés soon followed suit, forging new connections with business, agricultural and other interests.

For a time, it looked as though these efforts would bring forth a new breed of canny, deal-making democrat. Hara Kei (or Hara Takashi), who helped Itō to set up Seiyūkai, was a man with personal experience of operating pretty much every lever of power that modern Japan had to offer. He had worked in the state bureaucracy, in business and as a journalist. And hailing from Iwate prefecture, in northern Japan, he was also well placed to understand the needs of regional leaders and businessmen for whom Tokyo often seemed a far-off place.

These connections, together with tax money that he managed to funnel towards the pet projects of political allies across the country – a harbour here, a new road there – helped Hara to make his way up towards the very top of national politics. Moving government personnel around to ensure for himself a loyal base of support in the civil service, Hara waited patiently throughout the 1910s – both in and out of Cabinet – for his eventual chance at the top job. It came in 1918, amidst just the sort of mass riots that Japan's leaders feared.

Four years earlier, Japan had entered the First World War on the side of Great Britain, under the terms of the 1902 Anglo-Japanese Alliance. The Imperial Japanese Navy escorted hundreds of Allied ships in the Indian Ocean and the Mediterranean, while injured soldiers on the Western front occasionally found themselves being tended to by nurses from the Japanese Red Cross. But for the most part, Japan's activities during the war were governed by the pursuit of its own strategic interests: edging the Germans out of China and the South Pacific (the major Anglo-Japanese action of the conflict was a successful attack on the German colony at Tsingtao in 1914), and further expanding its influence on the Asian mainland. With the lease on the Liaotung Peninsula coming up for renewal, Japan presented a list of 'Twenty-One Demands' to China in 1915. These included the extension of Japan's lease on the South Manchuria Railway, recognition of temporary Japanese management of Germany's former Chinese possessions, and joint control of key mining operations in the country. Chinese leaders were in no position to refuse, leading furious student activists to declare a 'National Humiliation Day'.

Japan's leaders probably did themselves more long-term harm than good with these wartime manoeuvrings. In the US, political and public opinion began to shift against Japan and towards China, setting the stage for a difficult international decade to come. At home, meanwhile, the disruption suffered by commercial rivals during the war helped Japan's economy, as did contracts to produce arms and other goods for the conflict. But these economic gains brought inflation, and by the summer of 1918 public anger at rice prices – which had doubled since the previous year – turned into violence across the country.

Hara was no starry-eyed man of the people. He opposed calls for universal male suffrage, preferring instead to have the interests of lower-middle and working-class people voiced and dealt with co-operatively and out of the public eye, in worker–management councils. But he was adept at giving influential people what they wanted and had even managed to woo the stony senior statesman Yamagata, who now picked him, amidst the turmoil, as the country's first 'commoner' prime minister – and the first to have come up through the ranks of a plain old political party.

It was a tremendous and celebrated achievement, but it did not in itself change the fact that with little official encouragement for ordinary Japanese to participate in politics – beyond paying their taxes and reading a newspaper – the country's political parties remained relatively small, fee-paying clubs for the wealthy. Seiyūkai and their more progressive rivals in later years, Minseitō, were bankrolled by the Mitsui and Mitsubishi conglomerates respectively, with cooperation so close that it extended to inter-marriage between leading families on either side of the professional divide. Recognizing that the trend of the times ran in the direction of greater influence for the Diet, power-seekers from across the civil service, the military and big finance began to reinvent themselves as party politicians.

A young railway switchman by the name of Nakaoka Kon'ichi became so perplexed and outraged by what he saw as the cynical and highly partisan world of national politics that one autumn evening in November 1921 he approached Prime Minister Hara outside Tokyo Station and stabbed him to death. It seemed like a shocking relapse into the pre-civilized state from which the Meiji leaders had sought to lift Japan. In fact, it was a sign of things to come.

Was the answer to these constitutional and political crises *more* democracy – or less? For those who took the former view, the lifting of the ban on women's participation in politics in 1922 and then the granting of universal male suffrage in 1925 – quadrupling the electorate at a stroke – counted as major successes. For those inclined towards the latter view, the terrible prospect loomed of parties shaped by the masses enjoying Cabinet-level power. The chances of the country taking a radical, unwelcome direction were heightened further by a rocky economy in the 1920s: a stock market crash at the beginning of the decade, followed by a series of smaller shocks and the bankruptcy of businesses and banks saddled with impossible debt. A draconian Peace Preservation Law was passed the same year as the universal male suffrage bill, in an effort to ensure that this latest dubious democratic experiment enjoyed the safety net of enhanced police power.

Amongst those floating moderate alternatives to Western-style democracy was the Christian political scientist Yoshino Sakuzō, who worked at Tokyo Imperial University and worshipped just around the corner at Ebina Danjō's church. What Japan needed, he thought, was not government *by* the people but rather government *for* the people. Socialist prescriptions for Japan were wrong, because their assumptions were wrong: human beings are not merely the products of social environments. Instead, they possess a spiritual capacity – a blend of the moral and the rational – that transcends their environment, orients them towards the good, and should not be denied or downplayed. What they need is to be led by the right people: men of character (*jinkakusha*), who will respect and nurture these essential qualities, curb the power of the military and the state bureaucracy, and protect essential constitutional freedoms like free speech and the right to petition government.

Yoshino called this system *minponshugi*: people as the basis of, or focus for, governance. But though Yoshino's writings were widely read, alternative visions like his for Japanese politics failed to gain much traction across these crucial years. For some, they smacked too much of elitism and paternalism. For others, their idealism was at odds with the pragmatic materialism bequeathed by Japan's Meiji-era leaders: a natural-scientific view of the world, harnessed to the exercise of power by a small group of capable people in a narrowly defined national interest.

Two of the natural languages of subversive opposition to that Meiji settlement, religion and Marxism, had by the 1920s been successfully cast as marginal pursuits: the former at turns old-fashioned and potentially treasonous, the latter quite plainly beyond the pale given what Marxism means for monarchs. Throughout the 1920s, and especially once the new Peace Preservation Law was in force, left-wing activists found themselves periodically rounded up, beaten and imprisoned – some were murdered.

And yet these were not the only ways in which people of this period registered their views about Japan's present and its likely future, whether that was whole-hearted optimism, distress, dissent, suspicion of one another, or even a feeling that the country as a whole was heading for the rocks.

*

A man stands outside his pharmacy, boasting to his neighbours of how he couldn't bear to be parted from his unfaithful wife – so he chopped her into five pieces and, using a 'secret technique' involving a chilled wooden barrel, cleaned, treated and reassembled the parts as a waxwork dummy in his window. *This is it!* he tells them, pointing through the window pane. *Didn't you realize? Didn't you hear the water running at night?*

A student uses the ventilation shafts running through one of the new, anonymous apartment blocks being thrown up around the city to reach the room of an acquaintance of his. Silently, he makes a small hole in the ceiling, so that he can pour poison down a piece of string into the man's mouth while he sleeps. Didn't you realize? Didn't you know who your neighbours were . . . ?

A young writer, Yoshiko, is making her way through her post when she comes across a letter from a man – 'ugly beyond words . . . my lifestyle unsanitary' – who is intent upon confessing a crime. A chair-maker, he once made a large armchair so fine that rather than part with it he concealed himself inside before it was taken to its final destination: the lobby of a luxury hotel in Yokohama.

His plan was to crawl out of his tiny hideaway at night, and rob the hotel guests. But he soon discovered a quite unexpected pleasure:

> A girl in the hotel . . . sat on me. She was my first, and she kindled in my heart the most passionate love. I think she was European . . . she sang with such a sweet voice as she sat, for thirty minutes, moving her body and feet in tempo with the tune.
>
> I could hardly believe it. Me, who had always avoided the opposite sex on account of my horrifying face. And now my skin was almost touching hers through a thin layer of leather . . . oh, love in a chair!
>
> But, sadly, one day the hotel auctioned my chair off, and it ended up in the home of a high-ranking government official in Tokyo. Only, the chair turned out not to be for him: it was for the use of his young wife, in her room.
>
> Soon, I was with her almost constantly, joined with her as one. When she wasn't eating or sleeping, her soft body was always seated on my knees . . .

Yoshiko's brow begins to furrow as the description of this home unfolds. It is *her* home. And the room is *her* room . . .

Tokyo in the 1920s was a city where strange crimes of this sort happened all the time. But mostly in people's heads. Though Inoue Enryō, a generation before, had hoped to banish the fantastical from modern Japanese life, it turned out that the city fired people's imaginations as never before.

Feeding off – and further fuelling – these fears and fantasies was Edogawa Ranpo, a writer of mystery and detective stories, who took his inspiration and pen-name from Edgar Allan Poe and created the murky worlds of the mannequin wife, the apartment killing and the 'human chair'.

Edogawa drew his cast of characters from the rotten heart of modern Tokyo – and of modernity itself. Conspicuous amongst them were wealthy women, corrupted by or punished for their new-found independence: adulterous, sometimes murderous wives; an elderly moneylender killed for the cash she is seen stashing in a plant pot. Most of the men are weak, ugly, hapless or bored, falling into crime rather than exhibiting any great passion or talent for it.

Even Edogawa's wise and perceptive detective hero, Akechi Kogorō, succeeds not because he enjoys life in modern Japan but because he understands what makes its people tick. Their hopelessness and grasping is all too common, and all too easy to read. Life itself has become commodified, to the point where a man kills and dismembers his wife in order to truly 'own' her.

Writers like Edogawa enjoyed enormous success. Foreign detective fiction, with its feats of logical deduction, was considered a thoroughly wholesome grounding in rational thought for the nation's youth, so the likes of Sherlock Holmes and Arsène Lupin were welcomed with open arms. But with domestic writers like Edogawa, this central feature of the genre was subverted. Plot twists were thrown in that made a sudden mockery of what had come before – 'The Human Chair' ends with the letter-writer announcing in a second missive that the first was just an idea for a story, about which he is seeking Yoshiko's opinion.

Then again, why strive for narrative coherence in conjuring a city where so many people were living unfamiliar and unpredictable lives? The weird, the disturbing and the fantastical were far better suited to subject matter of this sort – as was a long-standing tradition of ghost stories, developed across centuries in a country where deceased relatives or friends at best watched over you, but at worst sought to do you harm. Ghoulish classics were reinvented for audiences not yet convinced that modern technology was entirely benign. Ghostly voices had, in the past, whispered on desolate winds. Now they could be heard emanating from dimly lit telephone booths.

People flocked to the cinema to see one of the six or so *kaiki eiga* – 'strange' or 'mysterious' films, often adapted from kabuki ghost stories – that were made every year, often released to coincide

A *bakeneko* dance party (Utagawa Kuniyoshi, *c*.1841)

with *Obon*, Japan's summer festivities to honour the ancestors. Newspaper editors with an eye to their circulation figures now and again splashed on 'news' stories about *bakeneko* – 'monster cats' or 'changed cats'. At one point, a very useful rumour did the rounds that a collection of *bakeneko* had found their way into tenement housing in Tokyo and broken into a *danse macabre*.

For critics tempted to read a great deal into what a society does with its leisure time, all this was a clear sign that Japan was going backwards. Not long ago, the country's driving slogan had been *bunmei kaika*: 'civilization and enlightenment'. Now there was critical acclaim for a story about a man groping a woman through a chair.

It was tempting, too, to regard an enormous earthquake that struck the Tokyo–Yokohama area in 1923 as a literal and figurative rupture with a more austere and purposeful past. Upwards of 100,000 people were killed, many of them dying in the fiercely destructive firestorms that swept through the city. In the building boom that followed, bars, tearooms and cafés proliferated. And where previously many

'Modern girls', *c.*1928

such places had played host to intellectuals engaging in serious conversation – often with one or two policemen looking on from a corner – newer establishments seemed premised instead on fun, frivolity and on testing the limits of the freedom this city gave them.

Two of the great symbols of the post-earthquake age were the free-wheeling *modan gāru* and *modan boi* ('modern girl' and 'modern boy'), and the café waitress. The former was an exaggerated take, by a scandal-hungry media, on young women and men who enjoyed dressing like Western stars of stage and screen and who seemed to their critics to live mainly for shopping and leisure. The café waitress 'type' covered a wide range of realities. Some simply served coffee. Others offered male patrons anything from a friendly smile through various grades of imaginatively thought-out erotic encounter – depending on the café, its owner and the girls themselves.

*

Sitting in one of Tokyo's cafés was Akutagawa Ryūnosuke's 'Mr A', steadily nearing the end of his tether:

> Opposite me were a couple who appeared to be mother and son. Though younger than me, the son looked almost exactly like me. The two were chatting like lovers, their faces pressed close together. Watching them, I realized that the son, at least, was conscious how much erotic pleasure he was giving his mother. This was a classic case of a kind of attractive force that I knew well. It was a classic case too of a kind of will that turns this world of ours into a hell.

These late encounters of Mr A's came as part of a tumble he was taking through a hallucinatory landscape of house fires, hotel rooms, basement restaurants, trains and tracks. Inside one train carriage, a man jabbers on at him about seeing a ghost; and a schoolgirl with a nasal whine plies a passenger with leading questions about what a 'love scene' is.

Mr A feels sick. His cultured, cluttered mind offers up Dante's *Inferno*, over and over again. Religion too – the image of bearing a cross. Something he wrote a while back returns to him: 'I have no conscience . . . all I have is nerves.' Aphorisms suit his segmented reality, steeling him just a little until he can get back to his room and his dwindling supply of sedatives. 'I don't have the strength to keep writing this . . .' he says at the end. 'Won't someone be kind enough to strangle me in my sleep?'

Akutagawa had long had an interest in Christianity, visiting the Oura church in Nagasaki where Japan's 'hidden Christians' had revealed themselves to Fr Petitjean. He brought a statue of Maria-Kannon back with him to Tokyo. His writings in the last hours of his life reflected on a religion so poetic and impossible that 'not even Christ himself could have fully practised' it. 'Foxes have their holes, the birds of the sky their nests,' he wrote, quoting from the Gospels, 'but the Son of Man has nowhere to lay his head.' Here was a person who had managed to point people beyond the 'mundane world', thought Akutagawa, and yet at the same time towards the core of its suffering. Here was someone, all those years ago, who hadn't needed the clatter and clang and shrieking intensity of an industrial city and a mass society to sense the homelessness that lay at the heart of the human condition.

Akutagawa Ryūnosuke passed away in the summer of 1927 with a bible open at his bedside. He left behind great sadness and trepidation – but also questions. Had he found the transcendence that he claimed no one could live without, or had he given up on it? And what did he mean by this – a final fragment of writing, apparently mistaken in its language, perhaps distorted by tiredness or barbiturates; or perhaps a last testament of sorts:

> Christ's life will always move us. It is a cruelly broken ladder for us to ascend to earth from heaven, left lying aslant in a relentless downpour from the grey sky.

7

Great Escapes

Kosawa Heisaku regarded his psychoanalytic rival Ohtsuki Kenji, with whom he was forced grudgingly to share a city, as a bit of a charlatan. Despite possessing no formal training or qualifications, Ohtsuki had successfully set himself up as an evangelist for Freud around Tokyo and beyond. He penned provocatively Freudian commentaries for the newspapers, scanning the urban landscape for items of phallic significance – from neckties to baseball bats – while uncovering entertaining sexual subtexts in the work of major authors of the day. His psychoanalytic discussion group boasted the popular writer of detective stories, Edogawa Ranpo, as one of its members. And he was even called upon to advise the police and the courts on criminal psychology.

Kosawa, on the other hand, had qualified first as a doctor and then as a psychiatrist at Tohoku Imperial University. But having torpedoed his university career by insulting his professor, Marui Kiyoyasu – from whom he learned about psychoanalysis only to announce that he was off to Europe to study it properly – he found himself, on his return to Japan in 1933, the unemployed father of a young and growing family. A little of Ohtsuki's entrepreneurial spirit was in order.

So up went a sign outside the Kosawa home, in Tokyo's busy and fashionable Den-en-chōfu neighbourhood, increasingly in demand since the earthquake a few years before. Kosawa's message was simple: '*Nandemo sōdan*' – 'Ask me anything'. Kosawa had posters put up at train stations, too, along with ads in the newspapers. Psychoanalysis was all but unknown amongst most Japanese, so talk of 'libido', or 'the Id', or sexual feelings towards one's parents was unlikely to bring any but a few oddballs his way. Instead, to an urban society at turns thrilled and overwhelmed by rapid change, and increasingly at home with soliciting and receiving advice, 'Ask me anything' promised to make simple, intuitive sense.

This was a city awash with potential clients. Across the late nineteenth century, and into the twentieth, more and more aspects of life had come to be assigned for a purpose: family relationships were semi-public, and self-consciously productive; education revolved around acquiring nation-strengthening skills and a communitarian ethic; and one's profession was to be pursued for the sake of the nation – whether that be weaving cotton, wielding a rifle or pushing a pen for the state's burgeoning bureaucracy.

One could even be distressed for the sake of the nation. Writing about his recovery from neurasthenia in 1909, the journalist Ishikawa Hanzan had modestly traced his illness back to his membership of more than 100 governmental and social organizations, together with 1,000 public speeches delivered across Japan for the edification of the masses. Likewise, when Japanese authorities in Korea discovered rising rates there of mental illness, their response was, in a word, 'Good'. One of their stated reasons for expanding their influence on the peninsula was to lift it out of its Chinese-traditionalist quagmire, and to forge a modern nation in Japan's own image. Psychological distress was a symptom of success.

Japan's most famous self-declared neurasthenic was the novelist Natsume Sōseki. While allowing that his condition was partly personal, a matter of excessive self-consciousness, he also blamed it on his country's faulty process of 'civilization' in recent decades. The country's 'firebell'-like awakening to the modern Western world had yielded hurried, superficial and 'extrinsic' change, and the creation of a society in which anyone who tried to cultivate true civilization within themselves would naturally become ill in the process.

A few miserable months spent in London between 1900 and 1902 helped Sōseki towards this conclusion. Hoping to deepen his understanding of English literature, Sōseki instead acquired a very different sort of education, courtesy of the almost daily humiliations that he suffered. He found himself on and mostly off two wheels around Lavender Hill and Clapham Common, as well-meaning friends tried to induct him into the latest craze: cycling. Policemen tutted, passers-by broke into ironic applause, and one man shouted 'Chink' when Sōseki nearly ran him over. Boarding-house landladies were by turn cold, sulky and overweening. He wrote of one:

[She was] far beyond any femininity . . . All the human weaknesses – bitterness, envy, obstinacy, rigidity, doubt – must have taken a delight in playing with that face to give it that ill-favoured appearance . . .Turning her black eyes towards the narcissi withering in the glass vase, she [said] that England, a cold and cloudy country, was not a pleasant place to live. No doubt she intended to point out to me that in this country even the flowers failed to bloom.

Meanwhile, London's industrial fog conjured for Sōseki a vivid visual and emotional sense of what modernity had done to England, and was now set to do to Japan. Settling onto roadways and lawns, it created a landscape in which the colour, energy and rich detail of human life was smudged and suppressed. All he could see of a nearby garden was its hard ornaments: modernity's pointless, lifeless artefacts freeze-framed in the damp gloom. Londoners seemed to be happiest when the curtain rose at the theatre, and they were transported, thanks to Shakespeare's *Twelfth Night*, to a sunny ancient Adriatic:

All of a sudden, the mist disappeared. Far off, on an expanse of greenery stretching out by the sea, sparkling under the hot rays of the sun, a handsome young man came in sight, wearing a yellow tunic and accompanied by a beautiful woman enveloped in a violet robe with long, billowing sleeves . . . She sat down in a marble seat in the shade of an olive tree. The peaceful sound of the orchestra came across the distant sea, its thin notes continuing without a pause. The whole hall trembled at the same time. In this darkness they were dreaming of Greece, which was all sweetness and light.

Living in London, Sōseki found that doubt and unease about the world, which had swirled relatively harmlessly around him back in Japan, now entered into him in the form of a profound culture shock and a deep challenge to his whole sense of self. 'What is modernity doing to us Japanese?' took on minute-by-awful-minute specificity as 'what is London doing to me?' A Japanese visitor calling on Sōseki around this time sent a telegram home about his visit. It read: 'Natsume has gone mad.'

Sōseki only ever experienced partial relief from the anxiety that he felt almost constantly 'in the pit of my stomach'. It came, he reported, when he finally found an authentic centre of gravity that was independent of borrowings, imports and the opinions of foreigners (crudely adopted by Japanese like 'glued-on peacock feathers'), or the excessive demands of Japanese leaders. 'What a horror,' he said to Japanese students in 1914, 'if we have to eat for the nation, wash our faces for the nation, go to the toilet for the nation!' One should instead strive to be 'self-centred': centring one's life and work clearly and firmly in oneself.

Sōseki warned his students not to try to avoid the stresses of modernization by centring their lives *on* themselves – a very different, and destructive, prospect. But he was too late. By the 1910s, a fad was emerging amongst highly educated young people for something called 'self-awareness', a trend marked by the intensive reading of poetry and philosophy while musing on one's own growth and relationships. In 1916, a student at an elite school in Sendai, northern Japan, which Kosawa would shortly attend, wrote in anticipation of a 'Taishō Restoration' which would match Meiji's external, materialistic revolution with an internal counterpart of 'mind and spirit'. European Romantic and Idealist philosophy, sometimes read in the original German by students

Natsume Sōseki (1867–1916)

whose education focused heavily on foreign languages, provided much of the inspiration. Drunken boarding-school mah-jong sessions were punctuated by renditions of 'De-kan-shō' – a student song celebrating their obsession with Descartes, Kant and Schopenhauer.

Critics claimed that all this was in danger of fostering a fatal detachment from social and political realities, on the part of otherwise promising young men whose expensive educations were being subsidized by an expectant state. The journalist Tokutomi Sohō wrote of his regret that where the good of that state had once been the national religion, too many people were now losing or questioning their faith.

But this apparent exchange of a national life for an inner life, especially in this younger generation, was far more political than perhaps some of its critics realized. Young people especially were developing a set of broadly overlapping misgivings about life in Japan. They felt there had been too much talk of the state and of a supposed collective good, and they worried about the loss of personal autonomy and spiritual depth that full-steam-ahead public service threatened to demand. They had been encouraged to rely too much on the head, to the neglect of the heart: surely objectivity, rational thinking and specialization obscured as often as revealed life's richness? And for all its pockets of innovation and patches of colour, urban life was still overwhelmingly characterized, for them, by cramped, mechanized drabness, with humans living at ever-closer quarters yet failing to generate between them much corresponding increase in happiness, empathy or solidarity. People's discomfort, and desire to escape, could not be written off as laziness or degeneracy. These things were loaded with moral and political judgement – and brimming with dangerous potential.

*

While Japan had accepted plaudits abroad for the remarkable process of modernization that had brought it victory over Russia in 1905, and for its humane treatment of prisoners during the conflict, back at home around 12,000 people had been locked up in cages. This was a system dating back to the Tokugawa era: the confinement at home of people with mental illness, often outside the house and open to the elements.

Tokyo University's Kure Shūzō, a student of Inoue Enryō and

famed as Japan's father of psychiatry, helped to produce a damning report on the system in 1918. He declared the mentally ill 'unlucky to have been born in Japan', a shocking turn of phrase given decades of political effort to build up the country's image. The government offered a belated promise to recognize mental illness as a medical rather than a law-and-order problem, and to construct proper treatment facilities in every prefecture.

In the meantime, Kure and his colleagues discovered, families were continuing to take sick relatives to Buddhist temples and Shinto shrines, where forms of treatment were being offered – albeit often in appalling conditions – that Kure recognized as paralleling contemporary Western forms of care. The practice of bathing under waterfalls resembled hydrotherapy, while the use of prayers and incantations could be understood as a form of psychotherapy.

Matching psychiatrists' scepticism about politicians and their promises was public scepticism about psychiatrists. Many feared being labelled with a diagnosis that might affect their family and future prospects, given uncertainty about whether mental illness could be inherited. There was a feeling, too, that psychiatrists were more interested in chopping up brains in university labs, or in warehousing (for profit) people who had become unwelcome in their own homes, than they were in listening to the problems that everyday life was beginning to throw up.

Starting in the early 1900s, philosophy, science, comparative religion and raw entrepreneurship – intellectual and commercial – came together to fill the gap left by public mistrust (and, in some cases, simple lack of awareness) of psychiatry. A range of new physical and psychological therapies emerged, offering to treat people via idioms they could readily understand. They were expansively holistic, discovering cosmic significance in personal complaints – the ultimate in the intimate.

Much was made of usefully flexible concepts like *kokoro* and *seishin*. '*Kokoro*' (心) could mean 'heart', 'self', 'personality' or the 'heart of things'. '*Seishin*' enjoyed an even richer strategic malleability, thanks to two *kanji* (精 [*sei*] and 神 [*shin*]) that hinted broadly at purity, mind, soul, gods and energy. Highly diverse ideas ended up sharing some of the same popular constituent parts, one borrowing from another its air of mystique or scientific credibility. The 'Japanese spirit', much talked about in the wake of the war with Russia, was *nihon seishin*. Spiritualism, idealism or spiritual effort might all be rendered as *seishin shugi*. One's inner, emotional currents were *seishin teki*. Psychiatrists called themselves *seishinkai* (doctors of *seishin*) while Kosawa's beloved discipline was *seishin bunseki* (*seishin*-analysis).

One of the first therapeutic pioneers was a man called Kuwabara Toshirō. He graduated from hypnotizing his maid at the age of thirteen – a feat the boy is said to have repeated on the poor woman more than a hundred evenings in a row – to publishing a bestselling book, *Seishin Reidō*, in 1903–4. The book laid out a technique, known as *seishin-reidō-jutsu* ('the art of the excellent movement of the mind') that seemed to give the Japanese public exactly what they wanted: physical and psychological healing that sounded modern and cutting-edge, featured a folksy first-person approach and an empathetic understanding of people in their suffering, and which was embedded in a quasi-philosophical account of the world. Hypnotism worked, Kuwabara claimed, by bringing the human psyche or individual *seishin* into tune with the greater universal *seishin*, or Mind, of which it was a part – and which has been known throughout history by many names: Brahma, God, Truth, Nirvana.

Within a few short years as many as 30,000 people in Japan had taken to calling themselves *reijutsuka* (spiritual practitioners). Medical doctors began to worry that if any old amateur could get away with practising a technique like hypnotism, then the reputation – and lucrative exclusivity – of their own profession, to which hypnotism evidently belonged, would surely suffer. They petitioned the government, who were only too happy to support Westernized professionals against what looked like quackery tinged with old-school superstition. The use of hypnotism 'without due cause' was included on a list of minor offences in 1908, alongside fortune-telling, exorcism, spells and incantations.

Non-medical hypnotists swiftly rebranded themselves as *seishin ryōhōka*, psychotherapists, some of whom aimed to cure the mind itself, while others promised to use the power of the mind to cure the body. For people looking to train in these new techniques, correspondence and short-stay courses were offered by institutions modelled on the traditional *Iemoto* system whereby precious skills were passed down through a familial or quasi-familial lineage. One of those destined to become known around the world was that of Usui Mikao. He opened a *reiki* – spiritual energy – healing clinic in Tokyo in 1922, and soon began to train others, first by passing the *reiki* ability on through direct touch and then establishing an organization capable of facilitating training on a much wider scale.

Though one of the great *reiki* missionaries to the West was a Hawaiian woman by the name of Hawayo Takata, within Japan therapy was for the most part men's work. Whether a therapist focused on familial, professional or more general social problems thrown up by new living and working environments (popular diagnoses soon included *taijinkyōfushō*: fear of interpersonal relations), it was widely thought that to be effective a practitioner had to be socially and educationally superior to the client. This would be conducive to the kinds of faith and trust that theorists like Inoue Enryō claimed were key components in healing.

But faith and trust in what – or whom? Many of these therapies seemed premised on a patient or client trustfully abandoning a malfunctioning, solitary self and story to something greater, whether a professional practitioner or 'Mind' itself. In a modern society shaped by its leaders to be deeply hierarchical – across politics, industry and education, and human relationships in general – how was one to distinguish therapeutic self-abandonment from simple conformity to authority or a particular set of values?

The problem was clear in another future Japanese therapeutic export to the West: Morita therapy, geared especially towards people suffering from nerves. Its founder was Morita Shōma, a one-time student of Kure Shūzō and a colleague of Akutagawa's psychiatrist confidante Saitō Mokichi. Morita started out in 1919 by inviting his first client to live with him in his family home, where he personally modelled for her the proper way to live and work and relate. Morita therapy soon evolved into a more structured, hospital-based cure, in which a number of Western therapies were combined and underpinned by a philosophical approach to life rooted in East Asian traditions. Patients moved from complete bed rest through to light and then heavier work, learning along the way how to operate in the world by accepting reality just as it is – *arugamama* – rather than seeking to push it around all the time (an attitude held largely responsible for their original troubles). But charismatic guidance, tinged with social and even moral superiority, remained a core part of the therapy. One of Morita's later clients described him as Christ-like. Ohtsuki Kenji, Kosawa's great rival, sometimes operated in a not dissimilar way, inviting young male clients to stay at his country home with him and his wife. He and the client would go for long walks, Ohtsuki standing in for the strong and attentive father that the client had never had.

How, in these sorts of situations, was a person to distinguish between liberation from troubling circumstances and merely their exchange for new ones, urged on them by intimately influential figures? A danger seemed to be looming, of 'great escapes' from modern predicaments leading merely into fresh forms of captivity.

*

One day a whole family went into the fields. In the evening, when they were about to return home, they found a woman crouching beside the river, smiling. The next day during the noon break the same thing happened again. This happened day after day, and gradually the rumour spread that someone from the village was visiting the woman at night. At first, the visits were only when her husband was away driving packhorses to the seaside. Later, the visits were made even when she was sleeping beside her husband.

Over time, it became evident that the visitor must be a *kappa* [a mischievous and deadly water spirit], and so the husband's mother went and slept at the wife's side. But late at night, when she heard the wife laughing and knew that the visitor had come, she found it impossible to move her body. There was nothing anyone could do . . .

When *kappa*-children are born, they are hacked into pieces, put into small wine casks and buried in the ground. They are grotesque.

What were modern readers to think of such a story? It didn't matter. 'Thinking' was quite beside the point. The pioneering folklorist Yanagita Kunio promised readers of *Tōno no Monogatari* (*The Legends of Tōno*) (1910) that he had written these stories down 'just as I felt them', when they were recounted to him by a resident of the rural town of Tōno. Sceptical about how far a reliance on logic alone was getting people in seeking to apprehend the world, Yanagita rendered the word for 'logic' as *rojikku* in his writing, the better to emphasize its foreignness and its questionable utility for Japan. Just as some Japanese Christians derided Western missionaries as *bata kusai* – stinking of butter – so, for Yanagita, the arteries of contemporary Japanese inquiry were becoming clogged with *gakusha kusai koto* – things that 'stink of the scholar'.

A graduate of Tokyo Imperial University, Yanagita resigned from the Ministry of Agriculture and Commerce in 1919 having seen at first hand government attempts to remake rural Japan in the interests of the state. First, the countryside's economic needs were subordinated to those of urban heavy industry, then its culture was steadily destroyed: old customs and practices were outlawed as magical or superstitious, to be replaced by the moralizing of imperial rescripts and of bureaucratic diktats from the Home Ministry in Tokyo. Shrines across the country were being merged, as local gods were dragooned into the service of a national system of State Shinto, focused on the Emperor and his imperial line.

With the alien corruptions of the modern city thus steadily making their way outwards into the countryside, like an ink-stain spreading across a map, one had, thought Yanagita, to draw on the saving wisdom of rural Japan while one still could. Inoue Enryō had looked at the countryside and seen *gumin*, stupid people. Japan's political leaders, it seemed, saw *kokumin*, a citizenry – tax-paying human resources on tap. Yanagita, instead, fancied that he saw *jōmin*, Japan's 'ordinary, abiding people', enviably immersed in nature.

Here were people who knew the limitations of attempting to describe the world objectively as though one somehow transcended it – trying to push and poke it, in the sorts of ways that had driven Morita Shōma's patients to collapse. To really understand life, you didn't try to describe it – you told stories about it. Of the seen and unseen intersecting: *kami*, goblin-like *kappa* and *tengu* ('heavenly dogs', a blend of the human and bird-like) rubbing shoulders with rich men, mad men and mountain women; of strange monkeys, wolves, foxes, spirits of the ancestors and deer who travel and mediate between worlds.

These were precisely the sorts of phenomena of which Inoue, with his *yōkaigaku* ('monsterology') hoped to help cleanse Japan. For Yanagita, they were the means of learning a different way of living. Where a client of Morita or Ohtsuki might be encouraged to closely observe their therapist, Yanagita advised readers to pay attention to and imbibe for themselves the *kokoro no hataraki* – the 'workings of the heart' – of the people of rural Japan, as revealed in the 'feel' of their stories. One would discover, Yanagita claimed, a 'consciousness of daily life' radically different from the one that far-off city existences now encouraged.

That urban consciousness seemed, to its critics, to be defined by the ticking of a clock. Ever-improving modes of production created a far-reaching impression of strict linearity about the world: of today surpassing yesterday; of the past as relevant and valuable chiefly as the necessary foundation for the present. People would soon forget that there was any other way to live. Modernity started out looming above you as epic buildings. Then it got under your nails as the debris of the industrial city, and into your head as the rhythms and logic of your new work life. It found its way into your home, too, in the form of altered relationships and routines, new clothes and furnishings. Finally, it wormed its way into your heart, until you could no longer remember what you possessed and were before.

Many Japanese thinkers of Yanagita's generation were looking for ways of redeeming what the German philosopher Martin Heidegger worried was a 'levelled-down' time emerging as part of modern life around the world: mere 'now'-points, evenly spanned, public, incessant – banal. The philosopher Miki Kiyoshi sought salvation in a 'foundational experience' of the world: some intuition or relationship or point of reference that would serve as an anchor, giving shape and bringing real meaning to the passage of time. Others placed their faith in high culture: its space and spaciousness could soothe minds addled and segmented by office deadlines, by rushed and noisy café conversations, and by a consumer culture that was constantly renewing itself. Still others, Yanagita amongst them, sought out parts and peoples of Japan not yet ensnared by moment-after-moment modern *chronos*, where life's rhythms were instead still set by *kairos* – a sense of the 'right' or the 'fitting' moment. These were communal, cooperative lives, defined and enriched by place and ritual, by seasons cycling and ancestors circling – returning to watch over their descendants.

But do ancestors and *tengu* really 'exist'? Again: it doesn't matter, Yanagita would respond. What a typically, tragically *urban* thing to ask. One should focus instead on the 'liveliness and freshness' of the people who feature in these stories, and on the dignity and honour they possess. In a round-table discussion with Akutagawa Ryūnosuke – who used *kappa* imagery in a satire on his society, written just a few months before he died – Yanagita repeated a speculation made by a teacher of his: one is less likely to do imprudent things if some 'unseen entity' might be lurking in the room, looking on and passing judgement.

Like Yanagita, the philosopher Watsuji Tetsurō, writing in the 1930s and 1940s, looked to rural life, human relationships and the distant past for purchase on Japan's uncertain present. He claimed that Japan's combination of a monsoon season with incoming Arctic air was crucial to understanding its people. These things had long made the country perfect for wet rice cultivation: a quintessentially cyclical and communitarian venture, tied to the tending of a particular patch of land. Watsuji was indebted to Heidegger, in his critique

A *tengu* (Ogata Gekkō)

of modernity. But he thought that Western philosophy as a whole was wrong to insist on taking the individual and his or her experience of the world as its starting point. Watsuji pointed his readers instead to the Japanese characters for *ningen*, 'human being': *Nin* (人) is 'person'; *gen* (間) is 'space' or 'gap'. To be human, he concluded, is in fact to be, at one and the same time, an individual person *and* in relationship. Meanwhile, the thick internal walls of a Western home reveal the unfortunate meaning there of 'family': just a bunch of individuals in pragmatic cohabitation. Contrast that with the ideal Japanese home, where thinner, movable partitions of wood and paper suggest a 'quiet but emotional and martial selflessness', where the illusion of being a single, lone unit of being can never really take root.

*

Great coffee, disappointing therapists. Such was Kosawa Heisaku's verdict on Vienna and on Sigmund Freud's psychoanalytic circle, reported to his brother (and financial backer) in a letter home. Kosawa had gone to Europe in 1932 hoping to encounter, in Freud, some cross between a father and a saviour. He once wrote to Freud, in rather gushing literary German, of his 'urge to experience my perfection through you'. But such dreams ended up dashed on the rocks of Freud's own frailty by the time they met, not to mention Kosawa's shaky command of the spoken language – to which Freud responded by suggesting that Kosawa find himself a German-speaking girlfriend, to help things along.

Unable to communicate well with Freud or afford his analytical fees, Kosawa instead received three short months of therapy with Richard Sterba, a disciple of Freud's, yielding only rather generic Freudian fare: Kosawa was too close to his mother, hated his father and harboured an aggressive dislike of his university boss (who had effectively just fired him). Nor does Kosawa seem to have received the hoped-for feedback on his new thesis about religion, culture and liberation: an adaptation of Freud's Oedipus Complex, which Kosawa called the 'Ajase' Complex, after a prince in Buddhist mythology.

The essence of Kosawa's argument was that Freud had misunderstood religion, as the wrong sort of 'escapism'. For Freud, religion had its roots in guilt and a fear of punishment. For Kosawa, a devout

Jōdo Shinshū Buddhist, what he called a 'religious state of mind' was in fact the ultimate therapeutic liberation. Its achievement was (or ought to be) the ultimate goal of psychoanalysis. To illustrate his point, Kosawa offered a short parable:

> The smash of a plate reverberates around a room, tiny fragments of ceramic skipping and tumbling across the kitchen floor. In the silence that follows a little boy – a good boy, already full of remorse – looks up to see his father's fury building: Why did you do that to a precious plate? Why the hell can you not concentrate?
>
> The boy apologizes, but the father's stubborn incomprehension is overwhelming. He shrinks back – starting, early in life, to repay fatherly remoteness in kind: fine then, I don't care anymore . . .
>
> But the boy's mother, too, is in the room: People are people, my love, and though what you did was wrong, never forget that I know you. And I know you can't help it with things like this, no matter how hard you try.

You can see religion as Freud understands it, Kosawa suggested, right there in how the child reacts to the father. But look at what happens when the mother steps in: the boy feels totally understood, completely accepted, and so is able to abandon himself to a healthy, reparative guilt. Freudian 'religion' gives rise to neurosis; *real* religion dissolves it away.

Kosawa Heisaku having tea with his home-stay host in Vienna (early 1930s)

Kosawa's ideas owed much to a Shin Buddhist monk he had met while at boarding school, Chikazumi Jōkan. A sometime assistant to Inoue Enryō, Chikazumi's was a more devotional, emotional form of faith than Inoue's. Like Yanagita, he was convinced by the power of stories to move people and to get a point across in the most direct way possible. He often used in his preaching a version of an old Japanese folk tale.

A son carries his ailing mother into the mountains on his back, with the secret intention of abandoning her there. Unbeknownst to her son, the mother has been laying a trail of twigs as they go: she knows her son's intentions. But the old woman harbours no hope of escape for herself. She wants to make sure her son finds his own way safely home.

The story of *Obasuteyama* – literally 'the mountain where the old woman is to be thrown away' – was, for Chikazumi, an allegory of the mercy of Amida Buddha. This was a mercy so complete that Shinran had founded the Shin sect, back in the thirteenth century, on the basis that a person needed only to recite a short prayer known as the *'nembutsu'* – *Namu-Amida-Butsu* ('Hail to Amida Buddha') – in order to be saved. This wasn't some magical incantation. It was a plea. It was an honest recognition of human weakness so profound that Shinran thought a person could not even recite the *nembutsu* without Amida's help, working away at the deepest level of their identity. As Kai Wariko, a modern Shin poet, put it:

The voice with which I call Amida Buddha
Is the voice with which Amida Buddha calls to me.

The distinctly modern element in all this was that Chikazumi and Kosawa focused on family relationships – as a tremendous salvific opportunity. For Chikazumi and Kosawa, the restoration of a damaged or dysfunctional relationship, achieved through realizing and confessing one's own deep vulnerability, was the very moment and the very means for Amida's mercy to break into mundane linear time, and into mundane human lives.

In a move of which Freud would surely not have approved had he known about it, Kosawa claimed that the great pioneer of psychoanalysis and ferocious critic of religion was nothing less than a twentieth-century Shinran. Freud had brought the tools of modern science to a perennial human task, offering people precisely the sort of vision of their fundamental frailty that was essential to allowing Amida's mercy to do its work.

What his clients therefore needed, Kosawa concluded when he returned to Tokyo to open his practice, was this: to experience a subtle blend of surprise and humiliation at the hands of someone whose love, compassion and insight were great enough to hold and guide them through the process. Kosawa would begin the work sitting behind his clients' heads as they lay on his couch, narrating aloud the ideas and images that came into their heads. *Do it as though you are a passenger on a train,* Kosawa counselled, *watching features of a landscape flash by: the sun hitting Mount Fuji, a farmer standing in a field, a schoolgirl on her way to school.*

Clients had to agree in advance to hold nothing back. In Kosawa's experience, people tended to filter what they told him, leaving out anything that seemed boring, irrelevant, embarrassing or liable to make the therapist angry. At some point, everyone started to resist the process. And yet here was the therapeutic gold. Just as Yanagita was sceptical of *rojikku*, so the way that clients *wanted* to present themselves to Kosawa was only of indirect interest to him. His role was to play, in turn, the provocateur and the open-armed mother.

Over time Kosawa evolved a particularly revealing means of accomplishing this with clients whom he treated via correspondence. He would ask them to send him, at regular intervals, two documents. The first was a covering letter, addressed to Kosawa. The second was a written record of a period of solo free association – all that had flashed through their heads when they obeyed Kosawa's command and let their thoughts and feelings go where they would.

The first document told Kosawa about the client's own self-understanding. The second was the really interesting one: it revealed something of what lurked in the client's unconscious. As therapy went on, Kosawa would hope to see material move from this second document into the first: unconscious elements making their way into conscious awareness.

One client confided in Kosawa that he recalled being embarrassed, as a child, when his parents forced him to wear a girl's rubber swimming cap at the seaside. Kosawa responded that he hadn't been embarrassed at all: he had liked it. *Covering up the ears symbolizes castration, which in turn suggests your desire to become a girl as a means of securing affection from your father. What's more, your recollection and sharing of that memory now may well be a sign of homosexual feelings towards me ...*

Maybe the client would spill his morning tea as he read this response. Maybe he would peer nervously over the top of the letter at his father sitting across the table. Whatever happened, this was part analysis, part carefully calibrated attempt to nudge a client who was beginning to over-intellectualize the process of therapy into gentle humiliation and the new self-awareness that might come with it.

Resistance is fertile: this was the modern core of a therapeutic style that Kosawa once described to a client in quasi-Buddhist terms as *Shinran no kokoro wo motte, seishin bunseki wo suru* – 'Doing psychoanalysis with the heart of Shinran'. If, as a client, you *really* don't want to share something ... then you probably should.

All of this lay in store for people answering Kosawa's *nandemo sōdan* – 'Ask me anything' – adverts. And plenty did. Nearly 400 clients from all walks of life walked through Kosawa's Den-en-chōfu doors during his first four years of private practice. A pharmaceutical salesman complained of domestic discord. The wife of a landowner had ended up lost in melancholy after the birth of a child. A company employee was driven to depression by overwork. A brothel owner and a confectioner were developing schizophrenia. A Buddhist monk, a fishmonger and a railway worker sought help with anxiety. Students struggled with erythrophobia (fear of blushing), which Kosawa suspected might be linked to masturbation. A paranoid bank worker came calling, as did a hysterical bonsai artist.

One day, a client reported to Kosawa a vivid experience of being momentarily outside of himself, or at least not quite 'in' himself in the usual way. Kosawa was overjoyed. 'That,' the client later recalled him as saying, 'is the real aim of psychoanalysis. Without it, psychoanalysis as a technique will not survive.'

From his client notes, written in the standard medical mixture of Japanese and German, to the decor in his consulting room, Kosawa endeavoured to be scrupulously neutral and scientific in his work. And yet, for him, psychoanalysis was totally unlike any other form of medicine. It didn't deal with just one part of a person, neatly separated out from everything else – like stitching a cut or setting a bone. In Kosawa's line of work, any single symptom was a statement about the whole person, their past as well as their present, and about the wider world in which they lived. He didn't introduce Buddhist language into the conversation because he didn't need to: its core concerns were already at the heart of everything he was doing.

Here was a tremendously influential set of early twentieth-century 'great escapes' more or less in a nutshell. People had to be lifted out of relatively new and unhealthily solitary ways of being in the world and put (back) in proper touch with one another – and, in turn, with some greater power, principle or source of value in the world. In this way, body and soul might be healed. Time might start to mean something. And the modernity that Japan's Meiji leaders had left as their legacy might be rolled back or redeemed.

Did that make people like Kosawa, Watsuji and Yanagita the past – or the future? In political terms, their ideas were deeply uncertain. They were potentially subversive, in that they refused to assume the rightness and inevitability of Japan's present direction of travel. But though they threatened to take the sheen off one of Japan's two great twentieth-century stories – that of Asia's first successful modernizer – Yanagita and Watsuji especially provided plenty of ballast for the second: Japan as a special, superior place, since time immemorial. If and when the public and political tide turned against the first story, modernity's foreign roots and damaging consequences becoming increasingly obvious, Yanagita's and Watsuji's ideas might become part of an attractive ideological alternative.

Depending on what you thought Japan needed in the 1920s and 1930s, people like Kosawa, Watsuji and Yanagita were radicals offering a path to freedom and flourishing, or they were reactionaries, seeking to put liberal democracy back in its box, returning it westward where it belonged. What they said about themselves here did not necessarily matter. More important were the future uses to which these and similarly subtle and complex schemes of thought might be put. A notable, worrying feature of these blueprints for a great escape – primordial authenticity, a timeless *Volk*, dynamic relationships that bind people together, encounters with Amida – was that in their romance they all reached out towards, almost seemed to crave, the same thing: power.

PART THREE

Leading Asia / Leaving Asia
(1920s to 1940s)

8

Self Power, Other Power, State Power

Eighteen-year-old Kikugawa Ayako stood patiently in line with the other young women. Each held a photo of a man in her hands – except for Ayako. After a while a group of men, all clutching portrait photos of their own, began to drift into the room, trying to match the images to faces in the line-up. Some checked the names etched into the women's luggage, just to be sure.

One man stopped in front of Ayako's willow-vine trunk. He looked up, smiling.

'Are you Ayako?'

'Yes.'

'OK, that's good.'

Without another word, he picked up her bag and left the room.

Ayako followed him out of the Honolulu immigration station to a nearby hotel, where they ate dinner, mostly in silence. The next day, they journeyed north around the coast of Oahu island. Ayako was surprised when it started to rain – people back home had talked of a tropical wonderland.

'So it rains in Hawaii . . . ?'

'Baka jya! [Ha! You fool!], of course it rains in Hawaii!'

Ayako would later remember the moment as their first real conversation.

The weather was really neither here nor there. Ayako had come to Hawaii simply to fetch this man, a distant relative by the name of Kikugawa Shitoku, home to his family in Kumamoto. Those other women, who like Ayako were just off the boat from Japan, were 'picture brides'. Families back home had been introduced to one another, had swapped 'exchange photographs', and now these girls had come out to Hawaii to meet their men and settle down in one of the migrant labour communities here.

Sugar and pineapple plantations would, after all, not run themselves. And since Europeans arriving in Hawaii in the late 1700s had brought with them diseases that devastated the local population, labour for the generally Western-owned plantations had to be shipped in from elsewhere. Beginning in the 1850s, Chinese workers from Guangdong and Macao were brought to Hawaii, where they were quarantined, fumigated and set to work. Japanese joined them after the Meiji Restoration in 1868; a trickle at first, but numbers rose rapidly after Hawaii's King Kalakaua visited his monarchical opposite number in Tokyo and struck a deal. By the turn of the twentieth century, nearly 100,000 Japanese labourers and their families had made the journey.

Young men who ventured to Hawaii alone, only to find themselves stranded there without the funds to return, called on their families to send them a wife – posting home a recent photograph to get the process going. Some sent photos of handsome strangers instead, the better to make a good match, meaning that a girl might set sail for romance in paradise, only to arrive tired and sea-sick into a rainy Honolulu, where a wrinkled old man was eagerly calling out her name. There was rarely a way back. The return fare would be prohibitive, and often the girls were already married to these men: the ritual exchange of nuptial *sake* cups had taken place back in Japan, in front of a photo of the beloved (or his better-looking stand-in, as the case might be).

Ayako made the most of the stunning coastline as they passed along it, the view occasionally jerking up and down amidst the jolting of her carriage. Her long journey from one volcanic archipelago to another was all for the sake of a very short stay. Or so she thought.

As soon as they arrived at Haleiwa, on Oahu's northern shore, Ayako and Shitoku were offered food. Only it was no mere casual snack: long tables had been specially laid out on straw mats. Someone loaned Ayako a Western-style dress, shoes and hat – and was oddly insistent that she put them on right away. Festive food was brought out. This was a wedding reception. Ayako's wedding reception.

It turned out that Ayako's family back in Japan had secretly sent a photo of her to Shitoku, who had agreed to marry her. And there was another surprise to come: soon after the wedding reception finished, Ayako's new husband revealed that he was deeply in debt. He had borrowed $400 to purchase a fishing boat, which promptly sank in bad weather. So instead of returning to Japan, later that summer in 1918, Ayako found herself being kitted out to work on a pineapple plantation, in order to help pay off Shitoku's debts.

A girl whose only experience of farm work up until now was feeding mulberry leaves to silkworms – her mother used to spin and weave the silk, sending it to Kyoto to be dyed and fashioned into kimono – now found herself working ten-hour days in the fields, before returning home to run her husband's bath and make dinner: *miso* soup, with boiled and seasoned pineapple-field weeds.

Against all odds, Ayako and Shitoku evolved into a happy couple, and from there into a happy family. A daughter was born in 1922, followed by a son in 1925, whose arrival in the middle of a working day left Ayako handling everything by herself. She laid out a futon and some newspaper, boiled water for the baby's first bath, gave birth, cut the cord, cleaned up and buried the placenta in a tin can under the house. The baby soon joined her in the fields; sometimes on her back, sometimes in a cracker box with a flour bag draped over the top to provide shade.

Twenty miles or so south of where the Kikugawas were shuttling between fields and home, Shitoku learning to whittle driftwood into toys for his children, US Navy vessels passed in and out of a dredged docking area. It was a sizeable operation, complete with shipyard, shops and other facilities. The days of King Kalakaua were by now long gone: he was dead, his kingdom had been overthrown and Hawaii had been a 'territory' of the United States since 1898. These particular docks now loomed large in American strategic interests, so much so that two vessels, the USS *Lexington* and USS *Saratoga*, were sent there in the early 1930s to stage mock attacks in order to see how prepared the defences were. The answer: not very. Pearl Harbor looked distinctly vulnerable.

Both the *Lexington* and the *Saratoga* had started life as battle-cruisers. Then, while they were still under construction, the US Navy found itself forced to turn them into aircraft carriers instead. Politics had intervened. Decades earlier, Commodore Matthew Perry had struggled to get the Japanese to open their doors. By 1921, the enthusiasm with which Japan was projecting its people and its military power out into Asia and the Pacific was becoming distinctly unwelcome. To try to forestall a potential naval arms race, Britain, the US and Japan agreed, in a Washington Naval Treaty signed in 1922, to maintain a 5:5:3 tonnage ratio across key parts of their seaborne fleets. There was to be a pause on the building of battlecruisers.

The Japanese were observing the situation closely. At home, the 1920s was a decade of experimentation in managing a mass industrial society. Abroad, it was a period – depending on one's level of optimism about international affairs – of fragile cooperation or of growing mistrust.

Japan-watchers had hoped that victories over China in 1895 and then Russia in 1905 might have represented the summit of Japanese ambitions. But it was not to be, and Western imperial powers that had for generations treated global cartography as a colouring-in exercise – British pink, French blue – increasingly feared for their cultural and linguistic homes-away-from-home in South East Asia and the Pacific.

The British were sprawled comfortably across such anglicized approximations of local people and place names as 'Burma', the 'Malay Peninsula', 'Singapore' and 'Hong Kong'. Territory nearby had been christened 'Indochine Française' and 'Nederlands-Indië'. And wars fought around the turn of the century by the soon-to-be staunchly anti-imperialist Americans had seen fall into their laps a string of islands named after the early modern Spanish monarch, Philip II. Spice, rubber and other valuable commodities poured out of these places, while Western administrators and educationalists, missionaries and military personnel poured in. It was a fine arrangement, and there was no room for newcomers seeking to muscle in.

Modern Japan's leaders had been empire-builders right from the start. The homeland of the Ainu, in the north, and the Ryūkyū Kingdom to the south had been assimilated early on as 'Hokkaidō' and 'Okinawa' prefectures respectively. Taiwan had been taken from China in 1895, and ten years later the Liaotung Peninsula lease, with its potentially lucrative South Manchuria railway corridor, was won from Russia. Korea went from contested peninsula to Japanese protectorate to fully annexed territory by 1910, a process whose violent latter stages cost nearly 12,000 Korean lives. For anyone beginning to sense a pattern, confirmation had come with Japan's clearing of German forces from East Asia and the South Pacific during the First World War.

By this point, some of Japan's leaders thought that expansion had gone far enough. Senior, semi-retired statesmen had succeeded in persuading government ministers to abandon some of their more inflammatory demands upon China in their 'Twenty-One Demands' of 1915, such as the acceptance on Chinese soil of Japanese advisers. These statesmen were disturbed to see a new generation of politicians and military men coming through who could be recklessly hubristic in their diplomacy – too young, as they were, to remember the acute vulnerability of the recent past, and too full of themselves to see the long-term dangers of diplomatic grandstanding.

And yet one of the lessons learned from the West early on was that a truly global power doesn't keep modernity's bounty for itself. It spreads it around, via a complex mixture of idealism, self-justification, avarice, and racial and cultural chauvinism. The French called it their *mission civilisatrice*. The journalist Tokutomi Sohō talked about Japan 'extend[ing] the blessings of political organization throughout the rest of East Asia and the South Pacific, just as the Romans once did for Europe and the Mediterranean'.

Bunmei kaika – 'civilization and enlightenment' – proved to be a domestic slogan easily repurposed for export. A raid on Taiwan in 1874, designed to create an early colonial toehold, had been whipped up by the media back home as the justified use of force against savages and cannibals. Woodblock imagery showed clean-cut Japanese accepting the surrender of grovelling Taiwanese. Later, it would be the turn of the Chinese to serve as the butt of Japanese and Western cartoon humour: lampooned as lumbering, lazy opium-junkies.

As media imagery began to make abundantly clear, a pan-Asian *mission civilisatrice* was not just about culture. It was also very much about race. Lecturing at Tokyo Imperial University, the Christian author of *Bushidō: The Soul of Japan*, Nitobe Inazō, argued for an

The popular press (*Tokyo Nichinichi News*) celebrate the Taiwan
Expedition of 1874

Satirizing Chinese military prowess across two conflicts:
'Jap the Giant-Killer' pictured in British magazine *Punch* (1894) during
the Sino-Japanese War; the American newspaper the *Tacoma Times*
(1904) on the prospect of China getting involved in the Russo-Japanese
War – harking back to 1894. China as a nation is here depicted as a
laundry operator, referencing popular stereotypes of early Chinese
immigrants into the USA.

open-ended commitment to sensitive, humanitarian guidance that would deal with Japan's less able neighbours strictly according to their own limited capacities. Meanwhile, over in Taiwan, Japanese governor Gotō Shinpei made a name for himself treating the island and especially its capital, Taihoku (Taipei), as a 'laboratory'. A quiescent, not to say grateful, local population could, it was thought, be relied upon for their forbearance as all manner of science-based techniques of administration were tried out, from the planning of wide, airy streets to civil engineering and public hygiene projects (Gotō was a German-trained doctor). Taiwanese demands for a degree of self-determination were mostly moderate enough to be ignored. It was a conspicuous feature of Japanese empire here, as elsewhere, that Japanese constitutional rights were not thought appropriate for colonized populations.

European visitors to Taiwan professed to love what the Japanese had done with the place. They lavished praise on colonial administrators for the manifest good they were doing. But Japanese imperial ideology was never entirely a European import. A Confucian distinction between civilized and barbarian, a *kokugaku* (nativist thought) concern with moral purity and impurity, and a resurgent interest in ancestry and bloodline linked to Shinto mythology all helped to entrench a view of racial discrimination, both abroad and at home, as perfectly in line with the facts.

One of the most infamous signs of this was a wave of extreme anti-Korean violence in the immediate aftermath of the 1923 earthquake. With much of Tokyo gone, and the rest of it in a febrile state, rumours spread – by word of mouth and in the newspapers – that Korean residents were taking the opportunity to start an uprising: poisoning wells, setting fires and carrying bombs around the city. Japanese vigilantes went looking for them, killing and brutalizing with an assortment of weapons ranging from guns to broken glass to fishhooks. People suspected of being Korean were tested on the national anthem or made to recite difficult Japanese phrases that would expose non-native speakers. Others were required to name all the stations on Tokyo's Yamanote train line.

Police and army personnel, some of whom had been involved four years earlier in quelling protests against Japanese rule on the Korean peninsula, largely stood aside at first – in some cases actually encouraging the rumour mill and joining in the violence. Only belatedly were thousands of Koreans gathered up and placed in protective custody. Others had been given refuge by Japanese neighbours. Up to 6,000 Koreans, perhaps many more, were less lucky – they were hunted down and murdered, in the space of just a few days. Later trials of the participants saw the accused, judges and onlookers exchange laughter and knowing looks. Many of those convicted received early parole.

And yet, while in Japan intellectuals pontificated about a superior Japanese bloodline and spirit, and how best to share its modern fruits with Asian neighbours, abroad the Japanese were not regarded quite so highly. For a few years, the United States had been happy to accept the likes of the Kikugawas on its soil. But then came the 'yellow peril'.

Cartoons in the *Tacoma Times* satirizing China's soldiery in 1904–5 were not primarily about foreign affairs. They had their real roots in local history. The 1870s and 1880s had seen laws passed and deadly riots break out in opposition to Chinese labourers in America. Much of Tacoma's Chinese community was hounded out of the city by a mob in 1885 – with the full support of its mayor, Robert Jacob Weisbach, who called them 'a filthy horde'. A local judge set the perpetrators free, allowing them home to a welcoming parade.

Then, in the early years of the twentieth century, attention had turned to the Japanese. A 'Gentleman's Agreement' was struck in 1907–8, under which the Japanese authorities agreed to restrict migration to the US. Though she didn't realize it at the time, Kikugawa Ayako had only made it to Hawaii under a rule that allowed picture brides to join husbands who were already living there. A few years later came the infamous 1924 Immigration Act. Henceforth no one who was ineligible for citizenship in the US would be allowed to enter the country as an immigrant – a category into which a Supreme Court ruling just two years before had explicitly placed all Japanese people.

The move met with vocal resistance both in Japan and in the US, where in the same month – December 1923 – that the Bill was introduced into Congress the American Red Cross raised $12 million in relief aid for victims of the Tokyo earthquake. But combined with an American military build-up in South East Asia and the Pacific, and

mutual suspicions over maritime power, the Act made the lives of internationally minded Japanese diplomats all but impossible back at home.

With Japan's economy seeing nothing like the economic benefits
promised by these internationalists – instead suffering in a global climate where big players like Britain could rely on their empires for raw
materials and markets – and with the limits of Western affection and
respect for Japan now finally laid bare, it was becoming progressively
easier to claim that the country's fledgling party politics was achieving very little. It was selling its people short, in fact, both at home and
abroad. For up-and-coming leaders like Konoe Fumimaro, the very
idea of 'internationalism' began to look like cynical rhetoric, designed
to blind people to an old and still enduring reality of 'have' and 'have-
not' nations.

*

On 17 July 1921, the ghost of Bertrand Russell appeared in Kobe,
Japan. All of a sudden, there he was: materializing in a temple dedicated
to Amida Buddha, and voicing his support for striking workers at the
nearby Mitsubishi and Kawasaki plants. Death having done nothing
either way for his ability to speak Japanese, a local strike leader by the
name of Kagawa Toyohiko helped out with interpretation.

In fact, Russell was very much alive when he gave his short speech
to the gathered activists. An over-zealous reporter for a Japanese
newspaper, the *Japan Advertiser*, had somehow inflated a bout of
pneumonia suffered by the great philosopher a few months earlier,
and pronounced him dead in Beijing. Japan's newsmen were slow to
offer a correction, so when Russell arrived in Japan his partner Dora
Black handed out notes to the Japanese media saying that Bertrand
Russell would be unable to give interviews, on account of being dead.

Still, journalists tried to sit next to the pair on trains, straining to
overhear their conversations and later making up stories about them.
On one occasion, the famous pacifist was reduced to chasing reporters away with his walking stick, after a throng of them caused Dora,
then pregnant, to stumble on some stairs and almost fall.

Undercover Japanese police were little better, booking the hotel
room next door to Russell's so that they could keep an eye on this

notorious foreign leftist. He had, after all, arrived in Japan at a particularly sensitive time. A post-war depression, mass lay-offs and
broader injustices in Japan's economic and political arrangements
together seemed poised to cast workers in great industrial centres like
Kobe into oblivion, and their families along with them. So they were
starting to organize and to ask an all-important question: who should
we look to – in what sorts of power should we invest our hopes – in
order to survive?

Cooperation with big business perhaps? A labour organization
called the Yūaikai, or 'Friendly Society', had grown to 30,000 members by this point, thanks to just such a gradualist approach to
building worker power. Its founder famously likened the relationship
between capitalists and labourers to that of husbands and wives.

But critics were increasingly asking where, precisely, gradualism
had got them. Kagawa Toyohiko looked like a better bet. 'Isn't it
time', he wrote, in a Yūaikai branch magazine called *Shin Kobe*
('New Kobe'), 'that capitalists started treating the workers at least as
well as their horses? Aren't we tired yet of [the Meiji-era slogan]
"Enrich the state, strengthen the military"? Shouldn't we move on
from being a civilization premised on wealth, to one rooted in human-
istic principles?'

Kagawa was soon elected president of the Kobe branch of the
Yūaikai, where he graduated from asking rhetorical questions to
campaigning on major issues and organizing strike action at Kobe's
dockyards, heading a march by 35,000 workers that stretched for
two and a half miles down the road. But an unprecedented moment
of hope for workers in 1921 was steadily worn down as management
first stalled (pretending that their top team was currently abroad, so
couldn't yet start negotiations) and then tempted some of the workers
back with retrospective bonuses. Legal provisions were invoked to
stop the remaining strikers gathering, and by the time Bertrand Russell came to town in the summer of that year activists were being
forced to gather at religious locations, under cover of 'worship'.
Kagawa was soon cut adrift by disappointed movement members.

In truth, he had never been fully on board, at least not with those
who were most committed to direct action. A philosopher and Christian convert, Kagawa didn't share the basic Marxist outlook of his

comrades in the labour movement. Instead, he understood the situation for Japan's workers as a balance between what Buddhists called 'self power' and 'other power': the power of human beings to sort themselves and the world out, versus the need to work with something greater and more mysterious.

Kagawa had been a lonely, introspective child who, having lost his father and mother early on, had on several occasions considered taking his own life. His sense of helplessness contributed to a profound attraction towards this greater, sustaining 'power'. Thanks in large part to friendships with two American Presbyterian missionary couples, Kagawa experienced that power first and foremost in terms of intimate love. 'Faith', he later wrote, 'means a realization of the fact that one is loved', and that the same power that runs through the universe 'is also at work within one's own being'. Buddhists understand this, and Christians understand it, he argued. The real obstacle to faith is not religious identity, but hopelessness. And yet so many in Japan are condemned by their conditions of life and labour to precisely this kind of alienating despair.

Kagawa began to develop his spiritual critique into a cultural and economic one. He spoke out against the misuse of technology in enforcing cruelly relentless regimes of mechanized work. And where other critics of Japan's modernity recoiled at the mistaken linearity that life was taking on, Kagawa's portrait of it focused on its relentless, entrapping pace:

'Busy, busy!' says the woman, as she shuts herself up in the rear of the house and sews away at finery she will wear, at the most, not more than three days of the year.

Businessmen there are who repeat the refrain 'Busy, busy' as they rush to and fro between their offices and the establishments where their illicit lovers live.

Military men take up the tune, 'Busy, busy' as they care for their cannon and polish their guns.

Students keep saying 'Busy, busy', as they sit up all night to prepare for examinations – and forget everything when the tests are over.

The liquor-dealer's bustle keeps the brothel-keeper busy.

The brothel-keeper's busyness keeps the physician busy.

The physician's rushing keeps the chauffeur on the go.
The chauffeur's activity in turn makes the liquor-dealer busy . . .
Without any aspirations, this living corpse obtrudes itself around
the earth . . . The window through which God would invade a life so
superficial and so completely absorbed in the present has been closed.

This 'busyness' was a form of self power, fostered by a standardized
education that did little more than bolt the required skills, attributes
and allegiances onto children who were expected to pass through
school mannequin-like in their blankness and availability to the
state's interests. Human beings were already intrinsically something,
Kagawa wanted to insist, part of a continuum of biological life by
means of which the Absolute is reaching for ever higher levels of creativity and perfection.

But cosmic contextualization of this sort – which was to surprise
international observers by becoming more rather than less prominent
across all points on the Japanese political spectrum in the 1930s –
was not everyone's cup of tea. Kagawa's union rivals in particular
were incensed by what they saw as his utopian gradualism and bourgeois time-wasting. 'Down with the hermit monk!' they shouted, as
his star waned across the second half of 1921. 'Down with the boss
of the beggars!'

These seemingly rather odd epithets were a dig at Kagawa's notorious living arrangements. More than a decade previously, he had
moved to Kobe's Shinkawa neighbourhood, one of Japan's most
notorious slums. There he took his place among around 10,000
people crammed without sanitation into tightly packed wooden hut-
like housing – a conflagration waiting to happen, homes heated as
they were by charcoal-burners and dimly lit with kerosene lamps.
Many of Shinkawa's residents were migrants from the countryside,
who had headed to Kobe in search of work, but who had found
instead various combinations of extreme poverty, exploitation,
gambling, alcoholism, prostitution, disease and crime.

Kagawa first gained a reputation in the neighbourhood as someone
who kept ghosts at bay, after surviving a few nights in a two-room
dwelling believed to be haunted by the ghost of a man recently beaten
to death there. He was soon room-mates with 'the copper statue' – an

alcoholic turned red and stuporous by drink – and with a bean-cake dealer who was sure he was being followed by the ghost of a man he had killed for overturning his cart. The latter could only sleep if Kagawa held his hand.

Kagawa became known, too, as an easy mark. People came seeking money or clothes at the point of a knife or gun. On one occasion, a well-aimed punch parted Kagawa from his four front teeth. On another, a man challenged Kagawa to hand over his shirt – claiming that if he did not, his Christianity would be proved a sham. Unable to think of a strong come-back, Kagawa took off his shirt and handed it over. The man duly returned the next day for his trousers and coat, leaving Kagawa sporting a red woman's kimono given to him by a neighbour – for the wearing of which he earned himself the nickname *Baka* (idiot).

If Taihoku was Gotō Shinpei's 'laboratory', the Shinkawa slum was Kagawa's. Both men used that same word, implying the application of experimental science, to describe their adopted homes. Kagawa's many institutional projects included experiments with cooperatives, designed to help people get hold of cheap food and medical care and eventually to work in a business they themselves owned. He set up a restaurant called Tengokuya (Heaven's Place), along with a toothbrush-making concern.

All of this, combined with a bestselling memoir, *Shisen Wo Koete* (*Across the Death-Line*), brought Kagawa a degree of fame both at home and abroad that after a while he found it hard to live without. He told one admirer that he was destined to become more famous than Itō Hirobumi – after all, even people in Sweden had heard of him. And he made numerous trips to the United States, where people on the lookout for a Far Eastern Tolstoy or Gandhi welcomed him with open arms.

The same criticisms that Mahatma Gandhi faced in India dogged Kagawa in Japan. His religious convictions might be genuine enough, but was he really the solution to the problems of modernity and a mass society? He struck some as a media-savvy egotist, adept at telling different people what they wanted to hear, diluting much-needed radicalism with spiritual platitudes, and in the end only too happy to work with an oppressive state when it suited him. He carried out research on social policy for the government in the mid-1920s, and participated in an official drive to teach rural people money-saving modern habits, including the use of a communal village clock. Years later, Kagawa dismayed his admirers by dining with one of Japan's arch-imperialists – the sincerity of whose '[Asian] continental policy', claimed Kagawa, 'almost brought me to tears'.

The truth, however, was that battle lines in 1920s and 1930s Japan – bosses versus workers, state versus its critics – were rarely clear or uncrossable. Both Kagawa and the workers of Kobe found themselves increasingly drawn, during these years, to some rather unlikely champions of radical change: civil servants.

This was a group of people associated, in the early Meiji era, with such close and cosy relationships to business that when in the mid-1880s fish started to float down the oddly coloured water of the Watarase and Tone rivers – either dead or so lifeless that they could be caught by hand – civil servants had first agreed to turn a blind eye. It was obvious that effluent from the nearby Ashio Copper Mine was causing the trouble, which extended in later years to dramatic floods when the mine's need for lumber resulted in major deforestation nearby. Denials and stalling from government and business alike brought some of modern Japan's first environmental protestors onto the streets. One group of farmers even tried to march on Tokyo, only to find that quick-thinking police had dismantled a major bridge along their route. The numbers that dribbled into the capital were, in the end, too small to make much of a difference. Only very belatedly was the mine-owner forced to spend more than a million yen cleaning up his operation.

But as the state and its power grew, so too did the number of civil servants. There were around 1.3 million of them across the country by the end of 1928 – roughly 5 per cent of everyone in work – ranging from police and teachers in government schools to diplomats and higher-level ministry bureaucrats based in Tokyo. These last were a class apart. They had been through Japan's top schools, on to Tokyo Imperial University (where the overwhelming majority specialized in law), and had passed higher-level civil service exams that were legendary for their exceedingly high failure rate. At the very top of the civil service were career bureaucrats fulfilling roles like bureau chief, prefectural governor and vice minister.

It was bureaucrats in the Home Ministry in particular who over time became known for a keen interest in managing Japan's process of industrialization, not least by addressing left-wing concerns and activism before they boiled over. The Ministry attracted few recruits from Japan's business-owning families; most were instead the sons of government officials or military men. And it was a sign of their growing independence from industrial interests that Japanese business leaders complained about young bureaucrats being sent abroad only to return home with the unrealistic ambition of grafting Western labour laws onto a Japanese system (part of an enduring trend in modern Japan for painting the inconvenient as culturally inappropriate).

Success in their social management endeavours required three things: good information, influence at all levels of society and a reputation for acting neutrally in the national interest. Home Ministry civil servants increasingly enjoyed the first two, at least. Behind some of the stand-out progressive moments of the 1920s, from universal male suffrage to poverty relief to support for workers' organizations, lay their research and negotiation and policy-making. Bureaucrats imagined their task in the grandest of terms. They favoured a concept of 'moral suasion' (*kyōka*), steeped in a combination of Tokugawa-era neo-Confucianism and more recent gleanings from American and European social policy. One of the leading lights of the Home Ministry's Social Bureau, Yasui Eiji, wrote proudly in 1923 of 'the state's transcendent position above the classes'.

Campaigns of mass cajolery dated back to a Local Improvement Campaign, beginning in 1906. Tokyo bureaucrats had worked then to rationalize local governance and worship alike, including the steady replacement of folk shrines with state-sponsored ones – a move which helped to inspire Yanagita Kunio's fondness for folklore. And they had done their best to chivvy the peasantry into working harder, paying their proper taxes and splashing less of their cash on alcohol and festivities. Critically important to success, they found, was collaboration with local interest groups, including youth organizations.

The state even took to creating its own interest groups. In 1924, a National Federation of Moral Suasion Groups was established, overseeing several hundred such groups just a year later. Civil servants' major target audience were the educated, professional urban middle classes – a demographic they well understood, since they were part of it themselves. When the Ministry of Education launched a daily life improvement campaign, presenting particular ways of living – from home economics to personal hygiene – as desirable in scientific and even civilizational terms, they were essentially reaching out to the kinds of people with whom they had gone to school and university.

Such close class and cultural ties (rather belying the fantasy of transcendence) helped these self-styled 'shepherds of the people' to become steadily more adept at giving particular groups in Japanese society what they wanted – or what they could be persuaded they wanted. Middle-class women pressing for access to politics found the House of Peers implacably opposed, but the civil service willing to work with them in reinterpreting 'politics': away from power (which they couldn't have) and instead towards influence (which they could). Leading women educators were persuaded to take on roles in the Ministry of Education's League for Daily Life Improvement, while more broadly the professional 'housewife' (*shufu*) emerged in state propaganda and allied media and consumer culture as a centrally important figure, not just in the family, but in Japanese life more broadly.

The feminist writer Hiratsuka Raichō had once eviscerated her country's familial arrangements, claiming that women were merely 'their husbands' slaves during the daytime and their prostitutes at night'. But she found later that the experience of bringing up two small children while looking after her ailing partner changed her view of the state, from patriarchal and backward to at least potentially benevolent. In particular, the idea that it might step in to offer financial help to mothers in pregnancy, childbirth and the early years of raising children seemed an eminently sensible one.

Yosano Akiko, famous for her anti-war poem during Japan's conflict with Russia, thought very differently: mothers who did deals with the state were accepting at best a very limited view of womanhood, and at worst a 'slave morality' of dependence. Mothers in need of help shouldn't be asking *Where's my handout?* but rather *Where's my husband?* Family life ought to be equal, and as little as possible of the state's business.

Such debates were had around the world during these years, but in Japan Hiratsuka's view steadily won out. Children, it was argued, were ultimately the property of society and the state. So the state contributing financially to the welfare of mothers, even providing incentives for them to have more children, represented both sound resource management – more troops on the way – and a means by which women could play a strategic role in the nation's affairs.

Christian social reformers were welcomed into the fold too – for their energy, education, contacts and on-the-ground knowledge of urban and rural poverty. When the economic devastation of the Great Depression in the early 1930s condemned countless rural girls to urban prostitution, the Women's Patriotic Association and the Women's Christian Temperance Union joined forces with bureaucrats to fight it, not least by helping the police to crack down on the westernized licentiousness of café culture. The police objected to the 'western' part, the WCTU to the licentiousness – and both were happy to call their stances 'patriotism'.

*

Even after Kagawa embarked on his limited cooperation with the authorities, he faced repeated arrest for his speeches and writings. In his ideal world, bureaucrats would end up on the side of the angels – state power in the end just another instrument of divine 'other power'. The reality was that across the 1920s, into the early 1930s, the Japanese authorities operated a pincer movement consisting of cajolery alongside compulsion. It had never been possible to say simply whatever came into your head. 'Preservation of the peace' was an aspect of the Meiji Constitution that the police were inclined to take most seriously. And as Japan's civil servants progressively co-opted causes that they could live with, they became less and less inclined to hear from those they couldn't.

From 1928, one could be charged – and face the death penalty – for 'crimes against the *kokutai*', the 'national body', with the Emperor at its head. Most of those targeted first were calling for left-wing revolutionary change. But the bounds of acceptable speech quickly contracted from there. It became possible for a Tokyo University law professor (Minobe Tatsukichi) who dared to suggest that the Emperor was an organ of the state, rather than mystically coterminous with it, to be denounced in the upper house of the Diet as an 'academic tramp', censured by both houses, attacked by army veterans, and even threatened with death.

Japan's law enforcement arrangements evolved in tandem with this narrowing national mood. Articles published in the *Keisatsu Kyōkai Zasshi* ('Police Association Bulletin') had once called for Japanese officers to develop a British-style tradition of policing by consent: maximizing authority while minimizing violent intervention. Instead, they were becoming known now, both at home and abroad, for extreme brutality and for a high number of deaths in custody – particularly of socialists and communists. The earlier desire for a *kokumin keisatsu* – a 'people's police', or 'a police for the people' – turned into a 1930s slogan of *tennō no keisatsu*: 'the Emperor's police'.

Most feared of all was the Special Higher Police (*Tokkō*), created back in 1911 after the attempt on the Meiji Emperor's life. Its brief was to tackle unwelcome ideologies and 'thought crimes' of all kinds. And its methods were appropriately psychological. One manual for interrogators warned officers to avoid politics, since radicals were often better educated than they were. Instead, they should play family off against comrades. A warm bowl of *oyako-donburi* (chicken and egg on rice) could be put in front of a recalcitrant detainee. *Your mother's worried about you*, the interrogator would say. *Why don't you eat up, forget all this silliness, and go home?*

With luck, *tenkō* ('conversion') and a confession would follow. Both were already features of Japanese law: philosophical principles of harmony and welcoming transgressors back into the fold dictated that punishment could be waived or leavened for the truly contrite. But they could also be useful in encouraging changes of heart in other detainees, as well as yielding additional arrests. And if homely cuisine failed to do the trick, there was always starvation, solitary confinement, physical torture and the sheer uncertainty and fatigue of indeterminate detention – the law on custody was circumvented simply by releasing a defendant and then re-arresting him or her at the door of the police station.

All this was about more than official detestation of left-wing politics, deeply concerned though the authorities were at the Russian Revolution and political uncertainty across Europe. By the early

1930s, decades of steady Japanese expansion in Asia and a progressive loss of trust with erstwhile Western allies looked like bringing international tensions to a head. Moral suasion, the co-option of prominent leaders and causes, the suppression of dissent: such things were no longer just about social management and salving modernity's wounds. They were about preparing to fight what might be a very long war.

9
Theatre

Into the darkness shone a light. Blue, artificial light, emanating from atop the waters of the Yangtze and Huangpu rivers. From the land picked out by its broad beams came a barrage of answering mortar fire. But the intense illumination remained steady, undimmed. The first hours of 23 August 1937. The stage was set.

It had taken nearly six years for the players and props to assemble, and for the script to take shape. Much of that activity was directed not from the Diet building or civilian ministries in Tokyo, but by small groups of army officers and civilian activists meeting in secret at home and abroad. They confided to one another their disgust at the lack of vision and backbone shown by their country's so-called leaders. And together they plotted small acts of violence – a blend of strategy and theatrical symbolism – that were designed to prepare the way for a much larger performance.

One of the first of those acts was the planting of a bomb near the tracks of the South Manchuria Railway (SMR) in September 1931, not far from Mukden, scene of the greatest land battle of the Russo-Japanese War. Damage to the track was negligible – a train passed safely across just minutes later. But bodies dressed in Chinese military uniform were 'found' at the scene, and immediately the cries went up. Sabotage! Revenge! Punishment!

The loudest of these voices belonged to the people who had in fact plotted the explosion: officers of Japan's Kwantung Army, who were responsible for security in the area. Lt Colonel Ishiwara Kanji was a convert to Nichiren Buddhism, and had spent the last few years turning that sect's teachings into predictions of an apocalyptic conflict destined to sweep the globe, drench it in blood, and finally make possible the peace that had for so long eluded humankind.

And if that sounds to you like the Great War, Ishiwara was fond of telling students at the Army Staff College, *then you're wrong.* The war to come would make the one just gone look like a stripped-back dress rehearsal. And this time Japan's role would be as principal player, pitted, at long last, against the United States – a conflict Japan had been destined to fight ever since Commodore Perry had sailed into its waters demanding peaceful relations at the point of a gun.

But for the apocalypse to go Japan's way, the country must first clean up its backyard. European imperialists were still crawling all over East and South East Asia. Chiang Kai-shek's Nationalists were steadily putting China's pieces back together. Godless Soviet troops were tramping eastward in ever greater numbers. And to top it all off, Asia-Pacific soil and seas were sprouting American bases and battleships at an alarming rate. What more did people want, by way of signs and omens? And could anyone doubt that without the rich resources of Manchuria, Japan was entirely without hope?

And yet Japanese diplomats, Ishiwara worried, remained incapable of saying 'no' to the Americans and the British, allowing them to pass off their self-interested bullying as 'internationalism'. The latest insult was the London Naval Treaty of 1930. A follow-on from the Washington Naval Treaty a few years before, it was intended to govern vessel numbers and tonnage for the world's great seafaring powers. But its terms put Japan in such a perilously weak position that even Diet politicians – for whom the likes of Ishiwara generally had very little time – condemned it as a betrayal of the country's security interests. Fights broke out in the chamber. Ashtrays were thrown. Then later that year a gunman took matters a step further, shooting and seriously wounding Prime Minister Hamaguchi Osachi at Tokyo Station – not far from where Prime Minister Hara had been stabbed to death nine years before. By this time, Ishiwara had had himself transferred to the Kwantung Army, where, with the help of funding from ultranationalist groups back home, he had spread his gospel of the coming apocalypse and helped to hatch the plan that opened with such a satisfying bang at Mukden.

The next stages of the scheme, following what became known as the Mukden or the Manchurian 'Incident', went equally well. While a new prime minister, Wakatsuki Reijirō, tried to reassure the international press that his country would not engage in hostilities in Manchuria, and urgent military orders to that effect came in from Tokyo, the commander of the Kwantung Army gave Ishiwara his blessing to do what had to be done. Amidst a flurry of new Chinese 'threats' and 'insults' to Japanese interests, the Kwantung Army began to take control of the region, bit by bit.

As politicians in Tokyo tried to find ways of convincing domestic and international audiences that goings-on in Manchuria remained under their control and within their definition of not gratuitously expanding hostilities, crowds in Osaka gathered in a park to cheer footage of the fighting – flown in especially by an enterprising news organization. Few newspapers questioned the Kwantung Army's version of events. The Chinese were the aggressors, and so must pay. Nor was there much sympathy for politicians' protestations. By December Wakatsuki realized that he had been outpaced by events, and overtaken by the public mood. He and his Cabinet resigned.

By 1 March 1932, the job was done. A new state, 'Manchukuo', was declared, with arrangements for governance entirely in keeping with modern Japan's turning of many centuries of East Asian history on its head. A man by the name of Puyi, the last of an illustrious line of Chinese emperors synonymous with the effortless pre-eminence in Asia of that country's culture, would serve now as Japan's puppet ruler and plaything.

The waters from where the blue light shone were a mystery to the Chinese forces on land. There had been no aerial reconnaissance of this portion of the coast. So they had no idea that thousands of Japanese troops were out there, waiting quietly aboard transport ships for the order to attack.

They found out just before dawn. From the direction of the light came artillery fire, ripping through Chinese positions. Navy planes suddenly appeared overhead, tearing up the roads to stop fresh units coming in to help these few coastal defenders – whom Japanese intelligence officers had promised would be far from the cream of the crop. Last came the crash and splash of amphibious landings, as soldiers rushed ashore to begin a thirty-mile push south towards Asia's second largest city after Tokyo: Shanghai.

Parts of that city, home to 3.5 million people, had turned into a war zone in recent days, with much of the violence focused on the district of Hongkou. 'Little Tokyo', as it was known, was home to Japanese businesses, the consulate and around 2,500 marines, entrusted with the security of Shanghai's 20,000 Japanese residents. Japan had left the League of Nations four years earlier in 1933, over the organization's criticism of events in Manchuria. The leader of the Japanese delegation had declared, as he stormed out, that his country was being 'crucified' by world opinion and, like Jesus of Nazareth, would one day be properly understood. Tensions in East Asia had risen further from there, to the point where in the end all it took for war to erupt in the summer of 1937 was a single, poorly timed toilet break.

After a brief exchange of fire in July, between Chinese troops and Japanese soldiers stationed near Beijing, as part of an international contingent in the city, a Japanese soldier had wandered off to relieve himself. An attempt to search for him had led to a second incident, which at first was settled, but which soon – with leaders on both sides under pressure to put on a show of resolve – deteriorated into all-out war. With Beijing in Japanese hands by the end of the month, Chiang Kai-shek had sent 100,000 troops into Shanghai to try to secure it. He had sent planes too, which consistently missed the Japanese warship *Izumo*, anchored in the Huangpu river, and instead hit civilian areas including a busy street near the six-storey Great World Amusement Centre. Hundreds were killed, joined by many more as Japanese planes targeted railway stations just as Shanghai residents were trying to leave for the safety of the countryside.

The global reach of Western imperialism, which so enraged the likes of Ishiwara, started to tell as foreign residents rushed to escape a city descending into chaos. British refugees left on an ocean liner that was made in Glasgow, named after one corner of the British Empire (*Rajputana*) and sailing now for another: Hong Kong. Americans, in similar fashion, escaped to Manila. Chinese residents had to make do with any foreign section of the city that would open its doors, or else drape British and American flags from their windows in hope of being spared the increasingly paranoid attentions of Chinese and Japanese forces on the lookout for enemy soldiers in civilian dress.

The Japanese marines in Shanghai set up barriers of concrete and barbed wire, hauled machine guns and sandbags into place, and deployed tanks and flame-throwers, hoping to hold out until their comrades completed their thirty-mile trek down from the north. But the Shanghai Expeditionary Force had become stuck near to where it had landed, pinned down by heavier than expected resistance from the Chinese. Its commander, General Matsui Iwane, found himself having to put in a request to Tokyo for more men. He was very nearly refused. For Ishiwara Kanji, now head of the General Staff Operations Division, the full-on conflict with China that he had helped to start had come too soon. The Japanese Navy should be asked to help out in Shanghai, he argued. We must leave the army free to secure Japan's position further north.

But permission was eventually given for three new army divisions to be sent over from Japan, alongside units from Taiwan. The provocateur Ishiwara resigned in disgust, as preparations were made for hundreds of thousands of men to receive a life-changing piece of post: an *akagami* ('red letter'), calling them up to serve.

Japanese Imperial Army soldiers during the Battle for Shanghai, summer 1937

*

One of the *akagami* of mid-1937 found its way into the hands of Sakaue Rikichi, the son of tenant farmers in the centuries-old Kosugi *mura* (Kosugi village) in Niigata prefecture. The more that Japan's leaders had seemed to lavish their love, time and resources on the country's growing cities in recent decades, the keener people in villages like this one had become to defend the agrarian way of life – as the true source of this 'Japanese spirit' about which their distant rulers never seemed to stop talking. It was a sign of just how wide the gulf in understanding between city and countryside could become that for one farmer from Ibaraki prefecture the great earthquake of 1923 appeared to be a cosmic judgement rendered against Tokyo by the earth itself:

> Of late, the vainglorious striving of [these] city people had reached extremes that caused poor, simple farmers no end of anxiety. With their elegant clothes and their gold teeth, gold rings, and gold watch chains, they flitted from one lavish social affair to another . . . But now all that has vanished as if in a dream, consumed by fire, and suddenly they find themselves reduced to misery. It seems that Heaven found it necessary to chastise them with a natural disaster in order to protect the nation.

The approving mention of the 'nation' suggested that, despite periodic eruptions of rural discontent, Japan's modern state-builders had not entirely failed in their task. Primary schools and tax offices had become accepted features of the rural landscape, binding the hearts of the young and the pockets of their parents to a series of previously unthinkable national goals.

Although rural boys and girls sat through similar lessons to their gold-toothed urban counterparts (albeit that attendance rates were generally lower in the countryside), and followed baseball just as avidly, there lingered a powerful sense that struggling rural communities were being asked to subsidize suspect urban aspirations. Anger peaked whenever the rural economy appeared most clearly to have been sacrificed for such things: when produce prices fell or were kept artificially low, or when the cost of essentials, from schoolbooks to silk-farming supplies, rose.

Alternately the object of swooning urban romanticism and

journalistic wonderment at the primitive 'rat's nest' conditions that prevailed in regions like Tōhoku – dubbed 'Japan's Tibet' – rural Japanese felt their vulnerability as never before in the early years of the worldwide Great Depression from 1929. Cash incomes fell from an index of 100 in 1926 to just 33 in 1931, climbing back only to 44 by 1934. Korean and Taiwanese rice imports had been keeping prices perilously low in recent years (urban stomachs apparently more of a political priority than rural ones), and then with a bumper crop in 1930 the floor fell away completely.

As a child, Rikichi had helped to produce boxes of silk cocoons to supplement his family's income: feeding the silkworms their mulberry leaves and shoots (often bought on credit), and keeping them at just the right temperature and humidity. Now, the price suddenly collapsed. Farm girls returned from closed-down silk mills. And as a flood of workless urbanites returned to the *furusato* – the 'home towns' often so misleadingly eulogized in city songs – a truly miserable migration got going in the opposite direction: young country girls were sent to work in the cities as prostitutes, some 16,000 from Tōhoku alone in the first half of 1931. Many more were taken away to labour as waitresses.

A father didn't have to be especially sentimental or politically aware to see that when city types first starved his family, then carted off his daughter to serve or service them, something had gone very seriously wrong with the world. Rural Japan needed to make its voice heard, now more than ever. And for that it needed allies. Fortunately, it had one very powerful ally indeed: the Imperial Japanese Army (IJA), which recruited overwhelmingly from the Japanese countryside and had a far better claim than the country's civilian leadership to be interested in its welfare.

The people who built Japan's new armed forces, from the late nineteenth century on, had made a deliberate break with the samurai past. The days of personal loyalty to a regional lord were over. They wanted a national organization populated by ordinary people who would take orders. Technology could take care of the rest. So farmers were recruited, force-fed stolid, starchy Western food, ordered to cram themselves into constricting Western trousers and boots, and introduced for the first time to everything from electric lighting and indoor stoves to the convenience of answering a call of nature indoors rather than squatting in some remote location with a few pages of the local newspaper to hand. Many conscripts even got their first taste of clock-time in the army, with classes arranged strictly according to a timetable composed of minutes and hours.

The army and navy's victories over China and then Russia had given their recruits and their civilian fans much to be proud of. And yet by the late 1920s they were struggling. Army and navy bureaux warred with one another over funds and strategic priorities, the former looking to mainland Asia for their enemies (Chinese and Russians) while the latter naturally saw danger on the high seas (British and Americans).

Inside the army itself, once its founding father Yamagata Aritomo left the scene, space opened up for a new generation of officers to fight over positions of power and over fundamental approaches to Japan's security predicament. An influential Kōdōha ('Imperial Way Faction') counted among its leaders General Araki Sadao, a man so fond of the army's samurai myth that he set up a foundry to produce Kamakura-era samurai swords (to replace the flimsy and unromantic French sabre favoured by officers in the modern army) and forbade the use in army literature of the words 'retreat', 'defence' and 'surrender'. Kōdōha insisted on the centrality of the Japanese spirit to the success, past and future, of the IJA, an idea that went back to the early Meiji army, whose leaders regarded surviving a lost battle as an indicator of poor or insufficient spirit, and an insult to the Emperor. Death was the gold standard.

Like many elements of what ideologues claimed was Japan's timeless uniqueness, this was a mostly modern and largely German idea. The famous refrain that 'duty is heavier than a mountain, death lighter than a feather' dated back not to some medieval hero but to 1882, and an Imperial Rescript to Soldiers and Sailors that demanded they be honest, absolute in their obedience – since their orders came ultimately from the Emperor himself – and fastidious about not involving themselves in politics. The emphasis on 'spirit' had been encouraged by a Prussian tactician by the name of Major Klemens Wilhelm Jakob Meckel, who worked as an adviser to the IJA in the second half of the 1880s. Even the best weaponry and fail-safe strategies are not enough to ensure victory, he claimed. One needs elan, fighting spirit and a hunger for making the first, offensive move. Such became the Japanese strategy against Russia in 1904: war was waged first and declared later.

Heirs to this wisdom, Kōdōha members insisted that Japan should plan for short, aggressive wars. Soldiers should be trained in the art of the breakthrough bayonet charge, the dawn attack and the rapid encirclement – the triumph of spirit over superior enemy numbers and armaments. Meanwhile, a loose-knit Tōseiha ('Control Faction') was formed to oppose these ideas, its members arguing instead that war was, now more than ever, an industrial endeavour. If Japan hoped ever to win a serious conflict again, it should play a cautious diplomatic game for a few years yet, taking its time to steer the economy towards the sustained production of the kind of modern weaponry the army still lacked. For the Kōdōha, such talk was close to defeatism.

One thing army officers did seem to agree on was the usefulness of violence, not just against the enemy but against its own soldiers. New recruits like Rikichi suffered brutal tests of discipline: soldiers forced to stand to attention all day, with no break, or given character-building beatings. And all this for mere pennies per month. No surprise, then, that very few people volunteered to serve and that some young men actively tried to dodge the draft – drinking soy sauce to raise their blood pressure, starving themselves so as to fail the weight qualification, moving to remote Hokkaidō or Okinawa, or making furtive shrine visits to pray to the gods to spare them any correspondence printed on red paper.

Of course, for a soldier to have complained about such vulgar topics as money or his own personal welfare would have been to invite yet more violence – by day on the training ground or by night inside the barracks. He served at the pleasure of the Emperor, after all, whose property he wore on his body and held in his hands – the breeches of army rifles were stamped with the imperial crest, lest anyone forget why they were holding them. He had been welcomed into a new home – commissioned officers served as parents, second-year soldiers as elder brothers. And recruited into his unit alongside others from his village it would be hard to forget the hopes invested in him by the community back home. Entering the army in the 1930s was, in any case, a natural transition from childhood: from an education that increasingly equated the military with the best of modernity; from martial exercises and games; from stagey military funerals that were sometimes hosted in school playgrounds.

'Every citizen a soldier' was, in Japan, not some last-ditch doctrine for when a war looked lost. It was a peacetime policy that went back to the years following the Russo-Japanese War, evident in education, in the local improvement campaigns beloved of Japan's bureaucrats, and most literally in the creation of the Teikoku Zaigō Gunjinkai, the Imperial Military Reserve Association (IMRA), responsible ultimately to the Army Minister. Once a young man had completed his required national service, he became a member of the IMRA, through whose thousands of local branches the life and values of that national service lived on: solidarity, cooperation and respect for the locally influential men – often mayors or school headmasters – who doubled as branch leaders. Here was a tremendously influential organization, boasting 3 million members by 1936. Many of those were increasingly angry at Tokyo politicians whom they regarded as starving the countryside to such a degree that enormous numbers of young men were now too malnourished to make the cut for military service. Here was graphic proof of the spiritual poverty of contemporary politics, and the urgent need for change.

At last, in the summer of 1937, dithering turned to action and rural Japan was about to get its say. Rikichi was one among nearly half a million boys and men – mostly from the reserves – seen off from their villages amidst celebrations that for some families cost as much as a wedding. *Sake* was drunk at the Sakaue home. A family photograph was taken at the local shrine, complete with rising sun banners inscribed with Rikichi's name and a promise to fight well. The next day, flag-waving children of the local elementary school turned out to see Rikichi off, joined at the local train station by white-sashed members of the Patriotic Women's Association – providing refreshment and encouragement.

Much was expected – and so much had to be promised. One new recruit, Nagatani Masao, recounted in his diary:

> Dad came to the 12 p.m. visiting hours. I promised that I would become a splendid man . . . I don't know where we're going, but when the faces

of those who came to see us off come to mind . . . unable to withstand the sincerity and emotion of the people of the prefecture, we were resolved.

From their regional barracks, Rikichi, Masao and all the others were funnelled onto trains and then cramped transport ships reeking of rotten food, unwashed bodies and the inevitable consequences of farmers taking to the sea for the first time. After a few days spent in extremes of heat then cold, soldiers landed in China and saw for the first time the reality of what faced them. The first thing many did was buy life insurance. Even the costliest policy suddenly seemed a grimly good bet.

*

Thirty-year-old Maebara Hisashi's war began in bathetic anti-climax, stuck in the mud with the expeditionary force, still a long way north of Shanghai. Then a Chinese artillery round came out of nowhere, sending shrapnel tearing through eighteen of his friends nearby. With barely any time to register what had just happened, Maebara was ordered to cremate their remains, say a prayer for them, and then bag up the bones to send back to their families. The easiest way to do it was usually to tear down a nearby farm building and use its beams for firewood. The method was 'like baking sardines', remarked one soldier – and just as anonymous: after rain stopped the bodies from burning, families back in Japan eventually received fragments of what was often the same dead soldier, each pack labelled as their loved one.

Fear, anger and a desire for revenge built quickly as battlefield scenes like this were repeated time and again, and soldiers were cut loose from their supply lines – forced to pick wild berries, steal chickens or hack away at the earth until they found some potatoes. The plunder of the local landscape soon morphed into attacks on Chinese passers-by, whether or not they were suspected of being spies. Maebara watched three young men have their heads inexpertly hacked from their bodies, by soldiers who promised to 'do better next time'.

Elsewhere, brutality was performed in order to give new recruits the necessary 'baptism of blood'. Sometimes it would be a 'live bayonet exercise' using Chinese prisoners. For Tominaga Shōzō, it involved a trip to a remote field, where he and others under consideration for officer rank were introduced to the 'raw materials for [a] trial of courage': starving Chinese prisoners, hooded, kneeling next to a hole in the ground, ten metres long by two metres wide. A senior officer took out his sword, poured water onto both sides of the blade, steadied his body as though for a golf swing, and beheaded the first of the kneeling men. Tominaga's turn eventually came. When it was over, he found his sword was slightly bent and wouldn't go back into its sheath quite as easily as before. But 'I felt something change inside me', he later recalled. 'I don't know how to put it, but I gained strength somewhere in my gut.'

As summer turned to autumn, creeks north of Shanghai started to fill with the still-kneeling bodies of beheaded Chinese soldiers, tumbling along in the water. Chinese morale was failing rapidly, but there were few desertions – for fear not of what might happen if their superiors caught them, but of what might happen if the Japanese did. Neither side in the conflict had the resources or the inclination to keep hold of the prisoners they took.

All the while, senior figures representing both armies gave daily press conferences in the city, taking care to time them so that one would not overlap with the other. Pacifying and persuading the press mattered a great deal. Hoping that a gesture of civility might help counter a growing reputation for brutality, the Japanese military served tea, coffee, whisky and beer at theirs. For the Chinese, the fighting around Shanghai was going so badly that by late October their best hope was that foreign outrage at the barbarism and death toll might prompt military intervention.

Most of these killings and cruelties were, on the Japanese side, the work of reservists hauled out of civilian life and thrown into what came to be called the 'meat-grinder' of the Shanghai conflict. But not all of them were. Alongside uniformed Japanese soldiers, foreign correspondents reported seeing on the streets of Shanghai roving bands of Japanese men in civilian dress, gathering intelligence for the military and murdering any Chinese whom they thought might be spies.

'Tough, long-haired, sly as snakes', with revolvers and knives tucked into their waists, these were *tairiku rōnin*, or 'continental adventurers': the export version of a modern domestic tradition of political violence, born with the mid-nineteenth century *shishi*, which by the time war broke out in China had helped to bring Japan's home islands to the brink of chaos.

Before they were great statesmen, many of the early Meiji leaders had been violent men. The ideal of righteous conflict that launched the imperial restoration of 1868 lived on afterwards in various forms: Saigō Takamori's 1877 rebellion; ultranationalist organizations like the Gen'yōsha (Dark Ocean Society) and the Kokuryūkai (Black Dragon Society); and *sōshi* – political thugs for hire. The new Diet building in Tokyo had been playing host, since the 1890s, to artfully dishevelled, swaggering young men with long hair and loud voices, carrying pistols, swords or swordsticks (canes with a blade embedded in the end). Some hung around outside, waiting for a particular politician to emerge – either a target or a patron in need of protection. Others wandered the corridors inside, intimidating politicians who, it was said, would often turn up to work in bandages. One politician had his *sōshi* beat a rival with brass candlesticks in the middle of a public meeting – for calling him a peasant. Soon the use of *sōshi* became so institutionalized that political parties actively and openly recruited them from Japan's criminal fraternity, gave them weapons training (including fencing classes), and incorporated them into bureaucratized 'pressure groups' that were straightforwardly divided into *interidan* (intelligence group) and *bōryokudan* (violent group).

The rise of communism and union activism helped to produce new groups, like the Dai Nihon Kokusuikai (Greater Japan National Essence Association), which brought together public figures (including Gotō Shinpei), construction companies and *yakuza* (gangsters) to intimidate workers and break strikes. The Kokusuikai had around 200,000 members by the early 1930s, and was very public about what it claimed were its patriotic aims – on one occasion showering bewildered Tokyoites with 10,000 promotional handbills, dropped from an aeroplane.

Links with political violence soon became yet another item to add to a charge-sheet against Japan's party politicians that already included greed, gratuitous squandering of the nation's energies in fighting one another (in the party-political sense, but often in actual Diet brawls) and gross incompetence of the sort that impoverished the countryside and imperilled national security. Nowhere did politics seem more broken and bereft of new ideas than in Hibiya Park one day when the Seiyūkai party reacted to a demonstration against Diet violence by sending along party thugs disguised as journalists (complete with fake business cards) to try to disrupt it.

Army idealists sought to combat this sorry state of affairs with violence of their own. In 1931, a group of civilians and young military officers calling themselves the Cherry Blossom Society made plans for a military coup whose scale of ambition bordered on the surreal: the centrepiece was to be an airstrike on the Prime Minister and his Cabinet. General Araki, of the Kōdōha faction, whose support the young officers expected, eventually persuaded them to turn themselves in to military police.

But a civilian 'Blood Brotherhood' – their slogan: 'One Member, One Death'– succeeded in early 1932 in killing a former finance minister and the managing director of Mitsui. This was one of four big conglomerates, along with Mitsubishi, Sumitomo and Yasuda, which survived the worst of the Great Depression only to fall foul of public opinion by making enormous sums of money betting against the yen just before Japan left the gold standard in late 1931. Such was the atmosphere in the country by this point that Mitsui's response to the assassination was not outrage but apology, and the doling out of large sums of money to patriotic charitable causes. Mitsubishi and Sumitomo quickly followed suit.

Two more acts of destabilizing, game-changing violence were to come. On 15 May 1932, a group of rogue naval officers shot Prime Minister Inukai Tsuyoshi dead in his home, while elsewhere in Tokyo police boxes, banks and political party headquarters were attacked with hand grenades. Then in February 1936, a coup attempt led by junior army officers linked to the Kōdōha faction got as far as encircling the Diet and army HQ with more than a thousand troops. Only when the navy brought forty ships into Tokyo Bay – guns aimed at the rebel soldiers – and loyalist army divisions arrived on the scene, did the coup start to falter. Finally, Emperor Hirohito, who had ascended the chrysanthemum throne a decade earlier (his era known as Shōwa or 'shining harmony'), took the unusual step of expressing his personal displeasure at the events unfolding in his capital. The coup came to an abrupt end, after three days of knife-edge uncertainty.

The 1936 plotters and others in Japan who hoped for a 'Shōwa Restoration' – overthrowing the democratic political order and returning Japan to 'true' imperial rule – never saw their wishes come true. But they managed nevertheless to nudge that political order in significant new directions. After the death of Prime Minister Inukai, the sense grew stronger that Japan's problems required a more specialized, technocratic approach than party politicians alone could offer. Only Cabinets of national unity, it came to be thought, could hope to contain the discontent and violence at home while steering an increasingly isolated nation through choppy international waters.

So the ultimate beneficiaries of violence at home were Japan's civil servants. The technocratic, managerial utopia for which 'reform bureaucrats' in particular had been longing – as free as possible from self-interested party-political meddling – seemed finally to be within sight. New super-agencies would soon be created to encourage cooperation across ministries, and between civilian and military planners. New laws would be passed, enhancing state power at the expense of employers and workers alike. Japan would see little of the demagoguery, pomp or mass rallying that marked political transformation in Italy and Germany. Nevertheless, its leaders were reaching similar conclusions: for newcomers to modern statehood, the difference between managing, controlling and coercing a population ought only to be one of degrees – a dial to be turned as the situation dictated.

*

The first hours of 5 November 1937: red lights, two of them, shine from atop the sea towards the land. They pick out locations on the coast, this time south of Shanghai. Thousands more Japanese soldiers are about to land, barely ten weeks after the original expeditionary force landed to the city's north. The 200 ships that carry them have approached with their lights turned off, radios silent. Once again, there has been no Chinese aerial reconnaissance. So once again the

Pro-government soldiers guard the Diet building during the
26 February incident, 1936

The Shōwa Emperor, pictured at his formal enthronement in 1928

few troops left defending the area around Hangzhou Bay have no idea what they are facing, until wave upon wave of Japanese soldiers appear in their midst.

Chinese commanders are convinced that all this must be a diversion from the fighting elsewhere. By the time they realize they are wrong, the incoming soldiers are advancing so quickly towards Shanghai that all they can do is turn and run, destroying the infrastructure around them as they go, in the hope of denying the enemy places to eat and sleep. The most that many Japanese soldiers see of their adversaries is a series of fires burning in the night.

Facing imminent encirclement, and with Western powers refusing to come to his aid – one of the last to say no is Stalin – Chiang Kai-shek orders his forces to withdraw completely from Shanghai. He has committed nearly half a million men to securing it, and the overwhelming majority of the conflict's 300,000 dead soldiers – not to mention countless dead civilians – lie on his side. But on 11 November 1937 the mayor of Shanghai makes the dreaded announcement: his city is now completely in Japanese hands.

Chinese forces beat a calamitous retreat westwards. Entire brigades desert, while other troops struggle to find good maps of the area, officers to guide them, or even the keys to the fortified structures from which they are expected to stop the Japanese from completing their long trek from Shanghai to their next target: the Nationalist capital, Nanjing. Much of China's government infrastructure – from employees to office equipment – has left Nanjing already. And at the beginning of December, Chiang Kai-shek decides that he too must go. He boards an aeroplane and flies out, leaving behind a contingent of Chinese troops to do what they can.

An enormous Japanese force is soon spotted approaching the city walls. Most of them are tired and hungry, better schooled in violence than young men like Rikichi could ever have imagined becoming. Discipline in the ranks is all but shredded. There will be no long-drawn-out battle for Nanjing, the way there was for Shanghai. These soldiers are not arriving, as they fear, at the gates of some fresh hell. They are bringing hell to the gates.

10

Divine Bluster

General Matsui Iwane made the same short journey every day. From his villa near the sea in Japan's Shizuoka prefecture he climbed a hill up towards a small Buddhist temple, not far from which stood a towering ten-foot statue of the bodhisattva of compassion, Kannon. She faced westwards in prayer, towards Nanjing.

It was her birthplace. Matsui had had her crafted out of earth brought back from the city, stained with the blood of the dead, in the hope that Kannon – literally 'the one who perceives sound' – would hear their cries and help their restless souls find peace.

On arriving at the great wall around Nanjing in early December 1937, Matsui had ordered his troops to stop and wait. More than ninety Japanese bombers had gone ahead, to soften up the Chinese defences inside the city and to assess the chances that a trap was being laid there. Matsui had a 'note of advice' dropped in by plane, counselling Chinese forces busy fortifying positions and barricading and sandbagging the city gates to surrender if they wanted to spare the city's beauty and their own lives. A deadline was set.

Both sides knew the Chinese position was hopeless; they were surrounded, with much of their leadership having left days and weeks before. Two dozen Japanese bombers were sent across from Shanghai, loaded not with ordnance but with champagne on ice: lubrication for the victory celebrations that commanders felt must be only days – perhaps hours – away. Back home in Japan, people in Tokyo were also feeling festive. Bunting was prepared for the façades of the War and Education ministries. Teachers made plans to march their pupils to the Imperial Palace.

But Iwane's deadline came and went without a response, and the first Japanese soldiers were ordered into the city on 10 December. Some scaled the surrounding walls by night, trying to win space atop them for machine-gun emplacements. The Chinese defenders consisted mostly of provincial troops, unpaid and armed only with basic rifles. Briefly they put up a level of resistance that surprised the Japanese, but soon they melted away. 'We are fighting against metal with merely our flesh and blood,' boasted their commander, before fleeing the city by boat.

Nanjing residents called for a short truce, so that shelters could be constructed for hundreds of thousands of people urgently in need of them. But their entreaties were ignored, and shortly after the Chungshan Gate fell on 13 December, the city was overrun.

Little news emerged at first of what was happening. Foreign journalists based nearby found that the usually solicitous and loquacious media representatives of the Imperial Japanese Army suddenly had little to tell them. 'Nanking's Silence Terrifies Shanghai', ran a headline in the *New York Times*.

But as international residents in Nanjing – journalists, missionaries, academics, welfare workers – scrambled to escape down the Yangtze River, many aboard the USS *Oahu*, they began to radio out news of a massacre. They had seen summary executions running into the hundreds, streets littered with corpses and abandoned Chinese uniforms. One journalist reported having dozens of guns thrust upon him by Chinese soldiers, anxious to surrender their weapons to the nearest foreigner before disappearing into the civilian crowd.

These were desperate strategies, and they met with mixed success. Many of the thousands of Japanese soldiers that now poured into Nanjing seemed uninterested in distinguishing combatants from noncombatants. Across the next few days and weeks, thousands of civilians of all ages were murdered, and countless women and girls were raped. City residents found themselves turfed out of their homes or forced to assist in the robbery of others. Wealthy-looking, Western-style properties were a first port of call. Soldiers used makeshift ladders to break in, stealing food, listening to records and ransacking rooms in search of gold.

Others roamed the streets looking for Chinese troops who might have changed into civilian clothes. Suspects – including people with what could be interpreted as army knapsack marks on their shoulders – were gathered together in groups of fifty or so, tied up and taken out beyond the city walls. Tank-fire, gunfire and bayonets were turned on them. Many tens of thousands were murdered – estimates would later rise to 200,000, even 300,000 and beyond – and large numbers of them went unburied, both outside and inside the city. *New York Times* correspondent F. Tillman Durdin wondered whether the point of allowing dead bodies to remain in the street, gradually ground into the dirt by Japanese vehicles passing repeatedly over them, was to 'impress on the Chinese the terrible results of resisting Japan'.

Such was the city into which Matsui trotted regally on horseback, at the head of a victory parade. He was joined by the Emperor's uncle, Lt General Prince Asaka Yasuhiko, along with 20,000 infantry, marines and mechanized units. The march passed down the East Road, from the Chungshan Gate towards the National Government Building, as warplanes flew overhead. The rising sun flag was raised, and Matsui led the gathered masses in turning eastward for three clipped shouts of 'Long live the Emperor'. *Sake* was drunk, dried cuttlefish eaten. Matsui later confessed to feeling deeply moved by the whole thing, but the rank and file were more ambivalent. Second lieutenant Maeda Yoshihiko wondered 'what the meaning of this ceremony is . . . a kind of self-indulgence, performed by high-ranking military men'.

The American journalist Hallett Abend sensed that Nanjing was set to become somehow exceptional, even in this era of horrors on the Asian mainland. This would be 'a page of history that the Japanese nation will always regret', he wrote. Officials in Shanghai were not trying to deny what was going on. And their accounts were clearly reaching Tokyo: Ishigari Itarō, Bureau Chief of the East Asia section of the Foreign Ministry, confided to his diary the news he was receiving of the 'atrocities of our army in Nanjing . . . [a] horrendous situation of pillage and rape. My God, is this how our imperial army behaves?' But Abend rightly suspected that further afield and into the future there would be attempts to cover all this up. He himself was first bribed, then intimidated, and then branded as 'anti-Japanese' over his reporting – the last a label to be applied almost reflexively,

General Matsui Iwane (*far left*) leads the Nanjing Victory Parade,
17 December 1937

for decades to come, to Japanese and non-Japanese alike who dared
to describe and seek to understand the scale and causes of what
Japan's armed forces did in Nanjing.

Matsui, for his part, certainly didn't grasp the implications. A big
believer in 'Pan-Asianism' – solidarity against the political and cultural
threat of the West – he spoke in February 1940, on the day that the
temple near his home was formally dedicated, of the carnage in China
as the 'mutual killing of neighbouring friends'. He still hoped that this
ongoing 'holy war' (*seisen*) would eventually result in the salvation of
East Asia. Dedicating his creation of bloody clay to that end and to the
souls of the dead on both sides of the conflict, he gave to statue and
temple alike the name *Kōa Kannon*: 'Kannon for a Prosperous Asia'.

*

For those around the world whose dismay at Japanese aggression in
Asia had now turned to disbelief at the extraordinary violence in

The *Kōa Kannon* statue

Shanghai and Nanjing, grandiose talk of peace, prosperity, cooperation and holiness rang understandably hollow. And yet in his appeal
to the divine – for cosmic context and moral justification – Matsui
was far from alone.

The 1930s saw the coming together in Japan of some of the most
radical philosophical critiques of Western modernity with some of
the most radical political ones. Nishida Kitarō, a man with a good
claim to being Japan's first modern philosopher and now entering the
final phase of a distinguished career, had long ago charged that Western culture was premised on two fundamental ideas – and both of
them were wrong. First, the notion that reality is ultimately 'something'. And second, that the natural mode of human be-ing is to live
and process the world as a rational individual.

Nishida claimed instead that reality is ultimately 'nothingness'.
Not in the sense of the once-was or the might-have-been, but *absolute*
nothingness: an unfathomable 'place', or horizon, upon which both

being and non-being arise. Look at a yellow flower, he said to his students at Kyoto Imperial University. But rather than noticing 'a flower' that is yellow, focus instead on the yellowness itself. Zoom in. Give it your full attention. Something interesting happens: your concern with the 'is-ness', the existence, of the flower – and also the 'is-ness' of yourself – begins to recede.

Once you're fully immersed in this yellowness, he continued, ask yourself where yellowness comes from. For some of you, the question won't make sense. But those of you who persevere will find that you end up imagining yellowness not in terms of substance but in terms of place. The question becomes not 'What is yellowness?' but 'Where is yellowness? Against what broader backdrop does 'yellowness' emerge?'

You may find that the answer arrives courtesy of a new and special sort of consciousness. Not the familiar kind, where you have various thoughts, but one where thinking 'has' – creates – you. And if you're prompted, finally, to ask 'where' this special consciousness 'is', the answer must be absolute nothingness, which produces and interpenetrates every plane of reality. You could say that absolute nothingness is God. And that God is absolute nothingness.

None of this will make any sense until you've had a taste of Zen – so claimed a friend of Nishida's by the name of Suzuki Daisetsu. Where Nishida was an occasional practitioner of Zen, Suzuki was a devotee and an evangelist: if Zen and an ideal of wordless insight were soon understood in the West as the very essence of Buddhism and Japanese cultural refinement, then Suzuki was one of a small handful of Japanese intellectuals who could claim credit.

A similar shift occurred at home in Japan, where laypeople in search of practices of self-cultivation amidst the strains of modern life demanded of Zen Buddhist monks a training in meditation, along with shared use of space in their temples. Those monks were struggling to keep their temples open and their traditions alive in the wake of anti-Buddhist feeling after the Meiji Restoration. Contributions to their coffers came now on a voluntary basis only. So if meditation was what people wanted, then meditation would be what they got.

This transformation within Zen, from a largely institution-bound set of specialized ideas into a widely intelligible resource for

D. T. Suzuki (1870–1966)

culturally and spiritually inflected political critique, proved extra-ordinarily influential in the middle years of the twentieth century. For a start, it possessed obvious nationalist and Pan-Asian potential. Suzuki suggested that in the face of Western culture, Buddhism in general provided a natural bond between the peoples of India, China and Japan. And, true to the legacy of Inoue Enryō, who derided religion in contemporary India as 'crystallized superstition' epitomized in bizarre and 'exceedingly filthy' cow-veneration, Suzuki insisted that Japan was where the Buddha's teachings, and human spirituality more generally, had so far reached their highest realization. Thanks to a meeting, centuries ago, of the samurai spirit (*seishin*) with Chinese Ch'an Buddhism, Japanese life as a whole, he claimed, had developed to become 'Zen-like'.

Across the 1920s, influential professors of law at Tokyo Imperial University used a different idiom to propose and promote strikingly similar ideas. Uesugi Shinkichi and Kakehi Katsuhiko argued that the essence of 'being' lay in the organic connectedness of beings within a community – living with one another, with the dead, and with the as-yet unborn. Only a community capable of realizing, in the sense both of recognizing and practising, these profound inter-relations could truly call itself a 'society'. And only a society consciously striving for perfection was entitled to call itself a 'state'.

In the West, they argued, you find only rather pitiful approximations of this, mere hasty constructs of convenience or control. The ideal form is to be found in Japan, where the state was not 'built' at all: it was divinely revealed. Amaterasu, the Sun Goddess, is the source and final goal of a polity animated by an organizational will provided by the Emperor himself – a 'god made manifest as man' (*arahitogami*). Such a state doesn't need laws, or politics, or compulsion of any kind: morality comes naturally, rooted in the conviction that man's most profound moment of understanding and self-realization comes when he merges – whether in life or death – with this will of the Emperor.

Such thoughts by themselves hardly amounted to a call for war. But an unsettling breeze was starting to pick up in Japan, strengthened by tributary gusts like these. Other contributions included Watsuji Tetsurō's claims about the intimacy of Japanese families versus the cold, pragmatic cohabitation found in the West. The novelist Tanizaki Junichirō suggested that whereas Japanese people experience the world as one might a room illuminated by the light of a candle – shifting shadows, the richness of ever-changing forms and feelings – Westerners live as though an electric light is either off or on: in total darkness, or in a blanched, bland world. Their inner lives are, in other words, artificial. Dead.

A surprising number of these gathering winds were in fact westerlies. Nishida and his 'Kyoto School' philosophical colleagues were profoundly indebted to German philosophy. Suzuki lived and worked in the United States for more than a decade around the turn of the twentieth century. Uesugi and Kakehi both studied the state in Germany – Kakehi in particular was steeped in Christian theology and regarded the Roman Catholic Church as an exemplar of man's desire for divine sovereignty. And one of the West's redeeming features, in the eyes of early twentieth-century Asian intellectuals seeking to push back against its cultural dominance, had been its capacity for forensic self-critique, bordering on self-sabotage – encountered colourfully in psychoanalysis, which suggested that somewhere beneath colonialism's starchy uniforms, pith helmets and high purpose there festered unspeakable thoughts and fantasies. Similarly, Japanese rejection of 'the West' often looked like the taking of sides in that region's internal cultural tussles – or else part of a global, cosmopolitan conversation about 'modernity'.

But audiences mattered more than origins in the late 1920s and into the 1930s, as Japan's diplomatic isolation worsened and the likes of Nishida and Suzuki – along with those who interpreted their work – got caught up in nationalistic drift. Uesugi and Kakehi's students included young men not just at Tokyo University but at the Army and Navy colleges. Kakehi had even devoted time, in November 1926, to personal tuition for a particularly privileged young man – who a month later became the Shōwa Emperor. Both Uesugi and Kakehi worked with ultranationalist discussion, pressure and propaganda groups opposed to liberal interpretations of Japan's constitution and to party politics, whose rise they feared and detested.

Japan's Criminal Investigation Bureau viewed such groups as potentially revolutionary – whether from right or left, hostility towards the status quo could not be tolerated – and so kept a close eye on them. They were right to worry. Here was a ready-and-waiting reservoir of support and coherent ideology, should violent political activists need to draw on it: in planning and preparing their attacks, and later in court, if and when they answered for them. The young military officers who assassinated Prime Minister Inukai Tsuyoshi at his home in 1932 travelled there direct from the Yasukuni Shrine, where they were seen 'doffing caps, clasping hands, and bowing towards the unseen mirror of the Sun Goddess'. One bought charms at the shrine and handed them around, a means of warding off police bullets.

And yet you didn't have to be a theorist or a theologian or a thug to feel included by the grand philosophical ideas of this age. Many were premised upon who you already were, by virtue of blood. Others appealed as earnest and ambitious attempts to gather in everything that seemed to threaten Japan and to lay it all at the feet of some higher principle, whether Amaterasu, the Emperor or 'absolute nothingness'. Nor did these great cosmic tamings of the country's troubles all boil down to forms of xenophobia. Suzuki's lauding of Japan and the Japanese was largely a matter of pride in his country, a sympathetic understanding of the spiritual emptiness felt by friends living in the West, and a frustration with lingering misrepresentations

there of Buddhism. And yet his words and the practices he championed could be – and were – taken up by warmongers, from 'Buddhist'
justifications for violent aggression to meditation retreats for army
officers. Nishida was attacked from the left after the war for his supposed nationalism, and from the right during it for taking too
enthusiastic an interest in European thought.

There was, then, hardly a straightforward progression from philosophy to a lust for foreign blood. But ideas that were at once inspiring
and capacious possessed enormous potential power, taking the complexity of Japan's situation in the 1920s and 1930s – the mixed
blessings of a mass society, unsettled politics, fluctuating economic
fortunes and uncertain international standing – and giving it grasp-
able contours. It might not be enough to make a person want war, but
it could help them to accept it when it came. Many would find themselves swept up, to look back in later years with a mixture of fondness,
puzzlement and grief.

In 1937, as the war in China spiralled out of control, sublime ideas
found their way into mainstream politics. The government published
a booklet entitled *Kokutai No Hongi* ('Fundamentals of Our National
Polity'). Written and revised by scholars including the philosopher
Watsuji Tetsurō, it blamed European Enlightenment thought – and
individualism especially – for the present world crisis, and for the
confusion into which many Japanese had innocently fallen. People
should ground themselves firmly, it said, in the Japanese spirit: a constant force in history, from the Sun Goddess down to the present
times. And they should shake off the shackles of their 'small selves',
in favour of the larger life to be found in the Emperor. Such was the
real meaning and magnificence of the *kokutai*.

More than two million copies of *Kokutai No Hongi* were printed,
including for use in schools. It became just one element in broad-ranging
and intensive efforts by bureaucrats and government-sponsored intellectuals to work out how Japan might survive the very hot diplomatic
water into which the military had plunged the country. The general
governmental trend was towards reining in energy-sapping contests –
from party politics to unfettered capitalism – and tightening state
control of the economy. A Cabinet Planning Board was established

in 1937 to coordinate economic policy, after which a wide range of further powers were gathered in by the state – concerning labour allocation and wage levels, prices and profit levels, industrial production, power generation, transportation, and the use of important land and buildings. An 'Imperial Rule Assistance Association' (IRAA) was established in October 1940: civil and military arms of government were to be united in a national party-like body, headed by the Prime Minister and reaching right down to the municipal level. Diet politicians, weary of being threatened by bureaucrats with their own extreme unpopularity in the country, and seeing in the IRAA a route to rehabilitation, gave their blessing, formally dissolved their parties and joined the new organization instead.

And yet none of this ever went as far as Rōyama Masamichi of Tokyo University would have liked. Part of a constitutional research group established in 1933, Rōyama advocated complete Nazi-style top-down control in Japan. But territorialism amongst Japan's bureaucrats, and criticism of the IRAA as effectively a new shogunate – and thus a competitor with the Emperor – helped to ensure that this much-hyped new body found itself effectively absorbed into the Home Ministry. The essentials of Japan's Meiji Constitution remained unchanged: the Diet continued to meet, populated by much the same people as before and used by business leaders, as ever it had been, to push for the interests of private enterprise against an overweening state. Japan ended up with watered-down statism, rather than full-throttle fascism.

Nevertheless, these years after the start of the war with China saw an impressive degree of political and cultural pressure applied throughout the country, bringing people ever more closely into the bureaucratic embrace. The Japan Federation of Labour met in Tokyo in the summer of 1940, and amidst cries of 'Banzai!' for the Emperor officially disbanded itself. Labour disputes from then on were settled by discussion under the auspices of an Industrial Patriotic Federation, on whose board sat a number of Home Ministry officials. Ichikawa Fusae's League for Women's Suffrage was persuaded to suspend its call for the vote, and was offered instead a sought-after law giving financial aid to struggling mothers. And where Hiratsuka Raichō once invoked the Sun Goddess as a symbol of women's radiant creativity, Ichikawa and a newly formed League of Japanese Women's Organizations now called for Amaterasu to be worshipped as part of a wider programme of reverence for the imperial family, sensible family budgeting and pragmatically modest dress.

Campaigners who had previously fought the government on a range of issues found themselves writing articles or touring the countryside to try to persuade people to save their money. Strategists had concluded that savings were an easier sell to the public than higher taxes, and they were useful for the war effort because they provided financial institutions with the funds they needed to buy government bonds.

With the raw material to keep up the fight in China falling into place by 1940, what the government needed was a sense of where a conflict that couldn't be stopped might ultimately be going. Two years before, Prime Minister Konoe Fumimaro, a one-time student of Nishida Kitarō at Kyoto University, had announced as his foreign policy aim a 'New Order in East Asia': regional stability achieved via cooperation between Japan, Manchukuo, and a China free of Chiang Kai-shek – who was in political hock to the West and so not to be trusted. Now, in the summer of 1940, his Foreign Minister Matsuoka Yōsuke proudly announced the creation of a 'Greater East Asia Co-Prosperity Sphere' (GEACPS).

War had broken out in Europe the previous autumn, so the potential availability of British and French colonial possessions in South East Asia had now to be factored into Japan's resource-seeking calculus. GEACPS was also the natural fulfilment of what the philosopher Miki Kiyoshi – like Konoe, once a pupil of Nishida Kitarō, and now a government adviser – called a need for 'grand ideas' to match the 'grand deeds' of Japan's armed forces on the continent. The state needed a story it could sell to parents sending their children off to war, and this, it was hoped, would fit the bill.

Early hopes for GEACPS, as something more than a fig leaf for Japanese imperialism, were revealed in later dismay. Both Miki and Nishida decried its swift appropriation by advocates of military expansion. Nishida reportedly told army leaders that a 'Co-Prosperity Sphere' that didn't meet the needs of people in the region was merely a 'coercion sphere'. Idealists had hoped that GEACPS might answer a dilemma posed by Fukuzawa Yukichi, one of modern Japan's founding fathers, all the way back in 1885: should Japan leave Asia for the warm and sophisticated embrace of the modern Western world – or should it aspire to lead it? Given an ever-widening chasm of misunderstanding and mistrust between Japan and the West, the latter option increasingly seemed the obvious and even urgent course of action.

By the time GEACPS was announced, more than 850,000 Japanese soldiers were active in mainland China, chasing Chiang Kai-shek from one provisional capital to another. Britain was looking like falling to Nazi Germany, with whom Konoe's army minister Tōjō Hideki managed to persuade reluctant naval colleagues to ally themselves in the autumn of 1940, in a Tripartite Pact with Italy. Japanese diplomats, meanwhile, had negotiated their country's occupation of northern French Indochina.

Hitler's invasion of the Soviet Union in the summer of 1941 briefly tempted Japanese strategists with a prospect long dreamed of: the Soviets too preoccupied with problems to their west to prevent Japanese forces surging through their eastern territories. But the Kwantung Army had in fact already started – and, to all intents and purposes, lost – a short war against the Soviets, near Nomonhan village on the Manchukuo–Mongolia border back in 1939. The memory of the humiliating truce that they had been compelled to accept helped to persuade Japanese leaders now to avoid renewed conflict with the USSR. A long-running 'northward/southward?' argument was won instead by those favouring a push down into South East Asia. Recent American embargoes on scrap iron and fuel exports to Japan – an attempt to rein in Japanese aggression and to punish the country for its choice of friends in Europe – were starting to bite. Tōjō worried that unless resources could be found elsewhere by the end of 1941, Japan would lose the opportunity to make GEACPS a reality.

So Japanese forces were sent into the southern portion of French Indochina in July 1941, further raising the temperature with President Roosevelt, who now froze all Japanese assets in the United States, banned all exports of oil (of which Japan's navy alone was said to be using 400 tons per hour at this point), and signed the Atlantic Charter with Britain's Prime Minister Winston Churchill. Konoe's suggestion of one-to-one talks with Roosevelt was rebuffed, and Tōjō, who soon replaced him as Prime Minister, found the going equally tough. The US wanted something the Japanese could no longer afford even to contemplate: Japan's full withdrawal from China.

It began to look as though the army ideologue Ishiwara Kanji's lecture-hall fantasies about an apocalyptic war with the United States might just be about to come true. If so, it made sense for Japan to throw the first punch: cripple American power in the Asia-Pacific region, and then strike a favourable deal. An attack scenario dreamt up a few months before, initially scoffed at, but then war-gamed with increasing seriousness, seemed now to be a desperate Japan's best – and perhaps last – hope.

*

Out of nowhere, on the Hawaiian island of Oahu, fierce fighting suddenly broke out. Kikugawa Ayako's family had grown from two children to four, and a favourite pastime now was playing samurai using wooden swords carved and polished by their father, Shitoku. Most of the rest of his time was spent ferrying American officers to and fro between the central Oahu town of Wahiawa, where the Kikugawas lived, and Schofield Barracks a few kilometres away. Shitoku knew very little English, so his little son Akimi would sit next to him in the car, reading the road signs for him.

Lots of first generation (*issei*) Japanese migrants in Hawaii drove taxis. So the sight of another, John Yoshige Mikami, taking a Japanese consular assistant on a tour around Oahu in 1941 was not unusual. His passenger, Morimura Tadashi, was not terribly popular with his colleagues at the consulate. They regarded him as completely useless at his job – which he was, because his expertise lay elsewhere.

Morimura's real name was Yoshikawa Takeo, and he was an intelligence officer in the Japanese Navy. At twenty-nine years of age, he had no prior experience as a field agent, but was gaining it rapidly from the back of Mikami's cab. Yoshikawa became especially fond of looking down on Pearl Harbor and Ford Island from nearby heights, noting that on Saturdays and Sundays large parts of the US fleet were at home in port. As he expanded his sightseeing to the central and northern parts of Oahu, he was struck by how thinly patrolled were the waters to the north of the island.

Yoshikawa became a fan of boat and plane rides too. One Sunday, he showed a couple of the maids from the Japanese consulate his version of a good time: taking them out to test the depth of the coastal waters off Kaneohe, on the eastern side of the island. He made the most, too, of a 'Gala Day' for the general public at Wheeler Army Airfield, just next to Schofield Barracks, noting details of hangars, runway lengths and widths, and the number of aircraft capable of taking off at once. He even knocked on the door at Schofield Barracks, on the off-chance that they would let him in (they didn't). Later, Yoshikawa joined yet another lady friend aboard a half-hour pleasure flight across the island, with beautiful and informative views across Wheeler and Hickam airfields. Straining in his seat, he caught a glimpse of Pearl Harbor to the south, an area about which Naval Intelligence was beginning to press him for detailed information.

The Americans knew that the Japanese must be conducting espionage in Hawaii, probably from the consulate in Honolulu. But there was little they could do about it. Basic restrictions were put in place – Yoshikawa hadn't been allowed to take a camera along to Wheeler's Gala Day – but you couldn't keep an eye on 160,000 Japanese and Japanese-Americans around the clock. And as tensions with Japan continued to rise, American leaders didn't want to do anything that might provide a pretext for war.

The next best thing was to know how much the Japanese knew. At the eventual cost of a nervous breakdown, Colonel William F. Friedman cracked a code used between Tokyo's Foreign Ministry and its embassies around the world. Soon, the resulting 'MAGIC' decrypting machines were doing intensive service, their wiring rarely given a chance to cool down. But there was a problem: the most devastating plans presently afoot in Japan were unknown to the Foreign Ministry. They were being put together by the Navy. And the Americans failed to break those codes in time.

Early in the morning of Sunday, 7 December 1941, aircraft incoming from the north were picked up by US radar. An officer, just days into his new job, insisted that all was well. A group of American B-17

Flying Fortresses were expected in from California, on roughly this trajectory. And local radio was playing Hawaiian music through the night, which it did when US aircraft were expected – a way of helping to guide them in. 'Don't worry about it,' he responded to his colleagues up at the radar station – who had failed to mention to him just how many aircraft they had spotted.

The people of Wahiawa awoke a little while later to the sound of all hell breaking loose. Japanese bombers and Zero fighters were emerging from the clouds in endless streams, diving downwards and destroying everything they could find at Wheeler Airfield, where American planes sat in convenient rows outside their hangars – close enough together that when one was struck it set off a chain of further explosions.

Wheeler had no anti-aircraft guns, and none of its planes were armed for immediate combat. Ammunition belts were removed each night and stacked in hangars, where they were now feeding a spectacular, deafening firework display. The best that the Americans could do was to get together to push undamaged aircraft out of the way of the Japanese planes, which were flying in so low that they rustled the sugar cane on their approach. Wheeler's commander later swore he saw the glint of gold teeth, as one Japanese pilot leaned out of his window, grinning at him as he swept past.

Well might he have smiled. Six Japanese carriers had made it undetected to within 200 miles of Oahu's northern coast, launching 183 aircraft in the space of fifteen minutes: a combination of fighters, high-level bombers, dive bombers and torpedo aircraft, forming a steadily expanding and intensifying arc of light in the sky, before heading south once everyone was airborne and ready to go. By the time US radar operators detected them and decided they were friendlies, a second wave had been lifted to the surface of the carriers and sent skyward to join them.

Even when the first bomb dropped, US military personnel still thought it must be their own side – a stupid error by some rookie pilot. Then the red discs on the sides of the aircraft came into view. One by one, visits were paid to the targets scouted by Yoshikawa: Wheeler Airfield, followed by various facilities around Pearl Harbor. All in all, a total of 350 Japanese aircraft sank five American

7 December 1941: Wheeler Airfield under attack (*above*) and the USS *Shaw* exploding in Pearl Harbor (*below*)

battleships, destroyed around 200 planes, and damaged or destroyed a dozen or so additional vessels. More than 2,000 Americans lost their lives, compared with just sixty-four Japanese killed in action.

Precisely how much real influence the Shōwa Emperor had in any of this would be argued over ever after. Certainly, great efforts were made by civilian and military officials to keep him informed, the better to give imperial weight to their actions. The Army and Navy sent separate daily briefings, with the effect that Hirohito as Supreme Commander represented the only level of command at which a full picture of the war was available. Apparently not quite trusting these briefings, Hirohito tasked his own personal army and navy aides, including his brothers, with collecting information independently of official channels.

One area in which the Emperor clearly did have influence, and for which he drew on his tutoring at the hands of his Tokyo Imperial University professor Kakehi Katsuhiko and others, was in the editing of an imperial rescript declaring war on the United States and the British Empire. Work on the document had begun in October 1941, and it was ready to go by the time news came in of the successful attack on Pearl Harbor. The Emperor donned his naval uniform that morning in tribute and celebration, and the rescript was promulgated at 11 a.m. Japan-time, on 8 December. At midday, a morning of patriotic music on NHK radio was brought to a close by a full reading of the document, and an address from Prime Minister Tōjō.

Blame was once again heaped upon the reckless Chinese for spurning Japanese neighbourliness, as well as on the Americans and the British for conspiring to dominate Asia. The rescript concluded:

> Patiently have We waited and long have We endured, in the hope that Our Government might retrieve the situation in peace. But our adversaries, showing not the least spirit of conciliation, have unduly delayed a settlement; and in the meantime, they have intensified the economic and political pressure to compel thereby Our Empire to submission.

This trend of affairs would, if left unchecked, not only nullify Our Empire's efforts of many years for the sake of the stabilization of East Asia, but also endanger the very existence of Our nation. The situation being such as it is, Our Empire for its existence and self-defence has no other recourse but to appeal to arms and to crush every obstacle in its path.

The hallowed spirits of Our Imperial Ancestors guarding Us from above, We rely upon the loyalty and courage of Our subjects in Our confident expectation that the task bequeathed by Our Forefathers will be carried forward, and that the sources of evil will be speedily eradicated and an enduring peace immutably established in East Asia, preserving thereby the glory of Our Empire.

*

Part of the problem for the United States at Pearl Harbor had been that its defenders were fat, drunk, cowardly and spectacularly inept. Such, in any case, was the version of events offered to young Japanese cinema-goers early in 1943. An animated feature called *Momotarō no Umiwashi* ('Momotarō's Sea Eagles') showed an American marine, based on a particularly portly Bluto from the Popeye films, guzzling from a bottle and then flopping around ineffectually on the deck of his ship as wave after wave of rabbits, monkeys and assorted other animals sporting rising sun bandanas piloted attack planes in the direction of his fleet.

In command of this surprise offensive was a young boy by the name of Momotarō – 'Peach Boy'. Everyone in the cinema would have known immediately who he was: the hero of an old Japanese folktale, who is born from a peach and later embarks on a quest to fight a band of ogres who are terrorizing the local population.

The Momotarō legend was a staple of Japanese literary life by this point, not just children's entertainment, but a source of insight into a primordial Japanese imagination. For Yanagita Kunio, just one of a legion of commentators on Momotarō, the tale revealed a profound but understated awareness in Japan of how the divine (the peach) gives rise to the human (Momotarō). The story also provided the perfect Pan-Asian allegory: a peace-loving country is menaced by ogres from far-off lands, a son of heaven strikes out to find and defeat them, and on the way he acquires a diverse and biddable set of comrades who come alive to his concerns and values.

As ever, Western culture was doing triple duty in Japan: inspiration, convenient foil and idiom of attack. A few years earlier, Japanese animators had scored a hit by pitting Momotarō against Mickey Mouse, the latter's face redrawn to reveal deeply malicious American intent. Now, *Momotarō no Umiwashi* opened by proudly announcing its sponsor: the Imperial Japanese Navy.

Momotarō no Umiwashi was a ground-breaking piece of animation for its day. It was also one of increasingly few options left available to Japanese in search of entertainment by this point in the war. Dance halls and jazz venues had been shut down and neon shop signs switched off, to save electricity. Japan's newspaper industry had shrunk from 454 titles to just fifty-four – including one per prefecture – while journalists and publishers alike lived in fear of reporting the wrong thing. Staff at *Chūō Kōron* ('Central Review') were arrested by the Special Higher Police, resulting in the rape of at least one woman, the deaths in custody of two male employees, and eventually the closure of one of Japan's most respected journals. One

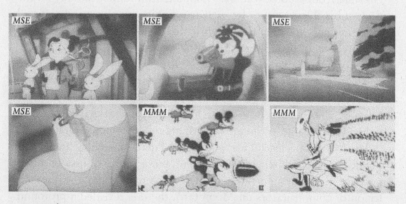

Scenes from *Momotarō's Sea Eagles* (MSE) (1943), showing Momotarō and some of his lieutenants, an American ship under attack, and a Bluto-like Marine, and from *Momotarō vs Mickey Mouse* (MMM) (1934)

Proof that the wartime co-opting of cartoons was a game that two
could play: Popeye enlisted for a US war stamp campaign

of its offences had been to serialize Tanizaki Junichirō's novel *The
Makioka Sisters*, which was judged to contain too much irrelevant
content about 'bourgeois family life'.

For people in search of something to do, there was still the officially encouraged shrine visit, or the enticement of an officially
approved ballet entitled 'Decisive Aerial Warfare Suite'. From 1942,
there was also an annual Imperial Edict Day, during which a stars-
and-stripes flag was drawn on the pavement in Tokyo and people
were encouraged to step on it – much as former Christians in Tokugawa Japan had once been required to tread on images of Jesus Christ
and Mary to show their disdain and thus prove their loyalty.

In the words of Prime Minister Tōjō: 'the masses are foolish . . . if
we tell them the facts, morale will collapse.' By the time *Momotarō
no Umiwashi* hit the cinemas, the facts had become distinctly
unfavourable. The war with the West had, in its first few months,
been a spectacular success. Pearl Harbor had been followed within

hours by a similar attack on grounded aircraft in the Philippines. Great colonial cities – Manila, Hong Kong, Singapore, Rangoon – had toppled like dominoes. In places like Burma and the Dutch East Indies, local nationalists welcomed the Japanese as liberators, before finding out what it meant to be Momotarō's pet helpers: their food and resources taken, their currency exploited to the benefit of the Japanese yen.

But just as the Japanese Empire reached its greatest geographical extent, the tide began to turn. In the summer of 1942, Japan lost a crucial naval engagement at Midway in the northern Pacific ('midway' between the Asian and American continents), rationing began at home, and American planners set to work on a post-war occupation.

Rhetorical appeal to 'national emergency' had been an almost constant feature of Japanese public life since the 1850s, with statesmen and military men barely letting a year pass by without seeking to persuade people of an imminent threat to the country's survival. The power of this idea to mobilize people, and to get money flowing in the right direction, was just too tempting. Now, however, Japan really was facing an emergency, to which the authorities responded with a combination of strictures designed to squeeze every last drop out of the country's natural, technological and human resources.

The definitions of extravagant spending, dress and personal grooming became steadily more encompassing. Boys and adult men could until recently be found sporting kimono whose colourful designs celebrated the country's military. One depicted men charging into battle, another showed biplanes soaring above the clouds, bearing the distinctive rising sun motif. But this fashion began to shift to the wearing of a national civilian uniform, while women sported ostentatiously unostentatious peasant pantaloons, or *monpe*. Young girls, meanwhile, were asked to send letters of encouragement to soldiers at the front – risking, in reply, a variety of coarse suggestions about how they might help the war effort, were they closer at hand.

An idea that dated back to the Tokugawa era was now tasked with helping to save the modern nation: groups of households collaborating as units. These neighbourhood associations – 1.3 million of them by the time of Midway, in groups of ten to fifteen homes – passed noticeboards between them, each providing a red stamp to confirm

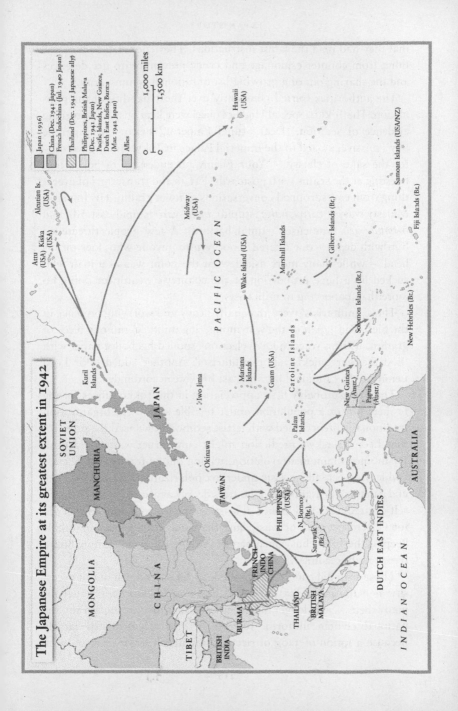

The Japanese Empire at its greatest extent in 1942

Japan (1936)
China (Dec. 1941 Japan)
French Indochina (Jul. 1940 Japanese ally)
Thailand (Dec. 1941 Japanese ally)
Philippines, British Malaya (Dec. 1941 Japan)
Pacific Islands, New Guinea, Dutch East Indies, Burma (Mar. 1942 Japan)
Allies

0   1,000 miles
0   1,500 km

SOVIET UNION

MONGOLIA

MANCHURIA

CHINA

TIBET

BRITISH INDIA

BURMA

THAILAND

FRENCH INDO CHINA

BRITISH MALAYA

Kuril Islands

JAPAN

Okinawa

TAIWAN

Iwo Jima

PHILIPPINES (USA)

N. Borneo (Br.)

Sarawak (Br.)

DUTCH EAST INDIES

Palau Islands

Caroline Islands

Mariana Islands

Guam (USA)

Wake Island (USA)

Marshall Islands

PACIFIC OCEAN

Attu (USA) Kiska (USA)

Aleutian Is. (USA)

Midway (USA)

Hawaii (USA)

Gilbert Islands (Br.)

Solomon Islands (Br.)

New Guinea (Austr.)

Papua (Austr.)

New Hebrides (Br.)

Samoan Islands (USA/NZ)

Fiji Islands (Br.)

AUSTRALIA

INDIAN OCEAN

that they had read the latest instructions. They cooperated on everything from counter-espionage and crime prevention to fire defences and the sharing out of a growing list of rationed commodities.

The authorities fretted constantly over the reliability of the population. The Tokkō (Special Higher Police) were kept busy by disturbing evidence of sedition. 'Dear Stupid Emperor,' began one Japanese boy's missive, posted to the Imperial Palace in Tokyo and signed off – for the sake of clarity – 'Your Enemy'. It ended up in police files bursting at the seams with postcards, letters and transcripts of everything from eavesdropped conversations to toilet graffiti. His Imperial Majesty was, at turns, *baka* (stupid), *baka-yarō* (stupid bastard), and *ō-baka-yarō* (immensely stupid bastard). A few people threatened him with death – one offered 2,000 yen to anyone who 'lops off his head' – while many more asked what the point was of a man who sucked up a huge proportion of the country's wealth for doing no more than pandering to militarists.

Those 'militarists' were an equally heavy and worrying presence in the files. 'Rid Japan of the war-mongering military' ran one piece of graffito, while a voter in local elections spoiled his ballot paper with 'End the war quickly, idiot militarists'. Another added 'Our Lord Lenin' to the candidate list and cast his vote accordingly.

There was probably little appreciation in the Tokkō offices for the resilient wit of a population under terrible strain. An organization traditionally preoccupied with leftist sedition now faced the prospect that Leon Trotsky's prediction might come true: war would push Japan into communist revolution, wiping out its fragile middle class and leaving behind a classic tinderbox polarization of a wealthy elite and a mass of peasants and labourers deeply aggrieved at the former's self-centredness. Asia looked at least as ripe for communism as it did for Co-Prosperity. Nor was it just the usual trouble-making rabble keeping the Tokkō busy: members of the elite Cabinet Planning Board were caught reading Marx.

Those who did end up toeing the line did so as much out of necessity as enthusiasm. Textiles ended up in such short supply that for many there was no longer much choice except to wear *monpe* and the national civilian uniform. Interest in entertainment fell largely because a ration of 330g of rice per day didn't leave a person with much energy for going out, while others were soon too preoccupied with foraging for food in the countryside. Fuel and matches were so hard to come by that people in Okinawa were said to be reading at night by the light of phosphorescent sea creatures. Neighbourliness was tested to its limits when young girls were discovered stuffing cushions up their dresses in hopes of procuring a pregnant woman's rations.

Cities like Tokyo and Osaka were becoming all but unrecognizable. Homes were losing their colour, their laughter and most of their valuables and metal goods, as pots and pans were handed over to the military for use as scrap. Streets lost their statues, their iron railings, even their temple bells. Only wood and paper remained.

But that was fine for American strategists planning the final stages of the war in 1944–5. Wood and paper were all they required for an endgame so brutally simple you could sum it up in a word: fire.

A young boy sat in the cinema marvelling at the sequel to 'Momotarō's Sea Eagles': *Momotarō: Umi no Shinpei* ('Momotarō's Divine Sea Warriors'). 'One day I'm going to make animated films,' he swore to himself. And yet Tezuka Osamu, future godfather of Japanese anime and manga, found he had almost no one with whom he could share his resolution. Much of Osaka had been devastated by America's new B-29 Superfortresses. And though the Shōchikuza cinema had so far been left mercifully intact, most of Tezuka's friends had been evacuated to the countryside. They were amongst more than 10 million Japanese civilians to flee the country's cities in the final months of the war, compared with around 1.2 million civilians from Britain's urban areas during the Blitz of 1940–41.

Across Japan, people were now being asked to throw everything into the war. Schoolgirls worked long hours creating enormous balloons to which incendiaries could be attached, in an effort to turn the jet-stream into a divine wind capable of raining destruction on the American mainland. Around 350 devices reached North America, with balloon fragments found as far east as Iowa. An explosion at a picnic in Oregon resulted in the only six wartime casualties anywhere on the US mainland.

But very little provision had been made in return for people's defence, especially in Japan's big cities. So while children's balloons floated hopefully away into the skies, hundreds of the most advanced bombers ever seen began regular flights over Japanese cities – each zoned by the Allies according to the flammability of its architecture. Thanks to Japan's lack of anti-aircraft guns, the B-29s were able to come in at chimney-top height, their defensive gun turrets taken out and replaced with extra quantities of incendiary.

A raid on 9 March 1945 against Tokyo, whose population density was around 103,000 people per square mile at the time, turned into the most destructive sortie in history. A quarter of one of the world's largest cities burned to the ground overnight. Canals boiled, glass melted, and up to 100,000 people were killed, most of them suffocating as firestorms sucked up the available oxygen.

Life for those who remained was a never-ending round of harsh, war-focused labour, to which ever younger men and, belatedly, women were recruited: enlisted in volunteer groups, drilled by soldiers in the use of bamboo spears, digging trenches and setting up barbed wire and pillboxes – getting ready for an imminent invasion. People were woken from their beds at 3 a.m. once per week for worship at local shrines. Schoolchildren were sent to the forests to collect pine stumps, so that the sap could be turned into aircraft fuel – it was claimed that 200 stumps could keep a single plane flying for an hour . . .

*

12 April 1945. Hayashi Ichizō had been a child of just nine when Japan's long war on the mainland started in 1931. He had made his way through typical Japanese schools of this period, in which maps of 'Japan' seamlessly blended its four main islands with disputed territory and recent conquests; ethics textbooks harped on Japanese values and spirit; swashbuckling stories were told of 'elder brother' making his way in the army; and the practice of martial sports and singing of military songs was common. He had attended one of the country's elite Higher Schools, in Fukuoka, and graduated from there to Kyoto Imperial University, where he had hoped to study philosophy, but had made do with economics. Now, he was pinned back in the cockpit seat of a navy plane as it screamed down towards an American ship off Okinawa.

Plenty of Hayashi's comrades in the *Tokubetsu Kōgekitai* (Special Attack Unit), better known as the kamikaze or 'divine wind', dreamed of taking as many Americans with them as possible when they went. Perhaps they would even pass beyond human into divine life: becoming a god, as both myth and the kamikaze manual promised. 'Aim for the smokestack,' the latter advised. 'Crash with your eyes wide open. Many have done so before you – they will tell you what fun they had . . .'

But as that glorious day approached, some pilots got drunk and rioted in their barracks. They took their *sen'ninbari* – 'thousand-knot [good luck] sashes' – and burned them in disgust. At least one pilot turned back on his final flight and strafed his commanding officers. Many more sabotaged their own planes or deliberately steered them into the sea.

Under a level of pressure at which later generations could only guess and wonder, the people and the pilots of Japan found themselves forced to think about what a 'nation' really is, in the end. It was a self-conscious endeavour in which few populations on earth can ever have been so well resourced. They had lived through more than a decade hearing stories about a phenomenally successful society now sharing its distinctly Asian modernity with its neighbours, listening to grand future plans, to heroic tales and to divine bluster of every kind.

And yet, when it came to it, young men like Hayashi Ichizō chose to imagine the nation as though none of this had ever existed, as though 'Japan' was better captured in a pre-modern poem or a wood-block print. They mused, in their last letters and diary entries, on the beauty of the moon, on the faces of family and on the flowers of their hometowns.

They had been told, in every way possible and via every means available to an increasingly unchallenged state, that Japan – and the world itself – was approaching the end-time. Yet they felt as though time was not ending, but turning: history was a force of nature, poised now to sweep away the nation's terrible mistakes and tragic misapprehensions of itself. Japan would lose this war. And they would die. But if nothing else they could be proud to have fed the fire that burned the field, making it fertile once again for the families they left behind.

'Dear Mother,' wrote Hayashi, by the light of a bonfire at his air-base in the far south of Japan:

The cherry blossoms here have all fallen. But the green leaves are lovely, reminding me of home.

This is like a dream. Tomorrow, I'm no longer alive. Those who went on sortie yesterday are all dead.

I'll be going ahead of you. I wonder if I'll be allowed to enter heaven. Please pray for me. I can't bear the thought of going to a place where you will not join me later . . . I just want to be held in your arms, and sleep.

PART FOUR

Modernity 2.0?
(1940s to 1960s)

11

Afterlives

Hell was much as the Buddhists had billed it. People staggered ghost-like along flaming streets, vomiting, as buildings ignited all around them and trees crashed to the ground. Steadily they lost more and more of their bodies to the soft, bubbling asphalt, as their flesh first drooped, then dripped, then fell away altogether. Finally, they collapsed, joining thousands of blistered and bloated figures already lying on the ground; some cried out for water, others were unable to speak through mouths filling up with maggots and flies.

On one point, however, Buddhist imagery had misled. Hell was not a realm, but rather a state of affairs. You didn't go there – it came to you, transfiguring your home, your family and your friends. For Nishimoto Setsuko, it arrived while she was sitting on the toilet. The old world simply vanished: at first bleached into white nothingness, then lost in utter black. An indescribable sound ripped through her, and then the new world arrived. The paper-and-wood partitions of her home had been repositioned. The wall outside was gone altogether. Neighbours discovered their roofs pitching upwards at odd angles, after a tremendous gust of wind forced itself inside and around their houses, sending everything sailing through the air.

The picture became stranger the closer you went into the centre of Hiroshima. Pushing empty carts along its burning streets, in search of lost loved ones, one entered a world fused together in the weirdest of ways. The flowers on women's kimonos had become imprinted on their bodies. Human silhouettes had appeared on the walls. Trying to make sense of it, some said that a shipment of oil drums must have exploded. Others blamed enemy saboteurs, parachuted in. It could be a gas attack: that would explain the 'electric smell' in the air. Or else this rain, just started, was gasoline being poured from the sky – ready to be lit up when the enemy made a second pass.

Setsuko scoured the streets and air-raid shelters looking for her husband, peering into the mouths of charred bodies in search of a tell-tale pattern of gold teeth. Tade Kinuyo did the same, with her baby on her back. She listened to him cycle through the same three words – 'hot!', 'milk!', 'bang!' – as her straw sandals were steadily worn away by the hot road.

Neither woman found anything. In place of a body, Setsuko burned her husband's tobacco pouch down by the river, burying the remains along with his pipe. That would have to do for a grave. A few days later, both she and her son Akio developed a fever. Smoothing her hair, she found clumps coming away with her hand. The same was happening to Akio. Rumours circulated about what this was, and how it might be cured. Setsuko's experiments included water infused with the *dokudami* herb.

Yokochi Toshiko, living nearby, heard that powdered human bones might soothe her son's burns. So she ground up the cremated remains of her husband in an earthenware mortar – both he and her nineteen-year-old daughter had faded away and died in front of her – and dabbed at her son's body with the powder. He died later that afternoon.

A sick and balding Akio got his call-up papers for the army. He and his mother set off again towards the city centre, back through all the bodies. Akio was given a little rice gruel when they arrived, served in a length of bamboo, and was told that he would be departing the following day. He slept that night at the railway station. Setsuko was all set to wave him off the next morning, when they heard an announcement: 'Discharged from military service'. They made their way home. Two days later, at noon on 15 August 1945, a voice was heard for the first time ever on the radio, offering one of history's great masterclasses in understatement. 'The war situation has developed,' reflected the Emperor, 'not necessarily to Japan's advantage.'

The surprising thing about heaven was how solicitously it catered to the voyeur. Down below, one could see Tokyo blackened by fire: buildings scorched, trees half burned away. The damned shuffled along what remained of the streets, emaciated and desperate. Up here, a curious sense of spaciousness persisted – and almost everything, naturally, was white. The chairs were covered in white slips; a throw of white bearskin adorned a davenport sofa. A large mirror hung on one wall, a life-size nude on another.

And there were women: Japanese, Russian, German and Italian. There was food and drink without end: shredded chicken in wine sauce, raw fish, fried shrimp, the very best whisky. And there were friends. So many influential friends, cultivated by way of the women and the food and the drink.

Such was the afterlife of Ando Akira. A lavish HQ and a lavish early post-war existence; a reward, you might say, for saintly service in his previous life, as 'Guardian of Korean Labourers and Protector of Korean Juveniles'. These protectees had formed a small army in the early 1940s, controlled by him and doing whatever Japan's wartime leaders required: dismantling munitions plants and rebuilding them, away from Allied airstrikes; setting up underground factories; digging tunnels.

The heavenly voice that drifted across the airwaves on 15 August 1945 had announced the end of that old world. Precisely how the new one would turn out, neither Ando Akira nor anyone else knew at that point. They understood only that a judgement of sorts was on its way, aboard American planes and ships, scheduled to reach these shores by the end of the month. All around the country, it was set to be a busy fortnight.

*

In the Imperial Palace, a family closed ranks. The Emperor's uncle, Prince Higashikuni, was appointed Prime Minister. Konoe Fumimaro, risen from the political dead, became his deputy. The war was lost, but the *kokutai*, the national polity rooted historically and spiritually in the imperial institution, could – must – be saved. It would come down to identifying the deadliest of enemies, and then working with the others.

Konoe had been giving much thought to this in recent months. In February, he had implored the Emperor to end the war. Since Midway in 1942, the United States had been on the counter-attack. A list had been building up, of locations previously all but unknown to most Americans, but destined to acquire iconic status in their own modern story: Guadalcanal, in the Solomon Islands (1942–3); Saipan (summer 1944); Leyte, in the Philippines (October 1944); Iwo Jima (February 1945); Okinawa (spring and summer 1945); Potsdam, from where at the end of July 1945 the Allies declared that only 'unconditional surrender' would forestall Japan's 'prompt and utter destruction'.

Defeat, Konoe had suggested to the Emperor in February 1945, was inevitable. But, he added, there were worse fates. A Japanese communist revolution was surely coming: fomented by the Soviet Union, preying on the population's exhaustion and deep disillusionment with their rulers, and working with lower-class elements in the army who naïvely believed that such a thing as Emperor-centred communism was possible. Japanese newspapers, meanwhile, were spreading rumours that the military was to be deployed to the country's central mountains, in preparation for a protracted battle to defend the homeland. The Emperor, they claimed, was to be evacuated to mainland Asia, and from there the struggle against Anglo-America would carry on.

The Emperor had listened to Konoe's plea, but had not acted. He still hoped that the Soviet Union would decide it needed Japan in what would surely be its next war – against Britain and America. In any case, what could he do? The only way to be rid of the militarists now was to sponsor a rival and equally untrustworthy faction in the army. The recent past had revealed that there were those in that vast and fragmented institution who understood loyalty to the *kokutai* as transcending obedience to any particular Emperor.

Some of these extreme elements had shown themselves early in the morning of 15 August. The incineration of much of urban Japan across 1944 and 1945 had not been enough. Nor had American use, twice in quick succession – on 6 August at Hiroshima and then 9 August at Nagasaki – of a devastating mystery weapon, with who knew how many more waiting to be deployed. A Soviet declaration of war against Japan on 8 August, and a swift march into Manchuria, had ruled that country out as an intermediary with the other Allies. Nearly half a million Japanese civilians were now dead, including around 140,000 at Hiroshima and 70,000 at Nagasaki. Still it was not enough. A small group of soldiers invaded the grounds of the Imperial Palace, intent on stealing or destroying the phonograph record bearing the Emperor's surrender message. The recording had to be smuggled out in a laundry basket, and delivered to a radio station which itself had suffered an army attempt at sabotage. Even once the broadcast had been made, rumours swirled of a planned attack on the approaching US fleet. Japan's few remaining aircraft had to be disarmed as a precaution, their fuel tanks emptied.

The imperial loyalists gathering around the throne were for the most part more level-headed men. One of the reasons why the Japanese Cabinet had waited so long before ending the war was deep uncertainty over whether the Emperor would be held accountable for it. The terrible possibility loomed that an august, even divine institution, stretching back countless centuries, might end with a man soiling himself, his neck broken in a hangman's noose. Now that the decision had been made to stop the war, the Emperor himself having intervened, the task for these imperial loyalists was to lay out a red carpet for the incoming conquerors, angling it carefully according to their own hoped-for direction of travel. The Allied leadership might just be persuaded to accept a version of recent history in which the Emperor was innocent of wrongdoing: held captive by a military clique whose prime mover, Tōjō Hideki, had been ousted more than a year before.

The case would be helped if inevitable concessions were made pre-emptively. It was clear, for example, from the Potsdam Declaration that Japan's armed forces would be disbanded. So by imperial order the process was begun. The manufacture of weaponry was sure to be outlawed. So the Ministry of Munitions did away with itself overnight. Adding to a haze over Tokyo produced by trucks and buses converted to run on wood, charcoal and household rubbish went the remains of hastily incinerated government documents, while former ministries with a more peaceful and constructive ring – Commerce & Industry; Agriculture & Forestry – were resurrected. Decades-old plans for land and labour reform were taken out and dusted off.

Enticements were prepared, too, for ordinary Allied soldiers. Advertisements were placed for Japanese women between the ages of

A devastated Tokyo, seen from the air (*above*) and from street level (*below*)

eighteen and twenty-five who would be prepared to offer 'comfort' in exchange for food and shelter. Around 1,500 candidates turned up to the first recruitment meeting for the new 'Recreation and Amusement Association' (RAA), ready to be put to use as 'shock absorbers' – as one of the scheme's organizers put it – for the more respectable women of the country.

Agents, crisscrossing Japan in search of other women who were similarly short of options, found themselves passing through a landscape where the view stretched far further into the distance than it had before. Whole sections of cities had all but vanished. It looked as though everyone had simply packed up one night – houses and all – and gone, leaving behind refuse, rubble and a few stray bits of wood. Only the occasional edifice remained standing, lonely and improbable. Railway stations that until recently had played host to the high emotion and flag-waving fanfare of wartime goodbyes – smartly uniformed schoolchildren singing songs, aproned women plying departees with snacks and warm words – were home now to children without parents, surviving under bridges, in underground passageways or inside the remains of trains and trams. They were joined by war widows, begging, and by girls doing whatever they had to in order to eat. Most of the other 9 million homeless people in Japan were taking refuge with relatives, or else cramming themselves into ramshackle shelters put together with wood or tar-paper or anything else they could find.

Millions more Japanese were sick – cholera, typhoid, dysentery, polio – or were reaching the final stages of starvation. In Osaka, world-class scientists had switched from developing weaponry to researching an emergency diet. People were shown how to make the best of acorns, peanut shells and even sawdust: a fermenting agent, they were told, could be used to break sawdust down into a powder to supplement flour in the making of bread or dumplings. They were advised that if cooked properly, the flesh of mice and rats was perfectly safe, perhaps even a little gamey and bird-like to the tongue. Blossoms, roses and silkworm cocoons, once part of a pleasing and productive natural environment, all now ended up on people's plates.

Someone was going to have to answer for all this. The race to say who – and to convince a population exhausted by lies – was already up and running. Arguing the Emperor's line, and taken on now as one of his advisers, was the rather unlikely figure of Ishiwara Kanji, preacher of the apocalypse and provocateur of 1931's Mukden Incident. Lean and tanned, with his head shaved, Ishiwara was busily touring the country on specially arranged trains. He delivered to crowds of up to 20,000 people at a time a message of repentance – theirs, not his. He had, he pointed out, advised against escalation in China in 1937, and against attacking the United States in 1941. Instead, it was traitors like Tōjō who had brought the nation low. The people of Japan must now turn their backs on the recent fight and join the Emperor in starting the post-war conversation – peacefully laying down their arms, reforming their society – so that they might hope to control it. All being well, Ishiwara told the gathered masses, in a decade or so Japan would be back in business.

For people of all political stripes, variations on this promise of rebirth kept them going over several difficult and otherwise hopeless months. Within days of the surrender, Ichikawa Fusae was busy setting up a Women's Committee on Post-war Policy. Women must, at long last, have the vote. And rather than bargaining with the country's bureaucrats, as they had before, they should now enter their ranks: Japan's state ministries, along with its Diet, must soon, at last, open their doors to women. For now, women should keep wearing their simple, wartime pantaloons, Ichikawa declared, because there was hard work to be done. Food production must be increased, and money must be saved. Japanese soldiers should be welcomed home with warmth, despite the rumours beginning to circulate about what they had done in China – where up to 20 million people had perished – and elsewhere in Asia. When the Allies arrived, they should be met with caution and with pride. Wartime government predictions of the bestial havoc they would wreak, should they make it to Japanese shores, might turn out to have been pure propaganda. Then again, it might not.

Tokuda Kyūichi spent these days in hopeful expectation of seeing daylight again soon, after eighteen years inside a prison cell. Together with Shiga Yoshio, the rambunctious Okinawan and former elementary school teacher had done what he could to run Japan's communist movement from behind bars. Friends sent them books, writing secret messages in the margins with starch. These could be read with the aid of iodine, obtained from guards on the pretence of injury. A splash of urine would then erase the evidence before the books were returned, now featuring replies written in flour paste. Communication within the prison itself was by means of Morse code. Shiga later claimed to have transmitted the entire text of the Soviet Constitution in this way to a comrade in the cell below him.

While the Emperor and his advisers struggled to get their story straight, in the hope of Allied absolution, the outcome of the war put Japan's communists in a strong position. They could claim to have been on the right side of history, imprisoned for championing the internationalism on which Japan's leaders had so disastrously turned their backs. Their very idea of 'history' had been vindicated. Time was not the romantic, quasi-mystical cycle proposed by Japan's pastoral fantasists. It was a linear path towards progress, its future course plottable by means of Marxist theory. In an 'Appeal to the People', published from prison while they awaited their release, Tokuda and Shiga claimed that history's next step was Japan's embrace of Allied occupation, as the basis for 'democratic liberation and world peace'.

Plenty of left-wing intellectuals agreed. They were soon calling for a new, 'objective' trend in literature: by portraying everyday conditions of life, popular momentum towards changing them would surely begin to build. Other writers focused not on a socialist future, but on what had become of people's inner lives in the recent past. These seemed to have shrunk and withered, displaced by state-sponsored 'public' values. The priority now should be to reverse that direction of travel. Individual will and conscience must be rediscovered, and then allowed to work its cleansing magic on the public realm. Japan's great political scientist and dissector of ultranationalism, Maruyama Masao, called for a new balance of self-sufficiency with public commitment, the latter dutifully rather than slavishly pursued. He took as his inspiration one of the leading lights of Japan's first, now soured, experiment with modernity: Fukuzawa Yukichi. The novelist Natsume Sōseki would have served equally well, having lectured his students half a century before on the right kind of 'self-centredness'.

For the writer Sakaguchi Ango, one of the pioneers of an emerging 'literature of the flesh' (*nikutai bungaku*), the making of new commitments had to begin with honesty about the old ones. Looking around, he saw a toxic brew afflicting the country, of schmaltz, depravity and fantasies of imminent social collapse. There was extreme despondency, at an almost superhuman effort expended by ordinary Japanese apparently for nothing, while the pre-war wealthy seemed to have come through unscathed – they could be heard singing war songs in expensive restaurants. A sentimental, pornographic *kasutori* subculture was growing up around a cheap alcoholic drink made from *sake* dregs (*kasu*), featuring images of naked Western women, alongside the spectacle of half-naked Japanese women creating 'live' versions of famous foreign works of art by posing inside huge picture frames.

Sakaguchi's essay 'On Decadence' addressed itself to all this. It offered one of the earliest post-war denunciations of the emperor system: look beyond the myth of divinely descended rulers, he wrote, and you find an ignominious history of weak men hauled out of obscurity by self-serving politicians bent on manipulating the easily impressed. In comparison to such false pieties, decadence had its relative virtues: 'We have become decadent not because we lost the war, but because we are human; we become decadent because we are alive, that is all.' The Japanese should embrace this fact, counselled Sakaguchi, and even encourage the process. Some amongst Japan's kamikaze pilots had understood the war as contributing to Japan's destruction and so its rebirth. Sakaguchi seemed to be hoping for something similar: degeneracy as generative, impurity as ultimately purifying.

*

The likes of Ando Akira spent the days after 15 August 1945 engaged in an ambitious process of wealth redistribution. The army had long been stockpiling the means for around 4 million men to fight an anticipated two- to three-year battle to defend the home islands. But on that day, its leadership issued Secret Instruction #363. Arms and ammunition aside, these supplies – billions of dollars' worth of food and clothing, fuel and state-of-the-art technology – could all now be 'civilianized': delivered 'free of charge' to local governments, and on promise of future payment to other interested parties. It was a licence to loot.

Some took along bicycles, and filled backpacks. But the real ben-efits went to the Andos of the world: quick-thinking bosses at the helm of big organizations, capable of mobilizing thousands upon thousands of trucks and railway cars. Everything from trousers to aircraft engines was scooped up, whisked away and then warehoused, buried, or wrapped up and stashed in lakes. To hide a really large haul, new buildings were constructed over the top. In this way, many a large Japanese company entered the afterlife with not one but two revenue streams: alongside enormous war indemnity payments lavished on business allies by the government soon after 15 August, they could slowly feed their stolen goodies onto a rapidly blossoming black market.

That market had been in operation since the late 1930s, when Japan's wars abroad first began to take their toll on living standards and people were forced to pay inflated prices for scarce commodities. It was hard to view something as criminal when there was little option and everyone else was at it, at some level or other. A special 'economic constabulary' set up to combat the practice made more than 2 million arrests in just fifteen months. Some were caught forging or transferring official price marks, as a way of getting around price controls. Others were making enterprising use of Japan's *omi-yage* gift-giving tradition: paying the required government price but offering a little present on top.

As life in the cities grew more desperate, trains began to fill up with urbanites making day-trips to the countryside to barter directly with farmers, or to forage for themselves. In mid-August 1945, hundreds of thousands of people boarded trains out of Tokyo every single day, crammed into carriages, hanging off the sides, lying on the top and holding on for dear life. Most were feeding their own families, but others had discovered an essential new source of income: smuggling. Women would coo lovingly at clothfuls of rice, strapped to their backs like babies, as they made their way to one of tens of thousands of open-air markets around railway stations and elsewhere.

The police all but gave up. 'Madam, your baby has wet itself,' warned one, with a knowing nod towards the leaky haul on a woman's back. And as they melted away to fend for themselves, armed gangs moved in. Japan had been home for centuries to pedlars (*tekiya*) and gamblers (*bakuto*). The former used a combination of sharp practice and outright intimidation to send customers away with a 'bargain' on everything from fake medicine to bonsai trees with no roots. The latter were more easily romanticized: itinerant rogues, swaggering along with swords at their sides, faces mysteriously obscured by sedge hats, capes blowing in the wind.

Both groups operated at the margins, part of parallel societies where an *oyabun* ('boss') lorded it over ranks of *kobun* (underlings, or apprentices). But some did profitable business with the mainstream. The modern reality of *yakuza*, as they sometimes called themselves – the word taken from a losing hand in a Japanese card game: 8 (*ya*), 9 (*ku*), 3 (*za*) – was one of violent strike-breakers, corallers of casual labour and practitioners of political thuggery. Like their samurai counterparts, the *shishi*, they mixed a heavily advertised concern for the 'little guy' (excepting recalcitrant trade unionists) with a fierce, foreigner-hating and frequently emperor-centred nationalism.

As of mid-August 1945, the foreigners they hated the most were the *sangokujin* ('third-country people'). Hundreds of thousands of Taiwanese, Korean and Chinese men had entered Japan in recent years, run by people like Ando as forced labour to replace army conscripts.

Kimura Ihei's *Tokyo Station* (1945): people cling to trains in Tokyo, heading out to the countryside to find food

Such was the reality of 'co-prosperity' in East Asia. Thirty thousand Koreans were now dead or dying in Hiroshima, while others were leaving Japan as fast as they could. Some of those who stayed began to fight for control of the increasingly lucrative black market stalls, against *yakuza* whose ranks were swollen by demobbed soldiers looking for any kind of work they could find.

Alongside the *bakuto* and *tekiya* lineages, a new strain of *yakuza* had emerged in recent years. *Gurentai* ('hoodlums') were self-made men inspired by nothing more than the opportunities of the war and its immediate aftermath. One such was Kodama Yoshio. Associated in the 1930s with populist, emperor-centred ultranationalism – including a group established by the Tokyo University law professor, Uesugi Shinkichi – Kodama spent much of the war in China and Manchuria. There he ran an intelligence network featuring hundreds of criminals, thugs and members of the Military Police, with whose help he obtained (through a mixture of barter and extortion) an array of war materials for the Navy: radium and nickel, cobalt and copper.

Serving his country served him well. By August 1945, Kodama had approximately $175 million to his name – in diamonds, platinum and cash – to add to the men he controlled, and his mines, fisheries and munitions plants in central China. Now he was turning his talent, money and contacts to empire-building at home. He looted army stores, helped to establish the government's Recreation and Amusement Association, visited the Imperial Palace to offer advice to the Emperor and struck up conversations with influential pre-war politicians hoping to become influential post-war politicians. A 'Nihon Jiyūtō' (Japan Liberal Party) was soon in gestation, with Kodama amongst those providing its financial spark of life.

Meanwhile, another of Japan's *gurentai*, equally adept at finding new friends and allies as the times changed, was busy with a pressing new project. Ando Akira was having his gangs of workers refurbish Atsugi airbase, in preparation for a flight due in from the Philippines on 30 August. Aboard was the man whose signed photograph would shortly be given strategic pride of place alongside the mirror and the nude on Ando's white office walls: General Douglas MacArthur, Supreme Commander for the Allied Powers.

12
Blue Note

The American jazz pianist Hampton Hawes, serving with the US military in Japan, had never expected to find Charlie Parker and Dizzy Gillespie's music making it all the way out here, 'over oceans, across rice paddies'. But then one day, in Yokohama's Harlem Club, as he later recalled, 'this little chick in a kimono sat right down at the piano and started to rip off things I didn't believe, swinging like she'd grown up in Kansas City'. One future jazz legend was encountering another. The girl at the keys was the Tokyo-Yokohama music scene's rising star: Akiyoshi Toshiko.

Born in Manchuria, Akiyoshi served as a nurse there towards the end of the war. Narrowly escaping murder by her own side – she overheard hospital bosses weighing death against the disgraceful prospect of their staff being raped by the advancing Russians in August 1945 – she made it back to her family home only to find it being methodically looted by Soviet troops. Everything but her piano was carried out of the door and sold off to a broker sitting in the village square nearby.

Akiyoshi and her sisters went unharmed. Their mother hurriedly cut their hair, dressed them up in boys' school uniforms, and hid them away downstairs. But by the time the family escaped to Beppu, on the southern Japanese island of Kyūshū, they had next to nothing left. Desperate to help bring in some money, Akiyoshi went against the wishes of her father, who wanted her to go to medical school, and answered an advert for an amateur dance-hall band, comprising accordion, drums, violin and alto saxophone – with Akiyoshi on piano, adapting her classical training as best she could.

Demand for musicians had never been higher. In late summer 1945, railway lines used just a few months before to whisk young Japanese out to the coast, boarding boats from there out to Asia-Pacific battle-fronts, began funnelling a quarter of a million jubilant GIs in the opposite direction. Sixty-five thousand American soldiers had been dying, getting wounded or going missing every month towards the end of the conflict. Tens – possibly hundreds – of thousands more were secretly projected to perish in Operation Downfall: the planned Allied invasion of Japan's home islands, scheduled to begin in November 1945 with Operation Olympic, directed against Kyūshū. Now able to leave their beds each morning with a reasonable expectation of seeing them again that night, US forces were in the mood to celebrate. Japanese musicians of all kinds found themselves waiting around at train stations, amidst the hungry, the homeless and the black-market buyers and sellers, for American servicemen to pick them up in their trucks. Some nights as many as 350 bands were needed in Tokyo alone, their musicians catching a glimpse of how the conquerors and the wealthy conquered were living – drinking, dancing, multi-course dining.

If you could sight-read, you could get gigs. After some early disappointments, a grading system was developed to sort the wheat from the chaff – 'Special-A' all the way down to 'D'. But for American GIs, jazz was ultimately 'their music'. Creative contributions on this side of the planet were not to be expected. A reasonably faithful facsimile would do: in this, as in so much else, Japan's education – or re-education – was regarded as only just beginning.

It was an attitude that Akiyoshi found maddening. She fell in love with the music of Teddy Wilson while in Beppu, and began working his fresh, nimble right-hand melodies into her own playing. But graduating from provincial Japanese-only dances to more discerning audiences in Tokyo and Yokohama, she encountered some infuriating distractions: dancers and jugglers, hired as part of the evening entertainment, and a seemingly never-ending stream of American soldiers who thought that jazz ran in their bloodstream or came with their passport. She tried to teach them otherwise, letting them sit in and play when they asked, then rattling through tunes like 'Fine and Dandy' so fast that they were forced to bow out.

Akiyoshi's deeper exasperation, widely shared in Japan, was the notion apparently held by some Americans that they were bringing real rhythm and melody to these shores for the very first time – even bestowing a new quality of humanity upon Japan, like Judy Garland's Dorothy in *The Wizard of Oz* (1939) helping Asia's Tin Man to at last find a heart. There was little interest in Japan's rich tapestry of musical styles, developed by a music industry with decades of experience combining instruments, scales, vocal techniques and lyrical themes in order to hit an ever-shifting audience sweet-spot: dashes of something new or foreign worked into a familiar existing weave.

In the autumn of 1945, that industry once again struck just the right note. '*Ringo no Uta*' ('Apple Song'), from the film *Soyokaze* (Soft Breeze), became a nationwide hit: not for its lyrics – 'the apple's lovable, lovable's the apple' – but for the deep resonance with an exhausted population of a glowing young actress (Namiki Michiko) skipping through an orchard, singing about the simple goodness of blue skies and luscious fruit. Blending a homely minor key with Western-style vocals, 'Apple Song' hinted at a revived readiness in Japan for new, incoming ideas about the world – if only, like Namiki and her apples, they could be presented in the right way: fresh rather than alien, natural and good, proffered, not forced.

The problem was that American Occupation forces arrived in Japan with plans for their defeated enemy already largely formulated, having started the process of preparing for war's end just months after it began at Pearl Harbor. Away from crude wartime propaganda depicting a simian collective lost in ignorant, scraping thrall to their Emperor, a subtler take on Japan had been developing in US intelligence and policy circles. The country's project of modernization had stalled, its journey out of feudalism putt-putting to a halt some way short of the universal human ideal that veterans of Roosevelt's New Deal saw as embodied – however imperfectly – in American society. US mechanics needed to be sent in to get the thing going again.

The grand, historic scale of this analysis found spectacular, deafening illustration on 2 September 1945 in Tokyo Bay (at the bottom of whose waters were rumoured to lie gold bars, recently ransacked from army stores). Aboard the battleship USS *Missouri*, Japan's leaders sat to sign the instrument of surrender while two flags fluttered overhead. One had been flying over the White House the day that

Pearl Harbor was attacked. The other had been flown by Commodore Matthew C. Perry when he arrived off Japanese shores nearly a century before. Now, as then, the words were warm but the choreography was as cold as ice. In Perry's day, three military bands had assaulted Japanese eardrums while ten steam-powered warships waited out at sea, packed with Marines. On this day, the sky itself bore the menace, blackened and rent by the roar of 400 B-29s alongside 1,500 fighter planes. There could be no mistaking the message: 'Gentleman, shall we try this again?'

*

Concealing herself now and then behind a pillar on the sixth floor of Tokyo's Dai-Ichi Insurance Company building was a young American woman not long arrived in the country. Beate Sirota had been working in New York for *Time* magazine when it issued its stark front cover in August 1945: Japan's rising sun flag, with its central red disc – the 'meatball', as GIs called it – crossed out in two simple but eloquent black strokes.

Beate's joy had been tempered by anxiety. Growing up in Japan, where her Ukrainian-Austrian father, Leo Sirota, was a sought-after concert pianist and teacher, she had been forced to move from the German to the American school in Tokyo in 1936 when her teachers started marking her down. The reason became clear only in retrospect: this was one end of a long continuum of anti-Semitism, at the other end of which lay Auschwitz. There, Beate feared, most of her European relatives had died. Her father and mother might now be all the family she had left, and the only way of getting back to Japan to find out what had happened to them was to join the Occupation.

Fluent in Japanese, and with experience producing wartime propaganda for the US government, Beate was the ideal recruit. Christmas Eve 1945 found her descending towards Ando Akira's refurbished Atsugi airbase. The pilot circled the area a few times before landing, letting his passengers congregate by the windows to take in the devastation.

'Occupied Japan' duly stamped in her passport, Beate made her way through Yokohama in a jeep, passing by blackened ruins amidst which people were trying to make onions and winter radishes grow. Her parents, it turned out, had been moved during the war, along with other members of the ex-pat community, to the summer resort of Karuizawa. There, life had become steadily worse, as food and fuel to heat the uninsulated cottages ran low and local police officers became convinced that someone must be using shortwave radio to communicate with the Allies. Beate's father had been on the verge of going to prison when he found the Japanese officers replaced by American military police – under whose noses Beate, with the help of a GI admirer, was able to smuggle stolen food to her parents.

Her family fed, and soon to be rehoused, Beate now focused on her work. On 4 February 1946, she was called into a conference room, along with other staff from the Government Section of GHQ (General Headquarters of the Allied Powers). General Courtney Whitney read out a three-part note, dictated to him personally by the six-foot-tall, corn-cob pipe-smoking boss from whom Beate now and again felt compelled to hide. General Douglas MacArthur's blend of simple speech, authoritarian cast of mind and enormous self-belief made many on his own side nervous of him. His Japanese interlocutors were frequently in awe of a man whom they were convinced ruled on personal whim: purging enemies, dishing out directives and barely leaving his corporate castle, chosen for the way it towered over the grounds of the Imperial Palace across the road.

But the man they called the Blue-Eyed Shogun did, technically at least, take orders like everyone else. His came in the form of a Basic Directive, issued by President Truman and worked up by the State-War-Navy Coordinating Committee (SWNCC) in Washington DC. It was a blueprint for a new Japan, and it boiled down to what became known as the 'three Ds': demilitarization, democratization and decentralization of power. The first was relatively easy. The second two were rather harder. Eventually, all three would go awry.

MacArthur's February note was characteristically terse:

I

The Emperor is at the head of the State.
His succession is dynastic.

His duties and powers will be exercised in accordance with the Constitution and responsible to the basic will of the people as provided therein.

II

War as a sovereign right of the nation is abolished. Japan renounces it as an instrumentality for settling its disputes and even for preserving its own security. It relies upon the higher ideals which are now stirring the world for its defence and its protection.

No Japanese Army, Navy or Air Force will ever be authorized and no rights of belligerency will ever be conferred upon any Japanese forces.

III

The feudal system of Japan will cease . . .

When he had finished reading out the note, Whitney announced that the people in this room were now a constituent assembly. They had until 12 February to turn MacArthur's words into a Constitution for Japan.

Much had already happened in the five months up to this point, since MacArthur landed in Japan. Gone was the Peace Preservation Law of 1925, restricting people's liberties – though its rescinding in October 1945 did not come soon enough for prisoners like the philosopher Miki Kiyoshi: disillusioned with what became of the Greater East Asia Co-Prosperity Sphere ideal, he had fallen out with the authorities and eventually been jailed, dying in prison in late September 1945, almost a month into the Occupation. Gone was the Special Higher Police Force, many of whose members simply melted away into other parts of Japan's vast bureaucracy. Gone were the Japanese Army and Navy, along with the empire they had built: Korea, Manchukuo, Taiwan and territories across mainland China and out into the Pacific. Gone – and in the process of going – were tens of thousands of politicians, police, teachers, publishers and other influential individuals whose names featured on a laboriously researched list of undesirables. And gone, already, were a large number of American

GIs: with Occupation turning out to be a much less bloody business than some had feared, one of the two American armies sent to Japan had promptly left again.

There were few signs of popular opposition in Japan to any of these American initiatives. Many people felt little but dismay, even hatred, towards their wartime leaders: for embroiling the country in conflict; for lying about Japan's prospects and progress as it unfolded; and for failing to protect people against unnecessary suffering by surrendering as soon as the cause was clearly lost.

And yet the language of MacArthur's February note was replete with bold talk of what 'is' and what Japan 'does'. How could he know? It was reminiscent of Yoshino Sakuzō's notion of *minpon-shugi* from a couple of decades before: offering government 'for' the people, catering to interests of which they were presumed to be too uneducated to be aware. So far, under the Occupation, 'by the people' involved the fairer hiring of functionaries – from December 1945, women could vote and be voted for in general elections – rather than a fair hearing for people's post-war aspirations before major constitutional suggestions were made.

Beate Sirota acquired an epoch-making role here, in the most casual of ways. The new Constitution was to have something of which generations of Japanese feminists had only been able to dream: a section on women's rights. Beate's boss turned around to her shortly after Whitney's constitutional announcement and said, simply: 'You're a woman. Why don't you do it?'

Beate did at least have a better claim than MacArthur to know how Japanese women lived and what they might want and need, having grown up in the country. And she took to her task with speed, dashing around Tokyo in an army jeep, ransacking every surviving library she could find for copies of constitutions – the Weimar Republic, France, the Soviet Union – while being careful not to borrow too much from one place, in case someone guessed what she was up to.

From the Weimar Constitution, Beate took ideas about marriage being based on the equal rights of men and women, and the duty of the state to support motherhood and families – something over which Japanese feminists like Hiratsuka Raichō and Yosano Akiko had wrangled before and during the war. From the Soviet Constitution,

Beate Sirota with Ichikawa Fusae

she borrowed an article on free 'medical, dental, and optical aid' for children. All too aware of how the Meiji Constitution had played out in practice, not least when it came to people's rights, Beate was determined to leave no room in her document for legal gymnastics by future Japanese lawyers – most of whom she expected to be fairly conservative men. The resulting draft was so long that Beate suffered a drastic editing down before the final version of the complete Constitution was presented to Whitney.

As Beate and the rest of the team worked away in an old ballroom, the newspapers carried news of their absent dance partner. US policymakers had decided early on – just as the Emperor and his advisers had hoped – that it made sense to try to govern Japan via, rather than in spite of, its existing institutions. So Japan's bureaucrats, together with moderate political leaders untainted by the war, had initially been tasked with preparing the new Constitution. But when newspaper leaks suggested they were tweaking the Meiji Constitution rather than tearing it up – imperial prerogatives all but untouched; people's rights still conditional; armed forces envisaged – MacArthur resolved to go ahead without his Japanese colleagues, and without telling them.

When GHQ officials arrived for a meeting on 13 February with the former diplomat and imperial confidant Yoshida Shigeru, along with Home Minister Matsumoto Jōji, they found the Japanese committee's draft Constitution spread out on a desk, ready for bargaining to begin. They ignored it, and revealed their own document instead: the Emperor removed from politics; an elected legislature empowered to hire and fire the Prime Minister; religion separated from state; any military capability out of the question; and a wider range of rights for Japanese people than even their American counterparts enjoyed – with guarantees on free universal education, public health and social security, and collective bargaining for workers.

The two stunned Japanese ministers were politely asked to accept all this. And then threats were made. General Whitney suggested that the American draft Constitution was the best way of protecting the position of the Emperor. And it could easily be released directly to the Japanese public – on the assumption, commonly made at GHQ, that Japan was a nation of natural liberals lumbered with conservative leaders. Taking a break in the garden, Whitney watched as a B-29 passed overhead, remarking to one of Yoshida's aides how much he was enjoying 'your atomic sunshine'. When he returned inside, the Japanese draft had vanished from the desk.

The threat against the Emperor had been a bluff. MacArthur had long intended to extend to the general Japanese population a version of the psychological warfare tactics that had worked against their military: parting the average Japanese private from his senior officers by appealing to the transcendent goodness (and implied innocence) of the man-god from whom he leased his gun. It was the same strategy used by the early Meiji leaders, and the very one derided by Sakaguchi Ango in his 'On Decadence' essay: unknown, barely legitimate leaders grateful for an imperial puppet whose strings could be discreetly pulled.

MacArthur's bluff went uncalled, and Beate was soon providing English–Japanese interpretation at an intense series of meetings aimed at hammering out a final draft of the Constitution in the latter language. The Japanese delegation used what wriggle room they could find. Concepts like 'the people' depended so much on America's own historical experience that they had only to wait until approximations like *shinmin* (subject) and *jinmin* (the public) were ruled out – as too servile and too socialist, respectively – before persuading their exhausted opposite numbers to accept *kokumin* (national), despite its heavy nationalist undertones. Similar moves had been made months before over the thorny issue of the Emperor's divinity. The English-language version of a rescript issued on New Year's Day 1946 had stated plainly that the Emperor was not 'divine'. The Japanese version said something rather different: he should not be regarded as an *akitsu-mikami*, a 'manifest god'. This left artfully open the question of whether Japan's emperors were or were not descended from the Sun Goddess.

Opinion polls in the spring of 1946, together with draft constitutions drawn up and circulated by ordinary Japanese (just as had happened sixty years before), suggested that although MacArthur had not been big on consultation, most people were at this point broadly in favour of what he had helped to engineer. They wanted inalienable popular rights. And they wanted to keep the imperial institution in some form, while curbing its power – no more than 5 per cent of the population shared the communists' radical republicanism. A series of country-wide imperial tours showcased the new arrangements, the Emperor appearing to his people as a socially awkward middle-aged man, in scuffed shoes and an ill-fitting everyman suit – the work of a tailor forbidden from touching his client. The old mystique was ebbing away. People spoke of a *shōchō tennō* (symbolic Emperor), even a *shiminteki tennō* – a 'people's Emperor'.

*

A few weeks after the announcement of the draft Constitution in March 1946, a man with a violin was sent packing. He had been caught performing a satirical song about MacArthur and Hirohito: 'Everybody is talking about democracy, but how can we have democracy with two emperors?' The authorities were starting to clamp down. American military police and Japanese police walked onstage at the Imperial Theatre together to halt a kabuki performance, over a concern about the risk of feudal backsliding. Cartoonists were forbidden from creating caricatures of MacArthur. A haiku that ran 'Small green vegetables / are growing in the rain / along the burned street' was banned, as 'Criticism of the United States'. Painters were steered away from depicting the distinctive *torii* gateways to Shinto shrines, because of their nationalist resonance.

Film directors embarked on a frustrating few years. They constantly had to reshoot scenes filmed in Tokyo, to avoid showing GIs, English-language signage, or other evidence of war and Occupation. A character in Ozu Yasujirō's *Late Spring* (1949) was forbidden from observing that Tokyo was filled with bombed-out sites. Despite the supreme obviousness of this to the city's millions of residents and visitors, his line had to be changed to 'Tokyo is so dusty'. Depictions of Mount Fuji were banned, because of its appearance in wartime propaganda (to news of which one director angrily replied: 'Why, in that case, did you not bomb Fuji, instead of Hiroshima and Nagasaki?'). And Kurosawa Akira saw his film *They Who Step on the Tiger's Tail* (1945) banned not once, but twice: first by wartime Japanese censors, as 'too democratic', and then by post-war American censors, as 'too feudal'.

Under the circumstances, a degree of control over the media was essential. The cumulative effect of years of hearing about Anglo-American evil and the necessity for holy war could hardly be expected to dissipate overnight. And with Ishiwara Kanji tipped by some to become Japan's *Führer* – plotting a humiliated nation's return to glory – there remained the prospect of people being cajoled into restarting the conflict. But the work of the Occupation's Civil Censorship Detachment (CCD) went well beyond what was required to ensure basic security. Six thousand – mostly Japanese – operatives checked around 330 million letters and packages (Ishiwara complained that it took three months for letters to reach him). They tracked 800,000 private telephone conversations. They subjected large numbers of newspapers, books and magazines to pre-publication censorship. And they vetted tens of thousands of publications and radio, theatre and film scripts.

Critics began to wonder why, if democracy was a natural state for human beings, it required quite this level of micromanagement – extending even to positive propaganda. At MacArthur's first meeting with the Emperor, a photograph was taken showing the former looming powerfully over the latter, who appeared uncomfortably overdressed and looked distinctly out of his depth. Such an image could not have been created during or before the war. Only Imperial Household photographers were allowed anywhere near the Emperor with a camera, and even they had to stay at least twenty metres back and use telephoto lenses, capturing just his upper body and avoiding shots from sideways on because of Hirohito's slight stoop. This latest photograph was a rare embarrassment, and the Japanese Cabinet quickly tried to ban the media from publishing it. But GHQ not only overturned the ban: they *insisted* that the photo be published, knowing full well the message that it would send.

For similar reasons, approved American writers and musicians were actively promoted, while the likes of John Steinbeck's *Grapes of Wrath* were forbidden. Film-makers were encouraged to show couples kissing, as a means of balancing out bowing: a practice that censors regarded as ingraining inequality and subservience but which they reluctantly reasoned could not be eliminated from Japanese culture by fiat. Soon, all this kissing, alongside a prevalence of escapist over politically incisive film-making, had Japanese conspiracy theorists wondering whether the Americans had secretly devised a 'three Ss' policy of cultural containment for their country: sex, sports and screen. Ironically, the Americans suspected something similar of the Japanese. After visiting the milky opulence of Ando Akira's HQ, along with his notorious Dai-An Club, the *Chicago Sun*'s foreign correspondent Mark Gayn found himself surer than ever of a 'shrewd, well-organized and well-financed Japanese campaign to corrupt the Army of the United States ... the weapons are wine, women, and hospitality, and the objective is to subvert the starch and purpose of the Occupation'.

Perhaps the most influential propaganda intervention of all was a sustained campaign to shape the way that the Japanese thought about the recent conflict. In the early months of the Occupation, GHQ's Civil Information and Education Section (CIE) put together an account of what it insisted had now to be called the 'Pacific War', emphasizing

America's place in it over that of East Asia – despite the latter's military theatre absorbing an overwhelmingly larger number of Japanese men, money and munitions. Beginning on the fourth anniversary of Pearl Harbor, this version of events was systematically disseminated in Japanese newspapers and via a radio series – 'Now It Can Be Told' – that purported to offer the Japanese the 'facts' of the conflict, at long last, so that they could draw their own conclusions. The narrative was as artfully contrived as the theme music, which blended the *shamisen* with the score from Hollywood's *Gone With the Wind*. This had been a war of pure, naked aggression, the Japanese discovered, in which their country's political and economic insecurities in the late 1930s and early 1940s had played no catalysing role. Militarists had silenced brave internationalists, and effectively made Hirohito their captive.

The Tokyo War Crimes Tribunal, convened in April 1946 to try 'Class A' war criminals – those accused of initiating and directing the war – largely ended up supporting this version of recent history. Critical reporting of its proceedings was forbidden, so Japanese audiences ended up hearing little of the concerns raised by a single dissenting judge, Radhabinod Pal from India: that some of the people who were putting Japan's leaders on trial had themselves violated the rules of war, by indiscriminately bombing Japanese cities and unleashing nuclear weapons on the world. News of what had happened in the months since those bombs were dropped – 'Little Boy' on Hiroshima, 'Fat Man' on Nagasaki – was meanwhile carefully suppressed. Japanese film footage of the aftermath was confiscated and flown to the United States for safe-keeping. Important accounts of the bombings did begin, belatedly, to emerge: in prose, poetry, painting and film. But the publishers of *Nagasaki no Kane* (*The Bells of Nagasaki*) (1949), written by a Catholic doctor, Nagai Takashi, who died from radiation sickness in 1951, found themselves forced to include in the book, for balance, an American-authored appendix detailing the Japanese army's 'Sack of Manila', in which 100,000 civilians were killed.

The terms of long-running, post-war conversations about East Asia's catastrophic mid-century conflict were thus effectively set by the exigencies of Occupation. A more balanced and transparent tribunal might have helped to begin the work of repairing relations in

East Asia. As things turned out, left-wing critics and Japanese neo-nationalists alike were later able to use claims of 'victor's justice' to bolster diametrically opposed positions on their country's political arrangements. And to add to perceptions that crucial details of the war were covered up or exaggerated, there was a sense that if suffering could be seen as equitably distributed – Hiroshima somehow balancing out Nanjing, Nagasaki traded for Manila – then apology or remorse from either party was beside the point.

In the short term, it was difficult for Occupation leaders to know how these various efforts at shaping Japanese attitudes were going to turn out. Japan's first post-war elections, held the same month that the Tribunal was convened, were regarded as a particularly risky affair. Some at GHQ had argued that a country still so polarized by war and hunger should not yet be sent to the polls. As it was, teams of American observers were dispatched, watching as ghostly white-haired adults and children – caught in a sanitizing spray of American DDT – milled around listening to endless soapbox speeches, often given by rival candidates standing side by side, in front of walls where the faded remains of wartime propaganda still lingered.

The country's two new conservative parties, the Japan Liberal Party and the Japan Progressive Party, found themselves in a novel situation. Just a couple of years before, socialists and communists had been under lock and key. Now they were legally campaigning (reinventing themselves as democrats, to match the national mood), and some of those in power – GHQ New Dealers in particular – seemed actually to be rooting for them. The focal point for much left-wing anger around this time was the portly pre-war internationalist Shidehara Kijūrō, serving as the country's Prime Minister since Prince Higashikuni stepped down in the wake of the debacle over the MacArthur–Hirohito photograph. Buildings were plastered with anti-Shidehara posters, and he was very publicly denounced at a mass rally of some 15,000 people in Hibiya Park, many waving red flags. The rally turned into a march on his nearby residence, and from there into an assault on it. Three hundred policemen struggled in vain to prevent first the outer gates and then the main door giving way. Punches and missiles were thrown, shots were fired by the police, and in the end a contingent of American military police in armoured jeeps had to be called in to break up the crowd and send them home.

To help bring that demonstration to an end, Shidehara had agreed to a meeting with the communist leader, Tokuda Kyūichi. After making a series of excuses via an unfortunate aide – he didn't want cameramen present; he didn't like floodlights; he didn't want his voice recorded – Shidehara finally appeared, and was treated to an unprecedented haranguing from Tokuda about conditions out there in the country. 'Look at you,' said Tokuda. 'You're so fat. You must be buying food on the black market.' A surreal encounter ended in a chaotic scuffle when one of Tokuda's delegation thought he spotted a secret service agent concealing a weapon, and Shidehara tried to make use of the diversion to escape from the room.

In the end, the April elections went reasonably smoothly, and thirty-nine women made a historic entrance into the Diet. The socialist and communist parties had failed to agree on a hoped-for progressive front, and instead the Japan Liberal Party took power, with Yoshida Shigeru becoming Prime Minister. For all the rhetoric of a 'new Japan' and excitement at the radical constitutional draft, which the newly elected Diet debated and then passed with only minor changes, it seemed to progressive critics very much as though the same old conservatives had ended up back in power, the wheels of their party machines greased by the same old business and landed interests. An American journalist was told by Japanese colleagues that this new Diet contained as many as 180 war criminals, while in other cases purged former politicians had succeeded in getting their wives or juniors elected in their places. Something similar was said to be going on in the press: an editor at the *Asahi Shimbun* admitted that an upstairs conference room at his newspaper's offices was reserved for purged staff members, who continued to draw salaries while loyal underlings took care of the day-to-day running of the paper.

Ongoing discontent spilled over into a new series of mass rallies. Tens – possibly hundreds – of thousands of people turned out for a May Day parade centred on a plaza right in front of the Imperial Palace. Demands were made for food and for an end to rationing (or at least its fair implementation). At a special 'food May Day', held three weeks later in the same place, Tokuda addressed a crowd of some 200,000 people. 'We are starving!' he shouted, before turning around to point out the Palace. 'Is he?' Mocking the Emperor's well-known awkwardness when confronted with the general public, he told the crowd that he had recently been refused an imperial audience. 'We were chased away. Is it because the Emperor can say nothing but "Ah, so. Ah, so. Ah, so?"' His delegation had, however, managed to enter the Palace, he said. There they had inspected the imperial fridges and perused the menu: plenty of fresh milk, chicken, pork, eggs and butter.

MacArthur finally intervened, publically denouncing the 'growing tendency towards mass violence and physical processes of intimidation under organized leadership' as a threat to orderly government and to the Occupation itself. It would not be allowed to continue. The limits of people's new freedoms were suddenly laid bare, but the high tide of left-wing radicalism was in any case beginning to pass. Food aid and a good harvest helped to take the wind out of socialist sails as 1946 wore on, but the most powerful factor by far – and one of the great achievements of the American Occupation – emerged in October that year: an economic revolution on such a scale that only someone with MacArthur's power, during a time of great flux in Japan's modern experience, could possibly have seen it through.

Where pre-war bureaucrats had tackled rural distress by offering aid and encouraging cooperation between landlords and tenants (the latter farming nearly half of Japan's cultivated land), a radical new Land Reform Law now all but did away with landlords. Believing that 'feudal' relationships and harsh agrarian conditions partly explained the rise of Japanese ultranationalism, strongly committed to a broad ideal of 'democratization', and concerned about the attractions of communism, GHQ introduced quotas for the amount of land that any one person might legally own or lease. They then bought all the rest at fixed rates and offered to sell it to the people who had been tilling it, via long-term mortgages whose burdens were soon eased by inflation. Some landlords appealed, but lost, and with ex-tenants now dominating the rural vote there was little chance that future Japanese governments would ever be able to risk trying to reverse the policy.

Back in the capital, meanwhile, as leftist ardour was cooling,

Women vote for the first time, in April 1946

MacArthur dug in. In cooperation with Japanese conservatives, he banned a national strike that had been called for 1 February 1947, in which 2.6 million people were poised to protest against low wages. He described it as a 'deadly social weapon' whose wielding Japan, in its present condition, might not survive. Politics seemed to be returning to a semblance of its former, pre-war self: a system of managerialism and negotiation, with police and strike-breakers held in reserve.

*

Akiyoshi Toshiko and Hampton Hawes quickly became friends after their meeting in Yokohama. They began to plan a tour together. But the American authorities in Japan proved less than enthusiastic. Junior officials had been thrilled at the PR potential of a Japanese girl playing alongside an African-American soldier, in proudly pressed and polished US uniform (Hawes admitted to a weakness, dating back to childhood, for braid and insignia). But then someone higher up vetoed the idea – 'One of those cracker Texas colonels,' Hawes suspected.

The turn of phrase was revealing. In theory, jazz should have been a great way for American Occupation forces to sell their broader political and cultural product in Japan. The US State Department clearly understood that for freewheeling, pan-ethnic Americana there was little that could touch it: they encouraged the likes of Benny Goodman and Dizzy Gillespie to make goodwill tours of Africa, the Soviet Union and the Middle East – from where Gillespie telegrammed President Eisenhower, trumpeting the effectiveness of 'our interracial group' against 'Red propaganda'.

The pre-war and wartime Japanese authorities had done their bit to set up an association of jazz with freedom, steadily clamping down on records and dance halls from the late 1920s onwards. The latter especially had been big business. Police had looked on with disapproval as men paid around two yen for a booklet of ten tickets, each of which got them a three-minute ride around the dance floor in the arms of one of the professional female 'taxi dancers' who sat waiting on chairs or benches. Fast, foreign music, intimate encounters in skimpy clothing and insufficiently patriotic venue managers – some of whom were a little too quick to dry their tears and dust off their cash registers following a period of closure to mourn the Taishō Emperor in 1926 – had occasionally been enough to earn a visit from Japan's swashbuckling political thugs. Sōshi came swaggering across the dance floor, samurai swords in their belts, determined to recall a trashy and effete clientele to the physical and sartorial standards of true Japaneseness.

The war turned jazz into a particularly creative form of passive resistance. The dance halls were closed, but listeners hoarded the records they were ordered to hand in, while musicians dutifully laid down their Anglo-American 'saxophones' and 'trombones' only to pick up instruments whose new Japanese names translated as 'bent metallic flute' and 'sliding bent long gold trumpet'. These they used to play a distinctly jazzy genre called 'light music' or 'national music'. One player later recalled that when they had finished recording a gunka (military music) track, which they were required to produce, they would jam in whatever way they wanted because the police officers outside the building couldn't tell Duke Ellington from Mozart.

Why, given all this, were the Americans not more enthusiastic in casting themselves as musical liberators? One of the reasons, hinted at in Hawes' comment, was that jazz shared with democracy some difficult, potentially dangerous characteristics. Ideally, both were transformative of minds and hearts. But they had a way of adapting themselves to fit an underlying social status quo – for better or for worse. For American jazz in the mid-twentieth century, that meant tensions of race and class. GHQ was already doing its best in Japan to hide these blemishes on a society that it hoped to offer up as exemplary. It censored all talk of race, even while the US military practised the segregation of black GIs stationed in Japan from white enlisted and officer comrades – in barracks and RAA brothels, in the intended audience for different radio programmes, and in the patronage of entertainment venues: Yokohama's Harlem Club, where Akiyoshi met Hawes, was a 'black' club.

The last thing the Americans needed was publicity of the sort generated by an incident during a tour of North American jazz talent around Japan. At one of the concerts, Benny Carter and the Canadian pianist Oscar Peterson ended up holding back some GIs in the audience while the jazz impresario Norman Granz punched another soldier in the face for abusing Ella Fitzgerald during her performance. The only upside was that for at least one Japanese member of the audience it became an unforgettable lesson in democracy: he recalled being 'impressed' to see a military figure taking a beating from a civilian – something utterly unimaginable a few years previously in Japan.

Jazz and democracy shared in common a broader dilemma for their exporters and champions. Both were about freedom and flourishing, improvisation and spontaneity. And yet if they failed to take quite specific forms when they travelled, they risked appearing fake, corrupt or superficial. Hence the temptation for Occupation personnel concerned with the state of Japanese politics not just to till the soil and sow the seeds, but to wait and watch and prune – to the point where Yoshida Shigeru began saying that 'GHQ' ought to stand for 'Go Home Quickly'.

Akiyoshi had anxieties of her own about jazz: where it came from, to whom it really belonged, how – and to what extent – it could be passed on or picked up. Despite being technically brilliant, and knowing bad jazz when she heard over-confident GIs play it, she worried that there might be some deeper source of inspiration into which Japanese like herself would struggle to tap. She confided as much in

Hawes, who advised her to eat 'collard greens, black-eyed peas, and corn pone and clabber'. Akiyoshi didn't realize he was joking. 'Where can I buy that?' she asked.

It took Akiyoshi until 1974 – much of that time spent living in the United States – to produce a piece of music that she was happy to say brought jazz and 'Japan' together. She accomplished it not by 'Japanizing' jazz, but by personalizing it. She allowed the music she learned to pass from her eyes and ears to her hands via her heart rather than her brain, setting aside calculations about national origins and ownership, and instead allowing her own needs and desires to drive the process. Only in this way could an idea of foreign origin truly be domesticated.

The breakthrough track begins with the steadily rising call of a Nō chant, and the clack of a *tsuzumi* (hand drum). Then the song's signature flute line starts up: a quivering glissando intended to mimic the sound of the *shakuhachi*, the Japanese bamboo flute. A close-harmony brass section takes up the melody from there, shifting the piece into a Western rhythm even while the Nō chant and drums carry through underneath. Akiyoshi called her creation 'Kogun' – 'lonely warrior' or 'forlorn force'. It was inspired by a news story of the time. A soldier of the Imperial Japanese Army, Private Onoda Hirō, had surrendered in the Philippines after twenty-nine years of hiding out – or, as he saw it,

Akiyoshi Toshiko (1929–) (*left*) and Hampton Hawes (1928–77) (*right*)

holding out. His former commanding officer had had to fly to his island and formally order him to stand down. 'Kogun' was in part about Akiyoshi as well, and her experience of trying to make it as a lone Japanese woman on the US jazz scene.

From hearing her first Teddy Wilson record back in Beppu, it had taken Akiyoshi nearly three decades of trial and error to get to this point. The rest of the Japanese population – democratic Constitution in hand and the first post-war elections now behind them – would enjoy no such luxury of time in experimenting with their American import. The end of the war had brought peace to much of the world, but it hadn't brought stability. America's leaders were setting new goals for themselves towards the end of the 1940s, and they had in mind a very specific role for their enemy turned ally.

13
Bright Life

Japan's new constitution was welcomed into the world on 3 May 1947, by a Japanese brass band playing 'The Stars and Stripes Forever' outside the Imperial Palace. GHQ having thus dropped a strong hint about the document's paternity, a thirty-page guide was produced, offering illustrated commentary designed to ensure that no one could miss the major points. The title of the booklet, of which 20 million copies were printed and distributed, was *Atarashii Kempō, Akarui Seikatsu* – 'New Constitution, Bright Life'.

The person destined one day to reveal to Japan and the world the true arrival of that life was at this point busy toddling around his house. Born near Hiroshima on the very day it was bombed, Sakai Yoshinori would one day be known around the globe as the 'Atomic Boy'. His legs would bear him, clad in purest white, up a seemingly never-ending flight of stairs, halfway into the blue heavens. In his hand, a flaming torch. In the sky above, fighter planes trailing coloured smoke, their pattern gradually resolving into five interlocking rings. On that day, *akarui seikatsu* would be a mere slogan no more. But first the bright life had to be built – and bought. The price would be high.

*

Summer 1949 found Morita Akio and a group of friends standing around in a leaky shack, frying oxalic ferrite in a pan. Their initial idea had been to turn their physics and engineering know-how, until recently devoted to Japanese military projects, towards the making of small parts for the large electrical companies whose fortunes they expected would soon rebound. They planned to drive the parts around Tokyo in their old Datsun truck, full of American army pet-rol procured on the black market from enterprising GIs. Military police had taken to dyeing their fuel red and making random vehicle inspections, to try to catch the culprits. But someone had discovered a means of using charcoal to cancel out the dye – hardship inspiring entrepreneurship – so that democratizing US Army supplies remained a relatively safe ruse.

Tokyo Tsūshin Kōgyō ('Tokyo Telecommunications Engineering Company': TTEC) was rather a grand name for a company whose headquarters was not yet waterproof. Nor was there any guarantee that their business model would work. Many of Japan's electrical companies were part of large, family-controlled corporate networks that had evolved over decades. They were connected via stock own-ership, interlocking directorships, exclusive and advantageous credit arrangements, and the buying and selling of one another's goods and services at preferential rates. Known as *zaibatsu*, they were regarded by liberals at GHQ – and out in the country at large – as having been complicit in Japanese militarism, and so incompatible with new democratic ideals. TTEC might find some of their largest potential customers taken off the board.

The challenge for those opposed to the *zaibatsu* lay in weeding out something so deeply rooted. These networks had expanded and diversified in tandem with modern Japan's economy. The career of a man called Iwasaki Yatarō offered a case in point. Active in shipping before 1868, he had assisted the Meiji leaders in some of their early seaborne adventures: the 'civilizing' raid on Taiwan in 1874 and the transport to southern Japan of the men and arms required to crush the Satsuma rebellion. Over the years that followed, aided by an emerging state inclined to trust large companies and combines to wield scarce capital well, Iwasaki and his successors at Mitsubishi added to their core shipping concern one new line of business after another. They got into coal, copper and gold-mining; banking, insur-ance and postal transport; farming and beer-brewing (the well-known Kirin brand); paper and chemicals; oil, iron and steel production; water and electrics; engine-building; and finally aircraft. The revol-utionary A6M Zero fighter, adapted for kamikaze missions in the last months of the Second World War, helped to bring them to the attention of American officers, one of whom posted a ditty to the bulletin board of his billet in Tokyo:

> There's something rather fishy
> About the Mitsubishi
> And the rest of the *zaibatsu*
> Are also not so hot-su.

It was a testament to the effectiveness of the red-carpet strategy pursued by the imperial house, conservative politicians and big business – starting compromise conversations before the Americans could get a word in – that the first US attempt at breaking up these *zaibatsu* was based on a policy actually put forward by one of the *zaibatsu* themselves: Yasuda, one of the 'big four' alongside Mitsubishi, Mitsui and Sumitomo. Under the plan, *zaibatsu* holding companies were dissolved, with most of their top executives forced out of their jobs and forbidden from purchasing shares when they were sold off.

The *zaibatsu* families could just about live with this – for now – while they set about gathering information on GHQ's longer-term intentions. Representatives all but camped out at MacArthur's Dai-Ichi building, while top American officials were wined and dined and their maids persuaded to spy on them. Eleanor Hadley, on whose *zaibatsu* research Occupation policy drew, was too junior to have a maid, and as a woman was thought unlikely to be susceptible to the charms of a geisha party. Instead, Sumitomo sent her roses.

Patience and persuasion soon paid off. By the time GHQ managed, in December 1947, to get through the Diet a more general measure to tackle 'excessive concentrations of economic power', the mood music from the United States was changing. Business opinion had become ambivalent about MacArthur and his mission. The first two years of the Occupation had set the American taxpayer back around $600 million in personnel costs alone – and for what? It was hard to imagine a country less favourable to future investment (or to achieving returns from existing ones): its economic recovery had stalled, while labour had been let off the leash and was causing no end of trouble. It was all deeply un-American. Putting those who had clearly colluded with militarism out of business was one thing. But GHQ seemed to want to go much further, punishing and purging the very people whose expertise was needed to get Japan's economy going again. Their timing was terrible: communism was on the rise across Eastern Europe, there was no guarantee that Chiang Kai-shek would hold off Mao Zedong in China, and yet here was the United States fettering free commerce and all but preparing the ground for a Japanese revolution.

Sympathy for this valuing of continuity was widespread amongst conservatives in Tokyo too: within GHQ, Japan's political parties and in various government ministries. There had been calls after the war for an overhaul of the state bureaucracy. But American faith in expertise, combined with sheer pragmatism had helped to ensure that very little was done. A measure requiring all officials of a certain seniority to be re-examined, to check their fitness for office, yielded only the 'Paradise Exam': candidates were allowed tea, cigarettes and an unlimited amount of time to complete the paper. For the most part, the same old 'shepherds of the people' remained at their desks, with some even trusted to screen candidates for MacArthur's purges – with the result that very few bureaucrats lost their jobs. Others pressed ahead with policy: the overwhelming majority of new bills introduced into the new Diet originated not with the political parties but with the ministries, in whose corridors every single Japanese prime minister right through to the mid-1970s began his career.

The Occupation's left-liberal idealists were beginning to feel that they had had their day. As the world's post-war battle lines became clearer, Japan in American eyes went from being a social experiment to a key Pacific ally. A strong economy and a robustly pro-American politics were the priorities, so rights to unionize and to strike were duly tempered, while the planned assault on large companies was first cut back and then quietly dropped. Joseph M. Dodge, a Detroit banker who had previously advised American Occupation forces in Germany, was sent out to Japan in 1949 to get the country moving. His prescription became known as the 'Dodge Line'. Inflation was to be tackled and the budget balanced, through taxes and public sector cuts. Extravagant government lending to business would be reined in, while subsidies and price controls were phased out. A workable fixed exchange rate would underpin foreign trade, control of which was now to be returned to private commercial hands (where previously it had been run through GHQ and the Japanese government). Last but not least, US aid to Japan would be scaled back.

Whatever their long-term benefits, in the short term these measures nearly took the country under, with a recession that put half a million people out of work. Japan managed to stay just the right side of the Dodge Line largely thanks to another being crossed, in the summer of 1950. Amidst a barrage of artillery fire, Kim Il-sung's Korean People's Army surged down over the 38th parallel dividing North from South Korea. A freshly formed United Nations mandated that a force be put together for South Korea's defence, and with the US contributing nearly 90 per cent of the troops, General MacArthur was selected as Commander-in-Chief.

The war ended early and badly for him: he was relieved both of his Korean command and his position as SCAP (Supreme Commander for the Allied Powers), for trying – in more or less open defiance of his superiors' wishes – to escalate the conflict into an attack on newly Communist China. But the conflict ended very well for Japan. Procurement orders from the US military for supplies and equipment repair brought between $600 and $800 million into Japan each year in the early 1950s. Prime Minister Yoshida Shigeru described the war as a 'gift from the gods'.

This unexpected windfall, together with a growing availability of bank loans – thanks to a Japanese population determined to save its money as soon as it could afford to do so – made it possible for Japan's wartime industries to refit for post-war production. Heavy and chemical industries were upgraded to supply the essential raw materials of economic recovery, especially coal and steel. Government tax incentives encouraged the importation of new technology to lower production costs, with the result that Japanese iron and steel production soon outstripped that of Germany, France and Britain. The years to come would see Japan reach one such milestone after another, helping to build a legend – at home and abroad – of a country floored by war, picking itself up again with incredible speed.

*

The talk around Morita Akio's navy lunch table on 7 August 1945 had been of a 'weapon that flashed and shone', used at Hiroshima the

'New Constitution, Bright Life': the front cover of a guide to the new Constitution (*left*). 'No more war' is helpfully illustrated (*centre*), as are the values intended for the new Japan: equality in marriage whatever the older generation think (*below right*), and freedom of religion (*above right*)

day before. A physicist by training, Morita knew what it must be. He was shocked, not just by its use, but by its existence. He had marvelled, years before, at film footage of the Ford Motor Company's Rouge Complex in Michigan. Iron ore was shipped in, turned into steel, shaped into automobile parts and assembled into the final product – all in one place. But he had thought that even the Americans must still be twenty years away from acquiring a nuclear weapon.

Japan's new Constitution meant that there would be no narrowing of that particular technology gap. But hidden away in their dripping shack, Morita and his friends were trying something else. Heated to just the right degree, the yellow powder in their pan turned brown: oxalic ferrite became ferric oxide. This was then mixed with a clear lacquer and applied, using fine, badger-hair brushes, to hemp-strengthened craft paper that had been painstakingly cut into strips with razor blades. The result: a crude form of magnetic tape, onto which voices could be recorded. The design was upgraded a year later when the team finally got hold of some plastic. Then, with great care, Morita was able to load up the company Datsun with TTEC's pride and joy: a 35-kilogram tape recorder.

Driving around Tokyo, looking for sales, Morita's pitch was

disarmingly simple. Who *doesn't* like the sound of their own voice? Who *doesn't* want to sing, and then play it back? But he went away disappointed for the most part. His company's machine was expensive, it was enormous, and in a country still more focused on needs than wants, there was no pressing case for it. Even when TTEC whittled down the size of their device to that of a particularly bulky briefcase, the only buyers they could find were schools, currently being cajoled by GHQ into using more audio material in classes. To broaden the market any further, TTEC would have to cut down the size, power consumption and price of their product substantially. It would take a technological revolution.

As luck would have it, just such a revolution had recently occurred at Bell Laboratories in the United States. The hero of the hour was no more than a few millimetres in diameter, and made from semiconductor materials. Its purpose was to amplify electronic signals – something that until now had only been possible with much larger and more energy-hungry vacuum tubes. An internal ballot at the lab to decide on a name for the new invention was won by the word 'transistor'. And in 1952, while on a sales visit to New York, TTEC's Ibuka Masaharu discovered that a manufacturing licence was now for sale. TTEC would buy it.

Or, at least, they would have liked to. Between TTEC and what Morita was convinced would be a fortune loomed the powerful and disturbingly interventionist Ministry of International Trade and Industry (MITI), to whom, in the wake of the Dodge Line, the Occupation authorities had steadily handed over control of Japan's international trade, technology imports and currency exchange arrangements. In theory, MITI's whole purpose in life was to fight the cause of Japanese industry, at home and abroad – employees liked to boast of their adherence to the old Tokugawa slogan of *jōi*: 'Expel the barbarian!' But in reality, civil servants tended to think that they knew better than the business people with whom they dealt. They saw it as their duty to steer them away from decisions that would be bad for them, and bad for Japan. TTEC's application cried out to be denied: a tiny, inexperienced company wanted to send $25,000 of precious foreign currency out of the country, in the vain hope of making serious use of a new and untried technology. Representatives of TTEC later recalled being 'laughed out of the room'.

Six crucial months passed – lost to potential competitors – before permission was finally extracted from MITI, at which point access to money became a problem. With the availability of finance not yet returning to pre-Dodge Line levels, companies were clustering around one of a small handful of banks, in the hope of getting at least some of the funds they needed. The banks, for their part, tended to regard big industrial customers and trading companies as their best bet for future prosperity. MITI encouraged the formation of these new combines (known as *keiretsu*), now with banks rather than family holding companies at their core and with shareholding and control more diffuse than before, for much the same reasons that its pre-war predecessors had championed the *zaibatsu*: to succeed in international trade and commerce, Japan needed to field powerful contenders. By the end of 1952, many of the Mitsubishi *zaibatsu*'s successor companies had been allowed to come back together. Mitsui's followed a few years later.

Fortunately for TTEC, they were able to hire as their chairman Mandai Junshiro: a former chairman of Mitsui Bank, who had initially been purged under the Occupation. The effect on TTEC's bank managers was magical. Before, they had struggled to get a serious hearing. Now, they strolled into Mitsui with its legendary former boss at their side, talking about TTEC as 'my company'. The taps were hurriedly turned on, and when Mandai mentioned in passing an upcoming share issue, employees at Mitsui took it as a personal command to invest.

A quarter of a million dollars could now be put into making hundreds of prototype transistors, eventually yielding a device capable of running a radio – something Bell Laboratories had cautioned would not be possible. Production remained deeply flawed: TTEC had to throw away ninety-five out of every one hundred transistors they made. But in 1955, their radio was finally ready for the shops. And though an American company beat them to the accolade of the world's first transistor radio by just a month, TTEC's was the world's smallest – and two years later they cut the size even further. Channelling the spirit of Japan's old-time pedlars of dodgy potions and rootless bonsai trees, Morita had special shirts made for his sales team, featuring slightly over-sized pockets. Their product thus became the world's first 'pocketable' radio – available in a selection of yellow, red, green or black.

Morita was determined not to pay double for his marketing, by having a brand name that was different from the company name. But 'Tokyo Tsūshin Kōgyō' was a long name to fit onto small products and to American customers it meant nothing – or at least nothing positive, so soon after the war. So Morita and his colleagues began to cast around for something else. Flicking through a dictionary, they came across *sonus* – 'sound'. It wasn't bad, but it reminded them of something better, a phrase the GIs used, its bright, fresh associations so attractive that Morita and co. had been applying it to themselves as they worked away in their shack. They were 'sonny-boys', so surely their company was Sonny. Better still, Sony. Yes, that would do.

The legend, as it built, was inseparable from America. The United States was Sony's inspiration in everything: from the shock of the advanced weapons used at Hiroshima and Nagasaki, through tape technology, the transistor and a vogue for abbreviated brands (IBM, AT&T), all the way to Morita's dream of establishing 'Sony America' and his proud unfurling of a Japanese flag on New York's Fifth Avenue when the company opened a showroom there in 1962. Along with his colleague Ibuka Masaru, Morita became one of Japan's first jet-setting businessmen. And while Morita went as far as setting up home in the US, Ibuka's son got used to his father returning from work trips with armfuls of slightly broken American toys – each one taken apart to see how it was made.

Japan had technical know-how in abundance, together with entrepreneurs of such talent and motivation that they would later be celebrated around the world as gurus, even gods. Hotel notepaper scribbles by Morita and Ibuka were treated as holy relics by Sony HQ, handled with trembling, white-gloved devotion on the rare occasions that they were brought out for display. But it was American commercial and diplomatic support that helped to release all this potential into the world. And that was not offered free of charge.

While Morita and Ibuka were busy building their company in the early 1950s, the United States was playing chaperone as Japan re-entered the international community. John Foster Dulles was tasked by President Truman in 1950 with agreeing a peace treaty with

Sony's 'pocketable' TR-63 radio (1957), a little over 10 centimetres high

Japan's former victims and enemies, most of whom gathered around a conference table in San Francisco the following year. South East Asian nations wanted reparations. Britain, like Japan, was improvising a transition from running a colonial trading bloc to accepting more evenly balanced terms of global trade. Its leaders wanted to limit Japanese competition in Asia, and especially on the Indian subcontinent. What the Soviet Union wanted more than anything was to have been included at a much earlier stage of the process. Its delegates were suspicious of plans to sign a US–Japan Security Treaty alongside the peace treaty: a remilitarized Japan, they argued, was being established as an American client state and Pacific staging area. Missing from the room entirely were the two Koreas, currently at war, and the two Chinas: the People's Republic, on the mainland, and the Republic, now sheltering on Taiwan.

Dulles also faced complications inside Japan, where a large chunk of the population wanted to see their country re-enter the world unarmed and neutral. There had been enormous disquiet at GHQ's decision, within weeks of the Korean War breaking out, to create a National Police Reserve (NPR) consisting of 75,000 men. The force was charged with tackling domestic insurrection only, and was run by former Home Ministry civil servants. But the Americans, who equipped it and sought its enlargement, regarded the NPR from the outset as the nucleus of a future Japanese army. And indeed it would have been an impressive domestic insurrection whose quelling required the use of bazookas, flame-throwers, mortars, tanks and artillery.

Where threats to the Emperor had helped to bring Japan's leaders to heel over the Constitution, now it was the turn of the country's economic prospects to be dangled over the abyss. Everything from loans and technology transfer to assistance with economic integration with South East Asia was made contingent upon Japan acquiescing to America's basic post-Occupation demands: US bases on Japanese soil and modest Japanese rearmament. Yoshida regarded economic recovery as the absolute priority for Japan, and thought it naïve to imagine that his country could do anything other than take America's side in world affairs while benefiting from its protection – such was the 'Yoshida Doctrine'. So although he pushed back as hard as he could against American demands for the NPR to grow, a San Francisco Peace Treaty and accompanying Security Treaty were duly signed in September 1951, coming into force the following year.

When the Occupation ended in April 1952, critics were hard pressed to tell the difference. Okinawa remained in American hands. GIs remained very much in evidence in many corners of the country. And Japan still lacked the ability to set independent economic and foreign policies. Just as GHQ had drafted Japan's Constitution, so Dulles had drafted a letter to himself from Yoshida, in which the latter stated unequivocally that his government had 'no intention' of concluding a treaty with communist China. Dulles duly made the letter public in January 1952, and that was that. The terrible chasm that existed between Japan and the mainland, opened up by successive wars from the late nineteenth century onwards, would go unbridged for a little while longer – officially, at least – while the country instead signed a peace treaty with the communists' archrivals down on Taiwan.

Opinion polls the following month suggested that half of the population thought that Yoshida was simply lying when he maintained that their country was not 'rearming'. In March, he admitted that he didn't think Japan's new Constitution prohibited 'war potential for self-defence'. Two years later there finally emerged, from a jumble of acronyms and agencies possessing strategically abstract names, the '*Jieitai*' or 'Self-Defence Forces', complete with land, sea and air components. The SDF were a far cry from the imperial forces of a decade before. They were under the firm control of the Diet, and the civilian bureaucrats who oversaw them, day to day, retained vivid and salutary memories of an era when men in uniform had been permitted real authority. But the new forces nonetheless faced a long and difficult struggle to earn public acceptance and trust.

With Japan's basic post-war arrangements settled, the country began to rejoin the international community, one institution at a time: the International Monetary Fund and the World Bank in 1952; the General Agreement on Tariffs and Trade (GATT) in 1955; the United Nations in 1956. The United States meanwhile tolerated a dollar–yen exchange rate that was advantageous to Japanese exporters and chose not to retaliate against Japan's harsh import arrangements for disadvantaging American products.

Those arrangements included tariffs that made the import of American cars prohibitively expensive, and regulations on foreign investment that prevented the likes of Ford and GM simply building their cars in Japan, as they had done before the war. Instead, the only way that they could now make money in Japan was to sell their designs and technology to Japanese partners. In this way, and with the help of wartime aircraft engineers left with little else to build, a Japanese automobile industry whose first product in 1907 had sold just ten units – eight of those to the police – began its slow emergence as a global player. Nihon Sangyō Corporation – 'Nissan' – had thrived making trucks and buses for the armed forces during the war. Now, it imported components and equipment from the British company Austin, built and sold the cars, and sent back around 3 per cent of the sale price to Austin.

By the early 1960s, companies like Nissan found that they had all the expertise they needed, and so terminated their external agreements. As the Japanese economy grew, demand for their products in the country's relatively large domestic market steadily picked up, as it did for a whole host of pre-war companies who had been busy reinventing themselves for the new era thanks to transistors and integrated circuits. Toshiba ('Tokyo Shibaura Denki'), NEC (Nippon Electric Company), Hitachi and Panasonic were all Meiji- and Taishō-era electrics companies, joined on the world stage as major Japanese brands by two other companies that had branched out and changed their names: a maker of 'Ever-Sharp' mechanical pencils had turned its hand to calculators and televisions as 'Sharp', while the camera-maker Precision Optical Industry Company had become 'Canon', named after the Buddhist bodhisattva Kannon.

A rare opportunity now appeared on the horizon for all these companies: a chance to reach a global audience with their names and products via the youthful, thrusting innocence of the world's greatest festival of international sport. The Olympics was coming to Tokyo. Japan would finally shake off old images of warmongering and poverty, becoming instead what the Americans had promised back in 1947: a beacon, at last, of the modern bright life.

*

The Mayor of Tokyo couldn't believe his luck. What better way of advertising a city's rapid recovery and re-entry into the global community than welcoming all the peoples of the world to visit, as guests and witnesses? Having a flame – lit in the ancient cultural crucible of that community – make a lavishly publicized journey all the way to your door? From Olympia along the old Silk Road, on foot and on horseback, via Athens, Istanbul, Tehran, Herat, Kabul, Peshawar, Delhi, Benares, Calcutta, Mandalay, Hanoi, Canton, Hankou, Mukden, Seoul and Pusan; and from there, across the water to Shimonoseki on Honshū, onwards through Okayama, Kobe, Nagoya and finally to Tokyo.

Thousands upon thousands of visitors would have their image of Japan finally moved beyond the exotic reductions of Mount Fuji and geisha. They would surely like what they saw, and once they spread the word back home a tourist industry would build. Predictably, there were worries about cost. Some asked whether a more modest torch relay might be in order. Couldn't we just send a Japanese warship to Olympia to pick it up? Perhaps a squadron of kamikaze pilots should make the trip, breaking aviation records along the way?

It was difficult to reconcile such suggestions with the ethos of the Games. But such were the times: the Tokyo Olympics were scheduled for 1940. The date was fortuitous, calculated long ago by Meiji-era bureaucrats as the 2600th anniversary of Japan's foundation by the legendary Emperor Jimmu, descendant of the Sun Goddess Amaterasu. The world could now be brought in on those celebrations: the West coming east, recognizing an ancient civilization to rival its own, and marvelling at a city gloriously reborn after the 1923 earthquake. There was historic significance even in the make-up of the organizing committee: its head was none other than Prince Tokugawa Iesato, heir to the last Tokugawa Shogun.

Soon, however, parts of the original relay route ran through war zones – some of them created by Japan. The International Olympic Committee (IOC) had been remarkably indulgent of Japanese foreign policy up to this point. Acutely aware that its 'global' games had not thus far been hosted outside Europe and the United States, the IOC eagerly awarded the 1940 event to Tokyo – three years after Japan's withdrawal from the League of Nations. For a while, the way seemed clear for Tokyo to follow in the footstcps of Berlin, where in 1936 Hitler and his film-maker Leni Riefenstahl set a high bar for using sport to spotlight a country's spirit, its genetically impeccable population and its shimmering sense of global purpose. Even all-out war with China, bloody violence at Shanghai and Nanjing making international headlines, failed to put the IOC off. In the end, it was Japan's sense of 'global purpose' that put paid to the 1940 Tokyo Olympics, and to the Winter Games scheduled for the same year in its northern city Sapporo. The country's leaders notified the IOC that they were regretfully giving up both sets of Games: China, they complained, was currently absorbing all their energies.

It was a while before the Olympic movement could put aside what Japan did with those energies. When the Summer Games were revived (in London) in 1948 after a twelve-year hiatus, even Japan's American sponsors failed to finagle the country an invitation. The Chicagoan head of the IOC, Avery Brundage, was a great enthusiast for Japanese art. But as he told a countryman in GHQ's Civil Information and Education Section in 1947, 'the English are very badly off . . . and it would be very harmful to all concerned if there were demonstrations during the Games due to the presence of Germans and Japanese'.

Japanese athletes instead made their return to Olympic sport at the 1952 Summer Games in Helsinki. That same year, just a few weeks after the Occupation officially ended, work began on a bid for the 1960 Games. In the end, Tokyo won the 1964 Games, the grand announcement early in 1959 firing the starting gun on a five-year race to be ready. As the organizers were only too well aware, the flipside of this unprecedented promotional opportunity was the unprecedented potential for embarrassing yourself – via the international media in the run-up to the Games, then amongst an estimated 120,000 foreign visitors once the Games began. Two billion dollars and a superhuman organizational effort were invested in making sure that didn't happen, right down to a citizen spring-cleaning of the city – involving more than a million people – and warnings against spitting or urinating in the street, or even using one's car horn unnecessarily.

For the British former Olympic athlete and sports journalist Chris Brasher, arriving in Tokyo at the end of September 1964, it was clear that Japan had defied the doubters. Contrary to expectations, the country was ready and the city was polished to a sheen – though not, he was pleased to see, to the detriment of its traditional charms. Having just read Ian Fleming's well-timed Japanese Bond thriller, *You Only Live Twice*, on the long flight over, Brasher was delighted to discover when he landed that Tokyo's famous 'kamikaze taxi drivers' had not been tamed by their changed surroundings: mile after mile of brand new highways, marked out with bright white lines, passing through new tunnels and ducking underneath twisting new expressways. His driver possessed so much of the old spirit, in fact – 'boring straight at a bus' – that Brasher began to wonder whether he would live long enough to see the Games.

The new Olympic architecture was a boon to an otherwise 'ugly' city, thought Brasher. Most impressive of all to him was the National Gymnasium, with its skin of steel and concrete draped between two tall masts. The Olympic Village had also been well thought out: adapted from US military housing, it offered greenery and calm just a 'javelin's throw' from the main stadiums and was free of the dust usually left around Olympic accommodation when it was thrown up at the last minute. Japan seemed to be getting everything right. Even when the Olympic Village was hit by a typhoon and then a minor earthquake, Brasher remained unshaken in his faith that the 'hard work, humility and charm' of his hosts would see things through.

At the opening ceremony, a capacity crowd of 75,000 people packed into the National Stadium were treated to what Brasher breathlessly claimed must be 'the most brilliantly organized spectacle ever held in international sport'. A group of young girls and boys drummed the Olympic flag into the stadium, before a young man, born the day of the Hiroshima bomb, ascended 160 steps up to an enormous urn waiting to be lit. Sakai Yoshinori's great moment would previously have been shared with the world by flying video-tapes out to various national broadcasters. This time, the images captured by three television cameras suspended from bamboo poles were beamed across to Europe and North America live and in colour via satellite, thanks to a technological tie-up between NASA, the Japanese government and Japan's national broadcaster NHK.

There was space-age technology on the ground too. Nine days before the opening ceremony, a brand-new train system had opened for business: the shinkansen ('new trunk line'). On its first day of operation, the world's fastest train carried more than 36,000 passengers along the Tōkaidō Line, named after the ancient travel route running from Edo to Osaka via Yokohama and Kyoto. Back when the Meiji Emperor had left Kyoto for Edo, the journey time along that road had been around a fortnight via palanquin. The first train service, in 1889, had cut the journey time between Osaka and Tokyo to sixteen and a half hours. Now, the shinkansen took four.

As with the Games, not everyone in Japan had thought the shinkansen a sensible way to spend money. A senior executive at Japan National Railways (JNR) described it in 1963 as the 'height of madness ... meaningless and destined to fail'. The disruption of laying brand-new track was enormous. A few enterprising people hurriedly built houses along the route, the better to benefit from government compensation money when they were torn down again. But around 50,000 bona fide families were also evicted in the building of the Tōkaidō Line alone. And where existing railway stations couldn't be enlarged, because built-up areas around them made it too expensive, a generation of new – 'Shin' – stations appeared. Osakans wondered why the money had been found to expand Tokyo Station, while at their end of the line some of the time saved using the shinkansen was lost again changing trains between Osaka and Shin-Osaka.

And yet the people leading the development thought of themselves as the 'dream team'. They were bringing to fruition an abandoned pre-war project to knit a country – and, back then, its empire – closer together through faster travel. In the 1930s, Japan's media had dubbed it the *dangan ressha* or 'bullet train' – a reference to its promised speed, though the line was also intended to carry ordnance to war zones.

Here, as with the car industry, military expertise was put to profitable peace-time uses. Matsudaira Tadashi's work on the Zero fighter persuaded him that Japan's terrible safety record for train derailments was due not to faulty track, as people had thought, but to vibrations caused by the trains themselves as they passed across. His new design for the truck underneath the railway carriages eliminated the problem. Kawanabe Hajime brought with him to the 'dream team' his Navy signals knowledge, from which he developed a system for regulating the speed of trains using low-frequency sound called ATC (Automatic Train Control). It would be used for generations to come.

From such technical feats, through futuristic contours and cockpits, to a space-age Centralized Traffic Control room, Japan's newspapers could barely contain themselves at 'the airplane that runs on rails' and what it portended for Japan's future. They would have relished, had they known, the reaction of a BBC commentator in 1964 as his train picked up speed after leaving Tokyo: 'I felt a surge in my stomach . . . I was looking around for a seatbelt.'

The importance of satellite broadcasting and the shinkansen went far beyond convenience or cheap nationalistic thrills. Before the war, 'Made in Japan' was so heavily associated with inferior products – paper umbrellas, pointless trinkets, toys that fell apart in children's hands – that in the early post-war era Sony had taken to confessing their products' country of origin on as small a label as they could get away with (on at least one occasion they were ordered by US Customs to make it larger). Now, Japanese electronics companies could boast about a hi-tech tradition in Japan, and expect to be believed.

Amongst the many products that the Olympics helped these companies to sell at home, one in particular stood out. It was a truly game-changing piece of technology. But it didn't come cheap. It needed grand, highly visual events to prove its worth and persuade people to part with significant quantities of their hard-earned money. Television had landed, and Japan was going to fall hard for it.

Much of the heavy lifting in first switching the public on to the new medium had been done a few years before. Emperor Hirohito's son, Crown Prince Akihito, caused a sensation in November 1958 when he became engaged to a commoner, Shōda Michiko. A 'Michiko boom' and spiralling public interest in the match, amidst hopes that the newly symbolic imperial institution might be about to take another step towards the people, gave an enormous boost to sales of television sets in the run-up to the wedding in April 1959. Nor did the nuptials disappoint. There was imperial mystique and splendour, with Michiko labouring under twelve layers of kimono – weighing nearly 15 kilograms in total, noted Britain's Pathé News ('Royal Romance Thrills Japs' had been their headline the year before). There were close-ups of the happy couple's faces at various points throughout the day. And there was a grand carriage ride through crowds in Tokyo, in the course of which a young man, incensed by the money being wasted on the wedding (when his fire-damaged school had yet to be reopened), threw a stone at the newly-weds and jumped up at their carriage, hoping to pull them out onto the road. He was quickly bundled away by police, later to be judged insane and locked up.

Where the royal wedding had been a great television event – with no less than ten and a half hours of coverage that day – the Olympics promised a whole series of great events: nine every day for a whole fortnight. Companies like Sony rushed to market new sets and to ramp up production. And while television sets had until recently been horrendously expensive, prices were coming down in the run-up to the Olympics, just as people were starting to feel richer. In December

1960, Japan's Prime Minister Ikeda Hayato announced a plan to take the nation's income and double it within a decade, through renewed state management of the economy: from investment in priority industries to various forms of encouragement offered to private companies. The era of wartime and post-war sacrifice was officially over. People would continue to save their money, but at the same time they could now, in good conscience, also focus on achieving and enjoying prosperity. In the end, Japan's leaders failed to fulfil this foolishly populist promise within ten years. They did it in seven.

Advertisers did what they could to encourage and capitalize on this feeling of wealth and material comfort in the early 1960s, which had 90 per cent of Japanese defining themselves as 'middle class' by the middle of the decade. They worked hard via the print media to persuade people that they could afford a television, then increasingly adapted their expertise to fit the potential of the new medium. TV advertising faced a steep learning curve around the world during these early years. The British public had been incensed when they found out that American coverage of Queen Elizabeth II's Coronation in 1953 was interrupted by a tea advert featuring J. Fred Muggs the chimpanzee. Early Japanese stumbles included a live, close-up advert for whale meat in which a fly landed on the food, and audience outrage at the cramming of no fewer than three advertisements into the minute-long men's 100-metre freestyle final at the 1958 Asian Games. But with the help of companies like the advertising giant Dentsū, Japanese businesses quickly became proficient in deploying a combination of direct advertising and programme sponsorship to boost their brands – the sponsorship, especially, intended to foster warm, long-term relationships with consumers.

Shabondama horidē (Soap Bubble Holiday) was ideal for these purposes: a lavishly produced musical and comedy extravaganza, sponsored by Milky Soap. It was the brainchild of Watanabe Productions, or 'Nabe Puro', a talent agency that started out touring its artists around American military bases and later morphed into the media equivalent of Ford's Rouge Complex. It acquired the raw material: song-writers, choreographers, costume consultants, music and television producers, and a regularly replenished store of telegenic and trainable young people. And then it beat, bolted and welded it all together into a wildly successful final product, which combined entertainment with strong publicity for a lengthy client roster of popular acts like The Peanuts, a duo of singing and dancing identical twins.

To its defenders, mass entertainment television like *Shabondama horidē*, together with NHK's New Year's Eve song contest *Kōhaku Utagassen* ('Red and White Song Battle') and its annual *Taiga Dorama* – an epic historical drama split into weekly episodes across a calendar year – played a powerful role in bringing people closer: the post-war nation was knitting itself together as a fabric of families whose individual members gathered in the same room at the same time to enjoy a shared spectacle. Programmes made with a live audience enhanced the effect of bringing hearts around the country into sync, the cameras lingering almost didactically on laughter, tears or shock. The country's numerous talent shows, meanwhile, were deeply democratic: 'ordinary' people were offered their shot at the big time. One of the first and greatest *tarento* – a term for mass-media celebrities, related to the English word 'talent' – was of course the commoner Crown Princess. Fans collected photos of the woman they preferred to call, simply, 'Michiko-san', and took coach tours around the town where she grew up.

The final boon provided by the Olympics was the chance for tentative steps to be taken towards restoring a broader national pride in Japan. Nearly thirty years before, the organizers of Tokyo 1940 had fretted over how the Emperor could possibly open the Games given that ordinary people were forbidden from hearing his voice. This time, he would speak. The dilemma was how to position him when he did so, along with all the imagery that in years past had been used to illustrate the national story. So much of that imagery was now tainted around the world, from former prisoners of war who relived Japanese brutality nightly in their dreams to many millions of families around Asia for whom the loss of loved ones in the 1930s and '40s was still similarly fresh.

No one in Japan was entirely sure what to do. What did it mean to say that the Emperor was a 'symbol of the state'? Was he *head* of state? The Constitution didn't specify. Rather than raise this as a legal question, Japan's conservatives pushed for him to be made sponsor of the Games, and so give the appearance of a head of state by officiating at their opening. Similar finessing was applied to the old national flag and anthem, neither of which officially enjoyed 'national' status anymore. Here again, rather than raise difficult questions or reopen wounds, flag and anthem alike were inserted into the proceedings as Olympic rather than nationalist symbols. Japanese people were democratically surveyed, in the lead-up to the Games, on what they thought was the best shade of red for the disc at the centre of the flag. The winning hue was affixed to Sakai Yoshinori's vest before he set off with the Olympic torch, and was used right across the Games. '*Kimi ga yo*', the former national anthem, was played twice: timed first to coincide with the arrival of the Emperor, then later with the release of the doves of peace.

The Self-Defence Forces provided 7,500 soldiers to help with security at the Games, along with Mitsubishi-built American F-86s to trace the Olympic rings. Here, too, great care was taken. The planes came from the SDF's aerobatic display team, harmlessly branded 'Blue Impulse'. And their appearance overhead was timed to coincide with the last of the doves, thereby enhancing a pacifistic image. Meanwhile, chrysanthemums festooned the stadium, and 28.8 kg of chrysanthemum perfume was pumped from dugouts as the ceremony unfolded.

It was all a sign of things to come. Here was a country severely limited in the means by which it could develop and project its own national image. In place of an independent foreign policy, Japan would have to express itself abroad by means of industry, high technology and visual culture – all three of which would inevitably be parsed for their politics by friends and enemies alike. The potential benefits here, of a prosperous and peaceful 'bright life', were immense: a release from poverty at home; and a release from the past abroad. And yet, as a pitch-perfect ceremony opened the most expensive Games in history, some in Japan were already asking awkward questions. What was the long-term cost to Japanese people of living in the kind of society that could afford and was willing to meet this Olympic price tag? And would they one day tire of paying it?

Crown Prince Akihito and Crown Princess Michiko,
on their wedding day in April 1959

Sakai Yoshinori opens the Tokyo Summer Olympic Games in October 1964

The launch of the shinkansen in October 1964

The Peanuts

PART FIVE

Twisted Visions
(1950s to 1990s)

14

Exhibitionism

Wasted forearms droop, bloodless and grey, from the sleeves of a dark kimono. Eyes bulge from a cold head, lolling forwards on the end of a snapped neck. A long, thin strand of mucus hanging from a nostril mirrors the long, taut rope on the end of which the elderly woman's shrunken body dangles. The only remaining signs of life are creaturely and degraded: a yellow-ribboned dog feeds from the corpse's nose; fish bob around a second dead body, which lies face down in a bloody pond.

The macabre visual language in which Yamashita Kikuji couched his denunciations of 1950s Japan was learned amidst the atrocities he had witnessed – and participated in – across southern China and Taiwan during the war. He created this particular painting, *The Tale of Akebono Village*, after the Cultural Brigade of the Japanese Communist Party tasked him with reporting on a violent dispute between a landlord and local villagers. An activist had been killed, and a woman had killed herself after losing her life savings when a local bank owned by the landlord collapsed. Yamashita's blend of socialist realism with a campaigning tinge of surrealism was typical of the 'reportage' painters of this era. He used it to bring out the scavenger-like existence to which the dead woman's surviving granddaughter had been reduced: deprived of the savings intended for her (a white document under a black kettle is all that remains of the elderly woman's bank account), she laps instead at the fluid streaming from her grandmother's nose.

Fewer than one fifth of Japanese surveyed in 1952 thought that the San Francisco Peace Treaty had brought them true independence. Signs of their country's much-vaunted graduation from defeated enemy to respected and protected ally were hard to spot. Instead, there was evidence everywhere of continuing subordination to American power and interests. Richly symbolic incidents kept stacking up. In the spring of 1954, the crew of a Japanese fishing boat, the *Lucky Dragon 5*, were irradiated in the fallout from an American thermonuclear weapons test at Bikini Atoll in the mid-Pacific. Disfiguring injuries resulted, from hair loss through to skin disintegration. When one of the twenty-three fishermen died, a furious political row broke out about whether radiation or – as American officials were inclined to argue – improper medical care for an underlying condition was to blame. A 'tuna panic' over potentially contaminated catches ran alongside rumours of radioactive cherry blossoms. And as Geiger counters became a new and unwelcome staple of editorial cartoons, a reported 30 million people – more than half the adult population of Japan – put their names to petitions calling for the eradication of nuclear weapons.

'Without military power,' Japan's Education Minister announced in a radio address back in September 1945, 'we go forward with culture.' His comment envisaged the country's peaceful reinvention via education and the arts. The reality was that during the 1950s and 1960s culture became the principal means by which post-war battles over the nation's identity, purpose and even ownership were fought. While the state, the Imperial Family, big business, advertisers and mainstream creative industries collaborated in the building of the 'bright life' story, the challenge for artists who opposed the bargain on which it appeared to be based – prosperity purchased at the cost of independence – was how to parlay an Akebono Village or a *Lucky Dragon 5* into a popular movement capable of changing the country's direction of travel. How to show people images of themselves and their society that they might not want to see. How to tell and garner attention for stories about Japan that were truer to its mixed reality than those one generally encountered while flicking through the television channels.

The first, fundamental task was to find and occupy some public space, within or without the mass media, and make suitably arresting use of it. The Yomiuri newspaper's annual '*Nihon Indépendant Art Exhibition*', established in 1949, offered an important early

The Tale of Akebono Village (Yamashita Kikuji, 1953)

opportunity. It represented a dramatic break from the past. Pre-war political leaders had dominated public space – literally and figuratively – via four national art institutions located in Tokyo's Ueno Park: the Tokyo National Museum (1872) stored and displayed works of art; the Tokyo School of Fine Arts (1887) taught an approved selection of 'traditional' techniques; the Tokyo Metropolitan Art Museum (1926) held exhibitions; and the National Research Institute for Cultural Properties (1930) carried out research. Government-sponsored art exhibitions were held annually from 1907 onwards, their influence magnified by extensive newspaper and magazine coverage.

The post-war artist and critic Okamoto Tarō charged the modernizing Meiji leaders who established much of this set-up with having been unable, or unwilling, to understand manners or morals or art except through Westerners' eyes. Those leaders had taken Japan's extraordinary cultural range, filtered out much that was primal and vital and self-aware, and sponsored instead an elite canon of fine art (put together with the help of scholars like Okakura Tenshin and the American Ernest Fenollosa) to be wielded for diplomatic ends abroad and conservative didactic ones at home.

The constituent parts of this official artistic tradition were impressive enough, in their own right. They included Buddhist sculpture and painting, alongside ceramics, textiles and exquisitely crafted swords. There was Yamato-e painting dating back to the imperial court of the twelfth century, which balanced spare depictions of pale courtly countenances with a playful 'blown-off roof' perspective that allowed viewers to spy into an interior room. Nō theatre, bunraku (puppet theatre) and a reformed kabuki were all eventually included, alongside court music and dance. But Okamoto felt sure that much of this left ordinary people cold, or engaged only at a respectful distance. It simply wasn't intimate or 'disagreeable' enough to fulfil the responsibility of art as he saw it: to supply a society with prophetic insight, and force it to pay attention; to continually register disbelief at the ingrained wrongs of the world; and to suggest, in the case of contemporary Japan, that material prosperity was a distraction from its demons (past and present) rather than an effective exorcism.

The *Yomiuri Indépendant*, held at the Tokyo Metropolitan Art Museum, upended this old model of elites carefully curating a national vision. In the spirit of early post-war democracy, the *Indépendant* opened its doors to all people and all styles. The youngest artist to be exhibited was a child of six. Paintings and mosaics by expensively trained professionals featured alongside a crayon drawing of a naked woman by a homeless man in Tokyo's Shinjuku neighbourhood. And just as anyone could be an artist, so anyone could be a critic: visitors to the *Indépendant* were encouraged to vote for their favourite piece, and to contribute reviews for the national newspapers. Okamoto was amongst those who took things a stage further in the mid-1950s, organizing a 'street debate' in front of the museum at which artists and members of the public met and discussed what was going on inside. Those hoping to swing the *Indépendant* towards the traditional canon objected to abstract art, on the basis that the public wouldn't understand it. The street debate was a chance to test that theory, and to ensure that such art – all art – engaged rather than alienated.

Other artists roamed the country, joining forces with political protestors. In 1955, the reportage painter Nakamura Hiroshi visited the village of Sunagawa, to the west of Tokyo, where residents were trying to prevent their land being cleared to make way for the expansion of the nearby US Tachikawa Air Base – its runway was at present so short that planes running missions to the Korean peninsula and South East Asia were unable to take off fully loaded. Whenever government surveyors arrived to assess their land, villagers would burn straw, throw buckets of human faeces and spray poisonous insecticide to try to chase them away.

Throughout the 1950s, the continued presence of US military bases on Japanese soil served as a lightning rod for discontent over the terms of the 1952 US–Japan Security Treaty. American Cold War military planners predicted that a first – possibly nuclear – strike by the Soviets might well be aimed at their interests in the Pacific. The case for maintaining, even developing, their bases in Japan seemed clear. To a good many Japanese, however, fed up with being asked to profess pacifism while tolerating foreign militarism in their midst, this kind of logic seemed circular and self-serving. Surely if the source of Japan's vulnerability to another atomic attack was the US military presence, then that presence – which by the end of the 1950s amounted to nearly 50,000 American troops spread across hundreds of installations on Japan's four main islands alone – ought to be ended, not expanded.

Sunagawa quickly became the kind of cause célèbre for which artists and protestors had been waiting. Villagers found their ranks swelled by artists and documentary-makers, along with leftist politicians, trade unions, the radical student organization Zengakuren, and even a number of Buddhist priests, beating drums to help lift demonstrators' spirits. Surveyors responded by bringing more police with them each time they tried to return, until in September 1955, a thousand policemen – accompanying an inspection team of just nine people – clashed violently with nearly 2,000 farmers and activists. With the national media looking on, protests spiralled from there.

The imagery at Sunagawa was perfect for whipping a local concern into a national tipping point. There was the injustice of simple farming livelihoods under threat. The poignancy, even Freudian resonance, of young girls sobbing as government surveyors drove stakes into their paddy fields. The tragic imbalance of the poor and the young, mostly unarmed, caught between a still-mistrusted Japanese police force and the military hardware of a rising imperial power. Nakamura captured it all in sketches and in one of the era's best-known

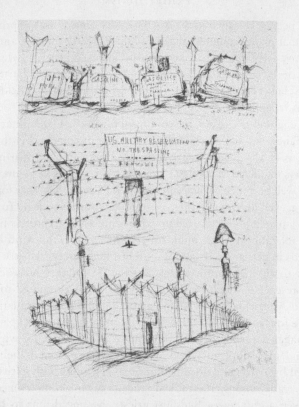

Sunagawa #5 (Nakamura Hiroshi, 1955): a sketch and the finished work

Gunned Down (Nakamura Hiroshi, 1957): a single incident turned into
a vision of a country prostrate and humiliated

paintings, *Sunagawa #5*. These he followed up two years later with
Gunned Down, after a middle-aged housewife named Sakai Naka
was shot dead – rumour had it, deliberately – while on a US army
firing range collecting brass shell-cases to sell for scrap.

In both the Sunagawa and the Sakai cases, the sense of drama created
by combining culture with protest was heightened by contributions
from the courts. Bitter, protracted arguments over whether William
S. Girard, the US serviceman involved in the shooting of Sakai,
should be tried under American or Japanese jurisdiction laid bare
Japan's subordination. Parallels were painfully apparent with the
'unequal treaties' of the nineteenth century, despised for the extraterritoriality arrangements that allowed foreigners who committed
crimes on Japanese soil to be tried by their own countrymen. The
case for trying Girard under Japanese law was eventually won. But

the outcome, a three-year suspended sentence, had the effect of intensifying public anger even further.

Where the Sakai case provided momentum to the campaign against
Japan's foreign policy arrangements, a more direct intervention in the
issue came in March 1959, when a judge in the Sunagawa case handed
down an extraordinary ruling. Acquitting seven leaders of the struggle,
who had been accused of trespass for entering Tachikawa Air Base
two years before, he declared that the presence of US bases on Japanese soil was unconstitutional because Article nine of Japan's new
Constitution forbade the maintaining of 'war potential' on its soil.

The US eventually dropped its plans for expanding Tachikawa.
But the swiftness with which Japan's Supreme Court reversed the
March 1959 ruling – reasoning that Japan's constitution did not
advocate 'defencelessness', while US bases could not be considered
'war potential' because Japan had no control over them – was used by
protestors to bolster their claims that powerful American influence
was at work behind the scenes in their democracy.

The timing of the controversy was enormously significant. The
widely disliked Security Treaty, to its critics the source and symbol of
Japan's semi-colonized state, was coming up for renewal in 1960.
Those planning to protest found in the main champion of treaty
renewal the perfect pantomime villain. A man whose name, less than
a decade before, the Americans had spelled out on a Sugamo Prison
placard as a potential war criminal was now Prime Minister, and the
Americans' best hope of saving the alliance with Japan.

Kishi Nobusuke had served in the late 1930s as the highest-ranking
bureaucrat in Manchukuo. There, as one of the most ambitious of the
era's 'reform bureaucrats', he had turned his genius for finance to
planning in detail the kind of state-controlled and total war-ready
economy that he and others advocated for mainland Japan. A prime
example of the kind of colonial abandon that can ensue when an
empire's officials live and work far from domestic scrutiny, Kishi's
less savoury activities ran to money-laundering, corralling millions of
Chinese – from the unemployed through to captured POWs – into
industrial slave labour, consorting with drug-traffickers and *yakuza*,
and making the most of his power over those around him to feed a
legendary libido.

After three years in Sugamo, where he broke prison bread and played board games with the wealthy gangster Kodama Yoshio (whose henchmen he would later use for crowd control), Kishi found himself released without trial. He drove straight to the Prime Minister's residence, where his brother Satō Eisaku – a future Prime Minister, currently serving as Chief Cabinet Secretary – helped him to change out of his prison uniform and into a business suit. 'Strange, isn't it,' Kishi commented, 'we're all democrats now.'

Officially de-purged from political life in 1952 and winning his first Diet seat the following year, Kishi set his considerable talents, contacts and personal finances to undermining Yoshida Shigeru, whose popularity with the voters was by this point in freefall. Yoshida finally resigned at the end of 1954, and the next year Kishi became one of the prime movers in a merger of the country's two conservative parties, from which was born the Liberal Democratic Party (Jiyū Minshutō). Electoral success followed swiftly, and in 1957 'war criminal Kishi', as opposition politicians liked to refer to him (others called him *yōkai*: monster), found himself at the helm of party and country alike.

Kishi's nostalgia for Japan's pre-war political arrangements showed itself quickly, in an attempt to re-empower the police to search private property at will and without a warrant – simply on suspicion that a crime might be committed at some future date. The thwarting of this measure by a broad coalition of Diet politicians (including some in the LDP), 4 million striking workers and a cross-section of Japan's newspapers offered a reminder – right on the eve of treaty renewal – of the lessons from recent protests: that a single issue could be used to highlight a wider national predicament, people could be persuaded to care, and that real policy change could be achieved.

Kishi tried to sell treaty renewal, the details of which were hashed out in Washington in January 1960, as a rebalancing of power in the US–Japanese relationship: the US would now have to negotiate with the Japanese government before making use of its troops stationed in Japan, and these forces could not be used to intervene in the event of a Japanese civil war (a scenario for which the previous version of the treaty had rather ominously allowed, deepening the sense of de facto occupation). He was unsuccessful. Protests against the treaty – its

Japanese name abbreviated to 'Anpo' – began to gather pace, encouraged by the Japan Socialist Party, the Japanese Communist Party, the General Council of Trade Unions (Sōhyō), Zengakuren, and prominent intellectuals including the political scientist Maruyama Masao. Events reached a climax on 19 May, the day that renewal had to pass through the Diet in order for President Eisenhower to be able to make his planned celebratory visit to Japan. As masses of protestors gathered outside the Diet building, Socialist Diet members trapped the Speaker of the House in his chambers in an attempt to stall proceedings. Kishi called in the police, and around 500 uniformed officers helped to drag his opponents away. Treaty renewal ended up being passed in the middle of the night, with no opposition Diet members in sight.

The country was pitched into turmoil. Millions now went out on strike, and weeks of large-scale demonstrations brought hundreds of thousands of people onto the street, shouting *'Anpo hantai! Anpo Hantai!'* – 'No to Anpo! No to Anpo!' On 10 June, student protestors surrounded, stoned and threatened to overturn a car carrying President Eisenhower's press secretary, who was in Japan to lay the ground for the presidential visit. He narrowly escaped by military helicopter and the presidential visit was promptly cancelled. A few days later, a Tokyo University student by the name of Kanba Michiko was killed during a confrontation with riot police outside the Diet building, further inflaming the situation and bringing 300,000 people out onto the streets around the Diet. Kishi was eventually forced by his LDP colleagues to resign. But the renewed treaty remained in place.

Three thousand protests during the Tokugawa era. Countless more from Meiji through to the 1930s. Farmers, tenants and teachers. *Shishi* and samurai. Feminists and freedom activists. Factory workers and young military officers. Putting up with perceived injustice and vigorously protesting against it seemed to run as two rich and sometimes complementary threads through early modern and modern Japanese culture, the pent-up energies of the former giving extraordinary physical and moral power to the latter. In all of this, the summer of 1960 earned itself a special place. Where the vast majority of those older protests had been sectional in their support – village, region, profession, class – and accordingly specific in their aims, the people on strike and surrounding the Diet, some trying to surge inside, came from all walks of life and had gathered at the heart of the nation to protest (and reclaim) its very purpose.

When those protests ultimately came to nothing, and the Anpo moment passed, the failure of an existential cause wrought existential consequences. Some tried to claim that with so many people taking an active part in the all-important contest for Japan's public realm – and in the most literal and vivid way, by filling the streets with bodies and flags and noise – democracy in Japan had at last been 'indigenized', as Maruyama Masao put it. Freedom, after all, is not something to be passively possessed, like an object. It is something you do, perform or exhibit. But for a great many of Japan's young especially, politics in general now lost its allure: it seemed no longer to be a route to meaningful change, or a worthwhile foundation of identity either for the individual or for society at large. Other avenues would have to be tried.

In any case, as participants in the protests pointed out, if this was 'Japanese' democracy, it was disturbingly open to hijacking by money and violence. Demonstrators had been attacked by hundreds of club-wielding counter-protestors, successors to the political thugs (*sōshi*) of the pre-war era. One drove a truck into the crowd. These people regarded themselves as anti-communist patriots, but they took part in – and were often paid for – the breaking of strikes and the beating up and intimidation of peaceful protestors. Most worrying of all was the broader nexus of business, politics, policing and gangsterism, of which they appeared to be a part. Brokering these post-war connections were the likes of Kodama, who was released from prison at the same time as Kishi and rapidly began expanding a customer base that was widely rumoured to extend to the CIA.

Meanwhile, to the dismay of anti-Anpo activists, Socialist and Communist Diet members had joined the newspapers in piously and simplistically condemning the violence on all sides. The leader of the Zengakuren accused the Communist leadership of frustrating a genuine mass movement by trying to contain and control it. The Anpo cause increasingly seemed not just to have been lost, but to be actively contributing to the fragmentation of the left into 'old' and 'new'.

Anti-Anpo protestors in 1960: Prime Minister Kishi Nobusuke's head on a stick, and 'We Dislike Ike!'

Worse was to come, with Japan's new Prime Minister Ikeda Hayato serving up his income-doubling plan in December 1960 as a soothing Christmas present for the nation. The LDP proved to have a talent for tacking towards the centre and offering domestic sweeteners whenever they were forced to put controversial policy goals on hold. They were assiduous, too, in courting ever broader voter support. Rice price regulation protected farmers – many of them now tilling their own land for the first time – from shifts in the market. And small businesses were taxed comparatively lightly and shielded from large corporation competition with rules preventing the latter from locating themselves in small neighbourhoods.

Japan's companies, for their part, were increasingly willing to woo workers with assurances over long-term job prospects and salaries, alongside an array of corporate benefits running from health-care to subsidized accommodation and holidays. Even the United States made efforts to pacify the Japanese public, launching a programme to reduce troop levels in Japan by 40 per cent, including the withdrawal of all ground forces.

Meanwhile, as the post-Anpo reckoning reverberated across the arts – with calls for the stereotyped imagery of much reportage painting to be exchanged for more penetrating analyses of power – it was becoming increasingly clear that Japan's culture war would have to be fought not just on canvas and on the streets but also on the airwaves and on screen.

*

'*Chūsha hantai! Chūsha hantai!*' – 'No to injections! No to injections!' The language of Anpo was filtering into Japan's schools, as children took to the corridors to protest against the inoculation schedule. Meanwhile, at religious ceremonies, little boys could be found exchanging traditional attire for turbans and capes, the costume of Gekkō Kamen ('Moonlight Mask'), Japan's first crime-fighting television superhero. Some even tried to emulate his feats of athletic bravery, leaping between tall buildings – leading to the common sight in hospitals around the country of pint-sized patients wrapped in towels, sheets and sunglasses being treated for cuts and scrapes and broken bones. It wasn't long before a child died trying to recreate one of the programme's stunts, resulting in the cancellation of the series in 1959, after barely a year on air.

As television spread across Japan, critical commentary in its old-media rivals – coloured, of course, by considerable envy and anxiety – focused heavily on the new technology's effects upon children. Some were trivial: children from television-owning households were said rarely to be bullied; instead they were guaranteed the best roles in sword-fighting games, while their friends were condemned to play the baddie – although it was reported that when the game was 'Anpo protest', no one at all was willing to be Kishi. Other observations were more worrisome. Children were spending less time exercising or doing their homework. At dinner, they gawped across the room at the TV, clutching their rice-bowls, rather than engaging with their parents or siblings – except to argue over the channel. At night, they went to bed late, and without doing much reading. Their use of language was increasingly vulgar and melodramatic. And imaginations that ought to roam free and far seemed to alight on characters like Gekkō

Kamen – whose theme song was sung incessantly – and become stuck there.

Alongside the disturbingly addictive nature of the new medium, claimed detractors, ran the terrible quality of its content. Television seemed to be struggling to escape its formative impulse: to attract pedestrians passing the first public sets by offering simple spectacle, from pro-wrestling to song contests. The critic Ōya Sōichi famously likened glancing at the television to spotting two dogs mating on a street corner: it was compulsive viewing, but you felt stupid afterwards. An early TV prank said it all. Someone was paid to enter the supporters' section at a baseball match and wave the flag of the opposite side, resulting in a fight. Japanese television, Ōya concluded, was creating a 'nation of 100 million idiots'.

Concern about the corrosive effects of modern mass culture – as dangerous or dumb, or both – did not begin with television. From 1925's 'Tokyo March' to the 'Apple Song' twenty years later, critics lambasted talented musicians and writers who were willing to shun refinement in favour of payment. A journalist at the *Asahi* newspaper had described the film *Soyokaze* (Soft Breeze), in which the 'Apple Song' featured, as being of value only to people seeking to make themselves physically sick – adding that the first ten minutes alone ought to do the trick. Namiki Michiko wasn't 'especially attractive' to begin with, the crude cinematography made her face look dirty, and the whole thing just reminded him of Japan's defeat.

Pop music in general, during and after the Occupation, was accused of blending banality with subservience to American styles and values: Japan as a mere cultural as well as political satellite of the United States. 'Yokosuka Dance' of 1952 was considered especially disturbing proof. Dreamed up by a local chamber of commerce to promote the city of Yokosuka, its lyrics revolved around sentimentalized intimations of sex – envisioned, it seemed, as taking place between a Japanese girl and an American GI, Yokosuka being home to a military base. One critic called it a 'masterpiece of colonial literature'. Alongside the sleaze ran the song's liberal use of imported Americanisms like *beri naisu* and *suīto hōmu*. This lyrical trend, together with the tendency of star singers like Eri Chiemi to mix Japanese and English phrases when they sang, raised the prospect of little girls growing up forgetful of, or at the very least confused about their own culture, singing songs that cast them unwittingly as the objects of American sexual appetites.

The days were gone when government bureaucrats could simply ban something they didn't like. Instead, they hosted a National Conference on Children's Culture. The Recording Industry Association of Japan (RIAJ) was persuaded to adopt an ethics code, which included a pledge to preserve constitutional values like public peace and wholesome living. Records should not promote bad customs, crime, injustice, indecency, or anything else that threatened 'child psychology'. A broadcasting ethics code followed a few years later, continuing a post-war shift towards artistic self-restraint under a combination of political and civil pressure.

Commercial self-restraint was rather harder to guarantee, and here too there were fears about the long-term impact of television. Viewers who found live broadcasts of the Anpo protests – put together by a first generation of intrepid, helmeted TV reporters – a little too harrowing had only to turn the dial to encounter a very different America. Sitcoms like *I Love Lucy* and *Father Knows Best* served as a powerful means of product placement – for American values and humour as much as for a hallowed ensemble of family possessions, from telephones and washing machines to fridges, air conditioning and cars. Modest material wealth like this came to mark you out in Japan – as it did in Western Europe during the same decade – as 'middle class'. And both the LDP and the advertisers who kept most of the country's television stations on air very much wanted you to have it.

Nothing seemed to stop the march of each new Western trend into Japanese life. Jazz and boogie-woogie gave way first to rockabilly and electric instrumental rock (*ereki*) and then to 'group sounds', thanks to visits to Japan by the American rock band The Ventures (in 1965) and The Beatles (in 1966). There was anger in some quarters at the use of the Budōkan, built to house Olympic judo, as a music venue for the Fab Four. But the wider concern, during the later 1950s and into the 1960s, was what the new styles of dress and behaviour that came with Western mass culture might be doing to the outlook of the nation's young. For music reviewers, live rockabilly concerts were a source of faint bemusement – one described a performer with his legs bent, guitar thrust outwards, 'waddling like a child with polio'. For Parent Teacher Associations (PTAs) and housewives' organizations, they threatened the transmission to Japanese children of a violent and sexualized disdain for the adult world. Boys were growing up wanting to be like the rockabilly star Yamashita Keijiro. Girls were rumoured to be throwing their panties at him.

Moral panic was good for business. In 1955, a novel called *Taiyō no Kisetsu* (*Season of the Sun*) became the surprise winner of the prestigious Akutagawa Prize for literature. Parental outcry at its content – sex, sailing, beaches, booze and bare-knuckle brawls amongst wealthy Japanese teenagers – helped to raise its public profile and it was optioned for a film, released in 1956. The book's young author, Ishihara Shintarō, was contracted by the studio to write a follow-up, and *Crazed Fruit* was released in cinemas later that same year. It launched the acting and musical career of Ishihara's brother Yūjirō, while helping Ishihara to establish a lucrative public profile as leader of the 'Sun Tribe' (*taiyōzoku*): young people sporting 'Shintarō crew cuts', wearing Hawaiian shirts and generally behaving badly.

Rebellion amongst the post-war young was not, of course, limited to Japan – Yūjirō was routinely compared with James Dean. But when Japanese children called their parents 'fascists' they were, in some cases at least, offering historical commentary rather than indulging in throwaway petulance. The political implications were different too. As the progressive politics championed by the likes of Maruyama Masao failed to gain the hoped-for traction, there was a danger that traditionalist voices on the right would dominate the response to moments of apparent social crisis like the *taiyōzoku* panic. The Japanese public realm, opened up after the war to so much fanfare, threatened to become trapped in a hopeless back-and-forth between an affluent mass culture that tested moral but not political boundaries, and a resurgent conservative establishment keen to use the more debauched elements of that culture as proof of the Occupation era's corruption of Japanese life – and the need to roll back some of those reforms.

For all that films in the *Crazed Fruit* mould might have appeared to play into the hands of youth-oriented commerce on the one hand (from Hawaiian shirts to hair products) and conservative politics on the other, they were also a sign of Japanese cinema finding a new voice. Even in the silent era, Japanese film had spoken to its audiences in a tone at once interpretive and didactic. Where Nō theatre had its chorus, bunraku its chanter, and kabuki its narrator, film had a *benshi*: a man who stood by the cinema screen, often in formal evening attire, describing the onscreen action, performing the voices of each character, and helping people to draw conclusions about what they were seeing.

Those conclusions were usually wholesome ones, but *benshi* were not strangers to a bit of misdirection, if it helped to preserve the freedom of their art form – in the face of authorities keen to keep an influential new medium in check, not least where foreign content was concerned. One *benshi* managed to reassure police that full-mouth kissing was simply a standard greeting in America. A second saved a 1907 French film about the Revolution of 1789 from being banned – the guillotining of a monarch being an unacceptable plotline – by miraculously unveiling a brand-new feature in its place. *The Cave King: A Curious Story of North America* told of a Rocky Mountains robber-baron who is brought to justice by a crowd of good-hearted local people and police who descend en masse on his hideout. Louis XVI had been recast as a criminal, with the storming of the Bastille his entirely lawful comeuppance.

And yet for some reviewers, film didn't always speak clearly enough. Ozu Yasujirō's *I Was Born, But* . . . depicted the boredom and insecurity of middle-class urban family life in the early 1930s: a father who is domineering at home but subservient at work; children who are as listless at school as their fathers are at the office, and no doubt destined to follow the same grim trajectory into adulthood. The subject matter was cutting-edge – the mixed blessings of the mass society – but detractors found the treatment ambiguous. They wanted a strong, provocative condemnation of modern life, rather than wistfulness and melancholy. They wanted polemic. Ozu offered portraiture.

Ozu's defenders might say that he was giving free rein to his audience's inner *benshi*, to narrate, interpret and draw moral conclusions – or simply to remain blissfully mute. It was thanks to precisely these sorts of qualities that *Tokyo Story* (1953) ended up helping to put Japanese film on the map. A retired couple make a journey from their rural home to visit their children in the big city, a place of smokestacks, telephone wires and trains trundling over iron bridges. It is soon painfully apparent that their son and daughter's busy urban lives – one a doctor, the other a beautician – have eclipsed any affection they might once have had for their provincial parents. Dramatic turning points are minimized all the way along, sometimes missed out altogether and simply referred back to later. The focus instead is on what is going on inside and around the characters: the quiet spaces into which brief spoken observations occasionally intrude, opening up more space in the process; the gaps between what is said and what is intended. In one scene, the two parents sit on cushions on the tatami-mat floor of their room at a seaside resort. Ozu uses his trademark low, lingering camera to enhance the sense of their children's lives, and of life itself, receding gently away from them. Drinking tea at a small table, the two contentedly exchange what would be non sequiturs were it not for all the silent connecting contributions of memory and emotion – as spacious, shifting and endlessly fertile as the expanse of sea onto which they are gazing out.

Respected though Ozu was, Japan's big film studios – Shōchiku, Tōhō and Nikkatsu prime amongst them – were, by the late 1950s, on the hunt for something new. They were beginning to worry – rightly – about what television was going to do to them. Movie-going in Japan peaked in 1958, with over a billion cinema visits that year, and then dropped precipitously over the decade that followed. The success of *taiyōzoku* films prompted studios to try promoting younger directors, in the hope of holding on to a youth audience. For this new generation, Ozu's artistry was never in question. Instead, it was the old problem, surfacing in a new era: where was the analysis, the anger, the call to arms?

One young film-maker, Ōshima Nagisa, summed up the work of predecessors like Ozu in a single, devastating word: congenial. A graduate of Kyoto University, where he had been heavily involved in student politics, Ōshima wanted his own films to be not 'products' but 'forms of action'. Here was one of the few ways, he thought, in which educated people like himself might reach out to a country in desperate need of painful reflection and radical change. After Anpo,

Japan could no longer afford congeniality. One of Ōshima's early films, *Night and Fog in Japan* (1960), rammed home the point, showing uninvited guests turning a wedding reception into an inquisition. It was a heated, claustrophobic examination of contemporary politics, group-think and personal culpability, with spotlights used to single people out as they spoke or cowered.

'New wave' directors like Ōshima drew inspiration from abroad: from Italian neo-realists like Roberto Rossellini, and from Alain Resnais and the French new wave. Here were two societies riven still – like Japan – by divisions between those who had supported and those who had resisted the totalitarian projects of barely a decade and a half before. But Ōshima's generation also set themselves up against domestic cinema, vying for movie-goers' attention not just with the likes of Ozu but with a syrupy and fatalistic war-film genre. Films like *Ningen no Jōken* (*The Human Condition*, made in three parts between 1958 and 1961) dealt seriously and unflinchingly with the war, and with what happens when individual responsibility bumps up against authority and big institutions. The latter concern was a major feature of Kurosawa Akira's films, too, both the period pieces for which he became famous abroad and contemporary dramas like 1952's *Ikiru* ('to live'). But a great many other directors threatened to frustrate the country's post-war quest for a more independently minded citizenry by focusing on the way that history sometimes stacks the odds against people, in terrible, inescapable ways. As one Japanese critic put it, submission to the 'world around' and to a 'collective self' began to be lauded again with surprising speed after the war. The romanticizing of the kamikaze was an especially egregious example, in films like *Beyond the Clouds* (1953) and *The Sacrifice of the Human Torpedoes* (1955).

Equally discreditable treatment of the recent past could be found in a series of films beginning with *Gojira* (*Godzilla* in its later US release). Appearing at the end of 1954, the year of the *Lucky Dragon 5* incident, *Gojira* was directed by an eyewitness to the aftermath at Hiroshima, Honda Ishirō, who envisioned his monster – its name a portmanteau of the Japanese for 'gorilla' and 'whale' – as nuclear disaster 'made flesh'. It was a huge box office success, thanks in large part to the special effects work of Tsuburaya Eiji, who had contributed to such an effective cinematic recreation of the Pearl Harbor attack in 1942 that the Occupation authorities had mistaken it for documentary footage. For *Gojira*, Tsuburaya exchanged *King Kong*-style stop-motion camera work for something much simpler: a man dressed in a big rubber suit mashing miniature cars and buildings underfoot, with high-speed footage, filmed under intense lights, slowed down to give the impression of a ponderous stomp.

Such features were to become a staple of both film and television in Japan, with fantastical heroes and villains conjured by outlandishly costumed human beings engaging one another in wrestling matches and martial arts-style fisticuffs. *Kaijū eiga* – monster movies – were critically important to the survival of studios like Tōhō in the television age. And to hostile reviewers, this was all too obvious in the genre's early years. Despite Honda's protestations, a film like *Gojira* seemed to be neither cautionary atomic tale nor pioneering piece of art. It was an attempt, pure and simple, to cash in on memories of Hiroshima and Nagasaki (increasingly to the fore as the end of Occupation censorship opened up public discussion), providing people with precisely the wrong kind of outlet for their anger and anxieties about nuclear weapons.

Up against these monstrous fantasies, with their monstrous ticket sales, Ōshima's *Night and Fog* had its work cut out. And in the end, it wasn't given much of a chance. Released on 9 October 1960, it was pulled from cinemas after just three days. The film wasn't at all the kind of thing that Ōshima's employers, Shōchiku, had envisaged when they assisted his rise through the ranks. But more importantly, it was gazumped by TV. People around Japan were suddenly glued to their screens at home, watching a spectacular piece of contemporary drama. A young man, all of seventeen years of age, and frustrated by his country's emptiness of purpose, was taking politics into his own hands. He rushed onto a stage where a left-wing politician was giving a speech, brandishing a short-blade sword, and ran him through with it, killing him almost instantly. Viewers were horrified. The attack was not just realistic. It was real. A prominent socialist, Asanuma Inejirō, had just been assassinated on camera.

*

Seventeen stares despairingly at his reflection in the mirror. 'I've turned bluish-black. That's the face of a chronic masturbator. People probably say: that guy's a full-time masturbator. Look at the colour of his face. Look at those cloudy eyes . . .' Only later, watching an ageing ultranationalist giving a speech, does he feel his self-loathing leave him, his anger turning outwards instead towards the targets picked out by the speaker. 'Petty officials! Pimps, selling out their country! Traitors! Shameless bootlickers!' When he hears a group of office girls behind him anxiously tut-tutting at this young 'Rightist', his epiphany is complete: 'That's it. I've touched the essence of myself. I am a Rightist! I scream out at them: "What about us Rightists, then, you bitches?!"'

Seventeen joins the old man's organization, the Imperial Way Party. He reads the Kojiki, the ancient chronicle of Japan's gods and emperors, and devours the poems of the Meiji Emperor. He takes to heart the central message of modern imperial ideology: 'devotion and selfishness are incompatible'. Blissful liberation, as impotence, indecision and the terror of death all melt away. Now, 'His Majesty the Emperor makes the choices'. From books the boy graduates to karate and judo. It is summer 1960 and he joins in the fighting against the Anpo protestors. He beats and tramples them, is arrested, then goes back for more. On 12 October that year, he takes up his sword and heads over to where a leftist politician is participating in a televised debate . . .

The young novelist Ōe Kenzaburō was inspired to create his lonesome, masturbation-obsessed character 'Seventeen' both by the murder of Asanuma in October 1960 and by his own sense of hopelessness and defeat at his country's politics. Characters like Seventeen – young men defined by impotence, voyeurism, sexual submissiveness or extreme sexual violence – appeared with increasing frequency in literature and film during the 1960s. Part of the reason was a turn, by increasingly cash-strapped film studios and distributors, towards the soft-pornography 'pink film' genre, which made up around half of new releases by 1965. But that didn't explain the themes running through some of these films. Takechi Tetsuji's *Kuroi yuki* ('Black Snow', 1965) told the story of nineteen-year-old Jirō, so traumatized by his mother's selling of sex to American soldiers at the nearby Yokota airbase that he struggles to form sexual relationships of his own, relieved of his impotence only by holding a loaded gun in his hand. Jirō ends up murdering an American soldier, and then his own mother, before being gunned down by military police.

Themes and protagonists like these reflected a real-life turn in the 1960s towards the primal, the fleshly and the violent. Establishment Japan, in which the Anpo protests had barely put a dent, was increasingly hard to identify simply with state institutions or even with the state in league with nefarious big business and a compliant media. An older generation of progressive intellectuals also had to be included in that category now, their blanket rejection of 'violence' during the Anpo protests having revealed to their critics a fear of change. Even ordinary citizens were starting to look like the enemy. They might not love the strictures of their school or working lives, but they could imagine worse – in many cases, they could remember it. Many of them therefore simply ignored the country's political travails, preferring the consolations of a book or a television programme, a holiday or film, or the ordinary joys of a family life where the risks of a member's sudden recruitment to a doomed war were now vanishingly slight.

Students and radical artists spent the decade trying to reach around what they saw as this modern, Western-influenced complacency, by exploring in its place a more vital Japanese past. They experimented with romantic cultural nationalisms of the left and right, in some cases dispensing altogether with ideas like progress or the nation. With the optimistic liberalism of the early post-war years tarnished by the Cold War and consumer capitalism – the wartime West's much-vaunted humanism seemed to have curdled into quiz shows and missile crises – the advantages had rarely been clearer of living in a country built upon more than a millennium's worth of creative contact around the world – with India, China and Korea, and only latterly with the modern West.

A pre-modern trawl for resources took some artists back to an Edo era fondly recalled as less sanitized than the present day. Others rewound all the way to Japan's Jōmon period (14,000–300 BC): Okamoto Tarō, enthusiast for the *Yomiuri Indépendant* exhibition, extolled the 'smell of Japanese soil' that Jōmon earthenware gave off.

Avant-garde traditionalists – such a thing was possible, in these times – reworked *ikebana* (flower-arranging), along with folk crafts and a range of Japanese and Chinese philosophies. The calligrapher Iijima Tsutomu talked about cleansing himself of the recent past and returning to the purity of 'a naked human being'. The work of the folklorist Yanagita Kunio, appropriated not so long ago by militarists, now found readers on the radical left: a means, they hoped, of rediscovering a connection with nature, whose sidelining by Japan's construction and entertainment industries was yet another source of the bleak present.

The *Yomiuri Indépendant* closed its doors for the last time in 1963, after complaints and attempts to censor a number of the exhibits. But some of the artists who had met under its auspices went out far beyond the exhibition space to confront and discomfit people with a new quality of directness. The Neo-Dada Organizers sold tickets in 1962 for a banquet marking the end of the war and the fall of the Japanese empire. Guests turned up expecting to eat, but found themselves treated instead to a taste of colonial-style exploitation: watching, stomachs empty, while the artists gorged themselves at their expense.

Two years later, another set of guests arrived in a room in Tokyo's Imperial Hotel to be fitted by members of the Hi-Red Center collective for their very own personalized atomic fall-out shelter. Body size was measured through immersion in a bath, the capacity of the mouth by seeing how much water it could hold. Photographs were taken from six angles, which were then turned into the six planes of what looked very much like a coffin. Few shelters were sold, but Hi-Red Center's satirical commercial pitch – billed as 'Shelter Plan' – was scarcely less ridiculous, they thought, than a society whose service industries blossomed while nuclear holocaust beckoned.

In a similar vein, the *angura* – underground – playwright Kara Jūrō set out to place his audiences in 'terrifying situations', some of which took place in public toilets, abandoned buildings, railway stations and even lily ponds – with stage entrances and exits a matter of emergence and submergence. He eventually settled on the use of a large red touring tent, which he first set up in the grounds of a Shinto shrine in Tokyo. It was the ideal location for a troupe of players whom Kara proudly described as *kawara kojiki* ('riverbed beggars') – after an unflattering Tokugawa-era descriptor for kabuki performers. The term referred much further back, too, towards the role of riverbeds as an ancient site of cosmos-changing drama. Gods and goddesses had once gathered in the sunless gloom of a dry riverbed to try to coax the Sun Goddess Amaterasu out of a cave in which she had hidden herself. They tried everything: banging drums, crashing cymbals, playing music, even bringing along a crowing cock – an exercise, perhaps, in sympathetic magic: trying to force the dawn through its most recognizable sound. Nothing worked. Finally, Ama no Uzume, Goddess of Mirth and Dawn, jumped onto an upturned tub, half-naked, and performed a bawdy, ecstatic dance. Everyone collapsed into laughter, and when Amaterasu took a peek to see what was going on, the Strong-Armed Man of Heaven hauled her from her hideout.

These ways of dealing with the divine – song and dance; entertainment and ecstatic trance; play and humour – defined Japan's performing arts ever after, from ancient court rituals to preserve the health of the Emperor (on which the Ama no Uzume story may have been based) through to kabuki theatre, whose disreputable first performers were so often involved in prostitution that women and children had to be banned from appearing on stage. Kara mourned the crushing of that spirit, first via Tokugawa clampdowns (the authorities uneasy about audiences having their passions inflamed by violent or romantic tales) and then by Meiji leaders reinventing kabuki for the purposes of cultural diplomacy: turning raucous all-day revelry into plush, gas-lit evening entertainment, to be enjoyed in elegant attire and complete silence. By the time kabuki had been made fit for Japan's imperial couple, and for a performance to be offered at Buckingham Palace (around the turn of the twentieth century), there was little left any longer that would have tempted Amaterasu out of her cave.

Kara's attempts to give theatre back its thrust and spontaneity must occasionally have had audiences missing their television screens. His restoration of the old kabuki walkways brought actors right out into the midst of people, performing plays that were centred on the actors' raw physicality and confrontational energy. If those plays could feel intimidating, they were also notoriously hard to follow, veering from lavatory humour to esotericism and offering plots and metaphors out of which little narrative sense could be made. One of the more straightforward pieces was *John Silver: The Beggar of Love*, written at the end of the 1960s about pirates and their nostalgia for the destructive sexual adventures of their youth. The setting shifted between a toilet in contemporary Japan back across the seas to Japan's wartime exploitation of Korea and Manchuria – in natural resources, money, conscript labour and organized prostitution. The 'new Japan', Kara wanted to remind people, has been built on the sins of the old one. And if we think that we cannot possibly become trapped and defeated by circumstance, in the way that our parents' generation did, then we are deluding ourselves.

The playwright Terayama Shūji and choreographer Hijikata Tatsumi were likewise steeped in the war years and their aftermath. Both grew up amidst desperate poverty in wartime northern Japan, Terayama losing his father and Hijikata watching one sister sold into prostitution while another died. So Terayama was deadly serious when he had members of his troupe jump into the audience, insult them, refuse to let them see the end of a play, spread them out at different locations across a city (so that they would see different performances), trap them in the venue, or even set fire to parts of the stage. He wanted to upset people, and to make them see the forces at work in controlling ostensibly free societies. Subservience in contemporary Japan, he thought, was far more ephemeral, even game-like, than people realized. It drew its real power from a deeply human exuberance that comes with alternately obeying and disobeying rules. One of his plays, *Nuhikun* ('Directions to Servants'), featured two contraptions on stage. A 'Saint–Master machine' was crafted to resemble the Meiji imperial throne, via which servants took it in turns to become the master – receiving the permission to discipline, punish and pleasure at will. A 'self-spanking machine' allowed the user to pull a string and receive a welcome wallop.

Hijikata rooted his Ankoku Butō – 'dance of utter darkness' – in the shamanic traditions of his part of Japan: blind female shamans called *itako* possessed the power to call up the spirits of the dead. Hijikata wanted people to encounter those spirits as real: in the slow, contorted movements of a semi-naked, white-painted body on a darkened stage; in fingers twitching and eyes rolling back in their

Hijikata Tatsumi on stage

sockets; and in a face grotesquely contorted, in possession and pain. Hijikata said he sometimes felt the spirit of his dead sister scratching around looking for him in the dark while he danced.

One of Hijikata's greatest performances was *Hijikata Tatsumi and the Japanese – Revolt of the Flesh*, in 1968. It cast him as a virgin on her wedding day, garbed in a back-to-front white kimono. The clothes came off to reveal a scrawny, naked man wearing a golden phallus, entering the convulsions of an ancient fertility ritual that culminates in him throttling a live rooster. Eventually, he himself becomes the sacrifice, hauled upwards off the stage and into the darkness.

But if this was a 'heretic ritual' – as the novelist and Hijikata fan Mishima Yukio said of Ankoku Butō – were the post-war, high-growth faithful paying attention? What if the people Hijikata and other radical artists most needed to reach were those least likely to exchange the cheery pop and easy-going humour of *Shabondama horidē* for the chance to see and hear and smell a chicken meet its maker?

Avant-garde audiences were made up, in large part, of students and young people, some of whom were turning, by the end of the decade, from the fleshly and the primal towards outright violence. Tensions over study and work conditions at home and Japan's support for its US ally abroad – despised military bases now being used as staging posts for a war in Vietnam – erupted into protests across more than one hundred

Members of Hi-Red Center scrubbing the pavement with tiny
toothbrushes, as part of a 'Be Clean!' event satirizing Tokyo's Olympic
preparations (16 October 1964)

university campuses in the late 1960s, paralleling student protests elsewhere in the world. One Japanese protestor described his school years as
like 'living in handcuffs', all for the sake of getting into a university
where classes were boring, overcrowded and increasingly expensive, and
the curriculum revolved around the needs of the country's employers.

Student activists on the 'New Left' during these years were clearer
than ever about their most difficult challenge: the sheer intimacy of
their enemy. University authorities could be barracked over miserably
functional curricula, professors cornered in classrooms over their
corrosive political or social views. But how was something as intangible yet pervasive as 'everydayness' – *nichijōsei* – to be tackled?
The control of parents, the complacency of privilege, the failure of
Anpo, the lure of affluence, the comforts of home, the opinions of
others, the glow of the television: the combined power of all these
things, as the dominating features of the day-to-day world, led some
students to conclude that only behind barricades could they live true,
honest lives – eating together, reading, talking and reflecting. Some of
the student protestors in the late 1960s put on helmets and took up
wooden staves against riot police who were made to stand in for all
of society's incorporeal wrongs.

Meanwhile, on both the left and right of politics there was desperate anger at the failings of comrades: on the left, an extreme political fastidiousness that contorted into paranoia; on the right, a display of romance and bloody patriotism choreographed to shame all those who witnessed it. Together, these impulses worked a turbulent era of protest to its savage climax.

In March 1970, nine members of a group called Sekigun-ha (the Red Army Faction) boarded Japan Airlines Flight 351 armed with samurai swords and dummy pipe bombs, concealed in the sorts of tubes used to transport fishing rods. They proceeded to hijack the plane somewhere above Mount Fuji, hoping to leave a country where political consciousness was low and police surveillance all too accomplished. They would train instead in Cuba, returning to Japan when they were ready to begin the revolution. Preparations had been extensive. The group had rented a hall, and arranged its folding seats according to the aircraft layout. They had brought along restraints for each passenger. What they hadn't done was check whether an internal flight would have enough fuel aboard to leave the country.

It didn't. Instead, an extraordinary series of events unfolded that began with the plane touching down in Japan's southern city of Fukuoka, where fuel was taken on and some of the passengers were let off (including one who said he planned to recommend the hijackers to Japan Airlines as cabin crew: they had changed the ashtrays, and given him something to read). The plane took off again, landing next in what the group were led to believe was North Korea. In fact, they were in South Korea, where fake signage had been hurriedly put in place by the American and South Korean military in order to support the illusion.

The plane remained on the runway for three whole days, amidst hijacker threats to blow it up: thanks to physics and chemistry students in their ranks, Sekigun-ha possessed genuine grenades made of dynamite and small metallic balls taken from a pinball-like gambling game called *pachinko*. Finally, Japan's Vice Transport Minister was swapped for the remaining hostages, and the plane made its way up to Pyongyang. The group still hoped to get to Cuba, but the North Korean regime had other plans for them, namely to assist their intelligence services, possibly with the notorious abductions of Japanese citizens that began later in the decade, many of them smuggled across the Sea of Japan aboard inflatables and ships. Nearly half a century later, some of the hijackers were still living in North Korea, in a dedicated 'Japanese village'.

Later that year, one of Japan's greatest and most self-consciously patriotic writers spat contempt for his countrymen:

> Post-war Japanese have opportunistically welcomed economic prosperity, forgetting the principles of the nation, losing their native spirit, pursuing the trivial without correcting the essential . . . leading themselves into spiritual emptiness. We have stood by like helpless bystanders, biting our teeth hard, passively witnessing the sell-off of our national politics over the last 100 years, deceiving ourselves about the humiliation of defeat in the war rather than confronting it. The Japanese themselves have assaulted their own history and tradition.

No longer willing to remain amongst the 'living dead', and having remarked to a friend after completing his masterpiece tetralogy, *The Sea of Fertility*, that there was little left for him to do, Mishima Yukio headed for the Tokyo headquarters of the Eastern Command of the Japan Self-Defence Forces. The feeble boy who had dodged physical exercise at school, the youth who had allowed a doctor's error to excuse him from fighting in the Philippines had now become the muscle-bound fantasy figure of Seventeen's rightist dreams.

Fifteen years before, Mishima had embarked on a body-building programme, regarding the classical Greek body as intimately bound up with the noble wisdom of that age: firm flesh, pure spirit (he kept a giant statue of Apollo in his garden). Mishima exchanged an interest in psychoanalysis – in the course of which he spent time with Kosawa Heisaku and published a novel on the subject (*Ongaku*, 'Music', 1965) – for SDF training, and then formed a small private army of his own, the *tatenokai* (Shield Society). Now, on 25 November 1970, with four members of that militia by his side, he entered the SDF barracks, grabbed the commandant (with whom he had done the courtesy of making an appointment) and bound him to a chair.

From the commandant's balcony, Mishima roared a speech at the soldiers below, inciting them to rise up for the Emperor – 'Is there no one who will hurl his body against the Constitution?' Then, having met with little more than silence and derision – which in his own disillusionment with his compatriots, he may well have expected – Mishima retired to the commandant's office, cut his stomach open with a sword, and had a man from his militia behead him. If the quisling so-called soldiery were immune to fine words, let them have a sacrament instead: *seppuku*, the classic samurai death, the ultimate selfless act.

Of the Sekigun-ha members who had stayed behind in Japan when Flight 351 took off, some left to form the globe-trotting and infamously violent 'Japanese Red Army'. Its activities over the next few years included an airport massacre in Israel (twenty-six people killed), an attack on an oil refinery in Singapore, assaults on embassies around the world and the hijacking of three passenger planes. Other members helped to create a larger Japanese group called the United Red Army, taking to the mountains to avoid the authorities.

Moving from base to base, a willingness to die for their cause and a determination to avoid the lure of comfort began to morph into the use of beatings – given or received – as a means of confirming commitment and enhancing self-critique. The process claimed its first life in late December 1971. Another member of the group died a few weeks later, after her comrades stepped in to help when half an hour of punching herself in the face failed to yield the desired results. Eight more deaths and two executions left only five people trudging towards yet another new mountain hideout in late February 1972. Expecting trouble, they made a hostage of a man they discovered in the lodge. The authorities found them and cut the power to the accommodation – the television blinked off, but it left a single, terrible image seared into their minds. US President Richard Nixon had landed in China to make a peace of sorts: it seemed the end of all they had fought for. The police outside soon began bombarding them with surrender pleas from loved ones, broadcast from loudspeakers. They used baseball pitching machines to fire rocks onto the corrugated iron roof of the lodge, creating a constant rattling sound that was intended to deprive them of sleep.

At home, tens of millions of Japanese sat back in their living rooms and watched as riot police moved in with a wrecking ball and took out a chunk of the lodge wall. Jets of water and tear gas shells were fired through the void, from which gunfire escaped, killing two policemen. After an eight-hour gun battle, viewers sighed with relief

Mishima Yukio (1925–70) addressing SDF soldiers on the day of his death

as the hostage was at last rescued and the group members taken alive. Court proceedings traced in intimate detail a journey from concern for society to apparent hatred of it; from radical political analysis, through asceticism, to spectacular barbarity.

What sympathy had existed in wider society for individuals of conscience who risked their own prospects to improve the lives of others was draining away fast. Students had tied up their teachers and donned improvised military uniforms. Distressed families had been seen hurrying down the stairs from a hijacked aircraft. Japan's first Nobel Prize laureate for literature, Kawabata Yasunari, had been spotted wading through reporters to reach the site of his friend's grizzly, puzzling final act. And young Japanese men and women had turned guerrilla, both in far-off countries and here at home, up in the mountains. If the search – the battle – for the soul of post-war Japan were to continue, other ways would have to be found of fighting it.

15

Pulling Strings

The *Lucky Dragon 5* tuna panic of the mid-1950s had barely subsided when news came in of yet more potentially contaminated catches, this time at the southern end of Japan's main islands. People living along the coast of the Shiranui Sea in Kyūshū reported seeing 'dancing cats' around their neighbourhoods: cats walking awkwardly, tripping, convulsing, running in circles and foaming at the mouth. Some of the cats threw themselves into the sea. Others were thrown in by locals – a combination of compassion and creeping anxiety. Meanwhile, birds were seen cruising into buildings, or falling out of the sky. Barnacles no longer clung to boats. Seaweed was losing its colour. Pine trees near the shore turned brown and died.

Then, in the last days of April 1956, children began to be hospitalized with symptoms ranging from speech difficulties and unusual shifts in voice pitch to numbness, loss of motor control, tunnel vision and trouble with hearing and swallowing. The human dimension of this bizarre, escalating crisis had so far been contained within family homes. Dying fishermen were roped to their beds to contain their thrashing. Now, at last, it was attracting clinical and public attention. By the end of the year, fifty-four people had been identified as sharing similar, unexplained symptoms. Seventeen of those had died.

Doctors and researchers cast around desperately for the cause. At first, they thought they might be dealing with some unknown infectious disease, because almost all the victims came from the same hamlets around the bay. But attention soon shifted to their diet of seafood, in which this area was famously rich: the boast was that if an unexpected visitor arrived, you could put the kettle on, go off to catch a fish or an octopus to feed them, and be back before the water boiled.

Suspect seafood led investigators to the waters of the bay, and in turn to a large chemical plant nearby. Shin Nihon Chisso Hiryō (New Japan Nitrogenous Fertilizers) had been operating since the beginning of the twentieth century. It loomed large enough in the nation's industrial and economic interests to warrant a pre-war visit from the Shōwa Emperor, thirteen Allied bombing raids and a privileged place in post-war economic planning. The city nearby was especially reliant on the plant. Minamata was known as Chisso's 'castle-town': a reference, drawing on a bygone samurai age, to the company's swaggering, feudal dominance in the area. Chisso employed more than half of the town's working population and contributed the lion's share of its taxes.

One of Chisso's most valued products was acetaldehyde. Widely used in industry, it was manufactured via a process whose waste products, dumped directly into Minamata Bay via a canal, were now thought likely to be the cause of people's symptoms. Sediment near the canal mouth was found to contain a wide variety of chemicals, amongst them a concentration of mercury so high – around two kilograms per ton – that you could mine it for profit. Chisso later did so.

But when researchers from Kumamoto University announced their conclusions about the links between people's symptoms and the chemical plant, Chisso concealed its own, similar results, and resolved instead to fight. It issued pamphlets casting doubt on the science behind the university findings. And when sales of seafood from the bay ended up being banned as a precaution, it used *mimaikin* (sympathy money) to buy the silence of local fishermen. One condition of the money was that recipients waived their right to compensation, even if Chisso's waste water was at some point found to be the cause of what was now being called 'Minamata disease'. Central government likewise suppressed its own findings, and rewarded the efforts of the university researchers by cancelling their funding.

*

While waste water continued to gush into Minamata Bay, Japan's leaders turned to more pressing concerns. The late 1940s and 1950s had seen the emergence of union activists, students and radical ideologues as the 'usual suspects' of street protest. The Anpo demonstrations of 1960 were different, and far more worrying for Japan's leaders, because they brought them face to face with an unexpected and fearsome new foe: the general public. A tide of first-timers, swelling the ranks of protestors around the Diet building and across Tokyo, watched on television and talked about in the newspapers, presented an unprecedented threat to the government's legitimacy and to its core claim: to be establishing the kind of 'new Japan' that the vast majority of people wanted.

Kobayashi Tomi regarded herself as the sort of person who, when discontented by the world, would usually just 'sit at home, becoming more and more annoyed'. But then she heard Prime Minister Kishi, in the course of berating the press for its one-sided and unrepresentative coverage of events in 1960, declare his intention to listen out for the 'voices of the voiceless'. The implication seemed to be that anyone not actively and vocally contesting the status quo must be happy with it. This persuaded Kobayashi to help form a protest group for the protest-shy. They took Koe Naki Koe no Kai (Voices of the Voiceless) as their name, and created placards that included slogans like 'Walk with us for fifty metres, or even ten!' Their marching song said it all:

> Come on Citizens, let's walk together . . .
> We know that you are busy at work every day
> And feel embarrassed to participate in demonstrations.
> But if we give up here and now, and fall silent
> Then Japan will never change for the better.
> Let's act now so that one day, when our children ask,
> 'What were you doing then?'
> We will not be ashamed . . .
> Come on Citizens, be brave!

The all-important word here was 'citizens': *shimin*. Anpo showed that you didn't have to build barricades, wield clubs or speak in mangled Marxist jargon in order to oppose injustice and help to achieve change. All you needed was a cause, knowledge of your constitutional rights, and a modicum of expertise in applying pressure in the right places. Nor did you have to agree that everyday life in Japan was now a web of odious, constraining economic and cultural attachments, from which only extreme vigilance, complete purification or violent self-marginalization would save you. Where radicals saw chains to be slipped, citizens spotted strings to be pulled. A rapidly expanding urban Japan offered no end of opportunity: it was densely populated, a hub for government and industry, and the scene of a rich – and therefore richly vulnerable – network of social and commercial transactions. It was here that battle would be joined.

A pre-war housing crisis, wartime bombing and mass migration to the cities required the building of 11 million homes during Japan's early economic boom years. Olympic visitors arriving in Tokyo encountered a landscape of concrete, cranes and half-structures – buildings in the process of either coming down or going up. By 1970, around 50 million people, or half the Japanese population, could be found living along the main section of the Tōkaidō corridor, running from Tokyo through Kawasaki, Yokohama, Nagoya and Kyoto to Osaka. People were soon talking about a 'Tōkaidō Megalopolis'. Across ever greater proportions of this famous rail route, train travellers found themselves struggling to say where one urban conurbation finished and the next began.

City-dwellers and their appetite for work and consumption were the life-blood of the new Japan. Couples dreamed of progressing from renting a home to living in a *danchi*, a government-built suburban apartment complex. These were soon joined by *manshon* – privately built city apartment blocks. The final step on the property ladder, if all went well, would be to stand one day, looking proudly on, as the constituent parts of a small prefabricated house were delivered to a newly purchased and freshly cleared plot of land.

Problems of space and sound-proofing in some of these homes were countered by the joys, new to many, of indoor toilets. Communal tatami-mat spaces were increasingly exchanged for wooden and vinyl flooring, with living and dining–kitchen areas separated out from private bedrooms – in which adults and children now slept separately. Tables and chairs vied for precious floor space with a rapidly expanding array of labour-saving gadgets. There were culinary innovations too: Chinese fried dumplings called *gyōza*, brought back to Japan by soldiers returning from war; Western-style bread (toast for breakfast; sandwiches for a quick lunch); processed foods including the instant classic, 'instant ramen' (noodles).

The year 1970 marked the country's point of peak material fulfilment. As Morita Akio's Sony became the first Japanese company to
be listed on the New York Stock Exchange, many Japanese could
look back on a decade of extraordinary growth that had allowed
them to graduate from encountering luxurious homes and lifestyles
on television to inhabiting and living them themselves. Where parents
and grandparents had yearned for peace and stability, the present
generation aspired to great careers and luxury clothes, fine dining
and foreign holidays. Health insurance and other welfare measures
launched in the early 1960s were helping people to enjoy all this for
longer than ever before – Japan would soon boast the longest-lived
men and women on earth.

Yet few of Japan's millions of new homes represented great victories for architecture. The emphasis had been on speed of construction,
cost-effectiveness of materials and the use of all available urban space.
And it showed. There was little in the way of coordinated planning:
residents found that electricity and telephone cables suspended
between poles and building façades ran mesh-like across their already
limited window views. And even those without a particularly keen
sense of smell found the provision of drainage and sewerage all too
conspicuously lacking. The air in some parts of Tokyo was so thick
with factory and car emissions that schoolchildren ended up being
hospitalized.

Two shocks in 1971 reminded people that even these rather mixed
standards of living might not be sustainable. First, US President
Nixon had announced – on live television, without forewarning the
Japanese – his plan to visit the People's Republic of China the following year. Then he had declared his intention for the United States to
leave the gold standard. The first move threatened Japan's long-term
value to the US as an ally in East Asia, while obliging it to reverse its
own longstanding post-war policy – originally forced on it by the
US – of keeping its diplomatic distance from China's communists.
The second pushed the value of the yen sharply upwards, rendering
Japanese exports suddenly more expensive (Nixon was not overly
concerned about this: angry at the country's leaders for their slowness in helping America with its trade imbalance, his economic policy
was – in his words – to 'stick it to the Japanese'). Two years later,

along came a third shock. Oil prices briefly rocketed four-fold, caused by conflict in the Middle East and resulting in a 'toilet paper panic' as people scrambled to hoard essentials before prices went up or supplies ran out.

In response to these setbacks, government planners prescribed more of the same, but with a few tweaks. Instability in the Middle East and the steady rise of competitor economies showed that Japan had to redouble its efforts at achieving a hi-tech economy, while becoming as self-sufficient in energy as possible. Investment was duly boosted in key areas from computers, bio-tech and robotics through to nuclear and hydroelectric energy. Electronics manufacturers worked to reduce the power consumption of their products.

Two – perhaps more positive – epoch-changing moments arrived the next year in 1974. In May, the first 7-Eleven franchise in Japan opened its doors. The nation was launched on a love-affair with the local convenience store, or *konbini*. A little over forty years later, Japan was home to no less than 60,000 stores. The standard arrangement involved around 100 square metres of retail space, open twenty-four hours per day, seven days per week. There was hot and cold food and drink, cigarettes and toiletries, manga and magazines. People could access an ever-increasing roster of services besides: paying bills, withdrawing money, buying concert tickets, dropping off parcels or laundry, making photocopies, using a massage chair, and even checking their blood pressure.

The second great consumer moment of that year was the national launch of Kentucky Fried Chicken's *Kurisumasu ni wa Kentakkii* ('Kentucky for Christmas') campaign. The manager of Japan's first KFC, Okawara Takeshi, had overheard two foreigners in his shop talking about how much they were missing turkey, being so far from home at Christmas. That night, it came to him in a dream: what if KFC were to offer a special 'party barrel' for the festive season? Within a few short years children had come to regard Colonel Sanders and Santa as more or less the same person, special KFC Christmas dinners were having to be ordered weeks in advance, and Christmas and chicken had become inextricably linked in the minds of the Japanese population. Okawara's dream eventually landed him his dream job: President and CEO of KFC Japan.

Amidst all the opportunities, shocks and innovations of the 1960s and early 1970s, there were echoes, still, of an older domesticity. The latest vacuum cleaners contended with traditional tatami rooms. Sliding panels (*fusama*) and paper screens (*shōji*) remained an artful means of opening up or closing off space. And a sunken, plain-floored *genkan* (vestibule) was still used to mark and maintain a transition between the dirt and distractions of the outside world and the cleanliness and relative safety of the home.

Housewives sitting at dining-room tables, drawing up lists of chores, no doubt detected rather more egregious continuities with the past. The Meiji Civil Code had been infamous amongst pre-war feminists for enshrining in law the *ie*: a 'household' whose headship, along with extensive rights over other members, passed exclusively from father to eldest son. That code very comfortably met GHQ's generous definition of 'feudal', and parts of it were updated in 1947 to ensure equal individual rights and shared inheritance of family property.

But here, as in many areas of life, Occupation reforms did not so much win thoroughgoing change as create the constitutional and institutional means by which people might one day win it for themselves. When it came to the family, women seeking a different deal had to contend with conservatives in government who were intent on ensuring a lengthy afterlife for the *ie*, both as a cultural ideal and an economic convenience. Government-backed, low-interest mortgages became conspicuous for their availability only to couples and families – not to individuals. Social security and taxation, too, were skewed towards establishing what LDP politicians referred to as a ('traditionally Japanese') 'welfare society' – contrasting it with the emergence of a 'welfare state' in parts of Western Europe. In Japan, government would offer a basic safety net, with adjunct roles played by employers and local communities. People would then look for care and social support primarily within the family – which more often than not meant mothers and grandmothers, aunts, sisters and daughters.

Citizen movements across the late 1960s and early 1970s were built on the realization that all of this – growth, consumerism, government attempts to connect social with civil engineering – depended upon the daily cooperation of ordinary people. It might not be every feminist's first choice, but even that list of chores in the housewife's hand was a weapon of sorts. It was an inventory of companies and service-providers who relied upon households like hers to survive, and in turn to drive the economic growth without which Japan's rulers lacked an impressive story to tell abroad or a mollifying one to offer an over-worked population at home. It was, in other words, as reliable a guide to Japan's pressure points as you could ask for.

In a battle for, and through, daily life, not every issue needed to be existential. Some of the most effective campaigns were fought on narrowly defined issues. *Danchi* complexes gave rise to citizens' associations intent on tackling sewerage charges and the corruption of local officials – one even tried to have their local mayor recalled. Other organizations got involved in discussions of train fares, waste disposal and Japan's shortage of high schools. Political study groups were set up, while veteran Anpo organizations like Voices of the Voiceless offered people advice on everything from campaigning tactics to dealing with the police (teaching them the legal difference between a threat and an actual arrest, along with a person's right to silence and a lawyer).

There was no shortage of participants. State enthusiasts for a post-war *ie* system soon discovered its downside: well-informed and influential women with time on their hands. They could present

A *danchi* housing complex near Osaka (1967)

A fresh culinary innovation: Morinaga's potato mash

themselves, as inclination dictated or context demanded, either as wives and mothers or as women seeking to liberate themselves from roles assigned to them by men. The former offered political traction with conservative voters and politicians, and carried significant moral weight. The latter, increasingly common amongst a younger generation influenced by new waves of American and European feminism, encouraged citizens to look at the structural problems in Japan from which so many of their particular concerns stemmed.

The speakers and topics at an 'Asian Women's Conference Fighting Against Invasion = Discrimination' in August 1970 demonstrated the broad and interconnected range of issues that women activists saw as having shared roots in discrimination, abuse of power and the failure of ordinary people – women and men alike – to wake up to their role in sustaining them. Alongside an opening statement later credited with kick-starting *ūman ribu* – 'women's liberation' – in Japan, there were discussions of the Vietnam War and Japan's relations with China, of the social problems that grew up around US and Japanese military bases and the food poisoning scandals that seemed to have their roots in businesses' lack of accountability.

Discussion and activism amongst citizens, in which women played a central role, seemed to represent a rejection of the idea – in part a hang-over from an earlier era – that governance was best left to specialists. There was also a growing realization that insisting on simple and uncross-able ideological battle-lines (politicians and bureaucrats versus the people, for example) was unrealistic in a complex society, and potentially counter-productive to a cause's prospects. An LDP politician and his or her family were no less at risk from air pollution or tainted cooking oil than anyone else. So why not make allies there, rather than enemies?

Citizens' movements had constantly to contend, however, with a powerful post-war story, which most wanted to believe and for which evidence had been piling up during the course of the 1960s: Japan finally making an unbridled success of modernization, from astonish-ing economic and export growth to standards of living that left the early post-war years seeming like another world. And yet there was profound potential here for abruptly confronting people with vivid evi-dence of the chasm that in some places loomed between grand narratives and shabby realities. It was used to devastating effect in 1970. The great, upbeat motto of that year was the one associated with a futuristic international Expo in Osaka: 'Progress and Harmony for Mankind'. To which a small group of citizens responded by dressing in the simple traditional garb of pilgrims (conical sedge hats and white robes, alms bags slung over shoulders), entering a shareholders' meeting in that city, and unfurling a banner on which was written a single word, freighted with scarcely imaginable anger and pain. It read, simply: 'Bitterness'.

*

Beginning in the summer of 1969, people in Minamata had found their windows being smashed, their houses urinated on and human excrement thrown at them. Thugs turned up at their doors to threaten them. Flyers were distributed denouncing Minamata patients as fakes: alcoholics or eaters of rotten fish, who were grubbing for undeserved money and endangering the local economy with vex-atious claims against its great benefactor, Chisso.

Patients and their families had lived for the past decade with shop-keepers who handled their money using chopsticks and bowls, and with people who mocked their symptoms or held their noses as they passed by.

But this was an escalation, and the reason was simple. The government had belatedly conceded, the year before, that Minamata disease was caused by effluent from Chisso's factory. And now, citizens were taking their cause on the road, into the national media, and through the courts.

Japan's legal system was based on adaptations of French, German and – since 1945 – American law, applied via the Supreme Court at the top, running down through high courts (primarily hearing appeals), district courts, summary courts (for minor offences) and family courts. For those who were sceptical about the government's interest in pursuing the progressive promise of 1945–6, the potential of the judiciary to rein in the legislature and executive was something to be explored and encouraged at every opportunity. Some of the richest sources of employment for the country's small cadre of lawyers lay with labour unions and opposition political parties in search of results like the sensational Sunagawa decision of March 1959, which had declared US bases in Japan to be unconstitutional.

Politicians and civil servants had good reason to worry about citizens resorting to the courts. Their power rested, far more so now than in the past, on tinkering, persuasion and public willingness to allow them a broad managerial remit. It was unwise to allow the legal boundaries of that remit to be tested too often or openly, or to permit too bright a light to be shone on the close working relationships between government and business – policy concessions and support abroad flowing one way, campaign funds and well-paid post-politics jobs the other. One of the many ways in which the wheels were greased in what green-eyed European and American observers took to calling 'Japan Inc.' was the phenomenon known as *amakudari* ('descent from heaven'): civil servants retiring in their early fifties and offering their expertise instead to grateful corporate contacts.

Contributing to government nervousness about the courts was the fact that Japan's studiously vague codes and laws left much to play for. In the late 1960s, pollution campaigners had begun to try their luck. By the time the Minamata legal action began in 1969, three other pollution suits had already been brought: for mercury poisoning in Japan's northern Niigata prefecture, resulting from a similar industrial process to that used by Chisso until recently; air pollution caused by a petrochemical complex near Yokkaichi City, in Mie prefecture (residents reported putting out their washing to dry, only to see it turn black almost immediately); and drinking water contaminated with cadmium in Tōyama prefecture.

These three cases were all won, yielding not just compensation but legal judgments that were wide-ranging in their implications. Definitions were provided for negligence and causality in liability cases. The burden of proof was shifted, so that plaintiffs had only to establish likely cause on the basis of epidemiological data (as opposed to the more difficult process of gathering and examining clinical and pathological data), after which it would be up to the defendant to prove them wrong. And the defendant's duty was established to use the best available technology in minimizing pollution – regardless of economic cost.

Political leaders were forced to act, too. A 'Pollution Diet' of 1970 passed no fewer than fourteen specific environmental measures, designed to cope with public disquiet and to forestall future lawsuits. Almost overnight, the country acquired some of the toughest environmental regulations in the world. Regulatory powers were laid out for central and local government and companies were made responsible for cleaning up waste.

The price of ensuring success for these measures would be constant pressure applied by the general public. Although the new measures looked impressive on paper, Japan's bureaucrats had done what they often did, right across the twentieth century: they had set out to wrest back control of a situation by wooing and working with interest groups who were clearly on the up, giving them just enough and no more. Arrangements hailed by the LDP as efficient and rooted in conciliation rather than contest were, to their critics, vague and toothless. Civil servants at MITI and the Ministry of Construction accepted the pragmatic need to answer protestors' concerns, but they could not tolerate having their or their business allies' hands tied too tightly. So no specific standards or emissions limits were written into law: it would be for the ministries to decide such things. And no money was provided for enforcement. American-inspired arrangements to involve the public in scrutinizing proposed development work, via impact assessments and planning meetings, were similarly shorn of legal force. Instead, *setsumeikai* ('explanatory meetings') were offered: people were invited to hear a lecture on the rightness and necessity of whatever was in the pipeline.

When the OECD rated Japan amongst the very best environmental performers in the world a few years later, it was a success for citizens' commitment to a cause long after it appeared to have been won. The ongoing publicity that they managed to generate persuaded MITI to persuade, in turn, Japan's businesses that pollution control was in their interests. Ministries advised on measures such as building taller smokestacks to avoid concentrating pollution in one area, and purchasing crude oil with lower sulphur content. In the same way, although Japan's new Environment Agency had little funding and even less independent power, it was able to play on fears generated by legal cases and by the negative press surrounding them to win important victories on automobile emissions and a 'polluter pays' principle.

Above all, no business wanted to become the next Chisso – vivid testament to what the Minamata protestors had achieved. Activists had worked to attract *masu komi* (mass media or 'mass communications') attention where they could, alongside producing their own *mini komi* (newsletters). Through the latter, support groups across Japan had been formed, one of which organized a well-publicized pilgrimage to the Chisso shareholders' meeting in Osaka, in 1970. Having stopped along the way in Hiroshima to join their cause with victims of the atomic bomb, eighteen patients and thirty-five supporters – each of whom had bought a single company share in Chisso – entered the shareholders' meeting.

Desperate executives shut the meeting down as soon as they realized what was happening. But newspaper and television cameras captured the unfurling of the banner nonetheless, with its compelling one-word denunciation. They also filmed protestors confronting the company president with memorial tablets of deceased relatives. Hamamoto Fumiyo, who watched Minamata disease kill both of her parents and cripple her brother, took him by the lapels of his suit jacket: 'You're a parent too . . . do you really understand my feelings? How much do you think I suffered? You can't buy lives with money!' Chisso had hired the advertising giant Dentsū to help it with its PR. But with Minamata support groups creating plays and documentary films about the disease, while photographers put before the nation graphic, heart-rending proof of its effects, it became clear that Chisso had lost the publicity battle.

They lost the legal argument three years later. The Minamata ruling in 1973 included a crucial observation: events outside the court had been influential in the progress of the case. Here was proof of the importance, for citizens' movements, of fighting simultaneously on a diverse range of related fronts. Thinkers like Ui Jun, an engineer at Tokyo University who set up the Independent Lectures on Pollution in 1970, helped to furnish first-timers with ideas on how. Some of them learned to embarrass Japan's leaders by publishing and disseminating internationally an English-language booklet called *Polluted Japan*, in 1972. Others took foreign journalists on a bus tour of Japan's most polluted sites. And in an industrial context where concealment was a common defence strategy, citizens uncovered and shared information. A housewife discovered a discoloured coin in a river, helping to identify hydrogen sulphide poisoning there. City residents mapped patterns of diseased pine trees, eventually locating a pollution source. Meanwhile, people were advised to look to their lifestyles as well. A campaigner against power-plant construction suggested a 'philosophy of the dark': one 'power-off day' per month would allow citizens to reflect on the costs of their culture of power consumption, while freeing them from the moronic television advertising that helped to sustain it.

The citizen spirit trickled down into local government too. Tokyo governor Minobe Ryōkichi encouraged Tokyoites and bureaucrats to exchange notes on the challenges that each group faced in using and providing city services. Across his long tenure, from the late 1960s through to the end of the 1970s, the fruits of Minobe's approach included free health insurance for elderly people on low incomes and the setting of 'civil minimums' – basic standards of life to which local government officials committed themselves.

People's energy for this kind of activity ebbed and flowed over the years that followed. In some cases, cooperation risked slipping into co-option – through the harnessing of citizens as a volunteer army by increasingly cash-strapped local authorities, as growth slowed during the 1970s. From assisting single mothers, the sick and the disabled to tidying up parks, a survey in 1976 revealed that 3.4 million people across the country were now working as volunteers. Was all this the beginnings of a distinctly, creatively 'Japanese' way of redeeming urban modernity, from which other countries might learn? Or had citizens' movements and volunteers ended up homing in *too* closely and exclusively on single issues that could be realistically tackled? As Japanese wealth continued to wow the world into the 1980s, new, more expansive visions began to be offered: exploring the greater meaning of Japan's – even humanity's – present situation, and starting to imagine what form redemption might possibly take.

Protestors, dressed in pilgrims' robes and hats, confront the Chisso company president in 1970, some carrying memorial tablets for deceased relatives

Uemura Tomoko, in the arms of her mother Ryoko, on the day (20 March 1973) that the Minamata litigants won their action against Chisso

16

Moving Mountains

A girl in a gas mask picks her way through dense forest, seething with botanical corruption. Sticky, distorted sacs litter the hard ground, from which brittle, barren flower-stems emerge, bent and dented like the limbs of a giant crustacean. Furred tendrils tower and sway. Soft, feathery spheres hang down from the forest canopy on hairy cords, leaking spores into the gloom. Five minutes without a mask in here would kill you. So the girl keeps hers on as she walks; a weapon over her shoulder, a test tube in her hand.

A siren tears the girl away from her work in the forest. Someone is under attack. She runs out, leaps onto her glider, and a modest ignition propels her skywards. Cruising along above dry, barren land, she finds an enormous beetle-like creature stampeding away from the forest. It is propelled along on a thicket of taloned legs, moving in a blur and churning up the dirt as it goes. The cascading layers of hard, protective shell that encase its body are studded with dome-like eyes, each glowing red with rage at a tiny human being desperately trying to outrun it on horseback.

The girl swoops in, and uses a stun grenade to bring the creature to a halt amidst a cloud of dust. Then she does something unexpected. She apologizes, for having had to use violence. And she pleads gently for it to return to the forest. After a pause, it does so. Together with the man whose life she has just saved, the girl heads home: to a small rural farming community protected from the poisons of the forest by a fresh wind that blows in from the ocean, funnelled between tall, rocky valley walls. It is a thousand years since the great industrial civilizations of the world all but wiped one another out in a seven-day nuclear war. And this isolated band of innocents is hanging on as best they can . . .

In this way, a young Marxist manga artist laid out the early frames of an epic adventure. His craft originated in China, as picture scrolls (*emakimono* in Japanese) up to fifteen metres in length, wrapped around a stick and tied with ribbon. The action on these scrolls took place from right to left, through a series of painted images sometimes accompanied by text. Themes ranged from cosmic cautions about the fiery tortures of hell to farting competitions amongst semi-naked, loose-fleshed men, and satire poking fun at Japan's Buddhist clergy (sometimes authored by clerics themselves).

Early scrolls were hand-painted, and too precious for most ordinary Japanese ever to lay eyes on. But a woodblock printing boom across the 1700s and 1800s made available combinations of images and words to almost anyone who wanted them. Edo bookshops and lending libraries boasted illustrated stories and series of scenic prints – Mount Fuji being a perennial favourite – alongside travel guides, encyclopaedias, books on fashion and medicine, adverts for local goods and services, portraits of kabuki stars, ghost stories, erotic *shunga* art and samurai adventures. A single print could be had for the price of a snack.

The Tokugawa authorities kept a close eye on the world of publishing, and especially the forerunners of modern satirical manga, the much-loved *kibyōshi*. These were tall tales told in sharp prose, packed tightly around lavish illustrations and then enclosed between hard yellow or blue covers. The market was enormous – some editions sold up to 10,000 copies – so that when the Western political cartoon found its way to Japan in the late nineteenth century, writers and audiences were quick to adopt and adapt. Where their predecessors contended with *kibyōshi*, the Meiji-era censors leafed carefully through publications like *Marumaru Chimbun* and *Tokyo Puck*. The latter's founder, Kitazawa Rakuten, created Japan's first comic strip around the turn of the twentieth century: two country people explore Tokyo, musing on the confusing wonders of the modern world.

Kitazawa became one of the earliest modern artists to use the word *manga* – 'whimsical pictures' – to describe what he was doing. It quickly became an industry, producing specialized comics for a youth audience: *Shōnen Club* (for boys) from 1914; *Shōjo Club* (for girls), from 1923; and *Yōnen Club* (for younger children), from 1926. All three were published by Kodansha, one of a small handful of publishers who managed to corner the manga market early on. After a grim interlude in which manga writers were compelled to follow their musician counterparts in producing narrowly patriotic and militaristic fare, the art form broadened and boomed once more in the 1950s, with stories of scientists, superheroes and ballerinas; futuristic fantasies; and a darker, realist genre called *gekiga* ('dramatic pictures').

The 'God of manga' was the man who once sat in an Osaka cinema watching 'Momotarō's Divine Sea Warriors' and vowing that he would one day do this sort of thing for a living. Tezuka Osamu created *Tetsuwan Atomu* ('Mighty Atom' – better known in English as *Astro Boy*) in the 1950s, alongside *Ribon no Kishi* ('Princess Sapphire'). Influenced by performances of the all-female Takarazuka Revue troupe, to which Tezuka's mother took him as a child, Princess Sapphire was one of the first characters to feature the large, sparkling eyes with which Japanese manga would later become synonymous around the world.

This formative generation of manga artists shared with their colleagues across the arts a deep distrust of adult authority, born from memories of the war. Knowing the world to be complicated and capable of terrible violence, they did not seek to dumb down or sugar-coat these things in their work for young audiences.

It was an approach that the Marxist manga artist took to heart as he set the scene for his heroine and her rural homeland. He didn't yet know where this story would go, but Miyazaki Hayao had a clear theme, inspired by the Minamata tragedy: human beings' ambiguous relationship with the natural world – at the same time abusing it and protecting it, in love with it and afraid of it, at one with it and estranged from it.

The heroine's name was Nausicaä. She was a leader, fighter, scientist and psychic, driven by a deep sympathy for life in all its forms. But precisely what Nausicaä ought to be fighting for was difficult for Miyazaki to discern. While others in Japan experimented with a sense of 'citizenship' forged through pragmatic action in the service of individual causes, Miyazaki was amongst those struggling to sketch out a bigger picture: a highly philosophical, even spiritual critique of his country's predicament – and that of contemporary humanity as a whole – along with a vision of what salvation might look like.

He was doing so in the early 1980s, at the end of a distinctly mixed decade. Miyazaki had witnessed elite complacency, violent incidents and economic shocks, but he had also seen signs of citizens' willingness to get involved in steering the ship.

So was Japanese modernity beginning to mature? Or was recent progress no more than life-support for a system that didn't deserve to survive? Miyazaki seemed to veer towards the latter, putting forward Nausicaä's small rural community as an attractive alternative: an apparently pre-industrial idyll with manageable numbers (around 500 people), where agriculture was pursued with simple tools and an open and communitarian spirit. And yet hidden away in a hut was an old fighter plane. This was a radically *post*-industrial world, apparently concealing this relic of a hi-tech, destructive past in the hope that it would help that era to rest in peace. Here was history as something ultimately beyond the power of humans to shape. A force of nature, even a malevolent spirit.

Nausicaä's community discovers this soon enough, in a series of events seemingly inspired by episodes from the broad sweep of Japan's modern experience. Nausicaä's innocent, pre-Meiji community avoids predation at the hands of far-off, militarily advanced powers only because its people are of little interest. But blissful anonymity doesn't last. Impossibly large aircraft appear overhead, hanging bulky and dark in the sky, cold bodies of riveted sheet metal dotted with the artificial yellow light of countless lonely windows. They tear up the pasture with heavy, bumpy landings. Then they disgorge imperial soldiers, anonymous in identical helmets, capes and satchels. Commanding these are a handful of leaders – callous and weak, intent on hiding behind a giant 'divine soldier' whom they are incubating as their ultimate weapon of war. An innocent Japan is being violated by its mid twentieth-century self, getting a taste of mainland Asia's pain before an all-too familiar punishment is meted out. From the divine soldier's mouth comes a furious torrent of nuclear fire.

Miyazaki was forced to conclude his meditation on modern Japan prematurely when the offer came in to create an anime version of *Nausicaä*. Its final scene, in which Nausicaä sacrifices her own life to save her world, struck him in retrospect as looking too much like a 'religious painting'. So while his new production company, Studio Ghibli, proceeded to turn out classics of sophisticated, child-friendly anime – *Laputa: Castle in the Sky* (1986); *My Neighbour Totoro* (1988) – Miyazaki poured his darker, more pessimistic energies into giving his *Nausicaä* manga a proper resolution.

Nausicaä had discovered early on that the poisonous forest – the 'Sea of Decay' – was in fact a living filtration system, gradually cleansing the world of the pollution to which the humans of the old hi-tech civilization had subjected it. Her job, in common with a number of Miyazaki's heroines and heroes, was to work with nature and confront those who would harm it. But later in the manga, Nausicaä discovers that in fact the whole world – human beings included – is artificial. None of this is 'nature' anymore. The old civilization is waiting, stored as eggs in a crypt, to be reborn once the forest finishes its purifying work and the artificial humans of Nausicaä's world – her amongst them – have all disappeared. The girl who started out as a messiah finishes as a killer: in order to save her own people, she has to destroy her ancestors in the crypt – even wielding the divine warrior as her personal weapon.

Miyazaki's final move in his Nausicaä manga was no mere twist in the story's tail. It was a twist of the knife. In declaring even Nausicaä's rural home to be the product of human fakery, he was calling into question one of modern Japan's oldest and greatest consolations.

The country's famously mountainous topography presented challenges for urban planners. But it offered cherished respite for those dismayed by the stuffing of plains and basins with artificial undulations of shabby white-grey concrete and prefab – cubes and cuboids latticed and linked together with those endless trails of black wire. Thankfully there was, in theory at least, only so much scope for this kind of destruction: the point soon came when the economic cost of reclaiming liveable land from water or mountain rock meant that it was no longer worthwhile. Places of escape, even redemption, thereby survived.

State-builders since the late nineteenth century had done much to encourage a view of rural Japan as pure and unspoiled. They set out to fabricate their new nation in urban factories, government offices, schools and universities, while relying on the countryside for sustenance: food, raw materials, a conservative corrective for foreign-inspired left-wingery, and finally a set of romantic symbols by means of which tired or culturally confused urbanites could gain access to a timeless 'Japan'.

Miyazaki's casting of doubt on the naturalness of 'nature', as *Nausicaä* progressed, stemmed in part from unease about the political and commercial distortion to which rural Japan was regularly subjected. From the pre-war pastoralism of the folklorist Yanagita Kunio to record companies around the same time offering to transport urbanites through music to some lost *furusato* (home town), rural romance was always at risk of recruitment into nationalist strategies that conflated modernity's flaws with unwelcome foreign influence – poisonous to the Japanese soul.

Similar concerns surrounded so-called 'spiritual intellectuals' of the 1970s and 1980s. The popular philosopher and historian Umehara Takeshi found in the Jōmon-era Japanese a hunter-gatherer people whose awe of the forest, coursing with spiritual life, represented, he claimed, Japan's primordial religion – and an antidote to contemporary society's atrocious mistreatment of the natural world. The Jungian analyst Kawai Hayao became well known for his exploration of the Japanese psyche via comparative analyses of Japanese and Western folk tales. Both faced accusations that their work – and their consecutive tenures as Director General at Nichibunken, a research institute for Japanese culture set up in 1982 – was at risk of serving neo-nationalist purposes. Miyazaki was critical of Umehara in particular. He was attracted by the idea of a spirituality rooted in environmental ethics, and in a purity of person and place, but he worried about the ethnically exclusive element in this kind of thinking.

Post-war commercial exploitation of a romanticized rural Japan was a decade old by the time Miyazaki created *Nausicaä*. Since 1970, large numbers of young urbanites had been heading off on train journeys around the country, hoping to discover some new dimension of themselves. The population had not, overnight, embraced philosophy or whimsy. These people were under direct instructions from the

Frames from the first instalment of Miyazaki Hayao's manga series
Nausicaä of the Valley of the Wind (1982)

advertising agency Dentsū. *Mō hitori no jibun wo mitsukeyō*, ran
their advertising slogan: 'Let's discover another self'. Colourful posters in trains and around stations featured young, urban Japanese
women, depicted in modern Western clothing and various states of
wonderment at scenes of old-time rustic beauty and tranquillity. 'To
go on a journey is to find a new home,' gushed one of the posters.

This advertising campaign, 'Discover Japan', was created for the
Japan National Railway (JNR), who were concerned about a likely fall-
off in train travel once 1970's Osaka Expo came to an end. Research
and in-depth interviews revealed a vanguard of the discontented in the
form of young, urban women. Old enough and wealthy enough to
travel, they were not yet caught up in making lists of chores or chivvy-
ing children along with exam preparations. They were looking for

recreation, remoteness and the 'old Japan'. Famous places were beside the point: what mattered was the travel and the atmosphere.

'Discover Japan' borrowed heavily from 'Discover America' just a few years before, even down to the use of weathervane symbolism. But it took for one of its slogans a telling twist on a famous piece of recent Japanese prose. Accepting his Nobel Prize for Literature in 1968, Kawabata Yasunari had entitled his speech '*Utsukushii Nihon no watakushi*': 'Beautiful Japan and Myself'. Dentsū's slogan replaced the possessive '*no*', which emphasized the sculpting of Kawabata's self and soul by Japan, with a simple '*to*' ('and'). *Utsukushii Nihon to watakushi* promised a 'Beautiful Japan' that would serve as an inspiring, anonymous backdrop – or even an instrument – for self-discovery. Sun-dappled forest pathways, tranquil temples, moving mountains . . .

For the choreographer Hijikata Tatsumi, 'the Japanese in front of their televisions' had portended a new 'dark valley'. With 'Discover Japan', critics sensed its arrival. Not content with shaping a nigh-on inescapable urbanized 'everydayness', the mass communications industry had created a follow-on product to complement and extend the shelf-life of the first: a carefully curated rural liberation. And where that first product had been all about sight and sound – magazines and music, cinema and television – this new one played on a much-neglected third sense. To experience something in a truly authentic way, you had to go there, reach out and touch it.

That the people who actually lived in rural Japan, always a majority up to and just after the war, occasionally felt somewhat used by urban fantasizing had become clear in periodic Meiji-era protests and then in the willingness of many to accept the military as their champion – against a distressingly resource-intensive urban decadence. Life for most rural Japanese improved rapidly after the war, thanks to land redistribution, politicians keen to shore up rural voting blocs with favours, and advances in agricultural materials and techniques. By the 1970s, relatively spacious rural homes accommodated much the same markers of middle-class existence as their more compact urban counterparts. Winter evenings could be whiled away in rooms lit by the same colour televisions and warmed with a combination of air-conditioning, *kotatsu* (a low table with a heater underneath and a blanket attached) and *sake*. At rest, somewhere in the dark outside, would be a piece of technology more revolutionary as a labour-saving device than any urban gadget: the power-tiller. Some 89,000 of these machines had been in use in 1955; by 1970, the figure was 3.5 million.

And yet, but for the sound of the television, many a country home in the 1970s would have been quieter than a generation before. During the 1950s and for much of the 1960s, Japan's booming population had been sufficient to keep the countryside well stocked with workers, despite great waves of urban migration. But from the late 1960s, it was hard to see the trend as anything but an emptying out of the young from the countryside. Home to just a quarter of the population by 1975, rural Japan was becoming for many little more than a blur of paddy fields and dilapidated outhouses seen from the window of a bullet train. In summer slower trains might be taken, as people visited small-town relatives for the festival of Obon, honouring the spirits of the ancestors. But for most of the year, such places had to fend for themselves: reviving, even inventing new festivals and foods, to put themselves on the tourist map.

Commenting on his ending for the manga version of *Nausicaä*, finally completed in 1994, Miyazaki expressed a deep pessimism about what happens when humans try to remake nature. He fantasized about the day when 'developers go bankrupt, Japan gets poorer, wild grasses take over', and Tokyo and Manhattan end up under water. For centuries in Japan, 'nature' had been intimately bound up with human desire and tinkering. Cherry trees were transplanted and cross-fertilized, to get the right blossoms flowering in the right places at the right times. Goldfish were bred for beauty rather than survival. Literature lauded highly stylized seasons and landscapes. Now, for the likes of Miyazaki, nature was imagined in a different way, offering a different sort of solace. 'Nature' was that which existed apart from all human meddling, truly flourishing only when left alone. This idea, and the shift from *Nausicaä*'s anime ending to its manga ending, seemed to reflect a trend in Japanese visions for the future – at least at the more expansive end of the story-telling spectrum. It was a movement from hope that the world could be redeemed, to a conviction that it must be destroyed; from seeking salvation to welcoming some form of apocalypse.

*

One of *Nausicaä*'s many fans was a young man in his late twenties by the name of Matsumoto Chizuo. The son of a tatami mat-maker, he was born blind in one eye and with severely reduced sight in the other. It was not uncommon for people in Japan with this sort of disability to work in healing professions, and this is what Matsumoto did, offering acupuncture, moxibustion and advice on herbal medicines. Later, he became interested in Japanese folk practices like divination, and in the array of spiritual ideas and practices available in Japan's hundreds of 'new' and then 'new new' religions, which ran alongside a more individualistic 'Spiritual World' movement. Books and seminars linked to the New Age in the West covered everything from yoga, meditation and psychotherapy to alchemy, near-death experiences and reincarnation.

The trend of the times, in the 1970s and 1980s, exchanged belief in grand metaphysical propositions for healing and purification (*kokoro naoshi*), as a means to both personal salvation and world renewal (*yonaoshi*). The creators of Dentsū's 'Discover Japan' campaign had done their homework. They well understood the power of a concept like *kokoro* – the heart, or heart of things – in a complex world. Combine that with *furusato* (hometown), and you had a slogan with considerable punch. *Tabi ni deru to, kokoro no furusato ga fuemasu*: 'Embark on a journey, and the hometowns in your heart will multiply.'

A combination of all these desires – for home, for adventure, for meaning and for change – led Matsumoto initially to one of Japan's new religions. Agonshū offered a revived Japanese Buddhist spirituality, rooted in contact with Tibetan Buddhism, the promise of psychic powers and the proper use of science and technology. The movement was opposed to the inhuman, destructive spirit of hyper-rationalism that science brought into the world when it confused methodology (which science was) with ideology (which it wasn't). Instead, the achievements of science – from computers to television and video – should be put to use, it was argued, to somehow lift the world out of its present materialistic dead-end.

In 1984, the year that *Nausicaä* hit Japanese cinemas, Matsumoto left Agonshū and started a yoga and meditation group for around fifteen people in the busy Shibuya neighbourhood of Tokyo. Two years later they set themselves up as the Mountain Hermits' Society and began to acquire rural land – including a tract near the foot of Mount Fuji – on which they could build communes. Many of those who came to live there were students and young professionals. They were drawn by Matsumoto's teachings and transformative personal charisma, just as they were repelled by the everyday world of rote, competition and corruption – despite having mostly, so far, succeeded in it. With his mission progressing, Matsumoto decided to change his name, along with that of his organization. He would be Asahara Shōkō. His group would one day be known around the world, as Aum Shinrikyō.

The people who signed up to Aum from afar – 4,000 by the end of the 1980s – or who handed over their worldly possessions in exchange for a place by Asahara's side in the commune, thought they had seen all they needed to of what Japan was becoming. Their fathers joined closely managed cohorts of salarymen trudging and slaving and pretending to enjoy their bosses' company on compulsory evenings out. Mothers sought light relief from domestic boredom by suing companies over dangerously defective products, adulterated juices and over-priced fuel. Children were placed, at an early age, on a conveyor-belt education system where testing at ever younger ages had now reached the point of evaluating the parents.

Meanwhile, the architects of all this seemed to be constantly, almost comedically, on the take. When Prime Minister Ikeda's successor, Satō Eisaku, was brought down in the aftermath of the Nixon shocks, Tanaka Kakuei took his place. He was a master practitioner of *kōenkai* politics, a system whereby national politicians built around themselves support organizations made up of local political and business interests, and accepted financial and logistical contributions to their campaigns in return for channelling assistance and central government spending the other way – often in public works – once power was achieved. It wasn't long before Tanaka, whose *kōenkai* boasted more than 100,000 members, found himself implicated in corrupt dealings both at home and abroad. He was forced to resign in 1974, after barely two years in the job.

Still, Tanaka remained so influential that he became known as the 'shadow shogun', while the administration of Prime Minister Naka-sone Yasuhiro in the 1980s, which he sponsored, was dubbed the 'Tanakasone Cabinet'. Tanaka managed all this despite being person-ally implicated when the vice-president of the US company Lockheed admitted in 1976 that during the 'jumbo jet wars' (which pitted his company against Boeing and McDonnell Douglas) millions of dollars had been paid in bribes to have All Nippon Airways and Japan's defence agency purchase more than a billion dollars' worth of aircraft.

Helping behind the scenes to shift cardboard boxes stuffed with Lockheed cash had been one Kodama Yoshio. Alongside stand-out political fixers like Tanaka, Japan's post-war *yakuza* were blossoming too. Gleaning sartorial inspiration from American gangster films, they became clearly identifiable in certain areas of the country's cities by their dark suits and shirts and their white ties, set off with sun-glasses, crew cuts and luxury American sedans. In the Osaka–Kobe area, the Yamaguchi-gumi had grown to 10,000 loyal members by the time of the 1964 Olympics. Tokyo had no single comparable organiz-ation. What it had instead, as an investigative series by the *Mainichi* newspaper made plain, was a nexus of power at whose heart was Kodama – helping to broker an association between the Yamaguchi-gumi and Yokohama's Inagawa-kai, which created a combine so large that it left only four of Japan's prefectures free of its influence. Inter-viewed by the *Mainichi* about these rumoured activities, Kodama replied that his only interest in life was fishing.

The Lockheed scandal proved, in the end, to be Kodama's down-fall. His home was first raided by the police and then, in a style entirely befitting a larger-than-life career, was half destroyed when a porn actor and former admirer – decked out in a rising sun bandana and screaming 'Long Live the Emperor!' – flew an aeroplane into his porch. Kodama survived the attack, only to be harried by prosecutors and tax officials until he died in 1984 following a stroke.

By this point the end was looming, too, for the LDP's long domi-nance of Japanese politics. Voters recognized that, whatever its failings, the LDP had overseen three decades of economic growth in Japan and taken the country's image around the world from one of poverty and hubris chastised to extraordinary affluence. But towards the end of the 1980s, an unpopular 3 per cent consumption tax was passed into law, intended to balance out falling income tax revenues as the population aged. Combined with a new scandal involving corporate payments to Diet members and bureaucrats, the measure dragged the LDP's ratings down to a disastrous 27 per cent – just 1 per cent ahead of the Japan Socialist Party (JSP).

A brief electoral comeback was undermined by an even bigger corruption scandal just a few years later, in 1992. A company called Sagawa Kyūbin was found to be linked to Inagawa-kai gangsters, and to have paid bribes worth billions of yen to around 200 politicians. A raid on a lavish Tokyo apartment belonging to one of the presumed beneficiaries, the LDP's vice-president and Tanaka protégé Kanemaru Shin (nickname: 'The Don'), yielded a made-for-television scene: a money mountain some $50 million high, in cash, bonds and even gold bars, hidden away in wardrobes and desk drawers. The public later heard of someone pushing a cart laden with $4 million in cash into Kanemaru's office.

When a court asked Kanemaru to part with only $1,600 as a fine for his wrongdoing, the country went into a paroxysm of protest at the state of its politics. Kanemaru did little to help, offering a single-sentence apology alongside some life advice regarding the importance of friends. 'My political philosophy', he declared, 'is to have some appreciation for a person who saves a drowning child in a river, even if that person happens to belong to a crime syndicate.'

More serious for Japan's long-term prospects was the dangerous upward spiralling of stock and land prices during the late 1980s. One of the causes was the Plaza Accord of 1985, an agreement made at New York's Plaza Hotel, in which the US, Japan, France, West Germany and the UK agreed to try to rebalance global trade by making currency markets interventions to devalue the dollar and help to boost exports to Japan. Japan also agreed to work to stimulate demand at home for foreign goods. Large-scale domestic spending by the Japanese government followed, contributing to serious asset inflation. Mortgage terms began to extend across three generations, and there were rumours in 1989 that Tokyo's combined real estate was now worth more than that of the entire United States.

Bureaucrats in the Ministry of Finance raised borrowing rates in late 1989, hoping gradually to deflate the bubble. Instead, it burst. The Nikkei stock exchange lost nearly half its value between late 1989 and the autumn of 1990, the world of real estate collapsed as loans went bad, and in 1992 Japan embarked on a period of recession that was soon dubbed its 'lost decade'. No one, it seemed, was in a position to kick-start the economy. Interest rates were hurriedly lowered again, but most banks lacked money, trust in potential borrowers, or both. A tumble in the value of the dollar, beginning in 1992, left Japan's famous export industry in crisis, as Japanese goods suddenly felt prohibitively expensive to American consumers.

Corruption was dispiriting, but incompetence was intolerable. A vote of no confidence in the LDP Cabinet was passed in the summer of 1993. They were returned as the largest party in the election that followed, but lost their majority. A coalition of opposition parties formed a government instead. For the first time since its creation nearly forty years before, the LDP was out of power.

Japan seemed to be on the cusp of dramatic change: from a country whose sense of economic purpose was so strong that it struck even the most ardent Western capitalists as vulgar or aggressive, to one that had lost its way. From a place defined by innovative technologies, business practices and labour–management relations, to one that commentators both inside and outside Japan increasingly sought to understand in terms of cultural and psychological quirks, most of them negative.

Attempts to use deficit spending to drag the country out of the doldrums contributed to another new set of images abroad: Japan as a country that couldn't make up its mind about nature – extolling, yet choking it, with chemicals and concrete. By 1993, more than 40 per cent of the entire national budget was being poured into construction, on which upwards of 6 million jobs came to depend. These were spread across more than half a million construction firms, most of them tiny sub-contractors. Japan was soon being talked about as *doken kokka*, a 'construction state': famous for ambitious projects that set out to tame its mountainous terrain, and for lucrative and widely publicized bid-rigging that meant each new road cost four times as much as the equivalent in Germany – or nine times the equivalent in the United States.

Japan's politicians were hardly the first in the world to practise pork barrel politics. And they had a hand in commissioning many necessary and impressive feats of civil engineering, including the world's longest tunnel with an undersea section: the Seikan railway tunnel, completed in 1988, was nearly 54 kilometres long and ran for 23 kilometres beneath the Tsugaru Strait, connecting Honshū and Hokkaidō. But critics railed at what they saw as flawed logic, dishonest pretexts and breathtaking costs. Kanemaru Shin had supplied one of the most vivid examples in 1989. As Construction Minister, he helped to win a contract for his own home prefecture of Yamanashi to host a testing project for maglev trains, despite the fact that Yamanashi was so mountainous that 85 per cent of the test track would have to pass through tunnels.

Many of the new projects across the 1990s were roads to nowhere, or bridges across to uninhabited islands. Natural rivers were straightened out, given concrete embankments, and sometimes dammed along their way to a coast whose length was strewn with concrete tetrapods in sterile, melancholy shades of beige and grey. And yet Japan faced no impending water or coastal erosion crisis that would justify such radical reworkings of its natural environment. Remote hillsides, far from populated areas where people might be at risk from landslides, were nevertheless dynamited or covered in concrete. Mountains were effectively moved from inner regions out to the sea, providing the raw material for filling bays and harbours, and creating artificial islands on which airports or offices or theme parks could be built.

For twenty seconds on 17 January 1995, the earth appeared to rebel against all this. Tremors measuring 7.2 on the Richter scale struck not far from the city of Kobe, continuing until 400,000 buildings had been destroyed, numerous roads and bridges ripped up or overturned, utility supply pipes and lines cut and hundreds of fires started. Nearly 6,400 people died in what became known as the Great Hanshin-Awaji earthquake.

As the nation looked on, the country's civil servants appeared to bungle their response. Relief centres turned out not to have been planned for. Japanese and American troops were kept from helping, despite American offers. And *yakuza* soup kitchens were up and running before official emergency food supplies found their way in.

A few weeks later, while the country was still reeling from the devastation and their leaders' apparent lack of preparedness, five of Asahara Shōkō's followers picked up umbrellas and bags of liquid wrapped in newspaper and left for the district of Kasumigaseki in Tokyo. Over the last few years, Aum Shinrikyō had grown in numbers and ambition. Asahara had morphed into a guru figure, advertising all sorts of special powers via the group's own in-house manga artists – including an ability to foresee Armageddon. In some of his sermons, this was depicted as a nuclear apocalypse, not unlike the *Nausicaä* backstory. And the date kept getting brought closer, as the list of the group's enemies got longer: the CIA, the Vatican, Japanese politicians and entertainers, even a member of the Japanese royal family. Trips to Russia helped the group to prepare, yielding many thousands of new converts along with weapons, machinery and even a military helicopter. There was a visit to Zaire, too, rumoured to have been an attempt to acquire the Ebola virus.

The Kobe earthquake, when it came, was interpreted as the opening, at last, of the war that would bring Armageddon. Asahara claimed that the tremors had been caused by earthquake machines developed by the great enemy, the United States. Fortunately his alternative government, made up of Aum members, was already in place, ready to take over if and when Japan's leaders succumbed.

The five people who headed into Tokyo on Monday, 20 March, were tasked with striking at the heart of the Japanese government, before a series of expected police raids on Aum could take place (the group had come under increasing media scrutiny of late, over suspected violent activity – and had in fact committed a number of murders, in protection of its interests). Kasumigaseki had been home to major state institutions in Japan since the Meiji era, which now included a Diet building opened in the mid-1930s as well as the country's central ministries and the National Police Agency headquarters. At approximately 8.30 a.m., in the middle of rush-hour, the five Aum members put their bags down on the floor of five different subway trains and punctured them with the sharpened metal tips of their umbrellas. Liquid sarin vaporized and began to fill the trains.

Twelve people died and thousands more were injured in the attack. Casualties would have been far worse had the sarin been purified to a greater degree. But still, Japan had earned a dubious honour: it was the first time, anywhere in the world, that weapons of mass destruction had been deployed by a private organization.

Asahara was arrested in May 1995 and soon began what would prove to be a long wait on death row. Meanwhile, sensationalist media coverage helped to stir people's anxieties, exaggerating the power and reach of a single 'evil cult' and covering in every last detail the hunt for the group's remaining members. Many of those details, as they emerged, really were unnerving: advanced computing and chemical weapons technologies hidden away inside compounds; strange, alien lives being lived just yards from ordinary society; and, above all, the resonance with so many people of Aum's core critique of Japan and the wider modern world – mired in materialism and stuck with soulless education and employment systems that left too many people bereft of higher purpose.

As millions of television viewers in Japan watched and re-watched commuters struggling with the after-effects of being gassed on their way to work, the broader shock was just how rapidly and hopelessly a country could be brought low. They were witnessing the collapse of a widely lauded and apparently invulnerable economic and social

Asahara Shōkō in custody

model. Devastation of the sort that Japan, home to a tenth of the world's earthquake activity, could never hope to secure itself against – but compounded by a vacuum of capable guidance at critical moments, as a large proportion of the nation's leaders were revealed as greedy, incompetent or both. Now there had been a fanatical, murderous rejection, by some of the country's brightest and best, of seemingly everything that Japan had once stood for.

Where would the country go from here to find an account of itself capable of energizing a beleaguered citizenry? As the fifty-year anniversary arrived of the country's wartime defeat and the end of its empire, it felt as though the answer was 'back' – back to a recent history insufficiently explored, and to regional relationships insufficiently restored.

PART SIX

Raising Spirits
(1990s to 2010s)

17

Telling Tales

4 September 1995. A car makes its way along a road, passing by sugar cane fields. In the back is a young girl. Her hands and feet are bound with duct tape. Her eyes and mouth have been taped shut . . .

This is happening at the southern end of an archipelago that stretches for 1,500 miles, from frozen earth and crystalline outcrops in the far north down to subtropical rainforest a little further south of here. Thousands of islands, some of them trodden and known over tens of thousands of years. Tales have been told, memories piled up.

A rippling rocky spine running down the largest of these islands kept the earliest settled communities mostly to its coasts – wearing bark and hemp and animal skins; living in thatched-pit homes dug into the ground and arranged in circles; hunting and fishing; cooking and storing acorns and nuts in some of the world's first pottery.

Forested land bridges to the nearby continent were soon submerged, but the neighbours continued to visit. Chinese records – dating from what Western calendars would one day mark as the early centuries AD – told of a 'Wo' or 'stunted' people living on these islands, grouped into around 100 small clan-kingdoms; of men tattooing themselves to ward off dangerous creatures when diving for seafood; of a female shaman ruling a people who baked animal bones then pondered their cracked remains for meanings and predictions, clapping to let the gods know where they were.

These people recorded their own stories, across the centuries, in pottery and in figurines with full breasts and pregnant stomachs; later in weapons, tools and precious objects of iron and bronze and silk. As one clan-kingdom, Yamato, began to dominate its neighbours, so the story told by its most powerful family began to win out

349

across a nascent nation: a tale of divinely descended imperial rulers, important enough that tons of earth were dug and piled up to create moated burial mounds on an epic scale. They were interred in stone chambers beneath, surrounded by the symbols of their story and power: mirrors, swords and bracelets. On top of the tomb were thousands of narrative clay figurines several feet high, arranged in a circle, marking the boundaries of the hallowed site – dogs and horses, shamans, maidens and armoured fighters. Two centuries later – the early 700s by Western calendars – these stories finally made it into writing, in the *Kojiki* ('Records of Ancient Matters') and the *Nihon shoki* ('The Chronicles of Japan').

. . . The girl in the car had been walking home from a stationery shop, carrying a new notebook bought for school. A man approached her, asking for directions. Suddenly, a second man grabbed her by the neck from behind, while the first hit her in the face. The two of them bundled her into the back of the car, beat her up and, together with a third man, drove off with her . . .

Those living in these far southern parts of the archipelago grew used, over time, to being bit-part players in other people's dramas – a point on the compass for mightier neighbours. They inhabited China's fabled eastern 'Liu-ch'iu' islands, or what Japan knew as its southern 'Ryūkyūs'. Their kings paid tribute to both powers for a while, before finally entering into the providential story of a third nation: an expanding United States of America. The menacing midsummer beach pageant to which Commodore Matthew C. Perry treated the Japanese in 1853 – Marines in tight formation, guns and cannons, the strains of 'Hail Columbia!' – had its dress rehearsal down here a few weeks before, when Perry extracted the use of a Ryūkyū port as a coal depot and safe harbour for American vessels.

The revolution in Japan whose fuse Perry helped to light soon spread south, in the form of a new state looking to mark out and secure its borders. The Ryūkyūs were annexed as 'Okinawa prefecture' in 1879, and an awesome logistical effort got under way aimed at making it, and its people, Japanese. Southwards across hundreds of miles of clear blue water went festivals, yen coins and criminal codes; post offices and portraits of the Emperor and Empress; merchants and industrialists; policemen and doctors; *jūdō* and *kendō*;

Japanese surnames and styles of dress. Land, much of it previously communal, was privatized. Sugar cane fields were planted.

The US had agreed to Tokyo's annexation of these islands. But a few short decades later, American ships returned, hoping to make Okinawa a staging post for a final push north against their former friends. Soldiers from mainland Japan were sent south in response, not so much defending the islands' people as defending the islands *with* the people: using them as human shields, taking their food, turning homes into billets and schools into barracks, raping some and shooting others as spies, and finally ordering them off cliffs in acts of mass suicide. A Peace Museum established near those cliffs later claimed that 100,000 civilians – up to a third of the island's population – had died during the Battle of Okinawa (April–June 1945), killed by Americans or Japanese, starvation or disease.

Roughly that same number of American service personnel remained on the islands after the US passed them back to Japan in 1972. Their bases occupied a full fifth of the main island, with much of what remained also not intended for the locals. Driving across that island, people passed by long stretches of barbed wire fence to the left and right, behind which American and Japanese flags flew from well-kept grassy banks and anonymous-looking military installations. There was vintage Americana: clapped-out bars and restaurants, forecourts full of rusting Fords and Chevys. And there were shiny new hotels and resorts, mostly built, staffed and patronized by mainland Japanese, rivalling the bases in the damage they did to the island's air, water, sea-life, soil and coastlines.

. . . The car stops on a quiet farm road. There is little to see through the windows beyond sugar cane and sky. The men, all three of them American military service personnel, climb into the back of the car, and take turns raping the Okinawan schoolgirl. When they've finished, they throw her out, half-conscious, onto the road and drive off. They dispose, in a nearby bin, of three sets of bloody underwear and one unused notebook.

Okinawa erupted. Eighty-five thousand people poured onto the streets in furious protest – the largest gathering in the islands' history – demanding an end to the abuse of this place and its people. Women began to come forward to say that they, too, had been assaulted by American servicemen. They were encouraged to speak out by a group called Okinawan Women Act Against Military Violence, jointly led by a local politician and an American missionary, whose delegation to an NGO Forum at the 1995 UN World Conference on Women in Beijing had returned home to news of this latest attack.

A clumsy American response spoke volumes about what the people of these islands meant to them. The commander of United States Pacific Command told a press conference that the three soldiers had been stupid – because for the price of the rented car they could have bought a prostitute. He was forced into early retirement. President Bill Clinton postponed a planned visit to Japan in order to avoid association with the incident, which came just days after First Lady Hillary Clinton had told the Beijing Conference that women's rights were human rights, and that military rape was a war crime. US–Japanese plans were set in motion the next year to move Marine Corps Air Station Futenma to a less central location, where schoolteachers would no longer have to shout to be heard above aircraft noise, and artillery would not be fired across civilian roads.

While life on Okinawa sometimes felt like being trapped in a Cold War museum, by the mid-1990s people further north in the archipelago were feeling afresh the weight of their mid-century wars. Ghosts long laid to rest – it was hoped – seemed to rise and rattle their chains. Others in Japan were more afraid of the future than the past. If China continued to grow, and the United States became less attached to its post-war Pacific ally, there was a danger that Japan's fortunes might end up locked into reverse gear: becoming slowly less prosperous and less significant in strategic terms – perhaps eventually ending up once again an exotic, insular curiosity at the world's 'Far Eastern' fringe.

*

'You cannot be asked to apologize every day, can you? It isn't good for a nation to feel constantly guilty.' Such were the sentiments of many a Japanese conservative in the 1990s, when faced yet again with talk of the war. But they were the words of Mao Zedong back in the mid-1950s, speaking to a visiting delegation from the Japanese

Okinawans protest against the rape of a schoolgirl in 1995 and its
roots in post-war US–Japan relations

Diet. Zhou Enlai offered similarly soothing noises: 'We should let go,'
he said, 'and ensure that history is never repeated.'

This wasn't absolution, of course. This was politics. Mao and Zhou
hoped to peel Japan away from the United States and its Asian allies –
South Korea, Taiwan and the Philippines – while easing their country's
isolation through bilateral trade and investment. Opinion within
Japan's ruling LDP was divided at this point, as it was within the Chinese Communist Party. But the next thirty years saw more cooperation
than conflict. Deals were signed boosting economic ties and allowing
thousands of captured Japanese soldiers to at last return home. Chinese authorities placed limits on the investigation and public discussion
of Japanese wartime violence. Even when a UN survey in the late
1960s hinted that a group of disputed islands – 'Senkaku' to the Japanese; 'Diaoyu' to the Chinese – might be home to huge reserves of oil,
the issue was dismissed as something for another day.

Finally, in September 1972, just a few months after President Nixon's epoch-making trip to China, Japan's Prime Minister Tanaka Kakuei boarded his own plane for Beijing. There were difficult moments. At a banquet, Tanaka apologized for the war using a turn of phrase in Japanese that his hosts deemed more appropriate for a spilled drink than a brutal and tragic conflict (Zhou Enlai later told him that his remark had 'bought the animosity of the Chinese people'). But an agreement was signed nonetheless, establishing diplomatic relations between Japan and the People's Republic of China and putting an end to a state of war which, on paper at least, had persisted up to that point.

Tanaka and Mao talked, when they met, about Richard Nixon, Henry Kissinger, and the Soviet Union. But they also discussed Buddhism, Confucius, incense and prayer. It was a reminder that their two countries were bound together by very much more than the violence of recent decades. And it was part of a post-war pattern for Japan: moving back and forth in how it thought about itself and presented itself to the world between history and culture – between time-bound stories, fraught with politics and freighted with difficult memories, and purer, putatively timeless ones.

Culture had its attractions right across the modern era. While Meiji-era thinkers reworked their national inheritance into a unique and globally competitive 'Japan', for reassurance at home and for retail abroad – land of the gods, way of the warrior, art of tea – foreign enthusiasts and critics embarked on a century and a half of trying to tease out the country's essentials. The writer and Japanophile Lafcadio Hearn encountered 'kindly' and 'fairy-like' people in the 1890s, living in a slightly miniaturized landscape. The Victorian designer Christopher Dresser found the Meiji Japanese 'genial' and 'loving', but saw an undercurrent of 'barbaric cruelty' revealed in their cuisine – in particular *ikizukuri*: a live fish sliced into quivering, edible chunks.

Decades later, the United States government employed the British anthropologist Geoffrey Gorer and his American colleague Ruth Benedict to unpick the supposedly alien psychology of a people with whom they had ended up at war. Gorer traced a speculative path from harsh toilet training through repression and guilt, ending at a disconcerting battlefield combination of extreme discipline and wild violence.

Benedict described a broader 'shame' culture, by no means utterly and irredeemably evil, but powered by concern for appearances, approbation and mutual indebtedness rather than unshakeable principles or a sense of inner freedom – these were characteristics of 'guilt' cultures, to be found largely in the West.

Benedict's book *The Chrysanthemum and the Sword* (1946), which contained these thoughts and many more besides on what made Japanese tick (in contrast to Americans) was criticized inside and outside Japan for its spectacular generalizations. The country's diversity – across time and region, war and peace, wealth and poverty, age and gender, ethnicity and personality – had, it seemed, been all but ignored. The result, both here and in similar works across subsequent decades, was a portrait of an improbably homogenous place, to which its painters were forced to add dashes of 'puzzling' and 'paradoxical' in order to explain away evidence of plurality.

And yet *Chrysanthemum* became an influential bestseller, read not just as a Japan primer by GHQ staff but purchased in translation by more than 2 million Japanese over the next half-century – even quoted in Japanese school textbooks. No doubt for some fans there was relief at seeing an American writer codifying Japanese culture where her wartime contemporaries had simply demonized it. But there was a broader pattern here, beyond any one book: a popular appetite, growing in Japan and abroad especially from the 1960s onwards, for work in a genre that became known as *nihonjinron* – 'theories about the Japanese'.

Claims included the importance of climate and ancestry in shaping a distinctively cooperative society and psyche; an aversion to confrontation; a preference for non-verbal communication (in contrast to Westerners' gauche and laborious verbosity); a flinty yet quietly understated Japanese 'spirit'; a balancing of rationality with sensuousness and deep feeling; and finally the rather circular idea that unless you were Japanese you could not hope to fully understand – or therefore convincingly refute – any of these claims. Point-by-point rebuttals by sociologists and anthropologists (including from within Japan) did little more than downgrade these 'theories' from shared shibboleths to quietly harboured assumptions or vague intuitions, across Japan and an increasingly Japanophile West.

One of the explanations for the staying power of these cultural claims was that however ideologically motivated, wrongly reasoned and extravagantly expressed, there were kernels of raw observational truth to some of them. Important too, for Japanese audiences, was that culture offered a useful distraction from history. Benedict's work had been very much concerned with the recent war and what it said about Japan. But many of its successors – the psychoanalyst Doi Takeo's writing on the concept of *amae* (presuming upon another's benevolence); the social anthropologist Nakane Chie on Japan's 'vertical society'; Ezra Vogel's *Japan As Number One: Lessons for America* (1979) – offered Japanese a reassuringly distinct and enduring sense of themselves, in the light of which mid-century events seemed not especially characteristic.

For Japan's post-war leaders, there was obvious political utility in persuading the population of the rightness and beauty, stretching back into antiquity, of a society that eschewed conflict and understood that unequal social relationships hold benefits for both parties. Promoting this same image abroad was an effective way of helping it to bed down at home, so closely did the Japanese media cover foreign discussions about their country. A condensed version of Nakane's work on Japanese society was distributed to Japanese embassies around the world for this very purpose, while the claim of harmony within hierarchy became one element in Japan's cultural diplomatic suite – alongside tea ceremony demonstrations, portraits of Mount Fuji's perfect contours, public displays of the art of flower arrangement (*ikebana*) and later the installation of talented sushi chefs in some of the more important foreign missions. Samurai swords were given an extended sabbatical, awaiting a new global generation capable of enjoying them at an aesthetic, fantastical or ironic remove.

The broader importance of these efforts to Japan's international fortunes was made vividly clear in 1962, when *The Economist* described an 'economic miracle' under way there – coining a welcome and influential phrase – only for French President Charles de Gaulle to be rather more disobliging, referring to Japan's Prime Minister Ikeda Hayato as 'that transistor salesman'. To have largely left behind – in some parts of the world, at least – a reputation as Asia's automaton butchers and slavers was an important achievement. But the prospect of replacing it with nothing more than a reputation for imitation, miniaturization and ruining other countries' trade balances was philosophically underwhelming, and clearly bad for business.

At the same time, reparations to South East Asian countries, under the terms of 1952's San Francisco Peace Treaty, were being made largely in the form of Japanese goods and services, alongside technical cooperation and overseas volunteering. The obvious economic self-interest in much of this, and in Japan's 'Official Development Assistance' generally – as a government stimulus to the domestic economy and a means of opening up overseas markets – did not go unnoticed by Japan's former colonial subjects. Despite Japan becoming the world's most generous contributor of overseas aid, opinion polls taken as late as the 1980s revealed that 70 per cent of the Thai population regarded Japan's economic activities as basically 'imperialistic'. Where Japanese capital was not universally trusted, Japanese culture, it was hoped, could step in.

Japan's cultural diplomacy proved phenomenally successful well into the twenty-first century, renewing itself as times changed so that each new generation of Japanophiles fell in love with a slightly different country. But culture could not hold the past at bay. By 1995 history seemed to be returning with a vengeance: in schools and bookshops, in the newspapers and in the Diet – above all in Japan's international relations. East Asia was entering an era of apologies and apologetics.

Japanese leaders had long worried about what went on in the country's classrooms. Having encountered graduates of Japan's highly ethnocentric pre-war and wartime education system on the battlefield, the Americans had resolved to dismantle it. From the summer of 1945, Japanese children were treated to the sight of some of their teachers being hauled away, while others were put to work – assisted by pupils – inking out sections of textbooks that were deemed 'undemocratic'. The teaching of moral education, Japanese history and geography was suspended completely, on the basis that these had been the principal means by which the indoctrination of the nation's youth had been effected.

New measures including a Fundamental Law of Education did away with the old Imperial Rescript on Education (to which pupils had bowed daily) and established a single-track education for girls and boys of all abilities: six years of elementary school and three of junior high school (*chūgakkō*), with an optional three more of senior high school (*kōtōgakkō*). Elected local education boards were given the power to oversee staffing and curricula. Classroom questions and debates were now vigorously encouraged.

Japan's remaining teachers, many of them grieving for students lost in the war, found themselves largely sympathetic to the new regime. Acting through the Japan Teachers' Union (JTU), allied with the Socialist Party, they became one of the country's most staunchly left-wing professional constituencies. They consistently opposed conservative critics of the new system, who claimed that an education stripped of its old pride in the nation was yet another debilitating legacy of the faulty, foreign post-war settlement imposed upon Japan. Teachers pushed back, too, against efforts to reinstate Japan's pre-war flag and national anthem.

Some battles were lost. Elections to local education boards were done away with in the mid-1950s, in favour of appointments by prefectural governors and local mayors. Around the same time, schools were instructed to set aside one hour per week for moral education, to be rooted in the country's 'unique culture'. A standard curriculum was reintroduced, and Ministry of Education (MoE) bureaucrats began reviewing the textbooks from amongst which boards could select.

This last mattered greatly to those in Japan who thought that inordinate and one-sided attention had been paid in early post-war textbooks to the wartime behaviour of Japanese soldiers. It had begun, they said, with a perfect storm of Occupation-era Americans seeking to paralyse the Japanese with guilt (or possibly shame), left-wing teachers uninterested in distinguishing patriotism from fascism and publishers intent on pandering to the teachers who used their books. Now, with MoE staff able to withhold approval of draft texts until desired changes were made, publishers could be advised to avoid undesirable usages and even entire topics. The use of the word 'invasion' in regard to China was discouraged. Talk of the Nanjing Massacre disappeared entirely until the 1970s. Historians including Ienaga Saburō took to the courts to challenge the constitutionality of this screening process. But though Ienaga won arguments over particular revisions, the legitimacy of the process itself was upheld.

Japan's textbook controversies became international news from the early 1980s onwards, attracting a degree of attention that was out of all proportion to the number of schools actually using any of the offending literature. This became part of a wider pattern to emerge from the 1990s onwards. There had long been a deep reticence in Japan, bordering on a taboo, about discussing the late 1930s and early 1940s in depth and in public. It remained a difficult, painful topic, and critics no doubt had a point when they suggested that avoidance was unhealthy in the long term. But by focusing heavily on neo-nationalist and revisionist commentary on that era – from Ishihara Shintarō's denial of the Nanjing Massacre in *Playboy* magazine to Kobayashi Yoshinori's *Gōmanism* and *Neo-Gōmanism* manga, satirizing modern Japan's capitulation to Western ideologies – the global media risked portraying the Japanese as a whole as somehow allergic to the taking of serious historical or moral inventories, in contrast to the exemplary process of self-examination through which West Germany had put itself.

In fact, anger amongst former members of the Imperial Japanese Army at books like *'Nankin gyakusatsu' no kyokō* ('The Fabrication of the "Nanjing Massacre" ') (1984), by a former secretary to General Matsui Iwane, had helped persuade some of them to come forward with diary accounts of what they and their comrades had done while in uniform. The death in 1989 of their former commander, Emperor Hirohito, made this a little easier to do. Memoirs produced by former prisoners of war of the Japanese added to the flow of new information, not least on notorious wartime episodes like the building of the Burma–Thailand 'Death' Railway by more than 60,000 Allied POWs and many more forced labourers from the region.

During the 1990s, an array of lawsuits – including a number brought by non-Japanese victims of the war – resulted in the Japanese courts becoming involved in affirming some of the wartime events questioned by revisionists. There had indeed been a massacre at Nanjing. Korean and other Asian 'comfort women' had been forced into sexual slavery in military brothels. And experiments in biological warfare (including human vivisection) had taken place at Unit 731 in Manchukuo.

Politicians with a gift for the gaffe or an eye to their support base helped to undermine all this. On 15 August 1995, Murayama Tomiichi – Japan's first socialist Prime Minister in half a century – issued a statement marking the fiftieth anniversary of the end of the war. His words, which carried considerable political weight thanks to unanimous Cabinet backing, left little room for interpretation:

> During a certain period in the not too distant past, Japan, following a mistaken national policy, advanced along the road to war, only to ensnare the Japanese people in a fateful crisis, and, through its colonial rule and aggression, caused tremendous damage and suffering to the people of many countries, particularly to those of Asian nations.
>
> In the hope that no such mistake be made in the future, I regard, in a spirit of humility, these irrefutable facts of history, and express here once again my feelings of deep remorse and state my heartfelt apology. Allow me also to express my feelings of profound mourning for all victims, both at home and abroad, of that history.

But a few days before Murayama's statement, the Education Minister Shimamura Yoshinobu had declared – on his first day in the job – that 'invasion' or 'non-invasion' depended on 'how you think about it'. Then, on the day of the statement itself, no fewer than eight Cabinet members made a visit to Tokyo's Yasukuni Shrine, deeply controversial in East Asia ever since it became known that the souls of fourteen Class A war criminals had been secretly added (in 1978) to the 2.46 million already enshrined there. Those who wished to maintain their insistence that Japan had never apologized for its past – or wasn't truly apologetic – could claim that Murayama's sentiments had in fact been purely personal.

As with Mao and Zhou's willingness to set history aside in the 1950s, so with the desire of Japan's former adversaries to do the opposite now: much of this was about contemporary politics. By the late 1980s into the 1990s, many Americans were far less favourably disposed towards Japan than even a generation before. They had had enough of the influx of Japanese cars and capital into their country, epitomized by Sony's purchase of Columbia Pictures and Mitsubishi's of a controlling stake in the Rockefeller Group, both in late 1989. 'Japan Buys the Center of New York,' declared the *New York Times*, while less reputable writers took the long view: a perennially aggressive people had exchanged bayonet blades for sharp suits, and tanks for Toyota Corollas. A new form of fairground-style entertainment emerged in Detroit and elsewhere: smashing up Japanese cars with baseball bats or sledgehammers – a dollar per hit.

US politicians enjoyed plenty of popular support in forcing trade quotas on Japan and in lambasting the country's contribution of $13 billion to the cost of the 1991 Gulf War as late in arriving, and both monetarily and morally inadequate. 'They pay in yen, we pay in blood,' ran the popular refrain, forgetting for a moment who had written a peace clause into Japan's post-war Constitution. When, after the war, the Kuwaiti government took out a large advert in the *New York Times* to thank the countries that had contributed to their liberation from Saddam Hussein, there was no mention at all of Japan. It was a devastating moment for the country's leaders, who had raised taxes to help foot their considerable share of the bill. The SDF began, the next year, to contribute to UN peacekeeping operations, with its first independent deployment outside Japan since the end of the Second World War coming soon after the end of the second Gulf War: around 600 Ground Self-Defence Force troops were sent to help with reconstruction in southern Iraq between 2004 and 2006.

In China, above all, attitudes towards Japan were hardening in the mid-1990s. In retrospect, an historic visit to Japan in 1978 by Deng Xiaoping – the first ever by a Chinese leader, over more than twenty centuries of contact – looked like the high point for post-war Sino-Japanese relations. Deng had cooed at car plants, marvelled at industrial robotics and smiled for the cameras aboard the shinkansen. A peace and friendship treaty had been signed the same year, and the two countries had even begun sharing intelligence about Soviet missile deployments – post-war East Asia was home more to shared enmities than it was real friendships. Japanese loans and TV dramas – including a classic *asadora* (morning serial) called *Oshin* (1983–4) – were warmly welcomed into Chinese bank accounts and onto Chinese screens.

Then controversies over textbook revisions and Japanese prime ministerial visits to the Yasukuni Shrine had intervened – visits that were partly a matter of personal politics, but largely related to pressure from veterans' groups to show some pride and respect. Popular protests across China in 1989, most famously at Tiananmen Square, brought brief respite from souring relations. Desperate for allies amidst worldwide opprobrium over the deadly violence with which the demonstrations were brought to an end, Chinese leaders reached out to Japan. In 1992, Emperor Akihito became the first Japanese emperor to visit China, taking the opportunity to express his own 'deep sorrow' at the 'severe suffering' inflicted on the Chinese people by Japan's armed forces. But China's leaders soon came to see that rapid economic change in their country, with all its unpredictable social consequences, required the ballast of a 'patriotic education'. Jiang Zemin (1989–2002) resolved to supply it, and from the mid-1990s a new curriculum from kindergarten upwards emphasized modern China's victimhood at the hands of Europeans and then Japanese. New dates were added to the national calendar, commemorating the Marco Polo Bridge incident, Nanjing and Japan's surrender. Historical daytrips became popular, not least to the Nanjing Massacre Memorial Hall, which was built in 1985 and then enlarged considerably in 1995.

Mao Zedong and Tanaka Kakuei meet, in September 1972

Neo-Gomanism Manifesto Special: On War, featuring 'colonial'
Allied flags trampled on by Japanese forces

*

Mixed feelings about Japan and its leaders abroad, across much of the
1990s and early 2000s, were mirrored by a worry at home that the
country was losing its way. Nowhere was that clearer than in the self-
interested and – to outsiders, at least – rather confusing party-political
machinations that resulted in something of a revolving door at the top
of national politics. Towards the end of Bill Clinton's presidency, US
Secretary of State Madeleine Albright and National Security Advisor
Sandy Berger passed around a piece of paper amongst themselves and
some aides, inviting one another to name – in the correct order – all
seven of the Japanese prime ministers with whom the Clinton administration (1993–2001) had dealt. None of them could do it.

From 2006 until 2012, Japan would get through another six prime
ministers, at the rate of roughly one per year. But during the period

from 2001 through to 2006, a single prime minister managed to keep his job for five and a half years, eventually relinquishing the role in accordance with LDP party rules rather than in disgrace or through losing an election. Koizumi Junichirō – affectionately known as 'Jun-chan' – was exceptional in all sorts of ways besides his political longevity, refreshingly direct communication style and trademark long wavy hair.

Abroad, East Asian relations were not helped by Koizumi's annual visits to Yasukuni. But his friendship with George Bush, forged in the wake of 9/11 and sealed at Graceland five years later (as Japan's most famous Elvis impersonator broke into 'Love Me Tender'), went a long way to bringing US–Japan relations out of the deep-freeze. At home, Koizumi offered 'pain' in return for modest gain. He acted against the bad debts afflicting Japan's banks in the wake of the economic downturn, and he cut government expenditure on public works – risking the wrath of the 'road tribe' of LDP members who owed their positions to construction contracts. He pushed through privatization of Japan's postal savings and insurance systems (home to hundreds of trillions of yen that Koizumi regarded as being wastefully and often corruptly invested) and moved to loosen up the labour market.

Greater flexibility for companies in employing workers on short-term contracts or hiring them via intermediaries was credited with enhancing

Prime Minister Koizumi Junichirō – as Elvis

competitiveness, but it was soon blamed for eroding old workplace guarantees over welfare and security of employment. When the global financial crisis of 2007–8 brought five years of respectable Japanese economic growth – around 2 per cent per year – to an end, companies responded by laying off temporary workers in large numbers.

The year 2009 began with stark televised images of tents, tarpaulin shelters and soup kitchens set up in Tokyo's Hibiya Park – just across from the Ministry of Health, Labour and Welfare. Drily named the 'New Year's Village for Contract Workers' (*toshi koshi haken mura*), it was one element in a partially successful civil society and media campaign to embarrass Japan's political and business community into a rethink. The eligibility requirements for unemployment benefit were softened, from one year of contributions down to six months – with those who remained ineligible offered welfare. Unused public housing was made temporarily available. And some Japanese firms reversed their lay-offs.

Insecurity of employment remained a fact of life, however, one which analysts were soon linking to Japan's accelerating demographic decline – on the basis that fewer people could now afford to start families. Some social critics pointed rather more speculatively to what they claimed was a broad malaise in the country, particularly amongst the young. People's emotional lives, patterns of behaviour or experiences of psychological distress had long been analysed in Japan for signs of what modernity was doing to the country – beginning with *shinkei suijaku* (neurasthenia) in the 1870s, which doubled as an individual diagnosis and a sign of stressful, breakneck modernizing times. This intertwining of suffering with sociology gathered pace in the late 1990s and early 2000s, via a remarkable series of new categories and buzzwords.

'Freeters' were those engaged only in casual, part-time employment. 'Parasite singles' usually referred to young women who were accused of sponging off their parents while indulging a taste for high-end consumerism. *Hikikomori* shut themselves away in their rooms or homes for months, even years on end. *Niito* had origins in the British acronym NEET: people 'not in education, employment or training'. *Sōshokukei-danshi* were 'herbivorous men', pushing hobbies or personal grooming to an advanced level of refinement, at the expense of relationships or work. Meanwhile, a general inwardness and lack of adventurism was detected in the youth of Japan, suggested by a sharp fall across the 2000s in the number of Japanese opting to study abroad.

Here, as with the real state of the economy and Japanese people's feelings about their past, perception – domestic and global – seemed to be at least as important as evidence. Quite different stories were told about these buzzword trends, all of which were real but most of which were amplified and distorted considerably by a sensationalist and sometimes catastrophizing media both at home and abroad. Some commentators were inclined to blame many of the trends on selfishness, weakness of will or a baffling reluctance to participate properly in a society which, for all its troubles, was still fundamentally kind, thoughtful, hospitable and secure. There were echoes here of the journalist Tokutomi Sohō, many decades before, regretting the late Meiji youth's apparent loss of faith in the nation-building project.

More sympathetic commentators blamed deteriorating living conditions, asking what it was about early twenty-first century Japan that compelled so many young people in particular to reject it in favour of a bedroom, a hobby, a handbag, perpetual single status, or some subcultural niche to be shared with a handful of the like-minded. Herbivorous refinement, or a temporary withdrawal from the world, could be read as a legitimate expression of dissent or even disgust – *hikikomori* might be staying at home because they knew there was nothing waiting for them outside.

Foreign visitors struggled to share the more pessimistic predictions about Japan's future. They encountered thriving and virtually crime-free urban public spaces, full of well-dressed and lavishly accessorized people eating in a fabulous array of restaurants, driving new cars, living the world's longest lives (life expectancy rose from around fifty-two in 1947 to over eighty in 2005) in a society with markedly less inequality than the US or UK, and enjoying along the way a wealth of high-tech gadgetry and high-quality entertainment, from Nō to detective novels to nightclubs. 'If this is a recession,' declared one British MP on a visit to Tokyo, 'then I want one.'

Gaijin ('foreigners') who stayed longer in Japan generally had a more mixed experience. They contributed to Japan's list of ambiguous modern maladies an affliction known as '*gaijin*-itis': a cycle of culture shock, adaptation and fresh culture shock, spiced with insufficiently acknowledged homesickness and a perpetual sense of being unfairly kept at arm's length by the locals, even actively discriminated against. No one could agree on how far the causes resided in the minds of each sufferer, and how far they were to be found out there in Japan – in some perpetually unfathomable blend of hospitality and xenophobia, and in a failing social and bureaucratic machinery.

But although long-term foreign residents tended to have a reputation amongst Japanese for complaining, and for comparing Japan to the countries of their birth (at least implicitly, and often to Japan's detriment), they were not the only ones worrying about their (adoptive) homeland's direction of travel. Many Japanese too were anxious about apparent stagnation and the ceding of the political and economic initiative in East Asia to their near neighbour. Away from the headlines and the history wars, China's growing economy had played an important role in Japan's partial recovery from its lost decade, with China overtaking the US as Japan's biggest trading partner in 2004. But in 2010, China became the world's second largest economy, bumping Japan down to number three. It was a widely expected change of places, but nevertheless one that almost seemed timed to complete the gloomy picture that critics were painting.

An important aspect of this gloom was that despite significant damage in recent years to the post-war story of a close coalition of politicians, bureaucrats and business people successfully co-stewarding Japan's fortunes, these general arrangements remained in place. Some of that damage had been sustained back in 1985, when Japan Airlines Flight 123 crashed in the mountains of Gunma prefecture, killing 520 people – the largest ever loss of life in an accident involving a single aircraft. Alongside loss of trust in a flagship Japanese company, the authorities were accused of a catastrophically slow response: four lives were saved, but people wondered whether it might have been more had Japanese rescuers not taken nearly fifteen hours to arrive at an admittedly remote and relatively inaccessible site – having turned down American offers of help shortly after the crash occurred. Ten years later, the Kobe response and the Aum attack compounded a sense of a state unable to keep its citizens secure.

Subtle shifts had occurred since in the country's balance of power, from a resurgence of interest in volunteering (given a degree of structure through a new Non-Profit Organization law in 1998) to efforts at increasing government transparency. The 'New Year's Village for Contract Workers' was just the latest proof of what intelligent activism could achieve. But it had so far proved impossible to dislodge what some called the 'iron triangle' of elected (especially LDP) officials, unelected civil servants and big business.

An example of its operations, not widely reported at the time, came on 7 March 2011. On that day, the Tokyo Electric Power Company (TEPCO) released to Japan's nuclear regulator, the Nuclear and Industrial Safety Agency (NISA), the results of research conducted three years before into safety at one of its coastal nuclear plants. The report concluded that existing sea walls were inadequate to prevent damage to the plant in the event of a large tsunami, but that the building of a higher sea wall would be too expensive when weighed against the imminent likelihood of what was regarded as a once-in-a-thousand-years event.

The promise of atomic energy had been familiar in Japan since the Meiji era, when the physicist Nagaoka Hantarō wrote a piece in the Yomiuri newspaper explaining the incredible efficiency of one day moving a steamship 'by destroying atoms, which constitute a slight amount of material, instead of burning several thousand tons of coal'. Atomic energy became a staple of Japanese science fiction from the 1920s (complete with atomic bombs and bullets), while radium *onsen* (natural hot-spring baths) were popular for their perceived health benefits.

Japan's military, too, took an early interest in the possibilities of nuclear warfare. But late-wartime claims that Japan possessed an atomic bomb, or that a fog-like beam could be fired from a cave inside a Japanese mountain, destroying Washington DC at a stroke, were little more than heart-warmers for a weary population. In fact, Japan's nuclear weapons programme had always lagged far behind the United States. 'We lost to the enemy's science,' declared the *Asahi Shimbun* newspaper on 20 August 1945. Weeks later, that enemy hunted down and did away with Japan's capacity for pursuing atomic research, taking its five cyclotrons to pieces and casting the parts into the waters of Tokyo Bay.

It fell instead to the British General Electric Company to build Japan's first nuclear reactor, at Tōkai village in the early 1960s. It was based on the design of a facility then under construction in Ayrshire, Scotland, but with a lower centre of gravity so as to mitigate the risk of earthquake damage. Local protests, fired by memories of the *Lucky Dragon 5* incident of 1954, marked the beginning of furious arguments between the government and the nuclear industry, on the one hand, and groups like the Citizens' Nuclear Information Centre on the other. Officials from MITI (after 2001, 'METI', the Ministry of Economy, Trade and Industry) took to visiting communities living near proposed nuclear sites and making presentations on the importance to the nation of nuclear energy. Beginning with Tōkai village, they offered to upgrade local infrastructure – moves welcomed by construction firms but denounced as *hakomono* (empty box) politics by detractors, who wondered what small and mostly elderly rural communities were going to do with football stadiums.

By the time of TEPCO's 2011 report, almost a third of Japan's energy was being generated by fifty-four nuclear reactors – fifteen of them in Tōkai village, which had long since acquired the nickname 'nuclear alley'. Another popular phrase was 'nuclear village' (*genshiryoku mura*), used to describe the extraordinary combined reach of pro-nuclear advocates across government, business, banking, academia and the media. Despite extensive and expensive cajoling, around three-quarters of the surveyed population in the late 1990s maintained misgivings about nuclear power. But it didn't matter. There was little prospect of policy change, and such was the regulator's reputation for warm relationships with the nuclear industry that its response to TEPCO's late and rather cavalier report on 7 March would probably not be overly draconian or demanding.

No one will ever know. Four days after its submission, the scenario described in the report as highly unlikely, and very expensive to plan for, began to play out.

18

Fragments

A devastated landscape. Dead trees. Poisoned produce. A defeated population. And yet, in the most unexpected of ways, regeneration. It came down to a boy with an apple for a head, sitting under starry skies with a man whose own head was made of bread, filled with red-bean paste.

'How come you're so kind?' asks Ringo Bōya, aka Apple Boy.

'When I see people in trouble, in my heart I just want to help them,' replies Anpanman (Bean-paste Bread Man).

Ringo Bōya is paying close attention. He wants to be a hero one day. But so far he has managed only to be selfish, quick-tempered, easily dispirited, and so desperate for grand adventures that he alienates his family and friends by refusing to get his hands dirty in the orchard on Apple Island.

This other man is the real thing, complete with cape, belt and booties. He isn't the hero for whom people might have hoped, in these toughest of times. Where Superman's nemesis substance was kryptonite, not readily obtainable by his enemies, Anpanman's is troublingly ubiquitous: water. His arch-enemy Baikinman – 'Germ Man' – has only to squirt a little at his face, cackling triumphantly at the controls of his tiny airship's water cannon, and Anpanman falls out of the sky. His friends have to rush in and bail him out: Shokupanman (Breadhead Man), Karēpanman (Currypanman), Meronpanna (Melonpanna), and all the rest. Jamu Ojisan (Uncle Jam) spends much of his time baking replacements for Anpanman's soggy head.

Vulnerability and a kindness that never wears thin: these are Anpanman's superpowers. Ringo Bōya learns fast, returning to the orchard to lavish patient love on a single sapling. When disaster strikes, destroying his hometown and poisoning its crop, the power of a single apple borne by this single remaining tree turns everything around. Enormous fragments of fractured earth-crust rumble back into place; a colossal lithic jigsaw puzzle magically gathers itself together and seals itself at the joints. The world returns to its natural state: clear skies, trees blooming, people smiling.

Anpanman's creator, Yanase Takashi, was old enough to have served in China towards the end of the war. He saw villagers starving and emaciated comrades staggering and then dropping out of their marching columns. That a war billed as 'righteous' could come to this made a pacifist of Yanase, for ever suspicious of traditional heroics. The only reliable righteousness, he decided, lay in compassion and in feeding the hungry. That ought to go for superheroes as well, he thought. Too often they tended to be distant figures, rarely touching anyone's life.

The resulting Anpanman character shocked teachers and reviewers at first. Here was a 'hero' who sought to soothe distraught children by tearing off a chunk of his own face and handing it to them with a grin. 'Please, never write something like this again,' commented one. 'We don't need more than a single book of this type,' said another. 'Cruel,' suggested a third. But the verdict from children themselves was quite the reverse, and soon there were more books, a stage show and an anime series.

The greatest accolade came in the wake of 11 March 2011. An earthquake powerful enough to shift Japan's main island 8 feet closer to the United States struck off its north-eastern coast, the region known as Tōhoku. A dark, deafening, putrid wall of water came surging inland, at a height of nearly 40 metres in places. Buildings and bridges, cars and people were sucked out to sea. Men, women and children were picked up and scattered across the landscape by a racing wave powerful enough to scrub urban infrastructure from the map. Others were caught in flood waters that appeared tame enough at first, but then wouldn't stop rising, and pushing and pulling.

Survivors struggled frantically to reach loved ones by phone, as helicopter news footage showed familiar parts of the landscape suddenly replaced by vast muddy lakes. Claims were emerging of explosions and possible meltdowns at Fukushima No.1 nuclear power plant. No one knew how far all this was going to go: how much death, how much harm from radioactive fallout – or how long it would take Tōhoku's agricultural communities to recover, assuming they ever did.

Amidst all the tragedy and profound uncertainty, reports began to emerge about how local children were coping. They were singing. A song about how wonderful it is to be alive, even amidst great pain. About the preciousness of existence – so fleeting for all things that even the shining stars will one day disappear. About a hero, his head made of bread, who never stops looking out for people and never gives up.

The song was the 'Anpanman March': upbeat drums and flutes, a chorus of cheerful childlike voices and sentiments that wove a charming sense of adventure with the deepest of human concerns. Yanase had always thought highly of his customer base, crediting them with being able to handle all sorts of ideas and emotions. At ninety-one years of age, he had been starting to think about retirement. But then he heard the reports about children singing in Tōhoku and started receiving letters – including one from a little girl in the disaster zone, who wrote: 'I'm not frightened; Anpanman will come and rescue us.' He set to work on three final stories.

Yanase's first two themes were restoration and hope. The third and last was homesickness and the rescuing of the homeland. Tōhoku's long association with apple-growing, now in doubt because of fallout from Fukushima, inspired him to set his story on Apple Island. Powerful images of regeneration were offered up to children and parents alike: a seed that is tended to, and flowers; a tree that sprouts even on the tongue of a terrible killing machine; an aspiring hero who abandons his isolation and reconnects with home. Placing himself alongside his audience for a moment, in the form of Anpanman talking gently with Ringo Bōya under a night sky, Yanase tells them that 'kindness' is not banal, not an empty piety. It is the only durable source of strength.

Some of the children reading and watching Yanase's crowning creations would later that day have eaten Anpanman curry from an Anpanman bowl, cleaned their teeth with an Anpanman toothbrush and gargled from an Anpanman mug, before changing into Anpanman pyjamas and climbing under an Anpanman duvet. Yanase's world was a commercial phenomenon. But this revealed more about

The tsunami of 11 March 2011, hitting the coast in Fukushima prefecture

Anpanman, Ringo Bōya and Meronpanna (©Takashi Yanase, Froebel-kan, TMS, NTV 2013)

Japan than a flair for the media franchise. The country had become newsworthy around the world, in recent years, for its apparent decline and confusion of purpose – a stagnant economy, poor job security and worsening work conditions, excessive overtime, a population worryingly reticent about reproduction. And yet in so far as the quality of attention lavished on its youngest members is a meaningful indicator of a society's underlying health, Japan had long been – and remained now – in more robust basic shape than either local or international critics tended to allow.

Young children were educated and entertained by some of the world's brightest and liveliest books and television. Programmes like NHK's *Okāsan to Issho* ('With Mother'), running since 1959, introduced children to the vast and eclectic cultural storehouse that they were set to inherit: folk songs, nursery singalongs, classical instruments, fiendish maths and word puzzles, ballet and kabuki theatre. A correspondence course featuring a little tiger-cub called Shimajirō offered carefully graded books, DVDs and toys to accompany children through their early years – from toilet training and care of younger siblings to tackling the formidable Japanese writing system and understanding the etiquette of train travel, via a 'Manners Ninja' whose skill-set included the statuesque stillness expected of a considerate commuter.

Older children were even more spoiled for choice, thanks to a huge array of manga, anime and games. *Kureyon Shin-chan* (Crayon Shin-chan) followed the comedy adventures of a precociously outspoken and unashamedly backside-exposing five-year-old called Shinnosuke, or Shin-chan for short. Doraemon was a blue robotic cat, sent from the future to befriend a struggling young boy. *One Piece* traced the fantastical voyages of Monkey D. Luffy and his Straw Hat Pirates, in search of the world's ultimate treasure. Meanwhile a company that started out manufacturing playing cards in Kyoto in 1889 had teamed up with an avid insect collector, Tajiri Satoshi, to produce one of history's most heavily trodden fantasy landscapes. Nintendo's Pokémon universe, appearing first on their handheld Game Boy console and later in books and anime, was populated by hundreds of species of small creatures to be collected, trained and then enlisted in battles with other trainers.

By 2011, these and countless other characters had found their way into homes around the world. Japanese childhood had gone global. If 1995 was Japan's *annus horribilis* – earthquake, Aum attack, history wars, the parlous state of the economy hitting home – 1996 seemed in retrospect to have begun a new era. That year saw the release of the first Pokémon game, the start of a Tamagotchi craze (a small digital pet on a key-ring), and the signing of a distribution deal between Disney and Miyazaki Hayao's Studio Ghibli, enabling the latter to play a central, celebrated role in an emerging worldwide Japan boom.

The Disney deal was briefly imperilled when a US producer suggested to a counterpart at Ghibli that edits to their material might be advisable, to make the stories more accessible for American audiences. He is rumoured to have received a samurai sword in the post, with a note attached to the blade: 'No cuts.' The medium aside, this was clearly the right message: foreign critics were enthralled by a culture where the borders between entertainment for children and for adults – and between childhood and adulthood more generally – were allowed to remain so excitingly, provocatively porous. Miyazaki's *Spirited Away* went on to win the Oscar for Best Animated Feature Film in 2003. Doraemon soon found himself influential enough to be accused of political subversion in China, and of corrupting children in India and Pakistan. And in the mid-2010s, *One Piece* became the most successful manga of all time, second only to *Harry Potter* as the world's bestselling book series.

Alongside Miyazaki, the work of the novelist Murakami Haruki served as one of the principal imaginative portals through which outsiders entered Japan and Japanese life. Becoming synonymous internationally with Japanese literature in the 1990s, while simultaneously accused at home of being neither truly Japanese nor truly literary, Murakami's work was remarkable for revealing contemporary Japan's doubts and woes in a way that drew foreign readers in rather than frightening them off.

Many of the young characters in novels like *Noruwei no Mori* (*Norwegian Wood*) (1987) were lonely, lost, bereft of optimism and uninterested in (or incapable of) making plans for the future. They struggled to sustain relationships or even coherent conversations. And yet there was an aesthetic attractiveness and a philosophical depth to their dismay at the world around them, and readers internationally found much that resonated with their own experiences of life. Murakami's writing, and the broader Japan boom, seemed to represent the latest and most easily accessible instalment of a gift that Japan had been giving the world for a century or more by this point: a wise and forensic look at modernity and what it does to people, combined with visions of alternative ways of living. Murakami himself was heartened to see the direction his country was going in after the wake-up call of 1995. He detected the emergence of a more free-wheeling society, of small-scale entrepreneurs and creative industries, out of the crusty old chrysalis of a complacent, corporate Japan now discredited by economic disaster.

Japan's politicians, no strangers themselves to crustiness or discredit, were quick to see the brand-renewal potential in this metamorphosis. Jumping on the 'Cool Japan' bandwagon, the Ministry of Foreign Affairs appointed the cartoon cat Doraemon as the country's 'Anime Ambassador' in 2008. When Japan's Prime Minister appeared at the closing ceremony of the 2016 Olympics in Rio de Janeiro, promoting Tokyo's 2020 Games, he was persuaded to do so dressed as Nintendo's Super Mario.

Yet it remained far from clear what this early twenty-first century shift from economic to cultural superpower would ultimately mean for Japan's standing in the world, particularly in the corners that mattered most. Young Chinese flocking to see a *Doraemon* film at the cinema, or embarking on tours of hallowed anime sites across Japan, was certainly a useful means of countering the negative imagery they were likely to find in their school textbooks or in the lurid war dramas churned out by Chinese studios. But there were few signs so far of the Chinese population at large warming to Japan as a result.

The same was true in South Korea. A ban on Japanese pop culture had gradually been lifted across the 1990s, but opinion polls suggested that a clear majority of Koreans still held negative views of their near-neighbour. To Tokyo's great frustration, Japan's past on the peninsula, including its army's sexual enslavement of women and girls, remained prominent in Korean politics and media. Culture and history, Cool Japan and the 'comfort women', appeared perfectly capable of coexisting.

*

This apparent disconnect between entertainment and politics in Japan deepened as the triple disasters of March 2011 – earthquake, tsunami and nuclear meltdown – turned into a dramatic and very public test of the country's key institutions over the weeks and months that followed. Nearly 20,000 people had lost their lives and 270,000 homes had vanished. Three reactors had melted down at Fukushima, spewing radiation into the air and contaminating the surrounding land, groundwater and streams: 110,000 people were forced to leave their homes. Meanwhile politicians and pop stars were enlisted to eat local produce in public, a woefully premature attempt at reassurance, at a time when little was known – and even less was being admitted, by TEPCO and government officials – about the tragedy's poisonous scale and scope.

The imperial institution came out of this grimmest of tests with its reputation enhanced. Emperor Akihito broadcast a message of reassurance to the nation, the first since his father's at the end of the Second World War. He and Empress Michiko, both casually dressed, made visits to evacuation shelters, kneeling to chat with people for whom a few square feet of sky-blue gym mat, bounded by cardboard and vinyl partitions, were all the home they had left.

Emperor Akihito and Empress Michiko visit survivors of
Japan's triple disasters in March 2011

The Japanese Self-Defence Forces, too, saw an improvement in their national standing, after the largest deployment in their history. Reconnaissance flights had been launched within minutes of the earthquake and emergency supplies had begun to flow. Around 100,000 SDF personnel – many wearing uniform patches or helmet stickers bearing the slogan *Ganbare Tōhoku* (Be Strong, Tōhoku) – were seen by the general public rescuing people, clearing roads and ports and constructing temporary facilities.

Support from around 24,000 US military service personnel, as part of Operation Tomodachi (Operation Friend), brought gratitude and acclaim for Japan's long-term and not universally welcome American guests. But there was also controversy over the risks to which people had been exposed. Crew aboard the USS *Ronald Reagan* recalled the metallic taste of the air on deck as they appeared to pass through the radiation plume. They showered in and ate food cooked in desalinated ocean water picked up off the Tōhoku coast. Of the many who soon began suffering major health problems – from leukaemia to tumours to thyroid malfunction – hundreds tried to sue TEPCO for compensation via the US court system, alleging that it had failed to inform the Japanese authorities of the seriousness of the radiation leak. While the legal back and forth went on, former prime minister Koizumi Junichirō set up a private fund in support of affected personnel, soliciting donations within Japan to help pay for their medical care.

Where newspaper surveys of public opinion revealed an 82 per cent favourability rating for the SDF response to the crisis, the figure for the government stood at just 6 per cent. A major reason was trust: ministers were widely thought to be covering up past incompetence (their own, and that of their industry allies), while minimizing the extent of the ongoing dangers from the Fukushima power plant. There were calls across the political spectrum for Prime Minister Kan Naoto to exercise some leadership – political, moral, emotional. And there were urgent calls abroad for greater transparency from Japan about how bad the situation was, and might potentially become.

Alongside obfuscation and slowness of response ran some ill-timed, opportunistic manoeuvrings in the Diet. Kan Naoto, desperately planning behind the scenes for the imposition of martial law and the evacuation of 50 million people from Tokyo – a mere 150 miles south of the Fukushima power plant – soon faced defections from col-leagues in his party, the left-of-centre Democratic Party of Japan (DPJ). He was eventually forced to resign, with the DPJ's Noda Yoshihiko becoming Japan's third prime minister in two years. Just over a year later, Noda was also out. The DPJ were swept from power by a resurgent LDP under a former prime minister, Abe Shinzō.

Beginning in December 2012, Abe's second term as premier showed, as Koizumi's had done before him, just how much a long-serving prime minister could bring their influence to bear on government. 'Abenomics' involved huge amounts of government stimulus spending ($100 billion in 2013 alone), the flooding of the economy with money by the Bank of Japan, and the further liberalizing of the labour mar-ket, with more women encouraged into work. By mid-2017, the International Monetary Fund was prepared to pronounce all this a success, citing modest growth and an unemployment rate running at just 2.8 per cent – the lowest in more than twenty years.

But Abe's ambitions ran broader than gradual economic recovery. Supporters told journalists that Abenomics was inspired by the Meiji-era slogan *fukoku kyōhei* – 'enrich the country, strengthen the army'. And the Prime Minister appeared serious about doing both, working to lay the foundations for a militarily more powerful and assertive twenty-first-century Japan. He established a National Security Coun-cil, centralizing security policy and removing it from parliamentary scrutiny. He announced a five-year project to expand the armed forces, with drone and amphibious capabilities. And he pushed through a highly controversial State Secrecy Law (2013), under whose terms a government could, with no external or judicial oversight, deem anything it desired to be a secret, thereby preventing its dis-closure. Investigative journalists could, in theory at least, now be jailed for soliciting secret information – whether or not they were aware of its secrecy.

The Secrecy Law threatened to worsen what was already a bad situation: Japan had recently been ranked fifty-third in the World Press Freedom survey, thanks to a combination of pressure applied by large advertisers and a culture of cooperative press clubs, in which journalists dealt closely with one another and with officials. Internet news and discussion sites enjoyed relative freedom from these traditional constraints on the media. But a notable trend was the use of that freedom by Japan's army of *netto-uyoku* or internet ultranationalists, who spent much of their time rehashing mid twentieth-century controversies, sharing thoughts and 'statistics' about alleged Korean criminality in Japan, and goading 'Abe-chan' (a generally affectionate but in this case derisory appellation) for not going far enough in his policies.

The greatest political sensitivities of all surrounded LDP plans to revise Japan's post-war Constitution: regularizing in law the existence of Japan's military and in addition – so some planners hoped – rethinking constitutional rights, re-emphasizing Japan's 'unique culture', and restoring the Emperor as head of state. Legislation in 2015 allowing Japan to exercise collective self-defence (coming to the aid of an ally where Japan itself was ultimately in danger) was seen as paving the way for some of these changes. It passed through the Diet amidst chaotic scenes in the Lower House, reminiscent of the chamber scuffles of May 1960. There were once again protests outside the building, drawing tens of thousands of demonstrators.

The Japanese public at large, whose permission for constitutional revision would have to be sought in a national referendum, remained for now narrowly opposed to the idea. But there were signs that world events might be turning in the LDP's favour. Japan was first trolled by US President Donald Trump for 'freeloading' under the American security umbrella, and then all but abandoned in 2018 amidst a rushed rapprochement between the White House and a nuclear-armed North Korea. China's premier Xi Jinping had established pre-eminence at home, with his ideology enshrined in the Communist Party Constitution and a presidential two-term limit scrapped in his favour. Now he was working to establish his country's pre-eminence in the world, the signs of which ran from Chinese-funded football stadiums in Africa to military bases on artificial islands in the South China Sea. Amidst all this, Japan's constitutional peace clause and the 'higher ideals' of which MacArthur had spoken in making the case for it were becoming easier to portray as a relic of the early post-war world, perilously out of touch with the times.

*

Abe packaged his plans for Japan as part of a 'significant rebirth' intended to coincide with the Olympics and Paralympics in 2020. And yet although Abe's own future as LDP leader looked uncertain, amidst scandals and persistently gloomy poll ratings for his Cabinet (alongside the occasional broadside from Koizumi Junichirō, resolutely anti-nuclear and anti-Abe), there was little sign of imminent change in the nation's fundamental political arrangements. The year 2020 would mark sixty-five years of the LDP's existence, during which time it had been in power almost continuously. Brief hiatuses had so far served more to discredit its opponents than to bring them electoral momentum. The LDP had its internal divisions and its legendary factional fights. But post-war Japan had yet to develop a credible two- or three-party system.

Japan's influential bureaucracy was even more deeply entrenched. A legacy of Meiji-era managerialism, its consensual conservativism and broad, shaping reach had at times encouraged in the minds of politicians and observers alike a conflation of state with nation; of paternalistic, sometimes ambitiously interventionist political and socio-economic leadership with the will of a supposedly unified and purposeful population.

Foreign commentary across a century and a half, much of it read and reflected upon in Japan, played a role in strengthening these perceptions. As the first Asian country to 'go global' in the modern Western mould, Japan was often treated as a mirror-image of Western societies: looked to for shining proof that those societies were fit for export and for cautionary illustrations – particularly from the 1990s on – of how they might, if improperly managed, go wrong. The flipside of this deeply self-referential search for 'Japan', unmatched in Western approaches to Korea or China, was the rather stark drawing of distinctions between Western and Japanese life found in Ruth Benedict's work and much of the *nihonjinron* ('theories about the Japanese') genre. The adjective 'Japanese' came to suggest something more cohesive and persistent across time – bound up with hard-to-access traditions and deeply ingrained psychological quirks – than was the case with 'American' or 'German', whose associations by contrast were more complex and more readily updated.

For the people of Japan, there were indeed moments when thoughts turned to the nation as a meaningful entity, in which their identity was heavily invested. August 1945 was one such moment. March 2011 was another. But for the most part, 'modern Japan' had emerged, and was constantly sustained, as a by-product of people doing other things: living lives in which family or community or the pursuit of knowledge, pleasure or success served as more intelligible and compelling ordering ideals than the 'nation' of their leaders' wishful and grandiose imaginings.

This difference, between the nation envisaged as a single unfolding story and the sum of countless smaller ones, could be found playing out on the cusp of the 2020 Olympics about 50 miles east of Tokyo. Often billed as the 'gateway to Japan', Narita International Airport was gearing up to funnel athletes and spectators into a hyper-modern and environmentally friendly national capital, full of new, energy-efficient buildings, low-carbon zones and cute mottoes and mascots. There would be hydrogen cars, driverless taxis ('robocabs') and facial recognition to improve stadium security. Competitor medals were to be struck using precious metals recycled from unwanted smartphones. There were even plans for an artificial meteor shower, generated by having satellites spray glowing pellets into the night sky. As in 1964, so in 2020: a capital would showcase a country defining itself through soft power and high technology. On the basis that first impressions count, five billion yen was spent replacing Narita Airport's old creamy-beige toilet facilities with brightly coloured new ones, complete with voice guidance systems and heated seats.

And yet just around the corner from the airport lay another gateway to Japan entirely. In July each year, the small city of Narita played host to an event of its own. Tiny temporary stalls lined the road, strings of hanging light bulbs illuminating their wares in the warm dark of the evening. *Yakitori* – chicken skewers – sizzled in salt and cayenne pepper, wasabi and thick, brown *tare* made from sweetened soy sauce. There was *yakisoba* (fried noodles) and *takoyaki* (minced octopus, mixed with onion and pickled ginger, then fried inside balls of batter). *Watagashi* (candy floss) and *ringo ame* (candied apples). Alcohol for the adults. Goldfish games and toys for the children.

The stalls and their thousands of milling customers together helped create a makeshift thoroughfare along which ornate festival floats passed slowly and with tremendous fanfare. Standing precariously on top, and sitting close together along balconies around the side, were elaborately costumed dancers and singers and drummers and flautists, all hauled along on huge ropes by young women and men in headbands and thin, coloured festival coats. The *kami* (gods) were passing through in their *mikoshi* (portable shrines). Men appeared to be holding these aloft, but in fact they were just about holding on: kicking their legs and smiling and shouting ecstatically, under the energetic power of the *kami* within.

Narita's Gion festival, or '*matsuri*' – from *matsu*, 'waiting [for the gods]' – was around 300 years old by this point, named after a Kyoto *matsuri* that was many hundreds of years older still. For a few precious hours, the modern state and the modern nation over which it presided were revealed as utterly contingent. Traffic lights went offline. The tarmacked roads beneath were tramped by wooden *geta* and rice-straw *zori*: sandal-like footwear from the Edo era and before. Business attire was left behind in favour of summer kimono crafted in a blaze of colours. The police were employed simply to protect all of this, keeping cars and buses at bay with white gloves and orange glow-wands. Here was something not merely far older than states, or professional politicians, or Olympic PR, but more fundamentally human too. Life lived intensely, shorn of its encumbering practicalities and pretensions. Time out of time.

Except, not quite. Narita's annual festival was the result each year of haggling between its supporters and the local authorities. What would the route be? How long could the traffic be held up? Could the organizers guarantee that things would not get out of hand? *Matsuri* elsewhere were often the product of what history and politics had given or taken away: some were desperate answers to rural depopulation, others more optimistic civic innovations encouraged by the success of events like the 1970 Osaka Expo. Traditional paper lanterns suspended from high wires or displayed in wooden frames bore the names of the companies and corporations on which *matsuri* depended for sponsorship. And everyday social politics fuelled arguments behind the scenes over which roles should fall to the young or old, men or women, this or that individual; who would sit or stand where in the procession; who would pay for the floats, and how much.

Narita Gion Festival, 2017

Olympic visitors who might find Japan's official 2020 story curiously sterile would glimpse in festivals like Narita's the real raw material out of which the modern nation had been forged: a never-ending push-and-pull within and between a richly complex civil society and an often rather remote and reactive managerial state, over the enduring concerns of everyday life and over the new ideas and attitudes – arriving from abroad or arising at home, across a turbulent century and a half – that promised or threatened to reshape that life.

The art of exercising political or bureaucratic power lay in separating these pressures into two broad groups: those that could be portrayed as outliers to some necessary core of national identity and purpose, and those that could or must be worked with, permitted in time to become part of that core. Into the previous category, at various points before 1945, had gone socialism, feminism, liberalism, Christianity, votes for women and militant trade unionism. Into the latter, across the post-war years: cooperative industrial relations, a pacifist stance in international affairs, a concern for the natural environment and a world-beating versatility in technology and entertainment.

For people seeking change, this meant that top-down was rarely a realistic direction of travel. It was more likely that incremental, bottom-up innovations might receive belated recognition and sponsorship from those with power. But the hurdles were many and high.

Defenders of the status quo were happy to encourage a collective amnesia about modern Japan's talent for transformation, and about just how new and even experimental – especially in the context of a millennium and a half of recorded history – much of Japan's present social and cultural settlement really was.

The varied meanings of the *hinomaru* flag by the late 2010s made clear how much a national push-and-pull could achieve in changing people's minds and sustaining multiple points of view. Across East Asia, and for some in Japan as well, the circular red sun on a white background remained powerfully associated with Japan's imperialist past and its traces in present-day politics. It had once been raised over Nanjing, and was now flown from the windows of black ultra-nationalist sound-trucks, blaring martial music (along with angry accusations against the nation's quisling politicians) at faintly embarrassed shoppers in Shinjuku and Shibuya, in western Tokyo. In 1999, Japan's teachers had finally lost their long-running battle to stop the *hinomaru* from becoming the official national flag, and 'Kimi-ga-yo' the national anthem. Some in Tokyo went to court to protest against what they saw as a new nationalistic and authoritarian order to face the flag and sing the anthem in school assemblies. They eventually lost the case.

But this same flag had been deployed with artful ambiguity at the 1964 Tokyo Olympics, associated with a peaceful sporting internationalism. And in the early 2000s, Japan's superstar photographer Ninagawa Mika had claimed it for fashion and pop: posing a model in front of it dressed in a bikini and a diaphanous crimson top, glittery-gold cowboy hat down low over her face, samurai sword slung over her shoulders. By the late 2010s, Japan's Olympic organizers felt at home enough with the flag to separate 'Tokyo' and '2020' in their logo with a bold red disc.

Something similar had happened with mental illness, and with depression in particular. The concept was unknown to most Japanese before public information and pharmaceutical campaigns in the late 1990s and early 2000s encouraged people to think about it as 'a cold of the soul' (*kokoro no kaze*): anyone could 'catch' it, it was nothing to be ashamed of, and it was eminently treatable with medication. The number of people diagnosed with a mood disorder in Japan duly doubled in just four years, while the market for anti-depressants boomed: in 2006 – the

Ninagawa Mika's *hinomaru*

year that a Basic Law on Suicide Countermeasures was passed, to help tackle the alarming rate at which people were taking their own lives in Japan – it was worth six times what it had been just eight years before. Related talk of *kokoro no kea* ('care of the heart') began to shift the image of mental healthcare in general, from a frightening and stigmatizing institutional intervention to the sort of help with emotions and relationships that to some degree everyone requires from time to time.

In the workplace, depression went from being unknown, to a personal problem, to a recognized outcome of overwork – for which companies could be held responsible, while government was forced to institute mandatory stress checks at work – finally to the subject of angry scepticism from workers whose colleagues had been signed off sick, thereby lumbering them with extra work. By the mid-2010s, Japan's suicide rate was at last beginning to fall, but there was talk of 'fake depression', along with a rash of high-profile *karō jisatsu* ('overwork suicide') cases that suggested too many companies were still dragging their feet in taming the country's overtime culture. One case involved a young construction worker who took his own life in March 2017 after putting in 190 hours of overtime in a single month on the 2020 Olympic stadium.

The history of the *hinomaru* and of depression in Japan showed that argumentation, flexibility and pluralism were built into Japan's

DNA. However much it sometimes suited leaders to downplay all three, as antithetical to the national character, periods of crisis and opportunity tended to bring them out. So it was conceivable that between the lingering trauma of March 2011 and the promise of Tokyo 2020 those seeking to nudge the country in new directions might find some means of doing so. The LDP and its allies had one vision of what Japan ought to look like in 2020 and beyond. But what others were there, and how might they gain a little traction?

*

A few weeks after Japan's triple disasters unfolded, a video was posted to YouTube. A man, in jeans, shirt, sunglasses and a hat, walks into a small, dimly lit room. He sits down on a stool, picks up a black acoustic guitar and launches into a slightly amateurish blues progression. The song is soon recognizable as a cover of 'Zutto suki dattandaze' ('I Always Loved You'), by the singer-songwriter Saitō Kazuyoshi. It featured in a cosmetics advert not long ago. But this is a cover version with a difference. In place of the romance of the original comes furious talk of Japan's fifty-four nuclear reactors, and of how television adverts have been saying for years that they are safe – when now we all know that they aren't.

The singer steadily warms to his theme. His vocals pick up. His playing seems to improve. And he builds to his chorus:

> It was always a lie!
> And now it's been exposed.
> It was always such a lie!
> 'Nuclear power is safe'.

Saitō Kazuyoshi would no doubt be consulting his lawyers. For someone to hijack his music in this way risked his own reputation by association, in an industry where the rules on acceptable conduct were very clear. Outright government censorship of music had ended with the Occupation. But the ethics code adopted back in the early 1950s, partly in response to worries about the corruption of young souls, was still very much in force. The body responsible for overseeing it, Recorin (Recording Industry Ethics Regulatory Commission), remained on the look-out for anything that disturbed national or public order, was disrespectful of life or justice, appeared to condone criminal or anti-social behaviour, or was sexually obscene or discriminatory. Record companies, careful of their liabilities and their artists' public image, checked all lyrics well in advance of a song's release. Previously rejected lyrics were circulated amongst producers, as examples of what to avoid lest they end up having to re-record their music and reprint their packaging.

Commercial broadcasters, under pressure from large and influential advertisers, imposed severe restrictions of their own: opposing anything, for example, that 'disgraced the authority of the government'. This cover song would be getting nowhere near a radio or a television – that much was clear. 'Radiation is on the wind,' the man was singing, knee pumping away with angry energy, 'When will the government wake up?!'

Few people would be interested in this sort of thing anyway. Conventional wisdom had it that young Japanese grew up expecting their entertainers to be friendly, companionable and empathic. They didn't want preachers or agitators.

Or did they? The YouTube cover song ended up going viral, shared and re-uploaded faster than frantic staff at Saitō's record label could have it taken down. 'Finally, a protest song!' exclaimed one fan on social media. 'His courage is exactly what we needed,' said another. Saitō himself turned out to be far from upset by it all. He would be launching no legal action – he was the man in the video.

It was a rare and risky thing to have done. Musicians had been known, on occasion, to take political matters into their own hands. The bassist for a band called Les Rallizes Dénudés had helped to hijack the Japan Airlines flight in 1970, and was still living in North Korea nearly half a century later. And yet a part of Japan's apparent disconnect between entertainment and politics was the fact that protest and mainstream pop generally had little to do with one another. The country boasted the largest music industry on the planet outside the United States, thanks to 'J-Pop' acts like SMAP and AKB48. Constant traffic between a honeycomb of musical and fashion subcultures and big corporate backers helped to produce stunning international success stories like Babymetal, an award-winning fusion of idol culture, Japanese

Gothic, Punk Lolita fashion and warp-speed heavy metal. But this creative and commercial trailblazing was combined with close control of artists by powerful management companies, both on and off stage.

Musicians working in Japan's enormous underground scene – ranging across punk, pop, heavy metal, folk and EDM – were less encumbered. But festival sponsors and venue owners could always turn them away if they started to cause trouble. 'Nine is a beautiful number' sang a punk vocalist in Tokyo's Kōenji neighbourhood, renowned for its small music venues, record shops and vintage clothes stores. His was not a genre known for subtle allusion. This was political code. It would be hard for anyone to object to the lyric, and yet fans would understand the reference: to the Constitution's peace clause – Article 9 – and by extension to Abe's grand plans.

Saitō Kazuyoshi's very public YouTube venture was a sign of its times. The disasters of March 2011 were so catastrophic, and claims about safety shortcuts and cover-ups so incendiary, that for a while people thought Japan might be entering a period of real transition. Saitō Kazuyoshi began to perform his 'cover' song at concerts, despite initial attempts by his management team to stop him. Sakamoto Ryūichi, part of the enormously influential Yellow Magic Orchestra and winner of an Oscar for the score of *The Last Emperor*, joined the novelist Ōe Kenzaburō in organizing a 'Sayonara Genpatsu' – 'Goodbye Nuclear Power' – rally in Tokyo's Yoyogi Park in July 2012. Alongside them was Setouchi Jakuchō, novelist and final client of Kosawa Heisaku, and now, to her many followers, Japan's modern conscience, exposing the psychological and moral damage done by Japan's 'vulgar' political class. Rallies like these attracted tens of thousands of people – numbers not seen since the Anpo protests of 1960. A veteran of those earlier protests, Sakamoto told the crowds of his pride at seeing Japanese people once again finding their voices.

Many others were active up in Tōhoku. The exhaustion suffered by local officials and emergency services in the region was testament to their ceaseless, all but sleepless work on behalf of their communities. But civil society showed a purpose and nimbleness that central government seemed once again to lack during the crucial first hours and days after disaster struck. Some sent money into the region. Others travelled there in person to clear dried mud and debris, and to help families settle into temporary housing. Bloggers, Twitter users and crowdsourced citizen science websites like Safecast took up the slack where information from the government and TEPCO fell short, sharing their own radiation readings (from devices placed, amongst other locations, on the tops of schools), along with concerns about unsafe food and its illicit distribution. Later, as the rebuilding process began and testing of agricultural produce showed that lingering public concerns were out of proportion to actual risks – which were very low for most parts of Tōhoku, and falling year on year – non-profit organizations assisted farmers in re-establishing the public trust that the inadequacies of official information had helped to undermine.

The difficulties of building momentum for systemic change quickly became clear. Sakamoto Ryūichi's outspokenness on the nuclear issue ended up costing him sponsorships and television appearances. He faced a barrage of criticism from people urging him to stick to his day job as a musician. The nationalistic *Sankei Shimbun* newspaper sneered at 'a stylish person of culture' who lived in a pricey condo in New York, yet saw fit to lecture people in Japan about where they got their electricity. And despite widespread public opposition and the deployment by protestors of everything from sound-trucks to SoundCloud in getting their messages across, nuclear restarts continued, while the LDP went all but unchallenged in the Diet. Meanwhile, those who

Anti-nuclear protest leaders: Setouchi Jakuchō (*middle*) and
Ōe Kenzaburō (*left*) (2012)

hoped that rebuilding in Tōhoku might persuade central government to make long overdue concessions of power to local authorities – both there and in general – had yet to see this materialize.

Across the later 2010s, an ongoing post-Fukushima opportunity began to merge with an Olympic one. As with Tokyo 1964, so with Tokyo 2020: the Games offered Japan both a platform for fresh national storytelling, in front of an international audience, and the prospect of global embarrassment if its claims rang hollow. This dual potential might end up being squandered. Japan might enter a post-Olympic funk, from which it would take some other, perhaps much less welcome, set of events for the country's twenty-first century challenges to find clear solutions. But for a short period before, during and after the Games, Japan's leadership would be susceptible to domestic persuasion and pressure of a kind that no opposition party or political movement by itself looked capable of generating.

*

Unity in Diversity

We live in a world that is diverse, rather than homogenous, and the differences among us span wide-ranging areas, from race, colour, sex, sexual orientation, language, religion, political or other opinion, national or social origin, property, birth, level of ability or other status. Readily accepting these differences and respecting one another allows peace to be maintained, and society to continue to develop and flourish. The Tokyo 2020 Games will foster a welcoming environment and raise awareness of unity in diversity among citizens of the world.

Tokyo 2020 Games Foundation Plan

Japan had, across its long history, been a diverse place in pretty much all the ways that the first line of 'Unity in Diversity' proposed. But modernizing leaders had developed a habit of treating difference as a national security issue: enfeebling or corrupting a national resolve without which the country would swiftly fall prey to Western power – military, economic or ideological. In 2005, Foreign Minister Asō Tarō offered a stark account of what critics called Japan's 'myth of homogeneity'. Japan, he said, is 'one nation, one civilization, one language, one culture, and one race – the like of which there is no other'. If diversity belonged anywhere, it belonged in the world of entertainment – in people's desires to explore and assert a range of lifestyles and identities, sealed safely away in the realms of private or shared fantasy and closely managed consumerism.

Asō was one of a handful of Japanese politicians with a knack for clumsy or controversial comments, from appearing to praise the Nazis to suggesting that Japan's elderly ought to 'hurry up and die'. But though few Japanese might have expressed it in the way he did, homogeneity in the sense of shared roots and shared ideals was one of modern Japan's most successful stories: a myth both in the colloquial sense of something untrue, and in the sense of something powerful enough to create new social and cultural facts on the ground, by shaping common-sense assumptions, thoughts and behaviour across many generations.

In these circumstances, people might be inclined to feel more than usually despairing of a phrase like 'Unity in Diversity'. Here was boilerplate Olympic banality, no more meaningful than Tokyo 2020's other two core concepts – Achieving Personal Best and Connecting To Tomorrow – and destined to join the physical detritus of the Games, swept up and disposed of in the hours after the closing ceremony.

Such scepticism would be well placed. 'Unity in Diversity' does not offer a straightforward successor to the older story, which boils down to unity *versus* diversity. It is not a vision of what Japan might quickly become – for many, it will raise the spectre of a collective loss of self. 'Unity in Diversity' could be useful instead as a puzzle and a timely provocation, helping to inspire once again in Japan the sorts of searching questions about how nations are built and sustained that had propelled astonishing progress at key points since the 1850s.

By the late 2010s, the time for searching questions had clearly come. Japan's working-age population was on a steep downward trajectory, with forecasters predicting that by 2040 a full third of a rapidly shrinking population would be over the age of sixty-five. The country's fertility rate had begun to fall below the level required to maintain the population back in 1974. Economic decline and deregulation had then exacerbated the problem, apparently leaving fewer young Japanese feeling wealthy or secure enough to take the risk of starting a family.

Women continued to suffer inequity in the jobs market, along with the worry that becoming a mother would effectively end their chances of further study or of forging a career. An Equal Employment Opportunity Law had been passed back in 1985, prohibiting gender discrimination in matters of training, benefits, dismissal and retirement, while encouraging firms to improve recruitment practices. But a report more than thirty years later ranked Japan lowest in the OECD for the proportion of women in management positions, lowest for the role of women in politics, and very near the bottom for its gender pay gap.

Japan's leaders were struggling to find and implement acceptable solutions. Survey evidence revealed a population yet to be convinced of the benefits of immigration. A modest wave of migration back in the 1980s had led to anxious talk of a 'foreign worker problem' in Japan. And although attitudes had since softened – helped by revelations in 2001 that this 'problem' extended to the imperial family: Emperor Akihito spoke publicly that year of his own family's Korean roots – people still worried about diluting or imperilling cherished social virtues, from very low crime rates (even in the hardest of economic times) to customary patterns and standards of behaviour which it was thought incomers would struggle with or not bother to learn. Politicians unwilling to risk a serious public debate about immigration were accused of creating backdoors into Japan for desperately needed foreign workers. A Technical Intern Training Programme, established back in the 1990s as a means of transferring technical skills to developing countries via time-limited internships, had since morphed into something resembling a guest worker programme, with poor pay and conditions.

Some in the LDP hoped, in any case, to meet the country's needs by other means: by getting more women and people of retirement age into work, and somehow raising the birth rate. And yet here too there were obstacles. The government established one of the world's most generous paternity leave schemes: up to a year, on nearly 60 per cent of full salary. But fewer than 3 per cent of fathers took up the offer, concerned about appearing cavalier in their work ethic and finding their prospects diminished when they returned to the office. Money was pledged for building more day-care centres, the pace forced thanks to a viral blog post – 'Drop Dead Japan!' – by a mother who risked losing her job because she had failed to find care for her child. But residents' organizations anxious about noise levels and traffic congestion routinely blocked plans for the construction of new facilities.

Humans were hard. Robots, at least, ought to be biddable. Japanese technology firms competed with one another in the course of the 2010s to create cuddly-looking 'care-bots' that could lift and assist the elderly and infirm, lead them in a gentle exercise routine, and increasingly interact with them as artificial intelligence research advanced. Alongside helping people to stay in their own homes for longer, and reducing pressure in the labour market (fewer foreign carers required; more Japanese adults freed from family duties to return to paid employment), the likes of 'Robear' offered Japanese industry a means of regaining its reputation for world-leading tech innovation, which seemed of late to have drifted across the Pacific to northern California's Silicon Valley. There was major export potential, too. China's ageing population was set to render it an eye-wateringly lucrative market for hi-tech care by the middle of the twenty-first century. Middle-aged Chinese presently caught between a love of Japan's pop culture and an inherited antipathy towards its past and its politicians might end their days being carried around by a Japanese robot or calling a self-driving Japanese toilet over to their bedsides.

But technology was set to be less a straightforward solution to Japan's demographic woes than part of a fundamental questioning process, a national push-and-pull now under way and heating up, over what the twenty-first century nation should become. The family had been at the heart of state power and national identity in the previous century: a social unit rooted in cooperation, care and a complementarity of roles, fundamental to a person's sense of self. The nature of those roles and relationships changed over time, but the basic definition of family had largely held across the modern era, as Japan moved from an inter-generational model to a conjugal one.

The question now was this: could – should – this definition of 'family' live on, as the shared cultural core across a growing diversity of households? The conjugal family had been in decline since the 1970s.

More homes now were made up instead of individuals, childless couples, single parents, or adults forced by circumstances to stay on with ageing parents. Robear was on the rise. Volunteer organizations were offering care and companionship for the elderly, increasing numbers of whom were taking their own lives rather than carry on in loneliness or poverty, or risk becoming a burden to their relatives. With few national politicians willing to champion LGBT rights, more and more local governments around Japan – beginning in 2015 with the district of Shibuya, in Tokyo – were taking it on themselves to offer official status to same-sex couples, for the purposes of renting apartments or consenting to one another's medical treatment. Did people still want to think in terms of a distinctly 'Japanese' family model? And if so, could those core values of cooperation, care and complementarity do the trick, bridging the gap even into an era of the human–robotic household?

What about 'community' – another pillar of modern Japan? The old conception was of something tight-knit and exclusive: neighbourhood; workplace; a national community rooted in a combination (shifting over time) of history, custom, blood, spirit and international embattlement. What were the core values here that might help women in the workplace, fathers seeking paternity leave or parents in need of childcare facilities?

If part of the puzzle of 'unity in diversity' was how to square the high value that people in Japan had grown up placing on unity with a pragmatic need, now, to embrace diversity, then Japan was enviably well resourced. A range of people across the country had spent much or all of the modern period living on the margins of Japan's mainstream stories, forced to weigh the sorts of questions that the country as a whole was now asking itself and to engage in a push-and-pull with the state and with society at large. Their experiences were mixed, their answers as yet incomplete. But there was food for thought here, perhaps even the seeds of some far-future Japan story.

Ainu land had for centuries served as the mainland's savage far-northern periphery. The Ainu were said to live in holes and nests, to drink blood, and to be dangerously swift on their feet. A few Japanese traders and settlers ventured across the Tsugaru Strait in search of salmon, animal skins and cultivable land, but for the most part the island was an exile destination with which domain lords threatened recalcitrant samurai.

Modernity had changed all that. Desperate to secure their new borders and to exercise – partly for international consumption – their responsibility to civilize the poor, the uncouth and the uneducated, Meiji-era leaders had set in motion a mass migration north. They seized Ainu land and destroyed their economy. By the turn of the twentieth century, the Ainu made up just 2 per cent of the population of what was now 'Hokkaidō' ('northern sea circuit'). Many of the Ainu were so mired in combinations of poverty and alcoholism that they were regarded as a naturally 'dying race' – as opposed to one being actively killed off.

A 'Hokkaidō Former Aborigines Protection Law', passed in 1899, revealed in its very name a degree of confusion and ambivalence about unity and diversity lying somewhere beneath the surface of Japan's modern story of homogeneity. There were attempts to assimilate the Ainu to a mainlander definition of 'Japanese': limited allotments of land were made (generously created from the stolen stock) to turn fishers and hunters into farmers; appearances and styles of dress were aligned with those down south; names were changed; and education was offered in Japanese while Ainu culture was laid to rest in museums. But differentiation and discrimination proved deeply attractive also. Many Ainu children were sent to special 'Native Schools', while those who attended general Japanese ones faced constant bullying long into the post-war era – including cries of 'Ah! Inu!': 'Ah – a dog!'

Ainu themselves, across the decades, were divided about how best to further their prospects in modern Japan. Some plumped for a mainlander conception of 'unity', moving away from Hokkaidō and leaving their Ainu identity behind. Those who preferred to maintain their own sense of community discovered some of the many ways in which 'diversity' could go wrong. An estimated 4.3 million visitors passed through the 'Hall of Mankind' at Osaka's Industrial Exhibition in 1903, gawping at a 'native Ainu village' while Ainu adults were paid to provide some theatre: stomping around, shouting and singing, and selling meat. A government tourist brochure in 1941 advised visitors to Hokkaidō to seek out one of two Ainu villages where, if they were prepared to 'defray the expenses of gathering them and giving them *sake*', Ainu would dance and sing for them. Other Ainu, the author warned, preferred to keep a lower profile.

'You are therefore requested, while looking at them, to refrain from laughing without any reason, or assuming an attitude of mockery.'

Fortunes only improved for the Ainu when they were able to exercise a degree of control over how their past and present were understood in Japan. An Ainu Cultural Promotion Law was passed in 1997, replacing the old Protection Law and marking Japan's first ever acknowledgement in legislation of an ethnic minority. Old place names were researched, and remnants of Ainu oral literature and craftwork were recovered and revived. In 2008, a Diet resolution officially acknowledged the Ainu as an indigenous people of Japan. Important problems of resource and land rights for the Ainu would take many years to settle. But Japan's basic understanding of 'unity' seemed to have been questioned, and found capacious and robust.

There was less cause for optimism elsewhere in the country. Nearly a quarter of a century on from the rape of 1995 and subsequent promises to relocate US Marine Corps Air Station Futenma, relatively little had changed for Okinawans. Relocation arrangements remained stalled: few people wanted a military base opening up near to where they lived. And while new cases came to light of sexual violence against Okinawan women by American servicemen and private contractors, and fragments of military hardware occasionally fell from the skies onto civilian areas below, politicians in Tokyo could do little more than go through a public ritual of protesting to their American allies. The great bane of Okinawan life could not be wished away: condemned to be the lynchpin – and main bargaining chip – in a US–Japan security relationship that neither party could yet afford to dispense with.

Periodic 'Okinawa booms' across the 1990s and beyond, in music, food and literature, helped to at least earn the region a recognized place in Japan's broader cultural mix. But too much of it happened on mainlanders' terms. The hit song *'Shima Uta'* ('Island Song'), in 1993, had used Okinawan musical instruments, notably the *sanshin*, and acknowledged both the region's beauty and its troubles. And yet it was by a band – The Boom – who hailed from Yamanashi prefecture, not far from Tokyo. Mainland films and TV dramas set in Okinawa tended to harp on the islands' rustic charms and laidback lifestyle, conflating poverty with simplicity, and underdevelopment with innocence or a purity of roots – Okinawa remained Japan's poorest prefecture, reliant on the '3 ks' of tourism (*kankō*), providing services to US bases (*kichi*), and carrying out public works projects (*kōkyō kōji*). Even Okinawan bands like Begin (from the Yaeyama Islands) and Orange Range found there was a fine line between sharing Okinawa's mixed musical tradition – folk, rock and rap, incorporating influences from South East Asia and the United States – and packaging it commercially for a main-land market in search of accessible authenticity.

The brief detention by US forces in 2016 of the well-known Okinawan novelist Medoruma Shun – while protesting the Futenma relocation – served as a reminder of how difficult it was to survive as a viable community when your cultural presence went unmatched by a political voice that could not be ignored. Koreans living in Japan knew this only too well. A 'Korean Wave' of K-Pop and television soaps washing over the country since the 1990s showed little sign of receding. And major cultural figures like the comedian, actor and director Kitano 'Beat' Takeshi were increasingly willing to discuss – and be proud of – their Korean ancestry. But just as the Ainu had lived for many decades with the ambiguity of a 'Former Aborigines Protection Law', so the vast majority of people of Korean descent in Japan (numbering more than half a million people in all) were stuck with the notion of '*zainichi*': Japan-resident. Used mostly for people who traced their family roots back to pre-1945 migration from the Korean peninsula (much of it forced rather than voluntary) and who now possessed permanent residency rather than citizenship, it sug-gested dwelling without belonging – either to state or to nation.

Official early twenty-first century rhetoric about 'multicultural co-existence' in Japan (*tabunka kyōsei*) had yet to ease this sense of homelessness amongst some Zainichi Koreans, or to do much about the discrimination they faced. *Tabunka kyōsei* struggled to compete with a very different idea about the country still found on the streets, online and occasionally in the mouths of prominent politicians: Japan as 'home' to a homogeneous people that welcomed any visitor who could produce a return ticket, while tolerating – on sufferance and at arm's length – the longer-term presence of non- or partially Japanese minorities. In 2014, as Okinawan and Ainu delegates joined the first UN-backed World Conference on Indigenous Peoples, a government committee had to be set up to investigate hate speech against Chinese, South East Asians and particularly Zainichi Koreans. As with Okinawans, many in these three groups continued to find their employment prospects confined to three 'ks': in this case, jobs that no one else wanted to do because they were *kitsui* (physically demanding), *kitanai* (dirty) or *kiken* (dangerous).

And yet popular interest in authenticity and roots is something with which Okinawans and other minority communities in Japan might be able to work – a glue of sorts, binding people together. Of interest too, for Japan's future, might be an apparent trend amongst young Okinawans towards going beyond assimilation versus differentiation – being 'Japanese' or being 'Okinawan'. People are talking about themselves as both, with the 'Japanese' part connecting them with other historically neglected regions of the country such as Tōhoku.

The possibility of being several things at once can also be a means for people still basically signed up to the idea – and the ideal – of homogeneity to begin to dissect it a little, and for 'diversity' to be thought of not in terms of a mainstream and its margins, but the multifariousness of every person's existence. Advocates for minority rights in Japan feel a pressing need for this to happen. They have found two things indispensable for success in their campaigns: power over how their communities and causes are represented, and change in how others see them and treat them. Disability rights campaigners welcomed Japan's belated ratification, in 2014, of the United Nations Convention on the Rights of Persons with Disabilities. It meant that in future, if companies and institutions failed to provide reasonable adaptations to their services – so that disabled people could exercise fundamental rights and freedoms on an equal basis – they could be penalized for discrimination. But physical or intellectual disabilities are still being compounded by a social one: a lingering understanding of disabled people's place in a community as that of supplicants and grateful recipients.

Japan's former outcast communities face a related problem. Once known by names like *hinin* ('non-people') and *eta* ('full of filth'), they are referred to in the modern era as *burakumin*, after the word for the hamlets (*buraku*) in which they had lived. But many in an estimated population of around 1.2 million do not want to be referred to as anything at all. Their minority status is based not on ethnicity or on a history of which they were proud, but on stigmatization stemming from their work in professions once regarded as unclean. The solution, said some, is for the concept and category of *burakumin* to cease to exist. By the early 2000s, some in the Buraku rights movement regarded this as having been achieved: decades of government 'assimilation' (*dōwa*) spending on homes, schools and other facilities in *burakumin* neighbourhoods, alongside compensatory education for Buraku children and social education for the general population, aimed at tackling old stigmas, has resulted in few Japanese thinking about the issue any longer. But in 2016 along came a reminder for rights activists of how precarious a position it was to have to rely on others to alter or forget their prejudices: a new law had to be passed, responding to new forms of discrimination, including the moving online of long-running attempts to locate the postal addresses of *burakumin* communities in order to vet potential employees or marriage partners.

There is no shortage, in Japan, of ways in which a person can be many things at once. There is scope for a more vital regionalism to return, moving from a carefully packaged sense of local produce and cuisine (give a person a prefecture and they could name you a *meibutsu* – 'famous product' – which the local airport would likely be selling as a souvenir) towards real devolved power. The global rise of identity movements might end up making contributions of its own: class and gender, sexuality and religion, subcultural hobbies and habits, even shared problems or medical diagnoses – depression and cancer blogs, and online support communities, were springing up around Japan in the 2010s.

Even food – a serious, and seriously diverse business in Japan – can offer inspiration. There is Chinese ramen; *karē raisu* (curry rice) from India by way of Britain (married to the long-ago Chinese import of sticky rice cultivation); *korokke* (croquette) and *tonkatsu* (pork cutlet) from France; *kasutera* (castella) cake from Portugal; hamburgers, pizza and spaghetti. Japan doesn't have a core national cuisine plus tolerated outliers Nor does it have a 'foreign cuisine problem'. It has a constellation of dishes that made up a recognizably Japanese whole, worked around a common cultural core of treating food with respect: in the choice of ingredients and presentation, in expertise (even culinary lineages) and service in restaurants, and in many a mealtime conversation all but exclusively devoted to what is on the table.

However Japan chooses to answer the questions it faces in the early twenty-first century, recent history suggests that it would take a combination of effort and artistry and the passage of time for the results to become part of what is a surprisingly – perhaps reassuringly – porous national identity and core. Just as 'Unity in Diversity' was best approached as a puzzle rather than a slogan or a piece of hectoring advice for immediate implementation, so an ultimately more significant moment for Japan than the summer of 2020 might well be 1 May 2019.

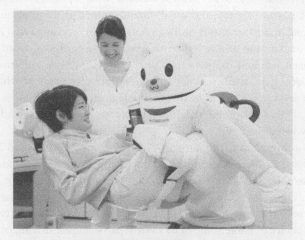

A demonstration of 'Robear' in Nagoya, 2015

Ainu celebrate the Autumn Ritual of Kotannomi, 2014

Eras and era changes mean a great deal in modern Japan. The former serve as chapters in the country's story – chronological, but each with a thematic flavour. The latter offer a chance to look backwards and forwards, taking stock of an ongoing search for the nation and mustering fresh resolve. The Meiji era, from 1868 to 1912, had seen a country pass through revolution to mourn a restored Emperor on his death. Taishō (1912–26) was associated with democratization, the rise of a mass society and an ill-fated attempt at internationalism. The long and tumultuous Shōwa era (1926–89) encompassed militarism, devastation and a return to new purpose. Heisei, from 1989, had been haunted by memories of the previous era's ambition and destructiveness, while seeing the fragmentation of much of what that era went on to build. But as the world's legions of Japanophiles would attest, it had also rendered the country more accessible and more widely loved than ever before.

On 1 May 2019, the sun rose on the Reiwa era. Crown Prince Naruhito, great-great-grandson of the Meiji Emperor, ascended the Chrysanthemum Throne following the long-planned abdication of his father, Emperor Akihito. This new era and this new reign will one day carry powerful associations of their own. For the moment, one can find in the choice of name some of modern Japan's deepest driving energies. There is confidence: an era name drawn for the first time not from classical Chinese poetry but from a Japanese anthology, the *Man'yōshū*. There is re-invention via fresh combinations of old and new: *wa* (peace) makes its twentieth appearance in an era name, while *rei* makes its first. And there is uncertainty. The poem from which Reiwa is drawn tells of an apricot tree blossoming in springtime. But though *rei* in that context means 'harmony' or 'auspicious', most Japanese know it from the word *meirei*: an order, or command. What might Japan's leaders require of their people in this new age?

As Japan prepares to find out, the most valuable reflections on how to sustain a nation – as a set of stories at once discovered and created; a set of clothes that we weave and wear at the same time – are to be found in what adults hope children will grow up to believe. All sorts of things happen in life, Anpanman seems to be showing Ringo Bōya as their adventure unfolds. We never know what will come next. But to hold on to hope, and to go forward together, is to find yourself 'home' at last.

Epilogue

It was a moonlit night in early summer. A thin fog hovered just above where the waves broke on the beach. Fukuji spotted two people walking: a woman and a man. He frowned. The woman was definitely his wife.

Following them as they headed off towards a cavern inside a nearby promontory, he called out his wife's name. The woman turned, and smiled. He saw now who the man was. He had been deeply in love with Fukuji's wife before Fukuji had married her. And he, like her, had died in the tsunami.

Fukuji's wife called back to him: 'I am married now, to this man.' 'But don't you love your children?' Fukuji cried out in reply. She paused at that, and began to sob. While Fukuji looked sadly at his feet, the woman and the man drifted quietly away.

More than six years on from the chaos and destruction of March 2011, the waters of the Pacific Ocean lapped gently at the Tōhoku coast; a deep, vibrant blue under a powerful sun. But roads around the Fukushima plant nearby still featured flashing signs at regular intervals. They informed passers-by not of speed limits or weather conditions, but of current radiation levels, measured in microsieverts. These went up and up, as you moved into a zone where you would have to stay inside your car if you broke down, then descended again as you left it for relative safety and normality. What looked like DIY gardening supplies were piled high on either side of the road: tightly filled plastic sacks shaped into taut, rectangular slabs. Inside was radioactive topsoil, stripped off the land in hopes of enticing former residents back to the area. But just as no one in Japan wanted these bags, so few of those residents could yet imagine making this place home again. Cars and corrugated iron roofs rusted amidst tall, untended grass, partially obscuring empty homes on which the paint was slowly peeling away.

Told to the folklorist Yanagita Kunio, the story of Fukuji and his wife became number ninety-nine in his *Tōno no Monogatari* (*The Legends of Tōno*), published in 1910. One hundred and one years later, in the wake of a new tsunami, people in Tōhoku had again seen and felt the presence of ghosts. Men and women dressed in winter coats, at the height of summer, walking on the beach. People hailing taxis, asking after a loved one, or checking 'Have I died?' before disappearing from the back seat. One survivor reported receiving a call on her mobile phone, using the ring-tone reserved for a close relative who had passed away. Another watched as a toy truck belonging to her lost child pushed itself haltingly around the room.

Writers in Tōhoku began collecting these accounts. They were the folk-tales of tomorrow. Fleeting moments of contact, with loved ones to whom goodbyes had not been said, seemed to these new chroniclers entirely natural. Certainly, fear was out of the question. As one put it, 'Thousands of people had just died at a stroke. What was left to be scared of?' Another wondered whether, now, as in Yanagita's day, urban Japanese might be in need of what this sparsely populated region, with its rugged, dramatic landscape, had long offered: exposure to nature, bestowing on people a closer apprehension of life's coming and going.

Reverend Taniyama Yōzō, a Buddhist monk and pioneer of disaster care, heard plenty of ghost stories. He also chanted sutras, removed rubble or made tea, depending on a person's needs. 'There may be things that Buddhism doesn't hear, or see,' he said. 'We should listen.' His friend Reverend Kaneta Taiō took the same approach with his triple entendre 'Café de Monk': a disaster-area drinks service run out of a pick-up truck, where a monk played Thelonious Monk records and listened to people express their *monku* – their complaints about life – in their own ways.

'Complaints' was a gently witty understatement. Kaneta had witnessed suffering so intense and so completely disorienting that it sometimes drew from people words and gestures that seemed to him diamond-like in their purity and preciousness – 'more beautiful', he recalled, 'than a sutra'. There were many other forces besides suffering in Tōhoku's landscape, some seeping slowly southwards towards Japan's major cities, and all unpredictable in their eventual consequences for the country. Sadness. A visceral anger, quiet but not likely to dissipate quickly. A profound mistrust of power. And an energy and determination to reconstruct, but not on the old terms.

At the Peaceful Love Rock Festival, in Koza City, Okinawa, the sun was going down, a warm evening was settling in, and a crowd of adults and children were drinking and fanning themselves, mopping their faces with hand-towels. A pudgy, balding man took to the open-air stage – an IT consultant from Tokyo. But there was something familiar, from another time and place, about the tight white trousers and white vest, the moustache and the exaggerated strut, the toying with the stem of a microphone stand. The man sat at a piano, a spotlight found him, and a hush came over the crowd as he began to work away theatrically at the keyboard:

I've paid my dues, time after time . . .

The ghost of Freddie Mercury, after a fashion. Drenched in sweat, and rising now from his seat as the key changed and the rest of the band joined in. He unfurled a huge Union Jack behind his shining head and across his back – and then revealed its reverse, to delirious cheers: the Okinawan flag. From one angst-ridden island nation, eastward across a vast continent to another, and down south here to a third; raising Ryūkyūan spirits just yards from a military base. 'We are the champions, my friend . . .'

Further north, the calm of morning. At the uppermost tip of Tōhoku, Mount Fear looms out of the landscape. Winding your way up its steep, densely wooded side, you arrive eventually at a plateau. Sulphur and incense mingle on the air. Here, in the caldera of an active volcano, lies one of Japan's fabled gateways to the underworld. A still, lonely lake, surrounded by a craggy, lunar landscape of blasted white-grey granite. Gentle puffs of steam, all but invisible, rise from gaps in the rock.

At the back of a small tarpaulin shack nearby, a woman sits in simple white robes, twisting and rattling a string of highly polished horse-chestnut beads in her hands. Her eyes closed, she mumbles away without pause, as though to herself. *I was so surprised to have died there I was looking forward to getting out of hospital and then I woke up here I've wanted to visit you in your dreams thank you for coming to find me don't worry I'm fine I'm looking out for you gosh but I was so surprised to have died how annoying here I am . . .*

Kneeling in front of her, in tears, are her clients. Stretching away from the tent, back in a line across the courtyard, are families waiting for their turn: to reach grandmothers, grandfathers, parents, brothers and sisters.

In the car park sit the very latest models: bodywork dewy, windscreens misted, as the sun sits on the horizon. Some of the consultations with the *itako*, or shaman, are being recorded on video camera. People tap away at smartphones in the queue. But what this woman in the tent is doing renders even the 1,200-year-old Buddhist temple in whose grounds she sits positively youthful by comparison.

Both traditions survive because they understand change, taking on new forms when they must. A senior monk here has joined a recent publishing trend for clerical self-help. But he doesn't believe in the solidity of books or streamlined bodywork, or perhaps even the temple's wooden walkway, standing on rickety stilts a foot or so above hot, sulphurous rocks, water trickling around them warm and yellow. You are not, today, he says, who you were yesterday. The same will apply tomorrow. People insist on making futile distinctions about death, he adds – either ghosts exist, or it's all about grief; either we appear again somewhere else, or we don't – because on the whole they have yet to understand life: its reality, and also its unreality.

Away from the temple, amidst the steam, stones of grey, white and black are piled up in several places – a metre high, several metres wide. At first sight, they look like deposits of rubble. In fact, they are cairns, dedicated to people who have led the shortest of lives. Young couples mill around, saying little.

Poked into the tops of the cairns, alongside statuettes of Jizō – protector of children and voyagers – are toy plastic windmills, in bright, glossy shades of pink and blue and yellow and white. Something for babies and children to play with, on the other side.

The very lightest of touches. In humour and feeling. In a taste for life's variety and vitality. In a talent for 'maybe', given an unknowable world.

A light breeze passes through, and the little coloured windmills respond: turning, squeaking into the silence. They come to a rest again. But never for long.

Chronology

1774   Sugita Genpaku's translation of a Dutch anatomy text appears, as *Kaitai Shinsho* ('New Text on Anatomy').

1787   Hayashi Shihei's *Kaikoku Heidan* ('Military Defence of a Maritime Nation') published.

1804   A Russian envoy, Nikolai Rezanov, arrives in Nagasaki seeking trade with Japan.

1808   The *Phaeton* Incident.

July 1853   Commodore Matthew C. Perry arrives in Edo Bay; hands over President Millard Fillmore's letter.

February–March 1854   Perry returns, and a Treaty of Peace and Amity is signed between Japan and the United States (the Treaty of Kanagawa).

1858   The first of Japan's 'Unequal Treaties' is signed in July: the United States–Japan Treaty of Amity and Commerce. The Commission for Foreign Countries is established.

1866   Under punitive pressure from authorities in Edo, Chōshū secretly signs a mutual aid agreement with Satsuma domain.

MODERN JAPAN

January 1868   Rebel forces, largely from Satsuma and Chōshū domains, take the imperial palace in Kyoto. The teenage Emperor Mutsuhito declares the restoration of imperial rule.

April 1868   Japan's new leaders issue the Charter Oath, as a statement of aims; the separation of Shinto and Buddhism begins.

May–October 1868   Edo falls to the rebel armies, and is renamed 'Tokyo'. The Emperor's reign name is decided: 'Meiji'.

1869   Tokyo becomes the capital city, home to the Dajōkan, the ruling Council of State. The abolition of the old domain system begins, with the return of regional registers to the Emperor. Old status groups abolished. The last of the Tokugawa forces surrender in the far north of Japan: the Boshin War is at an end. The Hokkaidō Colonization Office is set up, and the country's first Press Law enacted, encouraging the creation of newspapers and journals.

1870–71 Ministries of Public Works, Industry and Education are created. Telegraph and postal services are established. The yen becomes the national currency. Prefectures replace the old domains. A much-satirized 'Great Promulgation' campaign represents an early attempt to politicize Shinto.

1872 Ginza gutted by fire, a new-style rebuild in brick begins. Shinbashi Station is opened, to musical fanfare. A banking system is established, and Japan transfers from a lunar to the Gregorian calendar. Sunday becomes a day of rest. Christmas is a national holiday. A 'Fundamental Code of Education' creates a national education system, up to university level.

1873 Japan's warrior class is replaced by commoner conscription (via the 'Blood Tax'). A uniform land tax, payable in cash, represents the basis for Japan's future revenue. Saigō Takamori and Itagaki Taisuke resign from the government after a dispute over Korea. Proposal for the establishment of the *Meirokusha*: the 'Meiji 6 Society'.

1874 Demands are made for greater public participation in government. A People's Rights Movement is touched off. The Taiwan Expedition.

1875 A new Press Law gives the government limited powers over print publications.

1876 Samurai lose stipends. Gunboat diplomacy with Korea yields an accord similar to the unequal treaties under which Japan is labouring. Mitsui Bank – Japan's first private bank – and Mitsui Trading Company are launched.

1877 Satsuma Rebellion. Tokyo University established, becoming Japan's first 'Imperial University' in 1886. Tokyo Shōkonsha, established in 1869 to honour those who died fighting for the Emperor in the Boshin War, is renamed Yasukuni Shrine.

1878   Japan acquires elected prefectural and city assemblies.

1879   The last Ryūkyūan king is forced to abdicate, and 'Okinawa prefecture' is established.

1881   Under pressure from the People's Rights Movement, the government promises a constitution by 1890. Political parties begin to form: Jiyūtō in 1881; Rikken Kaishintō the next year.

1882   The Imperial Rescript to Soldiers and Sailors underscores their loyalty to the Emperor and the requirement for them to stay out of politics.

1883   Press regulations are tightened. The completion of the Rokumeikan.

1884   The Chichibu rebellion. The Gunma Incident.

1885   A Cabinet system replaces the Dajōkan, linking leaders to the bureaucracy – with which the district of Kasumigaseki becomes synonymous across the twentieth century. Itō Hirobumi becomes Japan's first Prime Minister; Inoue Kaoru becomes the first Minister of Foreign Affairs. The Osaka Incident takes place. Inoue Enryō turns his back on a priestly career.

1886   The *Normanton* Incident.

1887   A masquerade ball at the home of Itō Hirobumi becomes notorious in the press, for the foreign affectations of the 'dancing cabinet'. Publication of *Meiji Onna Daigaku* ('The Meiji Greater Learning for Women').

1889   The Constitution of the Empire of Japan is promulgated.

1890   First general election in Japanese history. Imperial Rescript on Education helps to entrench a conservative vision of Japanese values. Women are prohibited from attending political meetings or joining political organizations. Yamagata Aritomo tells the new

Diet of Japan's foreign policy aims, based around a line of sovereignty and a line of advantage.

1894–5 War with China ends in a Japanese victory. The Triple Intervention (Russia, France and Germany) forces the return of some of the gains, including the Liaotung Peninsula.

1897 Kyoto University established.

1898 The Meiji Civil Code becomes law, reinforcing Japan's *ie*-based family arrangements. Russia gains the lease to the Liaotung Peninsula.

1899 Formation of the Association of Japanese Motion Pictures, and the first public showings of movies – featuring geisha dances and recordings of kabuki performances. Hokkaidō Former Aborigines Protection Law.

1900 A new Public Order and Police Law is designed to combat industrial activism; Nitobe Inazō publishes *Bushidō: The Soul of Japan*. School fees abolished, and attendance rises above 90 per cent of girls and boys.

1901 Publication of *Katei no Kairaku* ('The Pleasures of the Home').

1902 The Anglo-Japanese Alliance.

1903–4 Publication of Kuwabara Toshirō's bestselling book *Seishin Reidō*, on spititual healing.

1904–5 A surprise attack by Japanese forces opens the Russo-Japanese War, which ends with an epoch-making victory for Japan. Despite key concessions in southern Manchuria, anger at the terms of the Treaty of Portsmouth contributes to rioting in parts of Japan.

1906 Itō Hirobumi becomes Japan's Resident General in Korea. Formation of the South Manchuria Railway Company. *Sermons of a Buddhist Abbot*, by Shaku Sōen, becomes the first book about Zen to be published in English.

1909 Itō Hirobumi assassinated in Harbin, by a Korean nationalist. Korea is fully annexed by Japan the following year.

1910 A socialist-anarchist plot to assassinate the Emperor is discovered, known later as the High Treason Incident. Publication of Yanagita Kunio's *Tōno no Monogatari* (*The Legends of Tōno*).

1911 Kanno Suga and Kōtoku Shūsui are executed for their involvement in the High Treason Incident. The Tokkō (Special Higher Police) is established, partly in response to the Treason incident. First issue of Hiratsuka Raichō's magazine *Seitō* ('Bluestocking'). A new Factory Law sets rules on safety at work and on the employment of young people, with a minimum working age established of twelve years old.

1912 The Meiji era comes to a close with the death of the Emperor. The Taishō era begins when his son Yoshihito ascends the throne.

1914 Japan declares war on Germany. Anglo-Japanese attack on German base at Tsingtao.

1915 Japan's 'Twenty-One Demands' on China.

1918 Japan participates in the anti-Bolshevik Siberian Expedition. Rice riots contribute to the rise of Hara Kei at the head of Japan's first ever party Cabinet. Kure Shūzō's damning report on the treatment of the mentally ill in Japan is published.

1920 Foundation of the New Woman's Association, by Hiratsuka Raichō, Ichikawa Fusae and others. Japan joins the League of Nations.

1921 Yamakawa Kikue and others found the Red Wave Society, focusing on women workers (in trade unions dominated by men). Large-scale strikes in Kobe, in which Kagawa Toyohiko takes a leadership role.

1922 Public Order and Police Law (1900) amended so that women can join political organizations. Establishment of the Japanese Communist Party.

1923 The Great Kantō Earthquake. Ratification of the Washington Naval Treaty, signed the previous year.

1924 Dissolution of the Japanese Communist Party. Foundation of the Women's Suffrage League by Ichikawa Fusae and others.

Immigration Act passed in the United States, undermining US–Japan relations and Japanese trust in the international order more generally.

1925 Universal manhood suffrage. Peace Preservation Law.

1925–6 Japan's first radio broadcasts, and the emergence of Japan's national broadcaster, NHK.

1926 New parties emerge: a reformed Japanese Communist Party, a Socialist People's Party and the Japan Labour-Farmer Party. The Taishō era comes to a close with the death of the Emperor. The Shōwa era begins when his son Hirohito ascends the throne.

1927 Akutagawa Ryūnosuke's short story *Haguruma* ('Spinning Gears') is published. Akutagawa dies in July.

1928 Mass arrests of leftists.

1929 New York stock market crash, develops into the Great Depression.

1930 *Sarariman: Kyōfu no jidai* ('Salaryman: Age of Anxiety') is published. The London Naval Treaty, its terms heavily criticized in Japan.

September 1931 Manchurian Incident.

March 1932 Establishment of 'Manchukuo'.

May 1932 Murder of Prime Minister Inukai Tsuyoshi.

1933 Japan withdraws from the League of Nations. Psychoanalyst Kosawa Heisaku begins private practice in Tokyo.

February 1936 Military coup attempted in Tokyo.

1937 Publication of *Kokutai no Hongi* ('Fundamentals of Our National Polity').

July 1937 Sino-Japanese skirmishes at the Marco Polo Bridge not far from Beijing, spreading to Shanghai the next month. The Second Sino-Japanese War begins.

December 1937 Japanese troops begin a rampage in Nanjing, lasting into January 1938.

1938 National General Mobilization Law. Konoe Fumimaro announces the aim of a 'New Order in East Asia'.

1940 Japan's Foreign Minister announces the government's plan to create a Greater East Asia Co-Prosperity Sphere. American embargoes on key exports to Japan. Japan's political parties dissolve themselves. Tripartite Pact with Italy and Germany. An 'Imperial Rule Assistance Association' is created, intended to unite civil and military arms of government. The Japan Federation of Labour disbands itself.

1941 Non-aggression pact signed with the Soviet Union. Japanese occupation of French Indochina is complete. Tōjō Hideki becomes Prime Minister.

7 December 1941 (local time) Japanese attack on Pearl Harbor.

1942 *Kindai no Chōkoku* ('Overcoming Modernity') symposium. Battle of Midway hints at a turning point in the war with the United States.

July 1944 Tōjō Hideki resigns as Prime Minister.

October 1944 First kamikaze attacks on American vessels.

February 1945 The Konoe Memorial to the Emperor, counselling an early end to the war.

March 1945 Firebombing of Tokyo.

April–June 1945 The Battle of Okinawa.

26 July 1945 The Potsdam Declaration.

August 1945 6 August: atomic bomb dropped on Hiroshima. 8 August: Soviet Union declares war on Japan. 9 August: atomic bomb dropped on Nagasaki. 15 August: Emperor Hirohito announces Japan's surrender. 30 August: General Douglas MacArthur arrives in Japan; the Allied Occupation begins.

October 1945   The film *Soyokaze* ('Soft Breeze') is released, becoming a nationwide hit.

December 1945   Women receive the vote.

1946   Japan's first post-war elections take place. Proceedings open at the International Military Tribunal for the Far East. Founding of Tokyo Tsūshin Kōgyō (TTEC) by Morita Akio and Ibuka Masaru. A radical Land Reform Bill is passed. Publication of Ruth Benedict's *The Chrysanthemum and the Sword*.

1947   MacArthur bans a planned general strike. The Fundamental Law on Education is passed, along with a Law for the Elimination of Excessive Concentrations of Economic Power. Japan's new Constitution comes into effect.

1948   A new Civil Code comes into effect. Verdicts handed down by the International Military Tribunal for the Far East. Former Prime Minister Tōjō Hideki and six others are hanged. The Summer Olympics are held in London – Japanese athletes are not invited.

1949   The Dodge Line and the creation of MITI. Morita Akio and his friends creating home-made reel tape.

June 1950   Outbreak of war in Korea, leading to calls the next month for the establishment of a National Police Reserve in Japan.

1951   General MacArthur fired by President Truman from his command in Korea and his position as SCAP in Japan.

1952   The San Francisco Treaty and US–Japan Security Treaty come into effect. The Occupation is over. Japan's return to the international stage continues with membership of the IMF and the World Bank, along with a welcome back to international sport at the Helsinki Olympics.

1953   Release in cinemas of Ozu Yasujirō's *Tokyo Story*.

1954   *Lucky Dragon 5* incident. Release of *Gojira* (*Godzilla*).

1955   Political parties realign: a Japan Socialist Party is formed, along with a Liberal Democratic Party. TTEC brings the 'world's smallest transistor radio' to market. The 'Sunagawa Struggle' begins. Ishihara Shintarō's *Taiyō no Kisetsu* ('Season of the Sun') wins the prestigious Akutagawa Prize for literature, helping to start a panic amongst parents about declining standards amongst the nation's youth.

1956   A Soviet–Japanese Joint Declaration ends the state of war between Japan and the USSR. Japan joins the United Nations. Minamata disease comes to public attention.

1958   *Gekkō Kamen* premieres on Japanese television.

1959   Crown Prince Akihito marries the commoner Shōda Michiko. The host city for the 1964 Olympics is announced – Tokyo.

1960   Anpo protests fail to prevent the ratification of a renewed US–Japan Security Treaty. Prime Minister Ikeda announces an 'income-doubling plan'. Release in cinemas (for three days) of Ōshima Nagisa's *Night and Fog in Japan*. Assassination of the Japan Socialist Party politician Asanuma Inejirō.

1961   Publication of Ōe Kenzaburō's novella *Sevuntin* ('Seventeen').

1962   Sony opens a showroom on New York's Fifth Avenue.

1964   The Tokyo Olympics and Japan's inaugural shinkansen journey. Hi-Red Center's 'Be Clean!' and 'Shelter Plan' events.

1965   Treaty on Basic Relations between Japan and the Republic of Korea is signed, after many years of talks. Takechi Tetsuji's controversial film *Kuroi yuki* ('Black Snow') is released.

1968   Kawabata Yasunari receives the Nobel Prize for Literature. Hijikata Tatsumi's performance, 'Hijikata Tatsumi and the Japanese – Revolt of the Flesh'.

1970   Kara Jūrō's play *John Silver: The Beggar of Love*. Japan's 'Pollution Diet': fourteen environmental measures are passed. The Osaka Expo and the launch of the 'Discover Japan' rail campaign.

1971   President Richard Nixon delivers two shocks to Japan, announcing his intention to visit the People's Republic of China and for the United States to leave the gold standard.

1972   Okinawa reverts from American to Japanese control. Normalization of relations between the US and China. Prime Minister Tanaka Kakuei makes a visit to Beijing, signing a normalization agreement with the People's Republic of China.

1973   The 'oil shock'. Minamata disease court ruling.

1974   Kentucky Fried Chicken's 'Kentucky for Christmas campaign' is launched, while 7-Eleven opens its doors: Japan's love-affair with Christmas chicken and the convenience store begins.

1976   The Lockheed scandal.

1978   China–Japan Peace and Friendship Treaty. Narita International Airport opens, after delays caused by protests. Deng Xiaoping visits Japan.

1982   The first instalment of Miyazaki Hayao's manga, *Nausicaä of the Valley of the Wind*, is published.

1985   Equal Employment Opportunity Law. Japan Airlines Flight 123 crash. The Plaza Accord.

1989   Death of the Shōwa Emperor; the Heisei Era begins. The Recruit Scandal.

1990   Dramatic fall in Japan's stock exchange. The (first) 'lost decade' is about to begin.

1992   Emperor Akihito becomes the first Japanese emperor to visit China.

1993   The LDP loses its government majority.

1994   Ōe Kenzaburō receives the Nobel Prize for Literature. The final instalment of Miyazaki Hayao's manga, *Nausicaä of the Valley of the Wind*, is published.

1995   The Great Hanshin-Awaji earthquake. Attack on the Tokyo Subway by Aum Shinrikyō. Arrest of Asahara Shōkō. Abduction and rape of an Okinawan schoolgirl by US soldiers. Prime Minister Murayama Tomiichi apologizes for Japanese 'colonial rule' and 'aggression' of a few decades before.

1996   Release of the first Pokémon game and the first Tamagotchi. Distribution deal signed between Disney and Miyazaki Hayao's Studio Ghibli.

1997   Ainu Cultural Promotion Law.

1998   Law to Promote Specified Non-Profit Activities.

1999   Law Regarding the National Flag and National Anthem.

2003   Miyazaki Hayao's *Spirited Away* wins the Oscar for Best Animated Feature Film.

2004   Japanese Ground Self-Defence Forces are sent to help with reconstruction in southern Iraq – the first independent deployment of troops outside Japan since the end of the Second World War.

2006   Basic Law on Suicide Countermeasures.

2007–8   The global financial crisis begins.

2008   A Diet resolution officially acknowledges the Ainu as an indigenous people of Japan.

2009   Images are broadcast across Japan of a 'New Year's Village for Contract Workers' (*toshi koshi haken mura*) in Tokyo's Hibiya Park, comprising tents and tarpaulin shelters.

2010   China overtakes Japan to become the world's second largest economy, after the United States.

11 March 2011   Japan's 'triple disasters': earthquake, tsunami and nuclear meltdown in Fukushima.

2012   A series of anti-nuclear rallies and protests take place across Japan.

2013   State Secrecy Law passed. The host city for the 2020 Olympics is announced: Tokyo.

2014   Okinawan and Ainu delegates join the first UN-backed World Conference on Indigenous Peoples. Government committee set up to investigate hate speech, dealing in particular with discrimination against Chinese, South East Asians and people of Korean descent living in Japan. Japan ratifies the United Nations Convention on the Rights of Persons with Disabilities.

2015   'Robear' unveiled. The district of Shibuya in Tokyo becomes the first local government in Japan to offer official status to same-sex couples, via 'proof of partnership' certificates.

2016   'Drop Dead Japan!' viral blog post reveals anger at inadequate childcare provision in Japan. Law on the Promotion of the Elimination of Buraku Discrimination.

2017   Abe Shinzō election victory brings constitutional revision within sight. The abdication is formally announced, planned for April 2019, of Emperor Akihito.

30 April 2019   Emperor Akihito abdicates.

1 May 2019   Crown Prince Naruhito ascends the Chrysanthemum Throne. The Reiwa Era begins.

Bibliographic Notes

PROLOGUE: HARUMI AND HEISAKU

The encounters of Heisaku with Harumi are based on Setouchi Jakuchō's autobiography (*Shishōsetsu*, 1985), an interview with Setouchi conducted by the author in October 2012, interviews with the son of Kosawa Heisaku, Kosawa Yorio (conducted 2007–2010), and on the private archives of the Kosawa family accessed by the author. On Denenchōfu, see K. T. Oshima, 'Denenchōfu: Building the Garden City in Japan', *Journal of the Society of Architectural Historians*, 55: 2 (1996). On the persistence of the 'special Japan' story, see Harumi Befu, *Hegemony of Homogeneity: An Anthropological Analysis of 'Nihonjinron'* (Trans Pacific Press, 2001) and (for modern psychological speculations) Nancy Rosenberger (ed.), *Japanese Sense of Self* (Cambridge University Press, 1994). On Japanese modernity: Harry Harootunian, *Overcome by Modernity: History, Culture, and Community in Interwar Japan* (Princeton University Press, 2001); Susan Napier, *The Fantastic in Modern Japanese Literature* (Routledge, 1995); Roy Starrs, *Modernism and Japanese Culture* (Palgrave, 2011); and Kevin Doak, *Dreams of Difference: The Japan Romantic School and the Crisis of Modernity* (University of California Press, 1994); James Phillips, 'Time and Memory in Freud and Heidegger: An Unlikely Congruence', paper given at the 7th International Conference on Philosophy, Psychiatry and Psychology, Heidelberg University, September 2004. Natsume Sōseki's quote comes from his novel *Kōjin* (1912) ('The Wayfarer'), and is reproduced in Susan Napier, *The Fantastic in Modern Japanese Literature* (Routledge, 1995). Kamei Katsuichirō's words are taken from Kamei Katsuichirō, 'A Note on Contemporary Spirit', translated in Richard F. Calichman (ed.), *Overcoming Modernity: Cultural Identity in Wartime Japan* (Columbia University Press, 2008).

I JAPAN GOES GLOBAL

On Commodore Matthew C. Perry's expedition to Japan, see Commodore Matthew C. Perry (compiled by Francis L. Hawks), *Narrative of the Expedition of an American Squadron to the China Seas and Japan* (1856; abridged edn, Big Byte Books, 2014); Centre for East Asian Cultural Studies (ed.), *Meiji Japan Through Contemporary Sources, Volume Two: 1844–1882* (Centre for East Asian Cultural Studies, 1970). On early modern Japan, see Marius B. Jansen, *The Making of Modern Japan* (Harvard University Press, 2002); James McClain, *Japan: A Modern History* (W. W. Norton & Company, 2002) and 'Japan's Pre-Modern Urbanism' in Peter Clark (ed.), *The Oxford Handbook of Cities in World History* (Oxford University Press, 2013). On Dejima and *Rangaku*, see Donald Keene, *The Japanese Discovery of Europe, 1720–1830* (revised edn, Stanford University Press, 1969); Marius Jansen, 'Rangaku and Westernization', *Modern Asian Studies*, 18 (4), 1984; Tatsushi Ueshima, 'Japan', in Robert William Thurston, Jonathan Morris and Shawn Steiman (eds), *Coffee: A Comprehensive Guide to the Bean, the Beverage, and the Industry* (Rowman & Littlefield Publishers, 2013). On the attack on Laurence Oliphant, see Margaret Oliphant, *Memoir of the Life of Laurence Oliphant and of Alice Oliphant, His Wife* (Harper & Brothers, 1891). On technological aspects of Japan's transition from Tokugawa into Meiji: Thomas C. Smith, *Native Sources of Japanese Industrialization, 1750–1920* (University of California Press, 1988); D. Eleanor Westney, *Imitation and Innovation: The Transfer of Western Organizational Patterns to Meiji Japan* (Harvard University Press, 1987); David G. Wittner, 'The Mechanization of Japan's Silk Industry and the Quest for Progress and Civilization, 1870–1880', in Morris Low (ed.), *Building a Modern Japan: Science, Technology, and Medicine in the Meiji Era and Beyond* (Palgrave Macmillan, 2005); E. Patricia Tsurumi, *Factory Girls: Women in the Thread Mills of Meiji Japan* (Princeton University Press, 1990) and 'Problem Consciousness and Modern Japanese History: Female Textile Workers of Meiji and Taisho', *Bulletin of Concerned Asian Scholars* 18:4 (1986). On Japan's postal system, see Andrew Cobbing, *The Japanese Discovery of Victorian Britain: Early Travel Encounters in the Far West* (Routledge, 1998). On women workers in Britain's General Post Office, see 'Women in the Post Office', <http://www.postalmuseum.org>. 'Vast village community': the words of Itō Hirobumi himself, reproduced in Andrew Barshay, ' "Doubly Cruel": Marxism and the Presence of the Past in Japanese Capitalism', in Stephen Vlastos (ed.), *Mirror of Modernity: Invented Traditions of Modern Japan* (University of California Press, 1998), p. 246. On self-definition and Japan's 'others', John Lie, *Multiethnic Japan* (Harvard University Press, 2004) and Richard M. Siddle,

Race, Resistance, and the Ainu of Japan (Routledge, 2012). On Japan's search for an acceptable cultural inheritance, Robert Sharf, 'The Zen of Japanese Nationalism', *History of Religions* 33:1 (1993). On Japan's modern army, see Edward J. Drea, *Japan's Imperial Army: Its Rise and Fall, 1853–1945* (University Press of Kansas, 2009). The Natsume Sōseki quote comes from Natsume Sōseki, *Wagahai wa neko de aru* ['I am a Cat'] (1905–1906), reproduced in P. N. Dale, *The Myth of Japanese Uniqueness* (Croom Helm, 1986). President Fillmore's letter is reproduced in Perry, *Narrative*. 'Riding on the Nagasaki road' comes from Hugh Cortazzi (ed.), *Victorians in Japan: In and Around the Treaty Ports* (Bloomsbury, 2012).

2 BLOOD TAX

On radical and campaigning women in modern Japan, Sharon L. Sievers, *Flowers in Salt: the Beginnings of Feminist Consciousness in Modern Japan* (Stanford University Press, 1983); Fukuda Hideko's autobiography *Half of My Life*, translated excerpts from which appear in Mikiso Hane (trans. and ed.), *Reflections on the Way to the Gallows: Rebel Women in Prewar Japan* (University of California Press, 1993); Fumiko Horimoto, 'Pioneers of the Women's Movement in Japan: Hiratsuka Raichō and Fukuda Hideko seen Through their Journals, *Seitō* and *Sekai Fujin*', MA thesis (University of Toronto, 1999); Sharlie Conroy Ushioda, 'Women and War in Meiji Japan: the Case of Fukuda Hideko (1865–1927)', *Peace & Change: A Journal of Peace Research*, 4:3 (October 1977). On Fukuzawa Yukichi and *jiyū* debates, see Douglas Howland, 'Translating Liberty in Nineteenth-Century Japan', in *Journal of the History of Ideas*, 62:1 (2001). On rural and violent discontent, Eiko Maruko Siniawer, *Ruffians, Yakuza, Nationalists: The Violent Politics of Modern Japan, 1860–1960* (Cornell University Press, 2008); Stephen Vlastos, 'Opposition Movements in Early Meiji, 1868–1885', in Marius B. Jansen et al. (eds), *The Cambridge History of Japan*, Volume 5: *The Nineteenth Century* (Cambridge University Press,1989); R. W. Bowen, 'Rice-roots Democracy and Popular Rebellion in Meiji Japan', *Journal of Peasant Studies*, 6:1 (1978); Marius B. Jansen, 'Ōi Kentarō: Radicalism and Chauvinism', *Far Eastern Quarterly*, 11:3 (1952); Daikichi Irokawa, 'Japan's Grass-roots Tradition: Current Issues in the Mirror of History', *Japan Quarterly*, 20:1 (1973). On samurai, Saigō Takamori and the Satsuma Rebellion: C. L. Yates, 'Saigō Takamori in the Emergence of Meiji Japan', *Modern Asian Studies*, 28:3 (1994); Oleg Benesch, *Inventing the Way of the Samurai* (Oxford University Press, 2014); John Rickman, 'Sunset of the Samurai', *Military*

History, 20:3 (2003); Edward J. Drea, *Japan's Imperial Army: Its Rise and Fall, 1853–1945* (University Press of Kansas, 2016). On the Japanese press, see James L. Huffman, *Creating a Public: People and Press in Meiji Japan* (University of Hawaii Press, 1997). On Chiba Takusaburō, see Daikichi Irokawa, *The Culture of the Meiji Period* (1969; English trans. Princeton University Press, 1985); Marius B. Jansen, *The Making of Modern Japan* (Harvard University Press, 2002); and Daikichi Irokawa, 'Japan's Grassroots Tradition: Current Issues in the Mirror of History', *Japan Quarterly*, 20:1 (1973). The figures for government arms during the Satsuma Rebellion come from Rickman, 'Sunset of the Samurai' and Jansen, *The Making of Modern Japan*. The quote from the American captain comes from Elizabeth Tripler Nock, 'The Satsuma Rebellion of 1877: Letters of John Capen Hubbard', *Far Eastern Quarterly*, 7:4 (1948). The words of Fukuzawa Yukichi and Itō Hirobumi on Japan's rural population are reproduced in Huffman, *Creating a Public: People and Press in Meiji Japan*. The Egypt comparison comes from Jansen, *The Making of Modern Japan*. 'Persimmon-coloured' comes from Fukuda Hideko's autobiography, *Half of My Life*, reproduced in Mikiso Hane, *Reflections on the Way to the Gallows*.

3 DANCING CABINET

For the Rokumeikan, see Pat Barr, *The Deer Cry Pavilion: A Story of Westerners in Japan, 1868–1905* (Harcourt, Brace & World, 1968); Toshio Watanabe, 'Josiah Conder's Rokumeikan: Architecture and National Representation in Meiji Japan', *Art Journal*, 55:3 (1996); Dallas Finn, 'Reassessing the Rokumeikan', in Ellen P. Conant (ed.), *Challenging Past and Present: The Metamorphosis of Nineteenth-Century Japanese Art* (University of Hawaii Press, 2006); Mock Joya, 'Women of Japan: Introduction of Western Fashions', *Japan Times*, 3 March 1928. The venue for the infamous party (at which Itō was rumoured to have tried to seduce a young married woman) is disputed: some writers place it at the Rokumeikan (Barr, *The Deer Cry Pavilion*; Sievers, *Flowers in Salt*); others locate it at Itō's home (Finn, 'Reassessing the Rokumeikan'; Joya, 'Women of Japan'). On Tokyo, see Edward Seidensticker, *Low City, High City: Tokyo From Edo to the Earthquake* (Alfred A. Knopf, 1983). On Kanagaki Robun: Donald Keene, *A History of Japanese Literature: Volume 3: Dawn to the West: Japanese Literature of the Modern Era* (Holt, Rinehart and Winston, 1984). Also on Japanese literature, see Joshua S. Mostow, 'The Revival of Poetry in Traditional Forms', in Joshua S. Mostow (ed.), *The Columbia Companion* to *Modern East Asian Literature* (Columbia University Press, 2003). On new fashions of the age, see James McClain, *Japan: A Modern History* (W. W. Norton & Company, 2002) and Seidensticker, *Low City, High City*. On early modern Japanese intellectual life, see Harry D. Harootunian, *Things Seen and Unseen: Discourse and Ideology in Tokugawa Nativism* (University of Chicago Press, 1988) and Marius B. Jansen, *The Making of Modern Japan* (Harvard University Press, 2002). For modern Japanese intellectuals: on Kuga Katsunan and Miyake Setsurei, see Bob T. Wakabayashi (ed.), *Modern Japanese Thought* (Cambridge University Press, 1998). On Home Ministry interventions in electoral politics, see Gordon M. Berger, 'Japan's Young Prince: Konoe Fumimaro's Early Political Career, 1916–1931', *Monumenta Nipponica*, 29:4 (1974). On saving the Imperial Rescript and portraits in times of crisis, see Linda K. Menton, *The Rise of Modern Japan* (University of Hawaii Press, 2003). On food culture, see Naomichi Ishige, *The History and Culture of Japanese Food* (Routledge, 2001). The Doodle San ditty is reproduced in Pat Barr, *The Deer Cry Pavilion*. 'A beautiful woman' is from *Jogaku Zasshi* magazine, reproduced in Donald Keene, *Emperor of Japan: Meiji and His World, 1852–1912* (Columbia University Press, 2002). 'Like luggage' is from the Tokyo *Nichi Nichi* newspaper, reproduced in James L. Huffman, *Creating a Public: People and Press in Meiji Japan* (University of Hawaii Press, 1997). For the 'fashionable crazes', see Basil Hall Chamberlain, *Things Japanese: Being Notes on Various Subjects Connected with Japan, For the Use of Travellers and Others* (John Murray, 1905). 'Rhymes too readily' is the observation of H. Paul Varley in *Japanese Culture* (University of Hawaii Press, 2000). 'Conducive to a spirit of bravery' is quoted in Mostow, 'The Revival of Poetry in Traditional Forms'. For an English translation of the Man'yōshū, see *1000 Poems from the Manyōshū: The Complete Nippon Gakujutsu Shinkokai Translation* (Dover Publications Inc., 2005). 'Contemptible imitation' is quoted in Keene, *Emperor of Japan*. 'Only values are fact-gathering and technique' is quoted in Jansen, *The Making of Modern Japan*. For the *waka* poem, note that in the Japanese original, the final line provides an example of *jiamari*: excess syllable(s), which were a feature of some *waka*.

4 HAPPY FAMILIES

On Hiratsuka Raichō, see Hiratsuka Raichō, *Genshi Josei wa Taiyō de atta*. An English translation is available: Hiratsuka Raichō and Teruko Craig (translation and notes), *In the Beginning, Woman Was the Sun: The*

Autobiography of a Japanese Feminist (Columbia University Press, 2006); Hiroko Tomida, *Hiratsuka Raichō and Early Japanese Feminism* (Brill, Leiden, 2004); Sharon L. Sievers, *Flowers in Salt: the Beginnings of Feminist Consciousness in Modern Japan* (Stanford University Press, 1983). On women, the state and radicalism, see Sharon E. Nolte and Sally Ann Hastings, 'The Meiji State's Policy Toward Women, 1890–1910', in Gail Lee Bernstein (ed.), *Recreating Japanese Women, 1600–1945* (University of California Press, 1991); Vera Mackie, *Creating Socialist Women in Japan: Gender, Labour, and Activism 1900– 1937* (Cambridge University Press, 1997); Sievers, *Flowers in Salt*; Tomoko Seto, 'Spectacular Socialism: Politics and Popular Performance in Shitamachi Tokyo, 1904–1918', PhD thesis (University of Chicago, 2014); Tomoko Seto, ' "Anarchist Beauties" in Late Meiji Japan: Media Narratives of Police Violence in the Red Flag Incident', *Radical History Review* (October 2016); Helene Bowen Raddeker, *Treacherous Women of Imperial Japan: Patriarchal Fictions, Patricidal Fantasies* (Routledge, 1997). On Shimizu Shikin, see Leslie Winston, 'Beyond Modern: Shimizu Shikin and "Two Modern Girls" ', *Critical Asian Studies*, 39:3 (2007); Rebecca L. Copeland, *Lost Leaves: Women Writers of Meiji Japan* (University of Hawaii Press, 2000); Fumiko Horimoto, 'Pioneers of the Women's Movement in Japan: Hiratsuka Raichō and Fukuda Hideko seen Through their Journals, Seitō and Sekai Fujin', MA thesis (University of Toronto, 1999). For domesticity, Iwamoto Yoshiharu, and the account of the 'family meeting' see Jordan Sand, *House and Home in Modern Japan: Architecture, Domestic Space, and Bourgeois Culture, 1880–1930* (Harvard University Press, 2005). The Kosawa family material is drawn from the private archives of the Kosawa family, accessed by the author, with thanks also to Ikuta Takashi and Takeda Makoto (see Takeda Makoto, *Seishin bunseki to bukkyō* ['Psychoanalysis and Buddhism'], Shinchōsha, 1990). On the Emperor, the imperial system, and its rituals and celebrations, see Takashi Fujitani, *Splendid Monarchy: Power and Pageantry in Modern Japan* (University of California Press, 1996); Norio Makihara, 'The Birth of Banzai', *Japan Forum*, 23:2 (2011); Donald Keene, *Emperor of Japan: Meiji and His World, 1852–1912* (Columbia University Press, 2002). On Ebina Danjō, see the memoir of Ōsugi Sakae, reproduced in Wm. Theodore de Bary, Carol Gluck and Arthur E. Tiedemann (eds), *Sources of Japanese Tradition, 1600 to 2000*, Volume Two, 2nd edn (Cambridge University Press, 2001). On Christian socialists, see Bob T. Wakabayashi (ed.), *Modern Japanese Thought* (Cambridge University Press, 1998). 'The home is a public place', reproduced in Nolte and Hastings, 'The Meiji State's Policy Toward Women, 1890–1910'. 'The flesh of her thighs' is from Tanizaki

Junichirō (translated by Paul McCarthy), *Childhood Years: A Memoir* (University of Michigan Press, 2017). 'Lord[ed] it over their wives and children' is from Shimizu Shikin's contribution to Ueki Emori's *Tōyō no fujō* (Women of the Orient, 1888), reproduced in Copeland, *Lost Leaves*. 'Ha!' is also reproduced in Copeland, *Lost Leaves*. 'The moment that any woman dies' is reproduced in Hiratsuka Raichō and Teruko Craig, *In the Beginning, Woman Was the Sun: The Autobiography of a Japanese Feminist*. 'The first enemy' is reproduced in Horimoto, 'Pioneers of the Women's Movement', MA thesis. 'Terrible toothache' and 'Ah, you men' come from Sievers, *Flowers in Salt*. The speculation about a Japanese Emperor seeing Mount Fuji for the first time comes from Keene, *Emperor of Japan*. 'Is your objective anarchism', in the *Yomiuri Shinbun* newspaper, is reproduced in Seto, 'Spectacular Socialism. Kanno's evidence to prosecutors and writings to friends comes from Mikiso Hane (trans. and ed.), *Reflections on the Way to the Gallows: Rebel Women in Prewar Japan* (University of California Press, 1993).

5 CONTESTING THE COSMOS

On the 1465 'Kanshō Persecution', see Mark L. Blum and Shin'ya Yasutomi (eds), *Rennyo and the Roots of Modern Japanese Buddhism* (Oxford University Press, 2006), especially Chapter 7. On Buddhism, modernity and the state in Japan, see Helen Hardacre, 'Creating State Shinto: the Great Promulgation Campaign and the New Religions', *Journal of Japanese Studies*, 12:1 (1986); Martin Collcutt, 'Buddhism: the Threat of Eradication', in Marius B. Jansen and Gilbert Rozman (eds), *Japan in Transition: Tokugawa to Meiji* (Princeton University Press, 1986); Christopher Ives, *Imperial Way Zen: Ichikawa Hakugen's Critique and Lingering Questions for Buddhist Ethics* (University of Hawaii Press, 2009); H. Paul Varley, *Japanese Culture* (University of Hawaii Press, 2000); Judith Snodgrass, *Presenting Japanese Buddhism to the West: Orientalism, Occidentalism, and the Columbian Exposition* (University of North Carolina Press, 2003); Jason Ananda Josephson, *The Invention of Religion in Japan* (University of Chicago Press, 2012); Gerard Clinton Godart, ' "Philosophy" or "Religion"? The Confrontation with Categories in Late Nineteenth Century Japan', *Journal of the History of Ideas*, 69:1 (2008); James Edward Ketelaar, *Of Heretics and Martyrs in Meiji Japan: Buddhism and Its Persecution* (Princeton University Press, 1990) and 'Strategic Occidentalism: Meiji Buddhists at the

World's Parliament of Religions', *Buddhist-Christian Studies*, 11 (1991); Winston Davis, 'Buddhism and the Modernization of Japan', *History of Religions*, 28:4 (1989). On Inoue Enryō, see Gerald A. Figal, *Civilization and Monsters: Spirits of Modernity in Meiji Japan* (Duke University Press, 1999); Miura Setsuo, 'Inoue Enryō's Mystery Studies', *International Inoue Enryō Research*, 2 (2014); Jason Ananda Josephson, 'When Buddhism Became a "Religion": Religion and Superstition in the Writings of Inoue Enryō', *Japanese Journal of Religious Studies*, 33:1 (2006); Gerard Clinton Godart, 'Tracing the Circle of Truth: Inoue Enryō on the History of Philosophy and Buddhism', *Eastern Buddhist*, 36:1–2 (2004). On Christians in Japan, see Thomas W. Burkman, 'The Urakami Incidents and the Struggle for Religious Toleration in Early Meiji Japan', *Japanese Journal of Religious Studies*, 1:2–3 (1974); Mikiso Hane, *Pre-Modern Japan: A Historical Survey*, 2nd edn (Westview Press, 2014); Stephen Turnbull (ed.), *Japan's Hidden Christians* (Curzon Press, Surrey, 2000); Kiri Paramore, *Ideology and Christianity in Japan* (Taylor & Francis, 2009); James M. Hommes, 'Baptized Bushidō: Christian Converts and the Use of Bushidō in Meiji Japan', *Journal of the Southwest Conference on Asian Studies*, 7 (2011); John F. Howes, 'Japanese Christians and American Missionaries', in Marius B. Jansen (ed.), *Changing Japanese Attitudes Towards Modernization* (Princeton University Press, 1965); George M. Oshiro, 'Nitobe Inazō and the Sapporo Band: Reflections on the Dawn of Protestant Christianity in Early Meiji Japan', *Japanese Journal of Religious Studies*, 34:1 (2007); George E. Moore, 'Samurai Conversion: the Case of Kumamoto', *Asian Studies*, 4:1 (1966); Tessa Morris-Suzuki, *Re-inventing Japan: Time, Space, Nation* (Routledge, 1997); Mark Mullins, *Christianity Made in Japan: A Study of Indigenous Movements* (University of Hawaii Press, 1998); Saburo Ozawa, *Bakumatsu Meiji Yasokyōshi Kenkyū* [Studies in the History of Christianity in the Bakumatsu and Meiji Periods] (Nihon Kirisuto-kyōdan Shuppankyoku, Tokyo, 1973); H. Byron Earhart, *Japanese Religion: Unity and Diversity*, 5th edn (Wadsworth Publishing, Boston, 2013); Emily Anderson, *Christianity and Imperialism in Modern Japan: Empire for God* (Bloomsbury, 2014). On the Russo-Japanese War, see Marius B. Jansen, *The Making of Modern Japan* (Harvard University Press, 2002); J. Victor Koschmann, *Authority and the Individual in Japan: Citizen Protest in Historical Perspective* (ISBS, 1978); Nobuya Bamba and John F. Howes (eds), *Pacifism in Japan: the Christian and Socialist Tradition* (University of British Columbia Press, 1978); David Wells and Sandra Wilson (eds), *The Russo-Japanese War in Cultural Perspective, 1904–05* (Palgrave Macmillan, 1999). On Yosano Akiko, see Laurel Rasplica Rodd, 'The Taishō Debate over the "New Woman" ', in Gail Lee Bernstein (ed.), *Recreating Japanese Women, 1600–1945* (University of California Press, 1991). 'In matters of electricity' is reproduced in Hommes, 'Baptized Bushidō: Christian Converts and the Use of Bushidō in Meiji Japan'. 'Oh my brother . . .' is an excerpt from Yosano Akiko's poem *'Kimi, shinitamō koto nakare'* ['Brother, Do Not Offer Your Life'] (1904). The translation used here appears in Steve Rabson, 'Akiko on War: To Give One's Life or Not: A Question of Which War', *Journal of the Association of Teachers of Japanese*, 25:1 (1991).

6 HAUNTING THE ORIENT

On Saitō Mokichi, see Amy Heinrich, *Fragments of Rainbows: the Life and Poetry of Saitō Mokichi, 1882–1953* (Columbia University Press, 1983). On Akutagawa Ryūnosuke, see Seiji M. Lippit, *Topographies of Japanese Modernism* (Columbia University Press, 2002); Kevin M. Doak, 'The Last Word? Akutagawa Ryūnosuke's "The Man from the West" ', in *Monumenta Nipponica*, 66:2 (2011); Akutagawa Ryūnosuke, Kevin M. Doak and J. Scott Matthews, ' "The Man from the West" and "The Man from the West: the Sequel" ', *Monumenta Nipponica*, 66:2 (2011); Rebecca Suter, 'Grand Demons and Little Devils: Akutagawa's *Kirishitan mono* as a Mirror of Modernity', *Journal of Japanese Studies*, 39:1 (2013); Murakami Haruki, 'Akutagawa Ryūnosuke: Downfall of the Chosen', in Akutagawa Ryūnosuke, *Rashomon and Seventeen Other Stories*, translated by Jay Rubin (Penguin Classics, 2006); G. H. Healey, 'Introduction', in Akutagawa Ryūnosuke, *Kappa*, translated by Geoffrey Bownas (Peter Owen Publishers, 1970). On Hayashi Fumiko, see Hayashi Fumiko, *Hōrōki* ['Diary of a Vagabond'] (1927); William O. Gardner, *Advertising Tower: Japanese Modernism and Modernity in the 1920s* (Harvard University Press, 2006). On the development of Tokyo's infrastructure and culture, see Elise Tipton, *Modern Japan: a Social and Political History*, 3rd edn (Routledge, 2015); Steven J. Ericson, *The Sound of the Whistle: Railroads and the State in Meiji Japan* (Harvard University Press, 1996); Hiromu Nagahara, *Tokyo Boogie-Woogie: Japan's Pop Era and its Discontents* (Harvard University Press, 2017); Alisa Freedman, *Tokyo in Transit: Japanese Culture on the Rails and Road* (Stanford University Press, 2010); E. Taylor Atkins, *Blue Nippon: Authenticating Jazz in Japan* (Duke University Press, 2011); Miriam Silverberg, *Erotic Grotesque Nonsense: The Mass Culture of Japanese Modern Times* (University of California Press, 2009); Christine R. Yano, 'Defining the Modern Nation in

Japanese Popular Song', in Sharon Minichiello (ed.), *Japan's Competing Modernities: Issues in Culture and Democracy, 1900–1930* (University of Hawaii Press, 1998); Barbara Molony, 'Activism Among Women in the Taisho Cotton Textile Industry', in Gail Lee Bernstein (ed.), *Recreating Japanese Women, 1600–1945* (University of California Press, 1991); Gail Lee Bernstein, 'Women in the Silk-Reeling Industry in Nineteenth-Century Japan', in Gail Lee Bernstein and Haruhiro Fukui (eds), *Japan and the World: Essays on Japanese History and Politics* (Palgrave Macmillan, 1988); Chiyoko Kawakami, 'The Metropolitan Uncanny in the Works of Izumi Kyōka', *Harvard Journal of Asiatic Studies*, 59:2 (1999); Michael Crandol, 'Nightmares from the Past: "Kaiki Eiga" and the Dawn of Japanese Horror Cinema', PhD thesis (University of Minnesota, 2015). On the politics of the period, see Richard Sims, *Japanese Political History Since the Meiji Restoration, 1868–2000* (C. Hurst Publishers, London, 2001); William Craig, *The Fall of Japan: the Final Weeks of World War II in the Pacific* (reissued edn, Open Road Media, 2017); Haruhiro Fukui, *Party in Power: Japanese Liberal Democrats and Policy-Making* (Australian National University Press, 1970); William R. Nester, *The Foundations of Japanese Power: Continuities, Changes, Challenges* (Palgrave Macmillan, 1990); Marius B. Jansen, *The Making of Modern Japan* (Harvard University Press, 2002); Peter Duus, 'Yoshino Sakuzō: the Christian as Political Critic', *Journal of Japanese Studies*, 4:2 (1978); Bernard Silberman, 'The Political Theory and Program of Yoshino Sakuzō', *Journal of Modern History*, 31:4 (1959). For insights into Japan's activities during the Great War, I am grateful for the advice of Ian Gow. On Edogawa Ranpo and crime fiction, see Edogawa Ranpo, *'Ningen Isu'* ['The Human Chair'], in *Kuraku* magazine, 1925; Edogawa Ranpo, *Japanese Tales of Mystery & Imagination* (Tuttle Publishing, Vermont, 1956; translations by James B. Harris); Mark Silver, *Purloined Letters: Cultural Borrowing and Japanese Crime Literature, 1868–1937* (University of Hawaii Press, 2008). 'As the night grew late' appears in Saitō Mokichi's collection *Tomoshibi* ['Lamplight'], reproduced in Amy Vladeck Heinrich, *Fragments of Rainbows: the Life and Poetry of Saitō Mokichi* (Columbia University Press, 1983). 'Dancing to jazz' appears in Taylor Atkins, *Blue Nippon*. 'My family was poor' appears in Linda K. Menton, *The Rise of Modern Japan* (University of Hawaii Press, 2003). 'A girl in the hotel' is from Edogawa Ranpo, *'Ningen Isu'* (author's translation). 'Opposite me', 'I have no conscience' and 'I don't have the strength' come from Akutagawa Ryūnosuke, 'Spinning Gears', in Akutagawa, *Rashomon and Seventeen Other Stories*. 'Which modernity', 'Foxes' and 'Christ's life' come from Akutagawa Ryūnosuke, 'The Man from the

West', translated by Kevin M. Doak and J. Scott Matthews, in Akutagawa, Doak and Matthews, ' "The Man from the West" and "The Man from the West: the Sequel" '.

7 GREAT ESCAPES

The details of Kosawa Heisaku's practice and correspondence are drawn from the private archives of the Kosawa family, accessed by the author, along with interviews with former clients of Kosawa, conducted by the author. Also see Kosawa Heisaku, '*Zaiaku Ishiki no Nisshu: Ajase Konpurekkusu*' ['Two Kinds of Guilt Feeling: the Ajase Complex'], in *Gonryō* magazine (1931); Kosawa Heisaku, *Seishin Bunsekigaku: Rikai no Tame ni* ['Understanding Psychoanalysis'] (Hiyoshi Byōin Seishin Bunsekigaku Kenkyūshitsu Shuppanbu, 1958); Christopher Harding, 'Japanese Psychoanalysis and Buddhism: The Making of a Relationship', *History of Psychiatry*, 25:2 (June 2014); Christopher Harding, 'Religion and psychotherapy in modern Japan: a four-phase view', in Christopher Harding, Fumiaki Iwata and Shin'ichi Yoshinaga (eds), *Religion and Psychotherapy in Modern Japan* (Routledge, 2015); Fumiaki Iwata, 'The Dawning of Japanese Psychoanalysis: Kosawa Heisaku's Therapy and Faith', in Harding, Iwata and Yoshinaga (eds), *Religion and Psychotherapy in Modern Japan*; Fumiaki Iwata, *Kindaika no naka no dentōshūkyō to seishinundō: Kijunten toshite no Chikazumi Jōkan kenkyū* ['Traditional Religion and Spiritual Movements in the Context of Modernization: Research on Chikazumi Jōkan as a Point of Reference'] (Osaka Kyōiku University, 2011). Yujiro Nagao, Takashi Ikuta and Christopher Harding, *Bukkyō Seishin Bunseki* ['Buddhist Psychoanalysis'] (Kongo Shuppan, Tokyo, 2016). On Japanese psychological distress and psychotherapy in general, see Yu-chuan Wu, 'A Disorder of Ki: Alternative Treatments for Neurasthenia in Japan, 1890–1945', PhD thesis (University College London, 2012); Akihito Suzuki, 'A Brain Hospital in Tokyo and its Private and Public Patients, 1926–45', *History of Psychiatry*, 14:3 (2003); Yasuo Okada, '110 Years of Psychiatric Care in Japan,' in Teizo Ogawa (ed.), *History of Psychiatry – Mental Illness and Its Treatments: Proceedings of the 4th International Symposium on the Comparative History of Medicine – East and West* (Shizuoka, 1982); Akira Hashimoto, 'Psychiatry and Religion in Modern Japan: Traditional Temple and Shrine Therapies', in Harding, Iwata and Yoshinaga (eds), *Religion and Psychotherapy in Modern Japan*; Junko Kitanaka, *Depression in Japan: Psychiatric Cures for a Society in Distress* (Princeton University Press, 2011);

Yoshinaga Shin'ichi, *Nihonjin no Shin-Shin Rei* [Japanese 'Body', 'Mind', 'Spirit'], Volume 4 (Kuresu Shuppan, 2004); Shin'ichi Yoshinaga, 'The Birth of Japanese Mind Cure Methods', in Harding, Iwata and Yoshinaga (eds), *Religion and Psychotherapy in Modern Japan*; W-S. Tseng, S. C. Chang, M. Nishizono, 'Asian Culture and Psychotherapy: An Overview', in W-S. Tseng, S. C. Chang, M. Nishizono (eds), *Asian Culture and Psychotherapy: Implications for East and West* (University of Hawaii Press, 2005); Gerald A. Figal, *Civilization and Monsters: Spirits of Modernity in Meiji Japan* (Duke University Press, 1999); Harry Harootunian, *Overcome by Modernity: History, Culture, and Community in Interwar Japan* (Princeton University Press, 2001); H. D. Harootunian, 'Disciplinizing Native Knowledge and Producing Place: Yanagita Kunio, Origuchi Shinobu, Takata Yasuma', in J. Thomas Rimer (ed.), *Culture and Identity: Japanese Intellectuals During the Interwar Years* (Princeton University Press, 1990); William Lee Rand, 'What is the History of Reiki?' <http://www.reiki.org>. On Natsume Sōseki in London, see Sammy I. Tsunematsu, 'Introduction' in Natsume Sōseki, *Spring Miscellany and London Essays*, translated by Sammy I. Tsunematsu (Tuttle Publishing, Boston, 2002). On Yanagita Kunio, see Ronald A. Morse, 'Introduction' in Yanagita Kunio, *The Legends of Tōno*, translated by Ronald A. Morse (Japan Foundation, 1975; new edn Rowman and Littlefield, 2008); Figal, *Civilization and Monsters*; Takehiko Kojima, 'Diversity and Knowledge in the Age of Nation-Building: Space and Time in the Thought of Yanagita Kunio', PhD thesis (Florida International University, 2011); Shun'ichi Takayanagi, 'Yanagita Kunio', *Monumenta Nipponica*, 29:3 (1974). On Yanagita's insistence upon recounting stories 'just as I felt them', see Figal, *Civilization and Monsters*. On Watsuji Tetsurō, see Harootunian, *Overcome by Modernity*. On Heidegger, James Phillips, 'Time and Memory in Freud and Heidegger: An Unlikely Congruence', <https://www.klinikum.uni-heidelberg.de/fileadmin/zpm/psychatrie/ppp2004/manuskript/phillips.pdf>. 'Far beyond any femininity' is from Natsume Sōseki, 'The Boarding House', in Sōseki, *Spring Miscellany*. 'All of a sudden' is from Natsume Sōseki, 'A Sweet Dream', in Sōseki, *Spring Miscellany*. 'Glued-on peacock feathers' and Sōseki's words to his students feature in '*Watakushi no Kojinshugi*' ['My Individualism'] (1914), reproduced in Jay Rubin and Natsume Sōseki, 'Sōseki on Individualism: "Watakushi no Kojinshugi"', *Monumenta Nipponica*, 34:1 (1979). 'One day a whole family' is from Yanagita Kunio, *The Legends of Tōno*. 'The smash of a plate' is from the author's translation of Kosawa Heisaku, '*Zaiaku Ishiki no Nisshu: Ajase Konpurekkesu*' ['Two Kinds of Guilt Feeling: the Ajase Complex'], *Gonryō* magazine (1931). See also Okonogi Keigo and Osamu Kitayama (eds), *Ajase Konpurekkesu* ['Ajase Complex'] (Sōgensha, 2001). Kai Wariko's poem features in Mark Unno (ed.), *Buddhism and Psychotherapy Across Cultures: Essays on Theories and Practices* (Wisdom Publications, Boston, 2006).

8 SELF-POWER, OTHER POWER, STATE POWER

For Kikugawa Ayako's story, and on picture brides in general, see Barbara Kawakami, *Picture Bride Stories* (University of Hawaii Press, 2016). See also Carol C. Fan, 'Asian Women in Hawai'i: Migration, Family, Work, and Identity', *NWSA Journal*, 8:1 (1996). On Pearl Harbor's vulnerability: J. J. Clark and Dwight H. Barnes, *Sea Power and its Meaning* (Franklin Watts, New York, 1966). On Japanese colonialism and relationships within East Asia, see Mark R. Peattie, 'The Japanese Colonial Empire, 1895–1945', in Peter Duus (ed.), *The Cambridge History of Japan*, Volume 6: *The Twentieth Century* (Cambridge University Press, 1989); Marius B. Jansen, *The Making of Modern Japan* (Harvard University Press, 2002); Kenneth B. Pyle, *The Making of Modern Japan*, 2nd revised edn (Houghton Mifflin, 1996); Aaron Stephen Moore, *Constructing East Asia: Technology, Ideology, and Empire in Japan's Wartime Era, 1931–45* (Stanford University Press, 2013); R. Siddle, *Race, Resistance, and the Ainu of Japan* (Routledge, 1996); Christopher Harding, 'State of Insecurity: Self-Defence and Self-Cultivation in the Genesis of Japanese Imperialism', in K. Nicolaidis, B. Sebe and G. Maas, *Echoes of Empire: Memory, Identity and Colonial Legacies* (I. B. Tauris, 2014); Sonia Ryang, 'The Great Kanto Earthquake and the Massacre of Koreans in 1923: Notes on Japan's Modern National Sovereignty', *Anthropological Quarterly*, 76:4 (2003); Joshua A. Hammer, *Yokohama Burning: The Deadly 1923 Earthquake and Fire That Helped Forge the Path to World War II* (Free Press, 2011). On American attitudes towards East Asian peoples, see Priscilla Long, 'Tacoma Expels the Entire Chinese Community on November 3, 1885', *History Link*, Essay 5063 (January 2003); Jansen, *The Making of Modern Japan*; Hammer, *Yokohama Burning*. On Bertrand Russell in Japan, see Bertrand Russell, *Uncertain Paths to Freedom: Russia and China, 1919–22* (Routledge, 2000). On Kagawa Toyohiko, see George B. Bikle, *The New Jerusalem: Aspects of Utopianism in the Thought of Kagawa Toyohiko* (University of Arizona Press, 1976); Robert D. Schildgen, *Toyohiko Kagawa: Apostle of Love and Social Justice* (Centenary Books, 1988); William Axling, *Kagawa*, revised edn (Harper & Brothers, 1946). On the Ashio Copper Mine and

Japanese state power, see Robert Stolz, *Bad Water: Nature, Pollution, and Politics in Japan, 1870–1950* (Duke University Press, 2014); F. G. Note-helfer, 'Japan's First Pollution Incident', *Journal of Japanese Studies*, 1:2 (1975); Sheldon Garon, *State and Labor in Modern Japan* (University of California Press, 1990) and Garon, *Molding Japanese Minds: the State in Everyday Life* (Princeton University Press, 1997); Robert M. Spaulding Jr, 'The Bureaucracy as a Political Force, 1920–45', in James William Morley (ed.), *The Dilemmas of Growth in Prewar Japan* (Princeton University Press, 1972); Bernard S. Silberman, 'The Bureaucratic Role in Japan, 1900–1934: the Bureaucrat as Politician', in Bernard S. Silberman and H. D. Harootunian (eds), *Japan in Crisis: Essays on Taishō Democracy* (Princeton University Press, 1974). On state–society relationships and cajolery, see Sheldon Garon in *State and Labor in Modern Japan*; 'Rethinking Modernization and Modernity in Japanese History: A Focus on State–Society Relations', *Journal of Asian Studies*, 53:2 (1994); 'Women's Groups and the Japanese State: Contending Approaches to Political Integration, 1890–1945', *Journal of Japanese Studies*, 19:1 (1993); and especially Garon, *Molding Japanese Minds*. 'Extend the blessings' is quoted in Peattie, 'The Japanese Colonial Empire, 1895–1945'. 'Isn't it time' is from Bikle, *The New Jerusalem*. 'Busy, Busy!' is from Axling, *Kagawa*. 'Academic tramp' is from Andrew Gordon, *A Modern History of Japan*, 2nd edn (Oxford University Press, 2008). On the police, see Elise K. Tipton, *The Japanese Police State: Tokkō in Interwar Japan* (University of Hawaii Press, 1991); Shunsuke Tsurumi, *An Intellectual History of Wartime Japan, 1931–1945* (Routledge, 1986); Patricia Steinhoff, 'Tenkō and Thought Control', in Gail Lee Bernstein and Haruhiro Fukui (eds), *Japan and the World: Essays on Japanese History and Politics* (Palgrave Macmillan, 1988); Patricia Steinhoff, 'Tenkō: Ideology and Societal Integration in Prewar Japan', PhD thesis (Harvard University, 1969).

9 THEATRE

On the Mukden Incident, see Marius B. Jansen, *The Making of Modern Japan* (Harvard University Press, 2002). On Ishiwara Kanji, see (for his thoughts on Perry) Roger H. Brown, 'Ishiwara Kanji's "Argument for an East Asian League", 1940', in Sven Saaler and Christopher W. A. Szpilman (eds), *Pan-Asianism: A Documentary History*, Volume 2: *1920–Present* (Rowman & Littlefield, 2011); Mark R. Peattie, *Ishiwara Kenji and Japan's*

Confrontation with the West (Princeton University Press, 1975). On Japan's armed forces, see Edward J. Drea, *Japan's Imperial Army: Its Rise and Fall, 1853–1945* (University Press of Kansas, 2009) and 'The Japanese Army on the Eve of War', in Mark Peattie et al. (eds), *The Battle for China: Essays on the Military History of the Sino-Japanese War of 1937–1945* (Stanford University Press, 2010); Theodore F. Cook, 'Making Soldiers: the Imperial Army and the Japanese Man in Meiji Society and State', in Barbara Molony and Kathleen Uno (eds), *Gendering Modern Japanese History* (Harvard University Press, 2005); Kawano Hitoshi, 'Japanese Combat Morale: A Case Study of the Thirty-Seventh Division', in Peattie et al. (eds), *The Battle for China*; Aaron William Moore, *Writing War: Soldiers Record the Japanese Empire* (Harvard University Press, 2013); Haruko Taya Cook and Theodore F. Cook, *Japan at War: An Oral History* (W. W. Norton & Company, 1992). On Japan and China, see Joshua A. Fogel, ' "Shanghai-Japan": The Japanese Residents' Association of Shanghai', *Journal of Asian Studies*, 59:4 (2000); Rana Mitter, *China's War with Japan, 1937–1945: the Struggle for Survival* (Allen Lane, 2013); James McClain, *Japan: A Modern History* (W. W. Norton & Company, 2002); Peter Harmsen, *Shanghai 1937: Stalingrad on the Yangtze* (Casemate, 2013); Yang Tianshi, 'Chiang Kai-Shek and the Battles of Shanghai and Nanjing', in Peattie et al. (eds), *The Battle for China*. On discontent in rural and urban Japan, see Ann Waswo, 'The Transformation of Rural Society, 1900–1950', in Peter Duus (ed.), *The Cambridge History of Japan*, Volume 6: *The Twentieth Century* (Cambridge University Press, 1989); R. Dore and T. Ōuchi, 'The Rural Origins of Japanese Fascism', in James William Morley (ed.), *The Dilemmas of Growth in Prewar Japan* (Princeton University Press, 1972); McClain, *Japan: A Modern History*. On Japanese gangsterism, see Eiko Maruko Siniawer, *Ruffians, Yakuza, Nationalists: The Violent Politics of Modern Japan, 1860–1960* (Cornell University Press, 2008); Sven Saaler, 'The Kokuryūkai (Black Dragon Society) and the Rise of Nationalism, Pan-Asianism, and Militarism in Japan, 1901–1925', *International Journal of Asian Studies*, 11:2 (2014); John Wayne Sabey, 'The Gen'yōsha, the Kokuryūkai, and Japanese Expansionism', PhD thesis (University of Michigan, 1972). 'Of late' appears in Waswo, 'The Transformation'. 'Dad came to the 12 p.m. visiting hours', is quoted in Moore, *Writing War*. The testimony of Tominaga Shozō features in Cook and Cook, *Japan at War*. 'Tough, long-haired' is the comment of a foreign journalist working in Shanghai, reproduced in Harmsen, *Shanghai 1937*. Ernest Satow's comments come from Sir Ernest Satow, *A Diplomat in Japan* (Seeley, Service & Co, 1921).

10 DIVINE BLUSTER

On Nanjing in late 1937 and early 1938, see Hallett Abend in the *New York Times* ('Ultimatum by Japan', 10 December 1937; 'Nanking Entered by Japanese Army', 11 December; 'Japan in Three Drives on Chinese Lines', 17 December; 'Reign of Disorder Goes on in Nanking', 25 January 1938); [No byline], 'Tokyo is Celebrating Capture of Nanking', 12 December 1937; [No byline], 'Nanking Occupied', 14 December 1937; [No byline], 'Nanking's Silence Terrifies Shanghai, 15 December 1937; [No byline], 'March of Victory into Nanking Set', 16 December 1937; [No byline], 'Conquerors Enter City in Triumph', 18 December 1937; F. Tillman Durdin in the *New York Times* ('All Captives Slain', 18 December 1937; 'Japanese Atrocities Marked the Fall of Nanking After Chinese Command Fled', 9 January 1938); Aaron William Moore, *Writing War: Soldiers Record the Japanese Empire* (Harvard University Press, 2013); Herbert Bix, *Hirohito and the Making of Modern Japan* (Gerald Duckworth, 2001); Kasahara Tokushi, *Nankin Jiken* (Iwanami Shinsho, 1997). On the ideals and realities of 'Pan-Asianism', see Peter Duus, 'Imperialism Without Colonies: The Vision of a Greater East Asia Co-prosperity Sphere', *Diplomacy and Statecraft*, 7:1 (1996); Brian Victoria, 'War Remembrance in Japan's Buddhist Cemeteries, Part I: Kannon Hears the Cries of War', *Asia-Pacific Journal*, 13:31 (2015). On Nishida Kitarō, D. T. Suzuki and the Kyoto School, see Robert Sharf, 'The Zen of Japanese Nationalism', *History of Religions* 33:1 (1993); Robert E. Carter, *The Kyoto School* (SUNY Press, 2013); James Heisig, *Much Ado about Nothingness: Essays on Nishida and Tanabe* (CreateSpace, 2015); Heisig, *Nothingness and Desire: An East–West Philosophical Antiphony* (University of Hawaii Press, 2013); Heisig, *Philosophers of Nothingness: An Essay on the Kyoto School* (University of Hawaii Press, 1996); James Heisig and John C. Maraldo (eds), *Rude Awakenings: Zen, the Kyoto School, and the Question of Nationalism* (University of Hawaii Press, 1995); Brian Victoria, *Zen At War*, 2nd edn (Rowman and Littlefield, 2005); Kemmyō Taira Satō (translated in collaboration with Thomas Kirchner), 'D. T. Suzuki and the Question of War', *Eastern Buddhist*, 39:1 (2008). On Koji Zen, see Janine Tasca Sawada, *Practical Pursuits: Religion, Politics, and Personal Cultivation in Nineteenth-Century Japan* (University of Hawaii Press, 2004). On Uesugi Shinkichi and Kakehi Katsuhiko, see Walter Skya, *Japan's Holy War: The Ideology of Radical Shinto* (Duke University Press, 2009). On the assassination of Prime Minister Inukai Tsuyoshi, see Skya, *Japan's Holy War*, and Hugh Byas, *Government by Assassination* (Alfred A. Knopf, 1942). On *Kokutai No Hongi*, see Ito Enkichi et al. (translated by John

Owen Gauntlett, with an Introduction by Robert King Hall), *Kokutai no Hongi: Cardinal Principles of the National Entity of Japan* (Harvard University Press, 1949). On the war, see Peter Duus, 'Imperialism Without Colonies'; Alvin D. Coox, 'The Pacific War', in Duus (ed.), *The Cambridge History of Japan*; Gordon W. Prange, *At Dawn We Slept: the Untold Story of Pearl Harbor*, new edn (Penguin, 1991). On the home front, see James McClain, *Japan: A Modern History* (W. W. Norton & Company, 2002); Robert D. Schildgen, *Toyohiko Kagawa: Apostle of Love and Social Justice* (Centenary Books, 1988); Sheldon Garon, 'Luxury is the Enemy: Mobilizing Savings and Popularizing Thrift in Wartime Japan', *Journal of Japanese Studies*, 26:1 (2000); Bix, *Hirohito*; 'Sensational Rumours, Seditious Graffiti, and the Nightmares of the Thought Police', in John Dower, *Japan in War and Peace: Essays on History, Race, and Culture* (HarperCollins, 1995); Ross Cohen, *Fu-Go: The Curious History of Japan's Balloon Bomb Attack on America* (University of Nebraska Press, 2014); Thomas R. Searle, 'It made a lot of sense to kill skilled workers: The Firebombing of Tokyo in March 1945', *Journal of Military History*, 66:1 (2002); Thomas Havens, *Valley of Darkness: The Japanese People and World War Two* (University Press of America, 1986). On Momotarō, see David A. Henry, 'Momotarō, or the Peach Boy: Japan's Best-Loved Folktale as National Allegory', PhD thesis (University of Michigan, 2009). On Japan's kamikaze pilots, see Emiko Ohnuki-Tierney, *Kamikaze, Cherry Blossoms, and Nationalisms: The Militarization of Aesthetics in Japanese History* (University of Chicago Press, 2002) and Ohnuki-Tierney, *Kamikaze Diaries: Reflections of Japanese Student Soldiers* (University of Chicago Press, 2006); Albert Axell and Hideaki Kase, *Kamikaze: Japan's Suicide Gods* (Longman, 2002); Hatsuho Naitao, *Thunder Gods: The Kamikaze Pilots Tell Their Story* (Kodansha, 1989). 'We are fighting' is quoted in Jonathan Fenby, *Generalissimo: Chiang Kai-Shek and the China He Lost* (Free Press, 2003). Maeda Yoshihiko is quoted in Kasahara, *Nankin Jiken*. 'Atrocities of our army' is quoted in Bix, *Hirohito*. 'None of this' is paraphrased from a comment recorded in Sharf, 'The Zen of Japanese Nationalism'. The 'Crystallized superstition' and 'exceedingly filthy' is quoted in Jason Ananda Josephson, 'When Buddhism Became a "Religion": Religion and Superstition in the Writings of Inoue Enryō', *Japanese Journal of Religious Studies*, 33:1 (2006). 'Doffing caps, clasping hands' is Byas, *Government By Assassination*. 'Coercion sphere' is reported in Heisig and Maraldo (eds), *Rude Awakenings*. 'Patiently have We . . .' was printed in every Japanese newspaper on 8 December 1941. Hayashi Ichizō's testimony is from Ohnuki-Tierney, *Kamikaze Diaries* and *Kamikaze, Cherry Blossoms*.

11 AFTERLIVES

On Ando Akira, Kodama Yoshio, and the Japanese underworld in general, see Mark Gayn, *Japan Diary* (1948; new edn Charles E. Tuttle Publishing Company, 1981); Richard Sims, *Japanese Political History Since the Meiji Restoration, 1868–2000* (C. Hurst Publishers, London, 2001); David E. Kaplan and Alec Dubro, *Yakuza: Japan's Criminal Underworld* (University of California Press, 2003); Eiko Maruko Siniawer, *Ruffians, Yakuza, Nationalists: The Violent Politics of Modern Japan, 1860–1960* (Cornell University Press, 2008). On Morita Akio, see Morita Akio, *Made in Japan* (Dutton, 1986); John Nathan, *Sony: the Private Life* (HarperCollins, 1999). On Japanese politics in the wake of defeat, see Herbert Bix, *Hirohito and the Making of Modern Japan* (Gerald Duckworth, 2001); John Dower, *Empire and Aftermath: Yoshida Shigeru and the Japanese Experience, 1878–1954* (Harvard University Press, 1988); James McClain, *Japan: A Modern History* (W. W. Norton & Company, 2002); Gayn, *Japan Diary*; J. Victor Koschmann, *Revolution and Subjectivity in Postwar Japan* (University of Chicago Press, 1996) and 'Intellectuals and Politics', in Andrew Gordon (ed.), *Postwar Japan as History* (University of California Press, 1993). On Sakaguchi Ango, see James Dorsey, 'Culture, Nationalism, and Sakaguchi Ango', *Journal of Japanese Studies*, 27:2 (2001). On army stockpiling and looting, see Theodore Cohen, *Remaking Japan: the American Occupation as New Deal* (Free Press, 1987). On black markets before and after the war, see Owen Griffiths, 'Need, Greed, and Protest in Japan's Black Market, 1938–1949', *Journal of Social History*, 35:4 (2002); Kaplan and Dubro, *Yakuza*; Siniawer, *Ruffians, Yakuza, Nationalists*; Edward Seidensticker, *Tokyo Rising: The City Since the Earthquake* (Harvard University Press, 1991). On women after the war, see 'Citizens', in Vera Mackie, *Feminism in Modern Japan: Citizenship, Embodiment and Sexuality* (Cambridge University Press, 2003); Mire Koikari, 'Exporting Democracy? American Women, "Feminist Reforms", and Politics of Imperialism in the U.S. Occupation of Japan, 1945–1952', *Frontiers: A Journal of Women Studies*, 23:1 (2002); Bix, *Hirohito*; Gayn, *Japan Diary*. For the broader post-war picture within Japan, see John Dower, *Embracing Defeat: Japan in the Aftermath of World War II*, new edn (Penguin, 2000). On first-hand experiences of the Hiroshima bomb, see Mikio Kanda (ed.), *Widows of Hiroshima: The Life Stories of Nineteen Peasant Wives* (St Martin's Press, 1989). On Koreans who died as a result of the Hiroshima bomb, see Michael Weiner, 'The Representation of Absence and the Absence of Representation: Korean Victims of the Atomic Bomb', in Michael Weiner (ed.), *Japan's Minorities: The Illusion of Homogeneity* (Routledge, 1997).

12 BLUE NOTE

On jazz in Japan, see Hampton Hawes (with Don Asher), *Raise Up Off Me: A Portrait of Hampton Hawes* (1974; new edn Da Capo Press, 2001); Akiyoshi Toshiko, *Jazu to ikiru* (Iwanami Shoten, 1996); E. Taylor Atkins, *Blue Nippon: Authenticating Jazz in Japan* (Duke University Press, 2011); Yusuke Torii, 'Swing Ideology and Its Cold War Discontents in US–Japan Relations, 1944–1968', PhD thesis (George Washington University, 2007); Kevin Fellezs, 'Deracinated Flower: Toshiko Akiyoshi's "Trace in Jazz History"', *Jazz Perspectives*, 4:1 (2010); Leonard Feather, 'Toshiko Akiyoshi: Contemporary Sculptress of Sound', *Down Beat* magazine (October 1977) and 'East Meets West, or Never the Twain Shall Cease, *Down Beat* (June 1976); Steven Moore, 'The Art of Becoming a Jazz Musician: An Interview with Toshiko Akiyoshi', *Michigan Quarterly Review*, XLIII:3 (2004); Rachel M. Peterson, 'Toshiko Akiyoshi's Development of a New Jazz Fusion', MA dissertation (University of Arizona, 2010); Interview with Akiyoshi Toshiko, conducted by the author, June 2017. On casualty projections for a land war on Japan's main islands, see D. M. Giangreco, *Hell to Pay: Operation Downfall and the Invasion of Japan, 1945–1947* (Naval Institute Press, 2009) and James McClain, *Japan: A Modern History* (W. W. Norton & Company, 2002). It was suggested that up to a million Americans might die in the assault, but such figures have tended to be regarded by historians as based on little evidence. On Beate Sirota, see Beate Sirota, *The Only Woman in the Room: A Memoir*, new edn (University of Chicago Press, 2014); Nassrine Azimi and Michel Wasserman, *Last Boat to Yokohama: The Life and Legacy of Beate Sirota Gordon* (Three Rooms Press, 2015); John Dower, *Embracing Defeat: Japan in the Aftermath of World War II*, new edn (Penguin, 2000). On life, politics, and censorship in Japan after August 1945, see Dower, *Embracing Defeat*; Elise Tipton, *Modern Japan: a Social and Political History*, 3rd edn (Routledge, 2015); McClain, *Japan: A Modern History*; Mark Gayn, *Japan Diary* (1948; new edn Charles E. Tuttle Publishing Company, 1981); Stephen Large, *Emperor Hirohito and Showa Japan: A Political Biography* (Routledge, 1992); Kyōko Hirano, *Mr Smith Goes to Tokyo: Japanese Cinema Under the American Occupation, 1945–1952* (Smithsonian Books, new edn 1992); Mark Sandler, *The Confusion Era: Art and Culture in Japan During the Allied Occupation, 1945–1952* (University of Washington Press, 1996); Donald Richie, *A Hundred Years of Japanese Film*, revised and updated edn (Kodansha America, 2012). On the musical accompaniment to the opening of Shimbashi Station, and on pre-war music in Japan more generally, see E. W. Pope, 'Songs of the Empire: Continental Asia in Japanese Wartime Popular Music', PhD thesis (University of

Washington, 2003). On popular music and protest, see Christine Yano, *Tears of Longing: Nostalgia and the Nation in Japanese Popular Song* (Harvard University Press, 2002); E. Patricia Tsurumi, *Factory Girls: Women in the Thread Mills of Meiji Japan* (Princeton University Press, 1990); Taylor, *Blue Nippon*; Hiromu Nagahara, *Tokyo Boogie-Woogie: Japan's Pop Era and its Discontents* (Harvard University Press, 2017). On the Paris and Vienna expos, see Yasuko Tsukahara, 'State Ceremony and Music in Meiji-era Japan', *Nineteenth-Century Music Review*, 10:2 (2014). On music and the broader Cold War context, see Penny Von Eschen, *Satchmo Blows Up the World: Jazz Ambassadors Play the Cold War* (Harvard University Press, 2006); Torii, 'Swing Ideology'. For an assessment of land reform by someone who witnessed it at first hand, see R. P. Dore, 'The Japanese Land Reform in Retrospect', *Far Eastern Survey*, 27:12 (1958). MacArthur's February note is reproduced in Dower, *Embracing Defeat*. 'Everybody is talking', is from Hirano, *Mr Smith Goes to Tokyo*. 'One of those cracker Texas colonels' is Hampton Hawes, in *Raise Up Off Me*. 'Our interracial group' is from Von Eschen, *Satchmo Blows Up the World*. 'We are starving!' reported in Gayn, *Japan Diary*.

13 BRIGHT LIFE

On the promulgation of the new constitution, see John Dower, *Embracing Defeat: Japan in the Aftermath of World War II*, new edn (Penguin, 2000). On the Occupation in general, see Dower, *Embracing Defeat* and *Empire and Aftermath: Yoshida Shigeru and the Japanese Experience, 1878–1954* (Harvard University Press, 1988); James McClain, *Japan: A Modern History* (W. W. Norton & Company, 2002). On Morita Akio and Tokyo Tsūshin Kōgyō/Sony, see Morita Akio, *Made in Japan* (Dutton, 1986); John Nathan, *Sony: the Private Life* (HarperCollins, 1999); Mark J. Stefik and Barbara Stefik, *Breakthrough: Stories and Strategies of Radical Innovation* (MIT Press, 2004). On Mitsubishi and the *zaibatsu*, see Hiroyuki Odagiri, 'Shipbuilding and Aircraft', in Hiroyuki Odagiri and Akira Goto (eds), *Technology and Industrial Development in Japan: Building Capabilities by Learning, Innovation, and Public Policy* (Oxford University Press, 1996); Eleanor M. Hadley (with Patricia Hagan Kuwayama), *Memoir of a Trustbuster: A Lifelong Adventure with Japan* (University of Hawaii Press, 2002). On the Japanese economy, see Chalmers Johnson, *MITI and the Japanese Miracle: The Growth of Industrial Policy, 1925–1975* (Stanford University Press, 1982); David Flath, *The Japanese Economy*, 3rd edn

(Oxford University Press, 2014); Yutaka Kosai, 'The Postwar Japanese Economy', in Peter Duus (ed.), *The Cambridge History of Japan*, Volume 6: *The Twentieth Century* (Cambridge University Press, 1989); James McClain, *Japan: A Modern History* (W. W. Norton & Company, 2002). On the SDF, see Akihiro Sadō, *The Self-Defense Forces and Postwar Politics in Japan* (JPIC, 2017); Dower, *Empire and Aftermath*; Thomas Alan Drohan, *American-Japanese Security Arrangements, Past and Present*, paperback edn (McFarland & Co., North Carolina, 2007). On Nissan and the automotive industry, see Hiroyuki Odagiri, 'Automobiles', in Odagiri and Goto (eds), *Technology and Industrial Development in Japan*. On Japan's Olympic history, see Christian Tagsold, 'Modernity and the Carnivalesque (Tokyo 1964)', in Vida Bajc (ed.), *Surveilling and Securing the Olympics: From Tokyo 1964 to London 2012 and Beyond* (Palgrave Macmillan, 2015), 'Modernity, Space, and National Representation at the Tokyo Olympics 1964', *Urban History*, 37:2 (2010), and – particularly on controversies concerning national symbols – 'The Tokyo Olympics as a Token of Renationalization', in Andreas Niehaus and Max Seinsch (eds), *Olympic Japan: Ideals and Realities of (Inter)Nationalism* (Ergon Verlag, Würzburg, 2007); Sandra Collins, *The 1940 Tokyo Games: The Missing Olympics: Japan, the Asian Olympics, and the Olympic Movement* (Routledge, 2008), 'Mediated Modernities and Mythologies in the Opening Ceremonies of 1964 Tokyo, 1988 Seoul, and 2008 Beijing Olympics Games', *International Journal of the History of Sport*, 29:16 (2012), and 'East Asian Olympic Desires: Identity on the Global Stage in the 1964 Tokyo, 1988 Seoul, and 2008 Beijing Games', *International Journal of the History of Sport* 28:16 (2011); Allen Guttmann and Lee Thompson, *Japanese Sports: A History* (University of Hawaii Press, 1998); Paul Droubie, 'Phoenix Arisen: Japan as Peaceful Internationalist at the 1964 Tokyo Summer Olympics', *International Journal of the History of Sport*, 28:16 (2011) and Droubie, 'Playing the Nation: 1964 Summer Olympics and Japanese Identity', PhD thesis (University of Illinois at Urbana-Champaign, 2009); Christopher Brasher, *Tokyo 1964: A Diary of the XVIIIth Olympiad* (Stanley Paul, 1964); John Bryant, *Chris Brasher: The Man Who Made the London Marathon* (Aurum Press, 2012); Jessamyn R. Abel, 'Japan's Sporting Diplomacy: the 1964 Tokyo Olympiad', *International History Review*, 34:2 (2012); The Organizing Committee for the Games of the XVIII Olympiad, *The Games of the XVIII Olympiad, Tokyo 1964: The Official Report of the Organizing Committee* (1964). See also Ichikawa Kon's documentary film about the games: *Tōkyō Orinpikku [Tokyo Olympiad]* (1965). On the shinkansen, see Christopher P. Hood, *Shinkansen: From Bullet Train to Symbol of*

Modern Japan (Routledge, 2006); Droubie, 'Playing the Nation'. 'There's something rather fishy' is reproduced in Theodore Cohen, *Remaking Japan: the American Occupation as New Deal* (Free Press, 1987). A 'weapon that flashed and shone' is from Morita, *Made in Japan*. 'Laughed out of the room' is from Nathan, *Sony*. 'Height of madness' and 'I felt a surge' are reproduced in Hood, *Shinkansen*. Note that 'divine wind' was a phrase in use during the early years of aircraft technology in Japan, distinct from the 'Special Attack Unit' formed towards the end of the Second World War (see Collins, *The 1940 Tokyo Games*).

14 EXHIBITIONISM

On Japanese public opinion concerning the San Francisco Peace Treaty, see James McClain, *Japan: A Modern History* (W. W. Norton & Company, 2002). On the *Lucky Dragon 5* incident, military bases and the US–Japan relationship, see Aya Homei, 'The Contentious Death of Mr Kuboyama: Science as Politics in the 1954 *Lucky Dragon* Incident', *Japan Forum*, 25:2 (2013); J. M. Miller, 'Fractured Alliance: Anti-Base Protests and Postwar US–Japanese Relations', *Diplomatic History*, 38:5 (2014); Andrew Gordon, *A Modern History of Japan*, 2nd edn (Oxford University Press, 2008); Donald Eugene Shoop, 'Sunagawa Incident', PhD thesis (University of Denver, 1985). On Kishi Nobusuke, see Mark Driscoll, *Absolute Erotic, Absolute Grotesque: The Living, Dead, and Undead in Japan's Imperialism, 1895–1945* (Duke University Press, 2010); Richard J. Samuels, 'Kishi and Corruption: An Anatomy of the 1955 System', Japan Policy Research Institute Working Paper 83 (2001). On post-war Japanese art movements, see Alexandra Munroe, *Japanese Art After 1945: Scream Against the Sky* (Harry N. Abrams, 1994); Linda Hoaglund (introduction by John Dower), 'Protest Art in 1950s Japan: The Forgotten Reportage Painters', *Asia-Pacific Journal*, 12:43 (2014) and 'ANPO: Art X War – In Havoc's Wake', *Asia-Pacific Journal*, 9:41 (2011); Peter Eckersall, *Theorizing the Angura Space: Avant-garde Performance and Politics in Japan, 1960–2000* (Brill, Leiden, 2006); David Elliott, *Reconstructions: Avant-Garde Art in Japan, 1945–1965* (Universe Pub, 1987). On protest, see Stuart J. Dowsey (ed.), *Zengakuren: Japan's Revolutionary Students* (The Ishi Press, California, 1970); Eiko Maruko Siniawer, *Ruffians, Yakuza, Nationalists: The Violent Politics of Modern Japan, 1860–1960* (Cornell University Press, 2008); McClain, *Japan*; Jansen, *The Making of Modern Japan*; David E. Kaplan and Alec Dubro, *Yakuza: Japan's Criminal Underworld* (University of California Press, 2003); Rikki

Kersten, 'The Intellectual Culture of Postwar Japan and the 1968–1969 University of Tokyo Struggles: Repositioning the Self in Postwar Thought', *Social Science Japan Journal*, 12:2 (2009); Takemas Ando, 'Transforming "Everydayness": Japanese New Left Movements and the Meaning of their Direct Action', *Japanese Studies*, 33:1 (2013). On pop and TV culture in Japan, see Jonathan E. Abel, 'Masked Justice: Allegories of the Superhero in Cold War Japan', *Japan Forum*, 26:2 (2014); Jayson Makoto Chun, *A Nation of a Hundred Million Idiots? A Social History of Japanese Television, 1953–1973* (Routledge, 2006); Hiromu Nagahara, *Tokyo Boogie-Woogie: Japan's Pop Era and its Discontents* (Harvard University Press, 2017); Carolyn Stevens, *Japanese Popular Music: Culture, Authenticity, and Power* (Routledge, 2008); Ian F. Martin, *Quit Your Band! Musical Notes from the Japanese Underground* (Awai Books, 2016); Deborah Shamoon, 'Sun Tribe: Cultural Production and Popular Culture in Post-War Japan', *E-ASPAC (An Electronic Journal of Asian Studies on the Pacific Coast)*, 1 (2002); Michael K. Bourdaghs, *Sayonara Amerika, Sayonara Nippon: A Geopolitical Pre-History of J-Pop* (Columbia University Press, 2012). On film, see Donald Richie, *A Hundred Years of Japanese Film*, revised and updated edn (Kodansha America, 2012); David Dresser, *Eros Plus Massacre: An Introduction to the Japanese New Wave Cinema* (Indiana University Press, 1988); Isolde Standish, *Politics, Porn and Protest: Japanese Avant-Garde Cinema in the 1960s and 1970s* (Continuum, 2011); David Dresser (ed.), *Ozu's Tokyo Story* (Cambridge University Press, 2010); Woojeong Joo, 'I Was Born Middle Class But . . . : Ozu Yasujiro's *Shōshimin Eiga* in the Early 1930s', *Journal of Japanese & Korean Cinema*, 4:2 (2012). 'Nation of 100 million idiots' and 'waddling like a child with polio' are reproduced in Chun, *A Nation of a Hundred Million Idiots?*. 'Masterpiece of colonial literature' is from Nagahara, *Tokyo Boogie-Woogie*. 'A picture is no good' is quoted in Richie, *A Hundred Years of Japanese Film*. 'World around' is Masumara Yasuzo, quoted in Dresser, *Eros Plus Massacre*. On Japanese consumption patterns, see Andrew Gordon, 'Consumption, Consumerism, and Japanese Modernity', in Frank Trentmann (ed.), *Oxford Handbook of the History of Consumption* (Oxford University Press, 2012); Penelope Francks, 'Inconspicuous Consumption: *Sake*, Beer and the Birth of the Consumer in Japan', *Journal of Asian Studies*, 68:1 (February 2009); Richard Ronald and Allison Alexy (eds), *Home and Family in Japan: Continuity and Transformation* (Routledge, 2011). On Japanese art and cultural diplomacy, see Noriko Aso, 'Sumptuous Re-past: The 1964 Tokyo Olympics Arts Festival', *Positions: East Asia Cultures Critique*, 10:1 (2002); Reiko Tomii, 'How *Gendai Bijutsu* Stole the "Museum": An Institutional Observation of the Vanguard 1960s', in Thomas J. Rimer (ed.), *Since Meiji: Perspectives on the Japanese Visual Arts, 1868–2000* (University of Hawaii Press, 2011). On Okamoto Tarō, see Elliott, *Reconstructions*. On avant-garde art more generally in post-war Japan, see Munroe, *Japanese Art After 1945*; William Marotti, *Money, Trains and Guillotines: Art and Revolution in 1960s Japan* (Duke University Press, 2013); Beth Noble, ' "This is not art": An Investigation into Explorations of Democracy and the Politics of Space in the Yomiuri Indépendant 1949–1963', MSc dissertation (University of Edinburgh, 2017). On Japanese theatre, see Brian Powell, *Japan's Modern Theatre: A Century of Change and Continuity* (Japan Library, 2002); Benito Ortolani, *The Japanese Theatre: From Shamanistic Ritual to Contemporary Pluralism*, revised edn (Princeton University Press, 1995); Eckersall, *Theorizing the Angura Space*; Miryam Sas, *Experimental Arts in Postwar Japan: Moments of Encounter, Engagement, and Imagined Return* (Harvard University Press, 2011); Carol Fisher Sorgenfrei, *Unspeakable Acts: The Avant-Garde Theatre of Terayama Shūji and Postwar Japan* (University of Hawaii Press, 2005); Ian Buruma, *A Tokyo Romance: A Memoir* (Penguin Press, 2018). On Ōe Kenzaburō and Mishima Yukio, see Yumiko Iida, *Rethinking Identity in Modern Japan: Nationalism as Aesthetics* (Routledge, 2002); Donald Keene, *A History of Japanese Literature*: Volume 3: *Dawn to the West: Japanese Literature of the Modern Era* (Holt, Rinehart and Winston, 1984); Susan J. Napier, *Escape from the Wasteland: Romanticism and Realism in the Fiction of Mishima Yukio and Oe Kenzaburo* (Harvard University Press, 1991); Gwenn Boardman Petersen, *The Moon in the Water: Understanding Tanizaki, Kawabata, and Mishima* (University of Hawaii Press, 1979); Ōe Kenzaburō (translated by Luk Van Haute; introduction by Masao Miyoshi), *Seventeen & J: Two Novels* (electronic edn Foxrock Books/Evergreen Review, 2015). On protest and resistance, see Ando, 'Transforming "Everydayness": Japanese New Left Movements and the Meaning of their Direct Action'; Patricia G. Steinhoff, 'Hijackers, Bombers, and Bank Robbers: Managerial Style in the Japanese Red Army', *Journal of Asian Studies*, 48:4 (1989); Yoshikuni Igarashi, 'Dead Bodies and Living Guns: The United Red Army and Its Deadly Pursuit of Revolution, 1971–1972', *Japanese Studies*, 27:2 (2007); William Andrews, *Dissenting Japan: A History of Japanese Radicalism and Counterculture from 1945 to Fukushima* (C. Hurst & Co Publishers, 2015); Mark Schreiber, *Shocking Crimes of Postwar Japan* (Yenbooks, 1996); Eiji Oguma, 'Japan's 1968: A Collective Reaction to Rapid Economic Growth in an Age of Turmoil', *Asia-Pacific Journal*, 13:12 (2015); Chris Perkins, *The United Red Army On Screen: Cinema, Aesthetics, and the Politics of Memory* (Palgrave Macmillan, 2015). 'A naked human being' is quoted in Munroe, *Japanese Art After 1945*. 'Postwar Japanese' is quoted in Iida, *Rethinking Identity in Modern Japan*.

15 PULLING STRINGS

On Minamata disease and Japan's post-war environmental crisis, see Mami Aoyama, 'Minamata: Disability and the Sea of Sorrow', in P. Block et al. (eds), *Occupying Disability: Critical Approaches to Community, Justice, and Decolonizing Disability* (Springer, 2016); Norie Huddle, Michael Reich and Nahum Stiskin, *Island of Dreams: Environmental Crisis in Japan* (Schenkman Pub Co., 1987); Frank K. Upham, *Law and Social Change in Postwar Japan* (Harvard University Press, 1989): Timothy S. George, *Minamata: Pollution and the Struggle for Democracy in Postwar Japan*, paperback edn (Harvard University Press, 2002); Jeffrey Broadbent, *Environmental Politics in Japan: Networks of Power and Protest* (Cambridge University Press, 1998). On citizenship, protest and the law, see Upham, *Law and Social Change in Postwar Japan*; Simon Andrew Avenell, *Making Japanese Citizens: Civil Society and the Mythology of the Shimin in Postwar Japan* (University of California Press, 2010); Hiroshi Oda, *Japanese Law*, 3rd edn (Oxford University Press, 2011); Patricia G. Steinhoff (ed.), *Going to Court to Change Japan: Social Movements and the Law in Contemporary Japan* (University of Michigan Center for Japanese Studies, 2014); William Andrews, *Dissenting Japan: A History of Japanese Radicalism and Counterculture from 1945 to Fukushima* (C. Hurst & Co Publishers, 2015). On urban population, see T. Ito, 'Tōkaidō – Megalopolis of Japan', *GeoJournal*, 4:3 (1980). On women and women's rights, see Yusuke Torii, 'Swing Ideology and Its Cold War Discontents in US–Japan Relations, 1944–1968', PhD thesis (George Washington University, 2007); Mire Koikari, 'Exporting Democracy? American Women, "Feminist Reforms", and Politics of Imperialism in the U.S. Occupation of Japan, 1945–1952', *Frontiers: A Journal of Women Studies*, 23:1 (2002); and Koikare, 'Rethinking Gender and Power in the US Occupation of Japan, 1945–1952', *Gender & History*, 11:2 (1999). On Japanese politics, see Richard Sims, *Japanese Political History Since the Meiji Restoration, 1868–2000* (C. Hurst Publishers, London, 2001); Morita Akio, *Made in Japan* (Dutton, 1986). On Minobe Ryōkichi, see Andrew Gordon, *A Modern History of Japan*, 2nd edn (Oxford University Press, 2008), and Avenell, *Making Japanese Citizens*. 'You're a parent, too' features in Upham, *Law*.

16 MOVING MOUNTAINS

On manga, see Brigitte Koyama-Richard, *One Thousand Years of Manga* (Flammarion-Pere Castor, 2014); Toni Johnson-Woods (ed.), *Manga: An Anthology of Global and Cultural Perspectives*, reprint edn (Continuum, 2009); J. B. Thomas, *Drawing on Tradition: Manga, Anime, and Religion in Contemporary Japan* (University of Hawaii Press, 2012). On Miyazaki Hayao and Nausicaä, see Shigemi Inaga, 'Miyazaki Hayao's Epic Comic Series: "Nausicaä in the Valley of the Wind": An Attempt at Interpretation', *Japan Review*, 11 (1999); Marc Hairston, 'The Reluctant Messiah: Miyazaki Hayao's *Nausicaä of the Valley of the Wind* Manga', in Johnson-Woods (ed.), *Manga*; Thomas, *Drawing on Tradition*. On Japan in the 1970s, see Andrew Gordon, *A Modern History of Japan*, 2nd edn (Oxford University Press, 2008); James McClain, *Japan: A Modern History* (W. W. Norton & Company, 2002); Morita Akio, *Made in Japan* (Dutton, 1986). On volunteerism, see Simon Andrew Avenell, *Making Japanese Citizens: Civil Society and the Mythology of the Shimin in Postwar Japan* (University of California Press, 2010). On Sino-Japanese relations, see June Teufel Dreyer, *Middle Kingdom and Empire of the Rising Sun* (Oxford University Press, 2016); Richard McGregor, *Asia's Reckoning: The Struggle for Global Dominance* (Allen Lane, 2017); Patricia G. Steinhoff (ed.), *Going to Court to Change Japan: Social Movements and the Law in Contemporary Japan* (University of Michigan Center for Japanese Studies, 2014). On the 'Discover Japan' campaign, see Marilyn Ivy, *Discourses of the Vanishing: Modernity, Phantasm, Japan* (University of Chicago Press, 1995). On 'new' and 'new new' religions, see Susumu Shimazono, *From Salvation to Spirituality: Popular Religious Movements in Modern Japan* (Trans Pacific Press, 2004). On Aum Shinrikyō, see Ian Reader, *Religious Violence in Contemporary Japan: The Case of Aum Shinrikyō* (Curzon Press, Surrey, 2000). On Japanese politics, see Richard Sims, *Japanese Political History Since the Meiji Restoration, 1868–2000* (C. Hurst Publishers, London, 2001); David E. Kaplan and Alec Dubro, *Yakuza: Japan's Criminal Underworld* (University of California Press, 2003); Jeff Kingston, *Japan's Quiet Transformation: Social change and civil society in the twenty-first century* (Routledge, 2004); Jacob M. Schlesinger, *Shadow Shoguns: The Rise and Fall of Japan's Postwar Political Machine* (Simon & Schuster, 1997). On Japan as a 'construction state', see Gavan McCormack, 'Growth, Construction, and the Environment: Japan's Construction State', *Japanese Studies*, 15:1 (1995); *The Emptiness of Japanese Affluence* (M. E. Sharpe, 1996), and McCormack, 'Japan: Prime Minister Abe Shinzō's Agenda', in *Asia-Pacific Journal*, 14:24 (2016); Alex Kerr, *Dogs and Demons: Tales from the Dark Side of Modern Japan* (Hill & Wang, 2001). On the

Japanese government's response to the Great Hanshin-Awaji earthquake, see David Pilling, *Bending Adversity: Japan and the Art of Survival* (Allen Lane, 2014). 'My political philosophy' and 'Every city, town, and village' are quoted in Schlesinger, *Shadow Shoguns*.

17 TELLING TALES

On Japan's pre-history, see Conrad Schirokauer, David Lurie and Suzanne Gay, *A Brief History of Japanese Civilization*, 4th edn (Wadsworth Publishing, Boston, 2012); Conrad Totman, *A History of Japan*, 2nd edn (Wiley-Blackwell, 2005). On Okinawa's history, see George H. Kerr, *Okinawa: The History of an Island People*, revised edn (Tuttle Publishing, 2000); Masahide Ota, 'Re-Examining the History of the Battle of Okinawa' and Koji Taira, 'The Battle of Okinawa in Japanese History Books', in Chalmers Johnson (ed.), *Okinawa: Cold War Island* (Japan Policy Research Institute, 1999); Richard McGregor, *Asia's Reckoning: The Struggle for Global Dominance* (Allen Lane, 2017); Laura Hein and Mark Selden (eds), *Islands of Discontent: Okinawan Responses to Japanese and American Power* (Rowman & Littlefield Publishers, 2003); Yoko Fukumura and Martha Matsuoka, 'Redefining Security: Okinawa Women's Resistance to US Militarism', in Nancy A. Naples and Manisha Desai (eds), *Women's Activism and Globalization: Linking Local Struggles and Transnational Politics* (Routledge, 2002). On the 1995 rape incident, see 'The Rape of a Schoolgirl', in Hein and Selden, *Islands of Discontent*; Carolyn Francis, 'Women and Military Violence', in Johnson (ed.), *Okinawa: Cold War Island*; Kevin Sullivan, '3 Servicemen Admit Roles in Rape of Okinawa Girl', *Washington Post*, 8 November 1995; Andrew Pollack, 'One Pleads Guilty to Okinawa Rape; 2 Others Admit Role', *New York Times*, 8 November 1995; [Associated Press], 'Sailor Testifies About Raping Japanese Girl', *Los Angeles Times*, 28 December 1995; Michael A. Lev, '3 GIs Convicted in Okinawa Rape, *Chicago Tribune*, 7 March 1996. On Japan's foreign relations, see June Teufel Dreyer, *Middle Kingdom and Empire of the Rising Sun* (Oxford University Press, 2016); McGregor, *Asia's Reckoning*; for the 1995 Murayama statement, see the website of Japan's Ministry of Foreign Affairs (<http://www.mofa.go.jp/announce/press/pm/murayama/9508.html>); for Education Minister Shimamura Yoshinobu's comment, see Ryuji Mukac, 'Japan's Diet Resolution on World War Two: Keeping History at Bay', in Edward R. Beauchamp (ed.), *History of Contemporary Japan, 1945–1998* (Garland Publishing, 1998); Tina Ottman, Zane Ritchie, Hugh Palmer and

Daniel Warchulski (eds), *Peace as a Global Language: Peace and Welfare in the Global and Local Community* (iUniverse, Indiana, 2017); for SDF deployments, see Wilhelm Vosse, Reinhard Drifte and Verena Blechinger-Talcott (eds), *Governing Insecurity in Japan: The Domestic Discourse and Policy Response* (Routledge, 2014). On arguments over wartime history, see Peter Duus, 'Introduction', in Michael Lewis (ed.), *'History Wars' and Reconciliation in Japan and Korea: The Roles of Historians, Artists, and Activists* (Palgrave Macmillan, 2017); Takashi Yoshida, *The Making of the 'Rape of Nanking': History and Memory in Japan, China, and the United States* (Oxford University Press, 2006); Ian Buruma, *Wages of Guilt: Memories of War in Germany and Japan* (Jonathan Cape, 1991); Matthew Penney, 'Manga from Right to Left', in *Mangatopia: Essays on Manga and Anime in the Modern World*, paperback edn (Libraries Unlimited, California, 2011). On education in Japan, see Kenneth B. Pyle, *The Making of Modern Japan*, 2nd revised edn (Houghton Mifflin, 1996); Leonard J. Schoppa, *Education Reform in Japan: A Case of Immobilist Politics* (Routledge, 1991); Hiro Saito, 'Cosmopolitan Nation-Building: the Institutional Contradiction and Politics of Postwar Japanese Education', *Social Science Japan Journal*, 14:2 (2011); Roger Goodman, Yuki Imoto, and Tuukka Toivonen (eds), *A Sociology of Japanese Youth: From Returnees to NEETs* (Routledge, 2012). On theorizing about Japan and the Japanese, see Sonia Ryang, '*Chrysanthemum*'s Strange Life: Ruth Benedict in Postwar Japan', *Asian Anthropology*, 1:1 (2002); P. N. Dale, *The Myth of Japanese Uniqueness* (Croom Helm, 1986); Harumi Befu, *Hegemony of Homogeneity: An Anthropological Analysis of 'Nihonjinron'* (Trans Pacific Press, 2001); Arthur Stockwin, 'Japanese Politics: Mainstream or Exotic?', in Jeff Kingston (ed.), *Critical Issues in Contemporary Japan* (Routledge, 2014). On the Japan Foundation, see Utpal Vyas, 'The Japan Foundation in China: An Agent of Japan's Soft Power?', *Electronic Journal of Contemporary Japanese Studies*, 5 (2008). On social problems in Japan, see Jeff Kingston, *Contemporary Japan: History, Politics, and Social Change Since the 1980s* (John Wiley & Sons, 2010); Anne Allison, *Precarious Japan* (Duke University Press, 2013). On Koizumi Junichirō, see Andrew Gordon, *A Modern History of Japan*, 2nd edn (Oxford University Press, 2008) and David Pilling, *Bending Adversity: Japan and the Art of Survival* (Allen Lane, 2014). On young people in Japan, see Roger Goodman, *Children of the Japanese State: The Changing Role of Child Protection Institutions in Contemporary Japan* (Oxford University Press, 2000); Sachiko Horiguchi, 'How Private Isolation Caught the Public Eye', in Goodman, Imoto and Toivonen (eds), *A Sociology of Japanese Youth*; Nicolas Tajan, 'Japanese Post-Modern

Social Renouncers: An Exploratory Study of the Narratives of Hikikomori Subjects', *Subjectivity*, 8:283 (2015). On mental healthcare after the 1995 earthquake, see Timothy O. Benedict, 'Heart Care in Japan: Before and After the 1995 Great Hanshin-Awaji Earthquake', *Inochi no Mirai: The Future of Life*, 1 (2016). On Japan's relationships with nuclear technology, see Maika Nakao, 'The Image of the Atomic Bomb in Japan Before Hiroshima', *Historia Scientiarum*, 19:2 (2009) and Nakao, *Kaku no Yūwaku: Senzen Nihon no Kagaku Bunka to 'Genshiryoku no Yūtopia' no Shutsugen* ['Nuclear Temptations: Pre-war Japanese Scientific Culture and the Birth of "Atomic Energy Utopia"'] (Keiso Shobo, 2015); John W. Dower, 'The Bombed: Hiroshimas and Nagasakis in Japanese Memory', in Michael J. Hogan (ed.), *Hiroshima in History and Memory* (Cambridge University Press, 1996); Charles Weiner, 'Retroactive Saber Rattling?', *Bulletin of the Atomic Scientists* (March 1978); Weiner, 'Japan's First Nuclear Power Station', *The Engineer* (6 March 1959); Daniel P. Aldrich, 'Revisiting the Limits of Flexible and Adaptive Institutions: the Japanese Government's Role in Nuclear Power Plant Siting over the Post-war Period', in Kingston (ed.), *Critical Issues*, and 'Networks of Power', in Jeff Kingston (ed.), *Natural Disaster and Nuclear Crisis in Japan* (Routledge, 2012); William Breuer, *Secret Weapons of World War II* (Castle Books, 2008); Jeff Kingston, 'Japan's Nuclear Village: Power and Resilience', *Asia-Pacific Journal*, 19:37 (2012). 'They pay in yen, we pay in blood', is from Penney, 'Manga from Right to Left', in *Mangatopia*. 'If this is a recession' is quoted in Pilling, *Bending Adversity*.

18 FRAGMENTS

On the tsunami of 2011, see Andrew Gordon, *A Modern History of Japan*, 3rd edn (Oxford University Press, 2014); Richard Lloyd-Parry, *Ghosts of the Tsunami: Death and Life in Japan's Disaster Zone* (Jonathan Cape, 2017); author interviews with survivors and families of victims (October 2017). On Yanase Takashi, see Nakamura Keiko, *Yanase Takashi, Meruhen no majutsushi: Kyūjyū nen no kiseki* ['Yanase Takashi, Wizard of Fairytales: A Ninety-Year Journey'] (Kawadeshoboshinsha, 2009); Yanase Takashi, *Jinsei nante yume dakedo* ['Life is But a Dream'] (Fureberukan, 2005) and *Anpanman Densetsu* ['Anpanman Legend'] (Fureberukan, 1997); '1945 nen natsu o tazuneru (3) – Yanase Takashi san: Anpanman kometa omoi' ['Enquiring after the Summer of 1945 (3) – Yanase Takashi: Thoughts on Anpanman'] in *Asahi Shimbun*, 15 July 2015; 'Jidai no shogensha (8)',

Yomiuri bukkuretto, 48 (2005); Fukuda Ikehiro, 'Itadakimaasu! Anpanman – nihonteki na inshoku no kansei o taigen suru hīrō'; Kuresawa Takemi, 'Bunshin to shite no kyarakutā'; Yokota Masao, 'Minna daisuki "Soreike! Anpanman" no shinrigaku'; and 'Interview: Yanase Takashi: subete wa un ni michibikarete – hīrō' no shōzō': all in *Yuriika: Yanase Takashi Anpanman no kokoro [Eureka* Special Edition: 'Takashi Yanase: the Heart of Anpanman'] (Seidosha, 2013); 'Yanase Takashi-san shibō: "Anpanman" sakusha, 94 sai', in *Asahi Shimbun*, 16 October 2013; 'Yanase Takashi-san shibō – 94 sai' in *Yomiuri Shimbun*, 16 October, 2013; 'Anpanman ni takushita yume – ningen – Yanase Takashi', NHK website, 30 October 2013. On Japanese pop culture, see Roland Kelts, *Japanamerica: How Japanese Pop Culture Has Invaded the US* (Palgrave Macmillan, 2006); Yasushi Watanabe and David L. McConnell, *Soft Power Superpowers: Cultural and National Assets of Japan and the United States* (Routledge, 2008); Douglas McGray, 'Japan's Gross National Cool', *Foreign Policy*, 130 (2002). On the SDF during the 2011 crisis, see Giuseppe A. Stavale, 'The GSDF During the Post-Cold War Years, 1989–2015', in Robert D. Eldridge and Paul Midford (eds), *The Japanese Ground Self-Defense Force: Search for Legitimacy* (Palgrave Macmillan, 2017); Yezi Yeo, 'De-Militarizing Military: Confirming Japan's Self-Defense Forces' Identity as a Disaster Relief Agency in the 2011 Tohoku Triple Crisis', *Asia Journal of Global Studies*, 5:2 (2013). On Operation Tomodachi and its aftermath, see Juan Carlos Rodriguez, '9th Circ. Agrees to Speed Up Sailors' $1B Fukushima Suit', *Law 360* (5 April 2016); Yuri Kageyama, 'Sick US Sailors and Marines Who Blame Radiation Get Support From Japan's Ex-Leader', *Navy Times*, 7 September 2016; Julian Ryall, 'US Sailors Who "Fell Sick From Fukushima Radiation" Allowed to Sue Japan, Nuclear Plant Operator', *The Telegraph*, 23 June 2017; Bianca Bruno, 'Judge: Sailors' Fukushima Radiation Case Doesn't Belong in US', *Courthouse News Service*, 5 January 2018. On the Fukushima disaster, see Gordon, *A Modern History of Japan*; Alexis Dudden, 'The Ongoing Disaster', *Journal of Asian Studies*, 71:2 (2012); Richard J. Samuels, 'Japan's Rhetoric of Crisis: Prospects for Change After 3.11', *Journal of Japanese Studies*, 39:1 (2013); Daniel P. Aldrich, 'Trust Deficit: Japanese Communities and the Challenge of Rebuilding Tohoku', *Japan Forum*, 29:1 (2017); Martin J. Frid, 'Food Safety: Addressing Radiation in Japan's Northeast After 3.11', *Asia-Pacific Journal*, 31:3 (August 2011) and 'Food Safety in Japan: One Year After the Nuclear Disaster', *Asia-Pacific Journal*, 12:1 (March 2012); Hrabrin Bachev and Fusao Ito, 'Agricultural Impacts of the Great East Japan Earthquake – Six Years Later', *Munich Personal RePEc Archive*, April 2017; on plans to evacuate Tokyo during the 2011 crisis:

Andrew Gilligan, 'Fukushima: Tokyo was on the Brink of Nuclear Catastrophe, Admits Former Prime Minister', *The Telegraph*, 4 March 2016. On the progress of Abenomics by mid-2017, see 'The Quiet but Substantial Successes of Abenomics', *Financial Times*, 1 May 2017. On Abe's strategic plans for Japan, see Lawrence Repeta, 'Japan's Democracy at Risk', *Asia-Pacific Journal*, 28:3 (July 2013); Carl F. Goodman, 'Contemplated Amendments to Japan's 1947 Constitution', *Washington International Law Journal*, 26:1 (2016); 'Abe's Master Plan', *The Economist*, 18 May 2013; Gavan McCormack, 'Japan: Prime Minister Abe Shinzō's Agenda', in *Asia-Pacific Journal*, 14:24 (2016); Mina Pollmann, 'Japan's Controversial State Secrets Law: One Year Later', *The Diplomat*, 9 December 2015. On plans for the 2020 Olympics, see <https://tokyo2020.org/en/>; Yukari Easton, 'Tokyo 2020 and Japan's Soft Power', *The Diplomat*, 31 August 2016; Danielle Muoio, 'Tokyo is Getting Ready to Host the Most Advanced Olympics Ever', *UK Business Insider*, 23 March 2016. On Japan's *matsuri* tradition, see Helen Hardacre, *Shinto: A History* (Oxford University Press, 2017). On depression in Japan, see Junko Kitanaka, *Depression in Japan: Psychiatric Cures for a Society in Distress* (Princeton University Press, 2011); Hiroshi Ihara, 'A Cold of the Soul: A Japanese Case of Disease Mongering in Psychiatry', *International Journal of Risk and Safety in Medicine*, 24 (2012); Christopher Harding, 'How Japan Came to Believe in Depression', *BBC News Magazine*, 20 July 2016. On the media and music, see David McNeill, 'Japan's Contemporary Media', in Jeff Kingston (ed.), *Critical Issues in Contemporary Japan* (Routledge, 2014); especially on Saitō Kazuyoshi, Noriko Manabe, *The Revolution Will Not be Televised: Protest Music After Fukushima* (Oxford University Press, 2016) and Manabe, 'Uprising: Music, Youth, and Protest Against the Policies of the Abe Shinzō Government', *Asia-Pacific Journal*, 12:32 (2014); Ian F. Martin, *Quit Your Band! Musical Notes from the Japanese Underground* (Awai Books, 2016); Carolyn Stevens, *Japanese Popular Music: Culture, Authenticity, and Power* (Routledge, 2008). On Japan's demographic time-bomb and associated attitudes, see Richard Ronald and Allison Alexy (eds), *Home and Family in Japan: Continuity and Transformation* (Routledge, 2011); 'How Does Japan Compare?', in *The Pursuit of Gender Equality: An Uphill Battle*, OECD Publications, 4 October 2017; Hirano Yūko, 'Foreign Care Workers in Japan: A Plan Without a Vision', Nippon.com, 13 February 2017; Hiroyuki Nakata, 'Attitudes Towards Immigration in an Ageing Society' (RIETI Discussion paper series 17-E-095, June 2017); Emma Jacobs, 'Out of Office: the Fathers Bringing up Baby', *Financial Times*, 13 March 2016. On 'carebot' technology: Jon Emont, 'Japan Prefers Robot Bears to Foreign Nurses',

Foreign Policy, March 2017; Leo Lewis, 'Can Robots Make Up for Japan's Care Home Shortfall?', *Financial Times*, 18 October 2017. On the history of LGBT rights in Japan, see Jeffrey Angles, *Writing the Love of Boys: Origins of Bishōnen Culture in Modernist Japanese Literature* (University of Minnesota Press, 2011). On Ainu history and culture, see Brett L. Walker, *The Conquest of Ainu Lands: Ecology and Culture in Japanese Expansion, 1590–1800* (University of California Press, 2001); Richard M. Siddle, 'The Ainu: Indigenous People of Japan', in Michael Weiner (ed.), *Japan's Minorities: The Illusion of Homogeneity* (Routledge, 1997); Katarina Sjöberg, *The Return of the Ainu: Cultural Mobilization and the Practice of Ethnicity in Japan* (Psychology Press, Abingdon, 1993); Kyosuke Kindaiti, *Ainu Life and Legends* (Board of Tourist Industry, Japanese Government Railways, 1941); Yoichi Tanaka, 'Ainu People Today', in *Focus*, 36 (Asia-Pacific Human Rights Information Center, 2004); Tessa Morris-Suzuki, 'Still a Way to Go for Japanese Minorities', *East Asia Forum*, 11 May 2015. On Okinawan history and culture, see 'Introduction' in Glen D. Hook and Richard Siddle (eds), *Japan and Okinawa: Structure and Subjectivity* (Routledge, 2002); Matt Gillan, *Songs from the Edge of Japan: Music-making in Yaeyama and Okinawa* (Routledge, 2012); Ina Hein, 'Constructing Difference in Japan: Literary Counter-Images of the Okinawa Boom', *Contemporary Japan*, 22: 1–2 (2010); D. L. Bhowmik and Steve Rabson (eds), *Islands of Protest: Japanese Literature from Okinawa* (University of Hawaii Press, 2016); Steve Rabson, 'Being Okinawan in Japan: the Diaspora Experience', *Asia-Pacific Journal*, 10:12 (2012). On Zainichi Koreans, see John Lie, *Multiethnic Japan* (Harvard University Press, 2004); Martin Fackler, 'New Dissent in Japan is Loudly Anti-Foreign', *New York Times*, 28 August 2010; Sonia Ryang & John Lie (eds), *Diaspora Without Homeland: Being Korean in Japan* (Global, Area, and International Archive, University of California Press, 2009). On the history of disability rights in Japan, see Carolyn Stevens, *Disability in Japan* (Routledge, 2013); Katharina Heyer, *Rights Enabled: The Disability Revolution, from the US, to Germany and Japan, to the United Nations* (University of Michigan Press, 2015); Shirasawa Mayumi, 'The Long Road to Disability Rights in Japan', Nippon.com, October 2014. On the Burakumin, see Christopher Bondy, *Voice, Silence, and Self: Negotiations of Buraku Identity in Contemporary Japan* (Harvard University Press, 2015); Ian Neary, 'Burakumin in Contemporary Japan', in Michael Weiner (ed.), *Japan's Minorities* (Routledge, 1997); 'New law to fight bias against 'burakumin' seen falling short', *Japan Times*, 19 December 2016. 'Vulgar' is from an interview with Setouchi Jakuchō conducted by the author in October 2012. 'Defray the expenses' and 'You are therefore requested' are from Kindaiti, *Ainu Life and Legends*.

EPILOGUE

On ghostly phenomena in the wake of the 2011 disasters in Japan, see Kiyoshi Kanebishi, 'Religious Layers of History Opened Up by the "Apparition Phenomena" After the 2011 Tōhoku Earthquake and Tsunami Disaster: Utilizing the Theory of the Gift Relationships of the Deceased Becoming Intimate' (working paper), in Kanebishi (ed.) *Yobisamaseru reisei-no shinsaigaku* ['Studying the Awakened Spirituality of the 2011 Tōhoku Disaster'] (Shin-yo-sha, 2016); Richard Lloyd-Parry, 'Ghosts of the Tsunami', *London Review of Books*, 36:3 (February 2014) and Lloyd-Parry, *Ghosts of the Tsunami: Death and Life in Japan's Disaster Zone* (Jonathan Cape, 2017); Okuno Shuji, *Tamashii demo ii kara soba ni ite* ['Stay With Me, Even as a Spirit'] (Shinchosha, 2017). On religion and distress in contemporary Japan more broadly, see Christopher Harding, Fumiaki Iwata and Shin'ichi Yoshinaga (eds), *Religion and Psychotherapy in Modern Japan* (Routledge, 2015). This chapter also draws on interviews conducted in Japan in October 2017 with Taniyama Yōzō, Kaneta Taiō, Kanebishi Kiyoshi, Okuno Shuji, Ioannis Gaitinidis, Murakami Aki, Kuroki Aruji and Matsuda Hiroko. 'It was a moonlit night' is the author's translation of 'Story 99' in Yanagita Kunio, *Tōno no Monogatari* (1910). 'Thousands of people had just died' is from Kuroki Aruji, interview with the author, October 2017.

Acknowledgements

Writing a book seems to involve drawing deeply on the generosity and patience of others while eroding – temporarily, one has to hope – those same qualities in the author. To everyone who has helped me, and put up with me – thank you. What follows are just a few of the countless contributions that people have made to *Japan Story*.

For their academic mentoring, I am forever in debt to the inspiring examples set by Martin Conway, Judith Brown and 'Ptp'. Ann Waswo introduced me to the extraordinary richness of Japanese studies, while Teikyo School United Kingdom put me in touch for the first time with Japan itself: working with impossibly lovely pupils and students, wielding impossibly advanced mobile phone technology (while braving the centrality to British cuisine of the humble potato), did much to fire a young man's curiosity about their country.

That curiosity would not have gone far without the award of a scholarship from the Daiwa Anglo-Japanese Foundation in 2004. The chance to live and study in Japan for a couple of years, and to actually be paid to do so, seemed then – and still seems now – a fantastically good deal. My deepest thanks go to the Foundation's Trustees, to Kono-san and Marie Conte-Helm for looking after me on the scholarship, and to Jason James and Susan Meehan for maintaining the relationship since.

I owe a great deal, in recent years, to the students and staff in the School of History, Classics and Archaeology at the University of Edinburgh. To my students in particular for your energy and joy; for the questions and insights that I scurried away and scribbled down; and for basically teaching me how to teach – thank you. May you all find gainful employment. And may you stay out of trouble.

Getting to know a new country involves its fair share of hurdles, and Japan is no exception. Having clipped my shins on some, and clattered to earth over others, I am all the more grateful to those who helped me clear the ones that I did. Akihito Suzuki at Keio University has been tireless in his encouragement of younger scholars. For buying me expensive sushi, for taking me through a list of people I really ought to have heard of already, and for everything else since – thank you. Junko Kitanaka, also at Keio, sets the very highest standards in studying culture and mental health, and is unfailingly warm and generous in helping others to try to meet them – for which thank you, Junko. Yorio Kosawa and Makoto Takeda got me started studying religion and the psy sciences in Japan. I hope their delight at seeing my expression, when first faced with the quivering, live-dissected fish we shared, served as some small compensation for their efforts. For later conversations about mental health and its place in the bigger picture of modern Japan, I am grateful to – amongst very many others – Takashi Ikuta, Fumiaki Iwata, Setouchi Jakuchō, Takeshi Kanaseki, Toshihide Kuroki, Kunihiro Matsuki, Yujiro Nagao, Yuji Sato and Shin'ichi Yoshinaga. For their trust in granting me access to the personal documents of family members, I owe thanks to Yorio and Makoto Kosawa, and to Nachiko and Atsushi Nagai.

Few academics write for colleagues alone. But sharing our ideas with a wider public often rests on a great deal of help from others. Alongside patient and forensic editors at various UK and Japanese publications, I owe a huge amount to the BBC and the Arts and Humanities Research Council: their fabulous 'New Generation Thinkers' scheme allowed me to embark on an extended apprenticeship in broadcast journalism, and helped to broaden considerably the scope of *Japan Story*. Mohit Bakaya, Matthew Dodd, Hugh Levinson and Robyn Read have offered me no end of opportunities to develop and share my Japan ideas, while Sheila Cook, Bob Howard, Luke Mulhall, Fiona McLean and Keith Moore have been saintly in their patience as essay and documentary producers.

For steering *Japan Story* through its planning stages and into the arms of Allen Lane, I am very grateful indeed to Robyn Drury and Martin Redfern at what is now Northbank Talent Management. First-class documentary and picture research came courtesy of Enzo

DeGregorio, Lesley Hodgson, Leo Howard, Yoshi Inoue, Hirō Saso and Yoshiyuki Wakida. My thanks also, for assistance with images, to Rosina Buckland, Timothy George, Marty Gross, David Humphries, Ninagawa Mika, Okamura Marie, Okamura Mihoko, Scott Ritchie, Jordan Sand and William Wetherall. Hiromi Sasamoto-Collins and Chris Perkins offered invaluable comments on the manuscript. My editor Simon Winder knows what my promises are worth when it comes to meeting deadlines, but has never let it dampen his enthusiasm for this project nor compromise his care in reading drafts and shepherding the whole thing through to completion. To Simon, and to everyone involved with the production of the book – including Ellen Davies, Matt Hutchinson and Jane Robertson – thank you for making the process so smooth and so enjoyable. For helping to fund the research on which the book is based, I am grateful to the British Academy, the Carnegie Trust for the Universities of Scotland, the Daiwa Anglo-Japanese Foundation, the Japan Foundation, the Japan Society for the Promotion of Science, the University of Edinburgh and the Wellcome Trust.

To anyone who has scanned down this far and spotted a name missing that really should have made it into even these much-abbreviated lines, rest assured that in the time since this book went to press I have probably had night-sweats over this and other omissions. Please accept my sincerest apologies, and of course my grateful thanks.

Finally, to my family, and especially to my wife Kae and our three children – Shoji, Yocchan and Hana: thank you for everything, and I'm sorry this all took so long. Let's go and play in the garden.

Illustration Credits

p. 12: Kosawa Heisaku (© Kosawa Family Archive); Setouchi Harumi (© Kyodo News)

p. 20: Edo Castle. Drawing by Kazuo Hozumi, from Akira Naito, *Edo no machi: kyodai toshi no tanjō* (1982)

p. 22: A street scene in Edo (© City of Edinburgh Council/Edinburgh Libraries)

p. 23: Ground-plan of Dejima (Courtesy of Koninklijke Bibliotheek, The Hague, shelf number KW 114 L 22, plate after page 264)

p. 24: *A Banquet on Dejima* (© Collection of Nagasaki Museum of History and Culture)

p. 26: Hokusai, *Great Wave off Kanagawa* (c.1830) (© H. O. Havemeyer Collection, Bequest of Mrs. H. O. Havemeyer, 1929/ The Metropolitan Museum of Art, New York)

p. 34: Portrait of Commodore Perry (© Honolulu Museum of Art, Gift of Mrs Walter F. Dillingham, in memory of Alice Perry); *Foreign Ship* (© Collection of Nagasaki Museum of History and Culture)

p. 37: Fukuzawa Yukichi (© National Diet Library, 'Portraits of Modern Japanese Historical Figures')

p. 41: Tsukioka Yoshitoshi, *Surrender of the Rebels* (c.1880) (© John Stevenson/Corbis Historical/Getty Images)

p. 42: Saigō Takamori (© National Diet Library, 'Portraits of Modern Japanese Historical Figures'); *Rumours About 'Saigō Star'* (© Chronicle of World History/Alamy Stock Photo)

p. 51: Kageyama Hideko (© Chronicle of World History/Alamy Stock Photo); Itagaki Taisuke (© National Diet Library, 'Portraits of Modern Japanese Historical Figures')

p. 54: The Rokumeikan (Courtesy of Wikimedia Commons)

p. 56: George Ferdinand Bigot, *Monday at the Rokumeikan* (1887) (© Chronicle of World History/Alamy Stock Photo); George Ferdinand Bigot, *Imitation* (1877) (© Chronicle of World History/ Alamy Stock Photo)

p. 64: Kobayashi Eitaku, *Izanagi and Izanami Creating the Islands of Japan* (c.1885) (© Art Collection 3/Alamy Stock Photo)

p. 69: Itō Hirobumi (© National Diet Library, 'Portraits of Modern Japanese Historical Figures'); Gotō Yoshikage, *Illustration of the Imperial Diet of Japan* (1890) (© 2018, Museum of Fine Arts, Boston)

p. 76: A family meeting: From Chokei Dōjin, *Katei no Kairaku* (1902)

p. 87: Toyohara Chikanobu, *A Mirror of Japanese Nobility* (1887) (© 2018, Museum of Fine Arts, Boston)

p. 88: Utagawa Toyukuni III, *The Origins of Sacred Dance at the Heavenly Cave* (c.1856) (© ART Collection/Alamy Stock Photo); Hiratsuka Raichō (Public domain, from Seitōsha, c.1913)

p. 99: Two Buddhist monks (© Chronicle/Alamy Stock Photo); Inoue Enryō (© Art Collection 4/Alamy Stock Photo)

p. 103: A *fumi-e* ceremony (© Chronicle of World History/Alamy Stock Photo); *Crucifixion* (*fumi-e* plate) (©Heritage Image Partnership Ltd/Alamy Stock Photo); staue of 'Maria Kannon' (Courtesy of Wikimedia Commons)

p. 109: Yamagata Aritomo (© National Diet Library, 'Portraits of Modern Japanese Historical Figures')

p. 112: 'Japanese Suicide Squad Fight Bravely in a Naval Battle at Port Arthur during the Russo-Japanese War' (© 2018, Museum of Fine Arts, Boston)

p. 119: Akutagawa Ryūnosuke (© National Diet Library, 'Portraits of Modern Japanese Historical Figures'); Hayashi Fumiko (© The Asahi Shimbun via Getty Images)

p. 126: Tokyo in the 1920s (© Bettmann/Getty Images)

p. 133: Utagawa Kuniyoshi, *Dancing Cats* (c.1841) (Courtesy of William Pearl)

p. 134: 'Modern girls' (Courtesy of Wikimedia Commons/Photographer: Kageyama Kōyō, 'Beach pyjama fashion', c.1928)

p. 140: Natsume Sōseki (© National Diet Library, 'Portraits of Modern Japanese Historical Figures')

p. 148: A *tengu* (Courtesy of the Humphries Family Trust)

p. 150: Kosawa Heisaku (© Kosawa Family Archive)

p. 162: Newspapers depicting the Taiwan Expedition of 1874 (Courtesy of Yosha Bunko collection, William Wetherall, www.nishike.com); 'Jap the Giant-Killer', from *Punch* (1894) (Courtesy of The Project Gutenberg EBook of *Punch, or the London Charivari*, Volume 107, 29 September 1894. Retrieved 16 May 2018 [EBook #46738]); 'Look Out John; It's Loaded' from the *Tacoma Times* (1904) (© Tacoma Times, courtesy of Washington State Library's Digital Newspaper Program)

p. 180: The Battle for Shanghai (© FLHC/Alamy Stock Photo)

p. 191: The 26 February incident, 1936 (© The Asahi Shimbun via Getty Images); the Shōwa Emperor (Courtesy of Wikimedia Commons)

p. 196: The Nanjing Victory Parade, 1937 (© Paul Fearn/Alamy Stock Photo)

p. 197: The *Kōa Kannon* statue (Courtesy of Wikimedia Commons)

p. 199: D. T. Suzuki (Courtesy of Okamura Mihoko)

p. 209: Wheeler Airfield under attack (© Time Life Pictures/US Navy/the LIFE Picture Collection/Getty Images); USS *Shaw* explodes during Japan's attack on Pearl Harbor (Courtesy of National Archives and Records Administration, War and Conflict Number 1135 (NAID: 520590, NAIL Control Number: NWDNS-80-G-16871). National Archives at College Park, College Park, MD)

p. 212: *Momotarō vs Mickey Mouse*, from *Omochabako shiriizu daisanwa: ehon 1936 nen* ('Toybox Series No. 3: Picture Book 1936'), J. O. Studio (1934); *Momotarō no umiwashi* (*Momotarō's Sea Eagles*), Geijutsu Eigasha (1942).

p. 213: Popeye war stamps advert (Courtesy of National Archives and Records Administration (NAID: 514862, NAIL Control Number: NWDNS-44-PA-1256). National Archives at College Park, College Park, MD)

p. 228: An aerial view of a bomb-damaged Tokyo (Courtesy of Wikimedia Commons); bodies and wreckage in Tokyo (Courtesy of Wikimedia Commons)

p. 234: A train taking Tokyoites to the countryside in search of food (Courtesy of Tanuma Takeyoshi)

p. 243: Beate Sirota with Ichikawa Fusae (Courtesy of the family of Beate Sirota Gordon)

p. 252: Women voting for the first time, April 1946 (© The Mainichi Newspapers/Aflo)

p. 255: Akiyoshi Toshiko (© Metronome/Archive photos/Getty Images); Hampton Hawes (© GAB Archive/Redferns/Getty Images)

p. 262: 'New Constitution, Bright Life' (© National Diet Library of Japan)

p. 266: Sony's TR-63 radio (© YOSHIKAZU TSUNO/Gamma-Rapho via Getty Images)

p. 278: Crown Prince Akihito and Crown Princess Michiko (© Bettmann/Getty Images); Sakai Yoshinori opening the Tokyo Summer Olympic Games, October 1964 (© AFP/Getty Images)

p. 279: The launch of the shinkansen, October 1964 (© The Asahi Shimbun via Getty Images); The Peanuts (© United Archives GmbH/Alamy Stock Photo)

p. 285: Yamashita Kikuji, *The Tale of Akebono Village* (1953) (© Gallery Nippon/Photo: MOMAT/DNPartcom)

p. 288: Nakamura Hiroshi, *Sunagawa #5* (1955): a sketch and the finished work (© Nakamura Hiroshi, image courtesy of The Museum of Contemporary Art, Tokyo)

p. 289: Nakamura Hiroshi, *Gunned Down* (1957) (© Nakamura Hiroshi, image courtesy of The Koriyama City Museum of Art)

p. 294: Anti-Anpo protestors in 1960 (© Courtesy and Copyright Keisuke Katano); 'We Dislike Ike!' (© Keystone/Hulton Archive/Getty Images)

p. 308: Hijikata Tatsumi on stage (© Onozuka Makoto, Courtesy of Keio University Art Center)

p. 309: Minoru Hirata, Hi-Red Center's 'Cleaning Event' (officially known as 'Be Clean!' and 'Campaign to Promote Cleanliness and Order in the Metropolitan Area'), 1964 (© HM Archive)

p. 313: Mishima Yukio: (© Bettman/Getty Images)

p. 321: A *danchi* housing complex in Tokyo, 1967 (© The Mainichi Newspapers/Aflo)

p. 322: An advert for 'potato mash' (Courtesy of Morinaga)

p. 328: Protestors confront the Chisso company president (© The Mainichi Newspapers/Aflo); Uemura Tomoko and her mother, Uemura Ryoko (© The Mainichi Newspapers/Aflo)

p. 335: Miyazaki Hayao, *Nausicaä of the Valley of the Wind* (1982) (© Studio Ghibli)

p. 345: Asahara Shōkō in custody (© JIJI PRESS/AFP/Getty Images)

p. 353: Okinawans protesting against the rape of a schoolgirl in 1995 (©TORU YAMANAKA/AFP/Getty Images)

p. 362: Mao Zedong and Tanaka Kakuei, 1972 (© Bettmann/Getty Images)

p. 363: *Neo-Gōmanism Manifesto Special: On War* (Courtesy of Gentōsha)

p. 364 Prime Minister Koizumi Junichirō – as Elvis (© ZUMA Press Inc/Alamy Stock Photo)

p. 373: The tsunami of 11 March 2011 (© SADATSUGU TOMIZAWA/AFP/Getty Images); Anpanman, Ringo Bōya and Meronpanna (© Takashi Yanase, Froebel-kan, TMS, NTV 2013)

p. 377: Emperor Akihito and Empress Michiko, March 2011 (© Newscom/Alamy Stock Photo)

p. 384: Narita Gion Festival, 2017 (Courtesy of Scott Ritchie)

p. 386: *hinomaru* (Mika Ninagawa) (mika 2004 C-print © mika ninagawa, courtesy of Tomio Koyama Gallery)

p. 390: Anti-nuclear protest leaders (© Aflo Co. Ltd/Alamy Stock Photo)

p. 401: A demonstration of 'Robear' (© JIJI PRESS/AFP/Getty Images); Ainu celebrating the Autumn Ritual of Kotannomi, 2014 (© The Asahi Shimbun via Getty Images)

Index

Page references in *italic* indicate illustrations.

ALLEN LANE
an imprint of
PENGUIN BOOKS

Also Published

Paul Davies, *The Demon in the Machine: How Hidden Webs of Information Are Finally Solving the Mystery of Life*

Toby Green, *A Fistful of Shells: West Africa from the Rise of the Slave Trade to the Age of Revolution*

Paul Dolan, *Happy Ever After: Escaping the Myth of The Perfect Life*

Sunil Amrith, *Unruly Waters: How Mountain Rivers and Monsoons Have Shaped South Asia's History*

Christopher Harding, *Japan Story: In Search of a Nation, 1850 to the Present*

Timothy Day, *I Saw Eternity the Other Night: King's College, Cambridge, and an English Singing Style*

Richard Abels, *Aethelred the Unready: The Failed King*

Eric Kaufmann, *Whiteshift: Populism, Immigration and the Future of White Majorities*

Alan Greenspan and Adrian Wooldridge, *Capitalism in America: A History*

Philip Hensher, *The Penguin Book of the Contemporary British Short Story*

Paul Collier, *The Future of Capitalism: Facing the New Anxieties*

Andrew Roberts, *Churchill: Walking With Destiny*

Tim Flannery, *Europe: A Natural History*

T. M. Devine, *The Scottish Clearances: A History of the Dispossessed, 1600-1900*

Robert Plomin, *Blueprint: How DNA Makes Us Who We Are*

Michael Lewis, *The Fifth Risk: Undoing Democracy*

Diarmaid MacCulloch, *Thomas Cromwell: A Life*

Ramachandra Guha, *Gandhi: 1914-1948*

Slavoj Žižek, *Like a Thief in Broad Daylight: Power in the Era of Post-Humanity*

Neil MacGregor, *Living with the Gods: On Beliefs and Peoples*

Peter Biskind, *The Sky is Falling: How Vampires, Zombies, Androids and Superheroes Made America Great for Extremism*

Robert Skidelsky, *Money and Government: A Challenge to Mainstream Economics*

Helen Parr, *Our Boys: The Story of a Paratrooper*

David Gilmour, *The British in India: Three Centuries of Ambition and Experience*

Jonathan Haidt and Greg Lukianoff, *The Coddling of the American Mind: How Good Intentions and Bad Ideas are Setting up a Generation for Failure*

Ian Kershaw, *Roller-Coaster: Europe, 1950-2017*

Adam Tooze, *Crashed: How a Decade of Financial Crises Changed the World*

Edmund King, *Henry I: The Father of His People*

Lilia M. Schwarcz and Heloisa M. Starling, *Brazil: A Biography*

Jesse Norman, *Adam Smith: What He Thought, and Why it Matters*

Philip Augur, *The Bank that Lived a Little: Barclays in the Age of the Very Free Market*

Christopher Andrew, *The Secret World: A History of Intelligence*

David Edgerton, *The Rise and Fall of the British Nation: A Twentieth-Century History*

Julian Jackson, *A Certain Idea of France: The Life of Charles de Gaulle*

Owen Hatherley, *Trans-Europe Express*

Richard Wilkinson and Kate Pickett, *The Inner Level: How More Equal Societies Reduce Stress, Restore Sanity and Improve Everyone's Wellbeing*

Paul Kildea, *Chopin's Piano: A Journey Through Romanticism*

Seymour M. Hersh, *Reporter: A Memoir*

Michael Pollan, *How to Change Your Mind: The New Science of Psychedelics*

David Christian, *Origin Story: A Big History of Everything*

Judea Pearl and Dana Mackenzie, *The Book of Why: The New Science of Cause and Effect*

David Graeber, *Bullshit Jobs: A Theory*

Serhii Plokhy, *Chernobyl: History of a Tragedy*

Michael McFaul, *From Cold War to Hot Peace: The Inside Story of Russia and America*

Paul Broks, *The Darker the Night, the Brighter the Stars: A Neuropsychologist's Odyssey*

Lawrence Wright, *God Save Texas: A Journey into the Future of America*

John Gray, *Seven Types of Atheism*

Carlo Rovelli, *The Order of Time*

Mariana Mazzucato, *The Value of Everything: Making and Taking in the Global Economy*

Richard Vinen, *The Long '68: Radical Protest and Its Enemies*

Kishore Mahbubani, *Has the West Lost It?: A Provocation*

John Lewis Gaddis, *On Grand Strategy*

Richard Overy, *The Birth of the RAF, 1918: The World's First Air Force*

Francis Pryor, *Paths to the Past: Encounters with Britain's Hidden Landscapes*

Helen Castor, *Elizabeth I: A Study in Insecurity*

Ken Robinson and Lou Aronica, *You, Your Child and School*

Leonard Mlodinow, *Elastic: Flexible Thinking in a Constantly Changing World*

Nick Chater, *The Mind is Flat: The Illusion of Mental Depth and The Improvised Mind*

Michio Kaku, *The Future of Humanity: Terraforming Mars, Interstellar Travel, Immortality, and Our Destiny Beyond*

Thomas Asbridge, *Richard I: The Crusader King*

Richard Sennett, *Building and Dwelling: Ethics for the City*

Nassim Nicholas Taleb, *Skin in the Game: Hidden Asymmetries in Daily Life*

Steven Pinker, *Enlightenment Now: The Case for Reason, Science, Humanism and Progress*

Steve Coll, *Directorate S: The C.I.A. and America's Secret Wars in Afghanistan, 2001 - 2006*

Jordan B. Peterson, *12 Rules for Life: An Antidote to Chaos*

Bruno Maçães, *The Dawn of Eurasia: On the Trail of the New World Order*

Brock Bastian, *The Other Side of Happiness: Embracing a More Fearless Approach to Living*

Ryan Lavelle, *Cnut: The North Sea King*

Tim Blanning, *George I: The Lucky King*

Thomas Cogswell, *James I: The Phoenix King*

Pete Souza, *Obama, An Intimate Portrait: The Historic Presidency in Photographs*

Robert Dallek, *Franklin D. Roosevelt: A Political Life*

Norman Davies, *Beneath Another Sky: A Global Journey into History*

Ian Black, *Enemies and Neighbours: Arabs and Jews in Palestine and Israel, 1917-2017*

Martin Goodman, *A History of Judaism*

Shami Chakrabarti, *Of Women: In the 21st Century*

Stephen Kotkin, *Stalin, Vol. II: Waiting for Hitler, 1928-1941*

Lindsey Fitzharris, *The Butchering Art: Joseph Lister's Quest to Transform the Grisly World of Victorian Medicine*

Serhii Plokhy, *Lost Kingdom: A History of Russian Nationalism from Ivan the Great to Vladimir Putin*

Mark Mazower, *What You Did Not Tell: A Russian Past and the Journey Home*

Lawrence Freedman, *The Future of War: A History*

Niall Ferguson, *The Square and the Tower: Networks, Hierarchies and the Struggle for Global Power*

Matthew Walker, *Why We Sleep: The New Science of Sleep and Dreams*

Edward O. Wilson, *The Origins of Creativity*

John Bradshaw, *The Animals Among Us: The New Science of Anthropology*

David Cannadine, *Victorious Century: The United Kingdom, 1800-1906*

Leonard Susskind and Art Friedman, *Special Relativity and Classical Field Theory*

Maria Alyokhina, *Riot Days*

Oona A. Hathaway and Scott J. Shapiro, *The Internationalists: And Their Plan to Outlaw War*

Chris Renwick, *Bread for All: The Origins of the Welfare State*

Anne Applebaum, *Red Famine: Stalin's War on Ukraine*

Richard McGregor, *Asia's Reckoning: The Struggle for Global Dominance*

Chris Kraus, *After Kathy Acker: A Biography*

Clair Wills, *Lovers and Strangers: An Immigrant History of Post-War Britain*

Odd Arne Westad, *The Cold War: A World History*

Max Tegmark, *Life 3.0: Being Human in the Age of Artificial Intelligence*

Jonathan Losos, *Improbable Destinies: How Predictable is Evolution?*

Chris D. Thomas, *Inheritors of the Earth: How Nature Is Thriving in an Age of Extinction*

Chris Patten, *First Confession: A Sort of Memoir*

James Delbourgo, *Collecting the World: The Life and Curiosity of Hans Sloane*

Naomi Klein, *No Is Not Enough: Defeating the New Shock Politics*

Ulrich Raulff, *Farewell to the Horse: The Final Century of Our Relationship*

Slavoj Žižek, *The Courage of Hopelessness: Chronicles of a Year of Acting Dangerously*

Patricia Lockwood, *Priestdaddy: A Memoir*

Ian Johnson, *The Souls of China: The Return of Religion After Mao*

Stephen Alford, *London's Triumph: Merchant Adventurers and the Tudor City*

Hugo Mercier and Dan Sperber, *The Enigma of Reason: A New Theory of Human Understanding*

Stuart Hall, *Familiar Stranger: A Life Between Two Islands*

Allen Ginsberg, *The Best Minds of My Generation: A Literary History of the Beats*

Sayeeda Warsi, *The Enemy Within: A Tale of Muslim Britain*

Alexander Betts and Paul Collier, *Refuge: Transforming a Broken Refugee System*

Robert Bickers, *Out of China: How the Chinese Ended the Era of Western Domination*

Erica Benner, *Be Like the Fox: Machiavelli's Lifelong Quest for Freedom*

William D. Cohan, *Why Wall Street Matters*

David Horspool, *Oliver Cromwell: The Protector*

Daniel C. Dennett, *From Bacteria to Bach and Back: The Evolution of Minds*

Derek Thompson, *Hit Makers: How Things Become Popular*

Harriet Harman, *A Woman's Work*

Wendell Berry, *The World-Ending Fire: The Essential Wendell Berry*

Daniel Levin, *Nothing but a Circus: Misadventures among the Powerful*

Stephen Church, *Henry III: A Simple and God-Fearing King*